Lionel Aggett's

ITALY

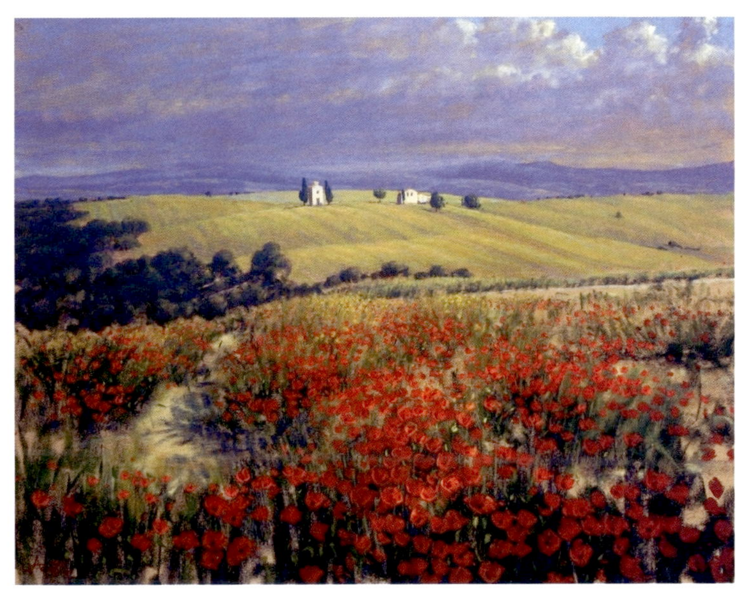

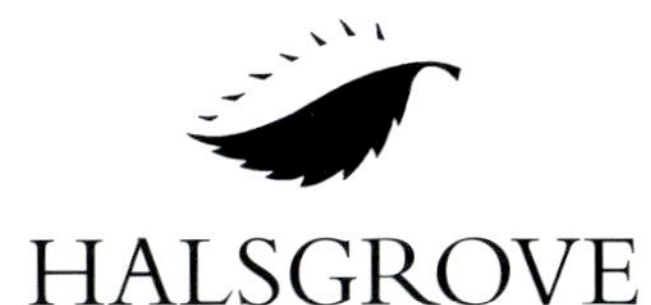

HALSGROVE

First published in Great Britain in 2007

Title page: *Chiesina di Vitaleta, Tuscany* Pastel 500 x 650 mm

British Library Cataloguing-in-Publication Data
A CIP record for this title is available from the British Library

ISBN 978 1 84114 606 5

HALSGROVE
Halsgrove House,
Ryelands Farm Industrial Estate,
Bagley Green, Wellington, Somerset TA21 9PZ
Tel: 01823 653777 Fax: 01823 216796
email: sales@halsgrove.com
website: www.halsgrove.com

Printed and bound by D'Auria Industrie Grafiche, Italy

Contents

ACKNOWLEDGEMENTS & DEDICATION 4
FOREWORD 5
INTRODUCTION 6
AN ITALIAN ROMANCE 8
RETURN JOURNEY TO THE SOUTH 14
PUGLIA 38
- Murgia and the Valle d'Itria 39
- The Gargano 56

UMBRIA 62
- Parco Nazionale dei Monte Sibillini 64
- Spoleto 69
- Bevagna 76
- Assisi 82

TUSCANY 96
- Sarteano and the Valle d'Orcia 99
- Siena and the Crete Senese 108
- San Gimignano 114
- Barberino Val d'Elsa and Chianti 123
- Florence 126

VENICE 130
- San Marco 132
- Dorsoduro 140
- San Polo 146
- Cannaregio 152
- Venice Lagoon 156

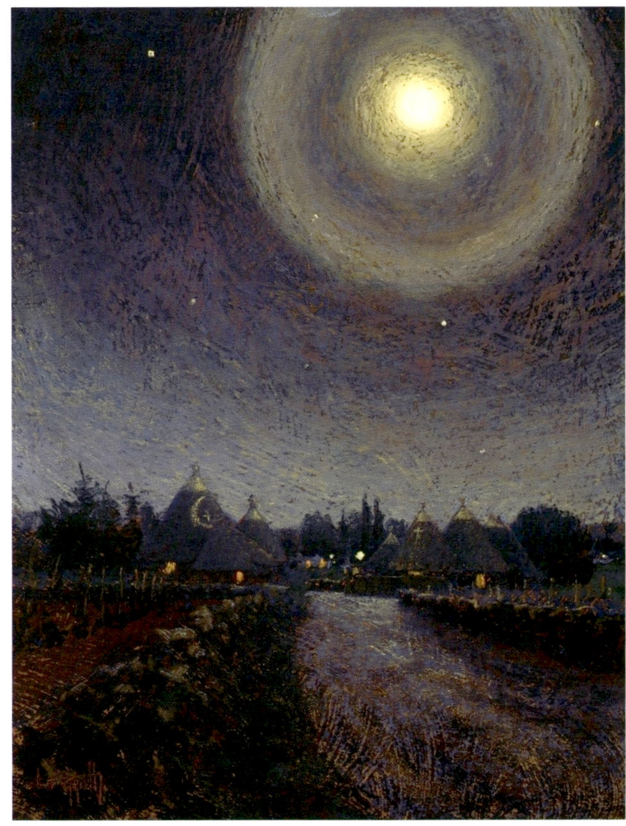

Moonglow, Valle d'Itria, Puglia Pastel 325 x 250 mm

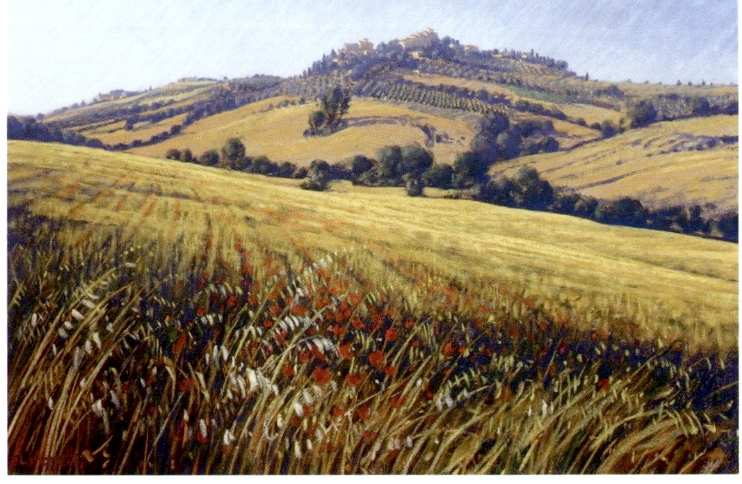

Cereale Dorato, Barberino Val d'Elsa Pastel 325 x 500 mm

Acknowledgements & Dedication

My thanks to W.H. Patterson Ltd, Fine Art Dealers of 19 Albemarle Street, London, W15 1BB, for hosting the launch of this book during my Solo Exhibition at the Gallery, held from 5th to 29th September 2007, and in particular to Cory Fuller, Director, for writing the introduction to this book.

Many of the paintings exhibited are featured in the following pages. The remaining paintings were sold during one person exhibitions held in the following galleries: – Llewellyn Alexander Gallery, London, John Davies Gallery, Stow-on-the-Wold, The Walker Galleries, Harrogate, North Yorkshire, and Sidbury, Devon, and Sarah Samuels, Chester and Rossett. My thanks to them all, and all patrons who have thus contributed to this book.

My appreciation to the Italian Ambassador His Excellency Signor Giancarlo Aragona KCVO for writing the foreword to this title.

My sincere thanks to Sue Reece for converting my hand written text to type, and also for the fourth time to Karen and Sharon and all at Halsgrove for their help and expertise.

My thanks once again to John Melville, photographer, for his excellent transparencies and digital work; also to Philip Bate of Calmar Picture Framing for framing the exhibition, and to Jane Henderson of the Gilders Workshop for her contribution.

This title is also dedicated to my darling wife Anne who accompanied me on various visits to this beautiful Country, and who has been so very supportive regarding my solo working tours. Also to our extended family, and all those who have encouraged me throughout.

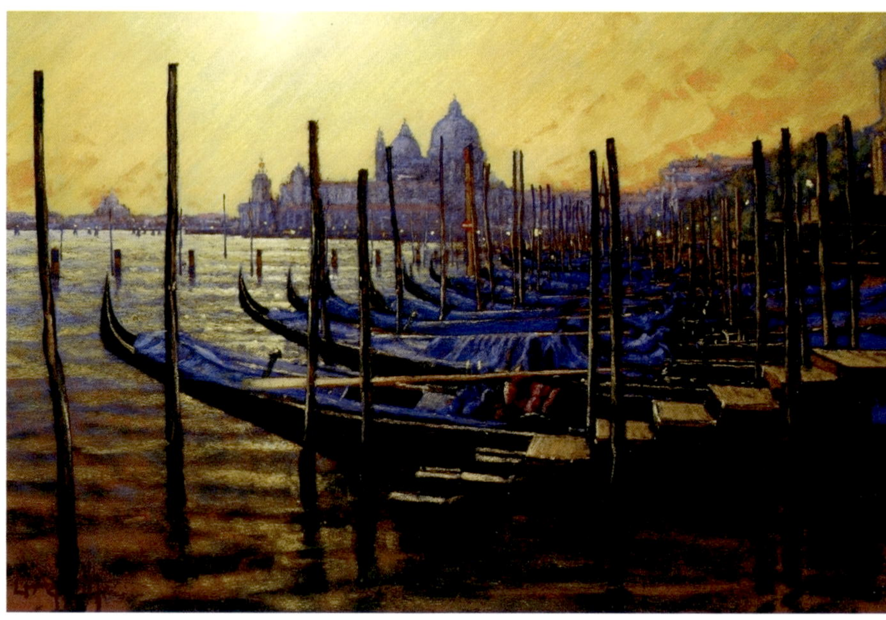

Blue and Gold Pastel 325 x 500 mm

Foreword

By the Italian Ambassador

Lionel Aggett's love of Italian landscapes and art are once again demonstrated by the handsome illustrations contained in this lovely book and by the works exhibited at the Patterson Art Gallery from the 4th September 2007.

It is a love which goes back in time a long way and, as for most English artists, was initially inspired by the regions of Tuscany and Umbria and the cities of Rome and Venice which, more than other parts of Italy, have fascinated artists and travellers over the centuries. But Lionel soon widened his horizons and discovered other parts of the peninsula, capturing their beauty and unique light and features in his beautiful paintings.

It is thanks to artists like Lionel Aggett that Anglo-Italian relations are nurtured and acquire a spiritual dimension which unites the two peoples.

H. E. Giancarlo Aragona KCVO
Italian Ambassador

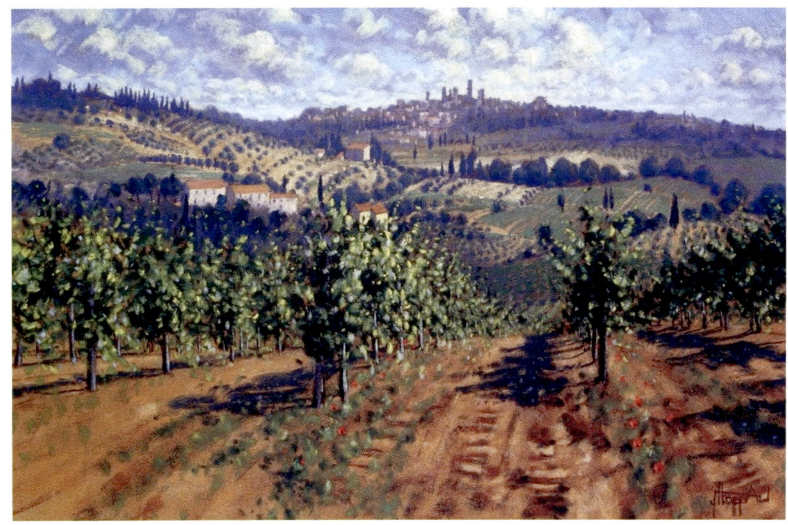

Vernaccia di San Gimignano Pastel 325 x 500 mm

Introduction

Lionel Aggett has been exhibiting regularly with the W.H. Patterson Gallery in Mayfair for the last eight years, culminating in a resoundingly successful first solo exhibition and book launch two years ago. Lionel has returned to Europe with his wife Anne, but this time has journeyed further South to Italy and we are delighted to be staging this greatly anticipated second exhibition.

Lionel is a dedicated artist whose ability to capture the atmosphere and colours of the Italian towns and landscapes has been perfected over the many years since he first visited Tuscany and Umbria in his student days

This book is a buzzing compendium of pastel drawings, sketches and notes which chart his travels on a day-to-day basis. Each page reveals another close observation and study of a stunning vista or quiet corner in a country steeped in cultural, architectural, artistic and gastronomic tradition.

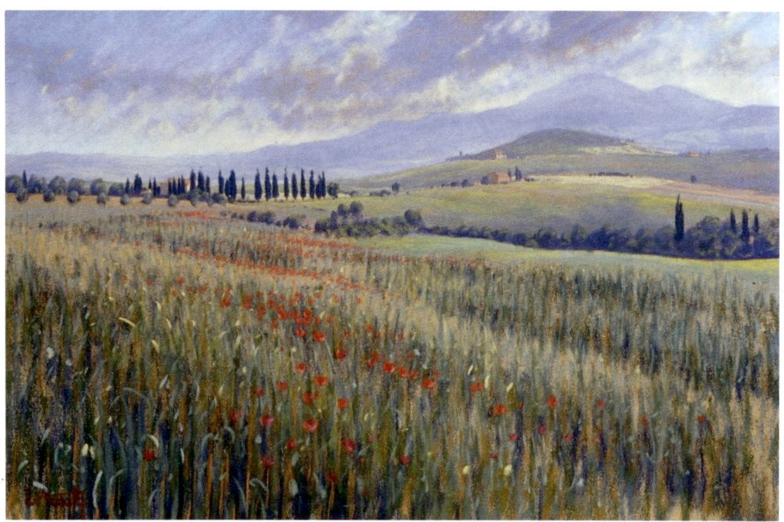

Val d'Orcia Pastel 325 x 500 mm

This book is a testament to Lionel's wonderful ability to discover hidden treasures and lifestyles.

Having travelled widely in Italy myself, and having rejoiced in finding those inspiring places upon which one oft' stumbles, if adventurous enough to stray from the beaten track, it is with absolute delight that I have been called upon to present a collection of paintings which capture the real heartbeat of Italy.

I first met Lionel four years ago, soon after he had completed a similar painting odyssey through undiscovered France which culminated in a delightful and treasured tome and a resoundingly successful first solo exhibition here at the W.H.Patterson. His skill as a pastelist is greatly respected by his peers and his success is reflected by the public appreciation of his evocative works of art.

Italy is a country which lends itself readily to Lionel's style of painting and drawing, colour leaps from the paper and changing lights are captured, from the fierce midday sun to the softer golden lights and long shadows.

Here, Lionel's travels have taken him from the top to the heel of Italy and upon the turn of each page is revealed another masterpiece or simple sketch, be it an expansive stunning vista or a close observation of rural life from a country steeped in cultural, architectural, artistic and gastronomic tradition.

Lionel first visited Tuscany and Umbria in his student days, where a love for Italy was clearly born. Lionel's ability to capture the atmosphere of the Italian towns and landscapes has been perfected over his many visits there and throughout this book I challenge you not to be infected by his enthusiasm, passion and joy for just being there in *"il Bel Paese."*

Cory Fuller
W.H. Patterson

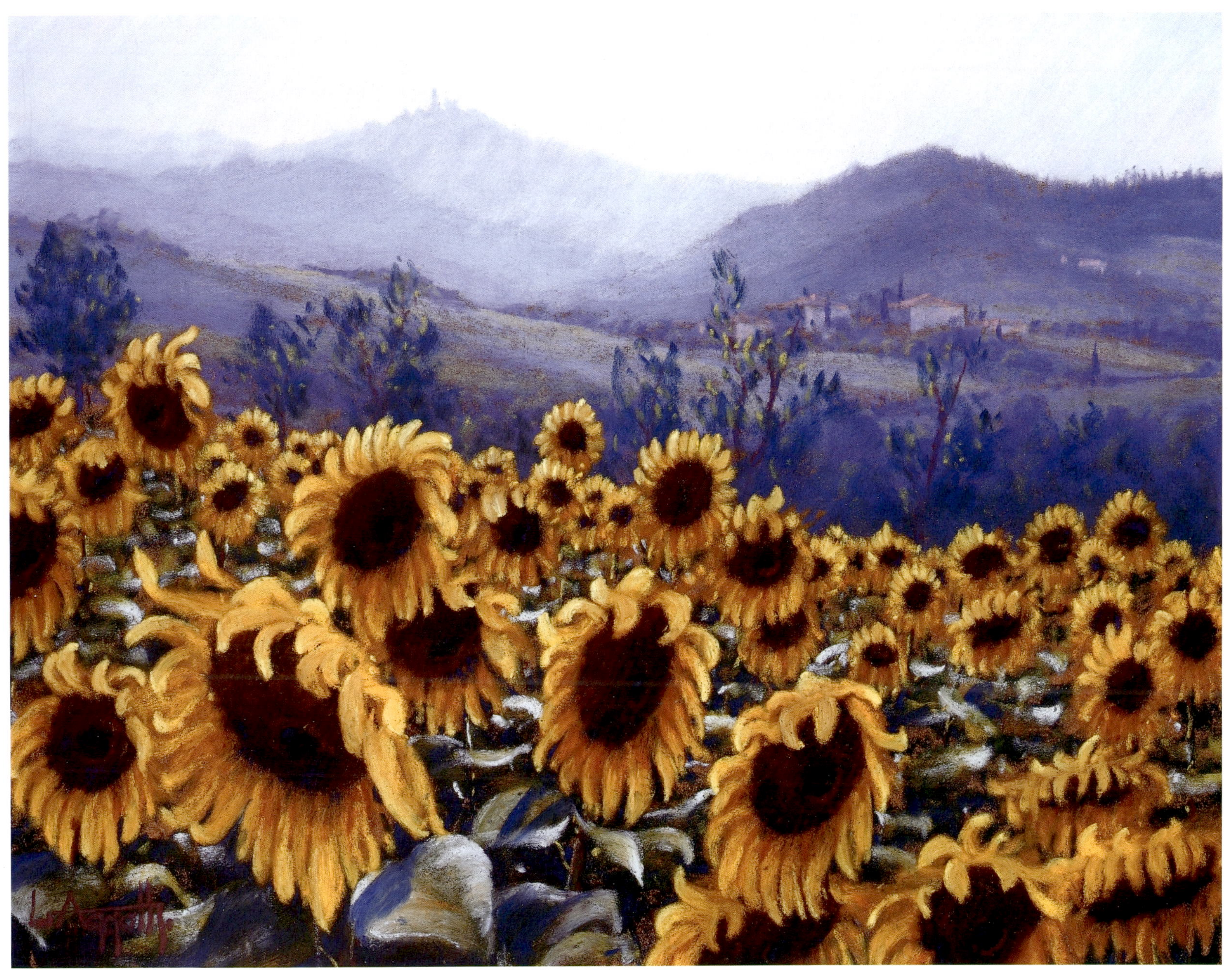

Evening near San Gimignano, Tuscany Pastel 250 x 325 mm

An Italian Romance

My love affair with Italy began during my architectural studies following enrolment as Probationer of the Royal Institute of British Architects in 1957, the year I left Exeter School. I was placed under Articles in the offices of J. Francis Smith and Partners, Architects and Surveyors (Exeter and London Wall). I worked at first in their Exeter office, with frequent visits to London for additional experience. Direct access to the superb Devon and Cornwall RIBA Library, housed at No 5 Cathedral Close, Exeter, on the first floor adjoining the office, and above Murray's Antiques, gave me every opportunity for studying the History of Architecture and Art.

The detailed study of the periods of Architecture culminating in drawn examples, in the form of History Sheets and presented as Testimonies of Study, was further broadened by my first visit to Italy in 1959 to experience the Renaissance masterpieces first hand. My employer and tutor, J. Francis Smith, paid the return train fares for myself and fellow student David Rhys, who was studying Building Surveying in the same office. We stayed at youth hostels, firstly in Perugia, Umbria, then Siena and finally in Florence, Tuscany, following a hike through glorious Tuscan countryside.

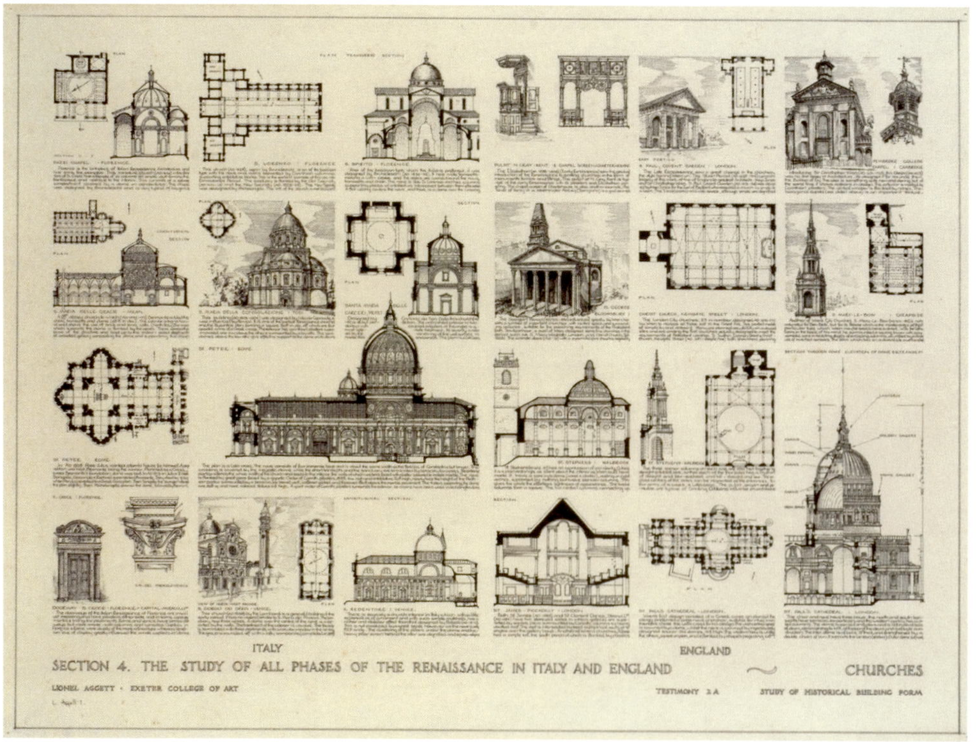

RIBA Testimony of Study. History of Architecture – Renaissance.

The architecture, landscape and paintings from those in the Uffizi, to the smallest country church have been etched in my mind ever since, to be re-kindled during every return visit. I still have those first Italian sketch books filled with rather scratchy Rapidograph pen drawings, and the more lively Fymo felt pen studies, made forty-eight years ago.

Although I was working in an office by day and studying by night, the salary was low due to the tutorage given. Additional means for further travel etc had therefore to be sourced through my own initiative. Following my Probationship and during the course of my studies, through the Intermediate and Final stages, I entered two RIBA Travelling Scholarship Design Competitions. I managed to win both; the first in 1961 for a self-planned visit to Northern Italy and Venice; the second in 1963 following the harsh winter, for the Rome School Easter visit. I was again accompanied by David Rhys for the first of these ventures. We travelled on my 1956 Lambretta to Venice for a month. The journey (quite an event in those days) was a memorable experience, and remains with me now as I pen these lines, having returned yesterday (1st April '07) from a working visit to that city. Much of the road network was unforgiving (the aftermath of the Second World War), for which the scooter's suspension and small wheels were rather unsuitable. The situation was exacerbated by the combined load of two lads and their large rucksacks. The bumpy ride from Le Havre down through France via Chartres, Auxerre and Dijon (where we sampled their gastronomic fare; we could only afford the starter, an omelette), resulted in mechanical failure. The rear suspension torsion bar sheared as we crossed the French-Swiss border. An extra day in Montreux was accepted with dutiful resignation and a painting of Chateau de Chillon ensued, which was later sold. Over the Simplon Pass, and down to Baveno for our YHA stop beside Lago Maggioré. Youth Hostels provided our accommodation throughout the journey.

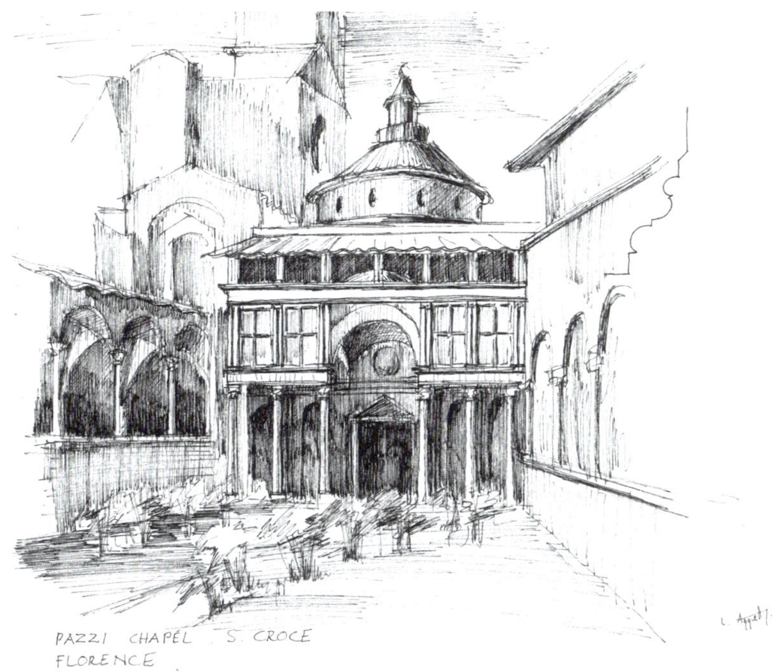

Pazzi Chapel, S.Croce, Florence Ink *Completed during the 1959 study tour.*

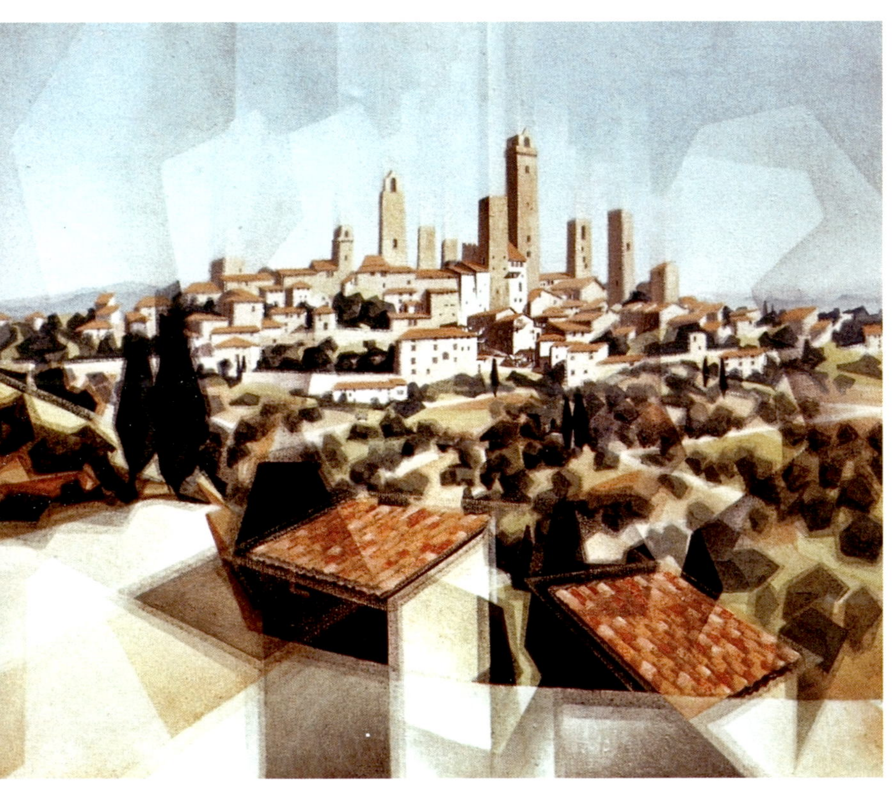
San Gimignano Acrylic *Painted in 1968 following the earlier study tour. Many works were painted in the '60s and '70s using this approach.*

On to Milan and The Last Supper; onward to the architectural and planning masterpieces of the grand northern towns: Cremona, Mantua, Padua, Vicenza, and finally across the causeway to Venice. The Youth Hostel was (probably still is) near Palladio's great church of the Il Redentore, on Giudecca. We were there, coincidentally, for the Feast of the Redeemer, and by design for the art and architecture. More about this amazing city later.

The visit to Rome with other RIBA students, who had won similar scholarships, with the Easter weekend in the middle of our stay, also made a lasting impression, and encouraged my development as an architect, architect planner, and artist. Much inspiration was gained from the topography, architecture, sculpture, murals, paintings and planning, both old and new. The 1960 Olympic complex, with many buildings designed by Pier Luigi Nervi are breathtaking and, for me, equated well with their Roman counterparts. I returned with over 50 watercolours, sketches and drawings, which were bound into a report for presentation to the RIBA.

The natural flair of the Italians has enabled them, over the centuries, to create a seamless fusion of architecture, sculpture and painting. The manner in which the whole organically relates to the topography through sensitive hard and soft landscaping has created "art" of an exemplary nature. This natural propensity for creating something that is "just so" is evident from the simple but correct placing of a sculpture in the smallest village square, usually adjacent to a gem of a church with an exquisite fresco inside, to the more ambitious and resplendent creations to be seen in and around Tivoli.

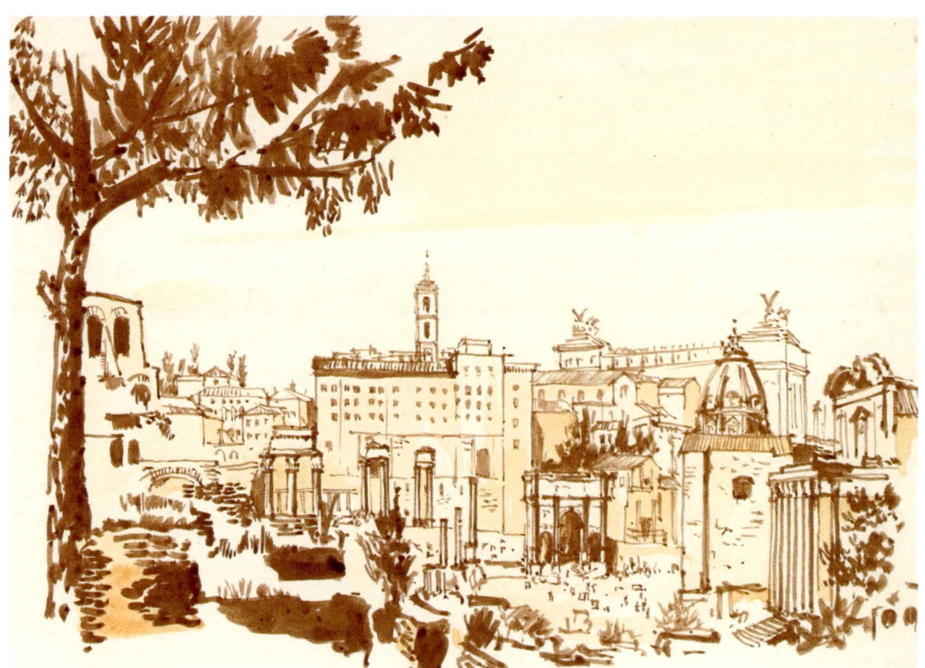

The Forum, Rome Ink & brush 240 x 240 mm.
Completed during the 1963 Rome Scholarship Easter Tour.

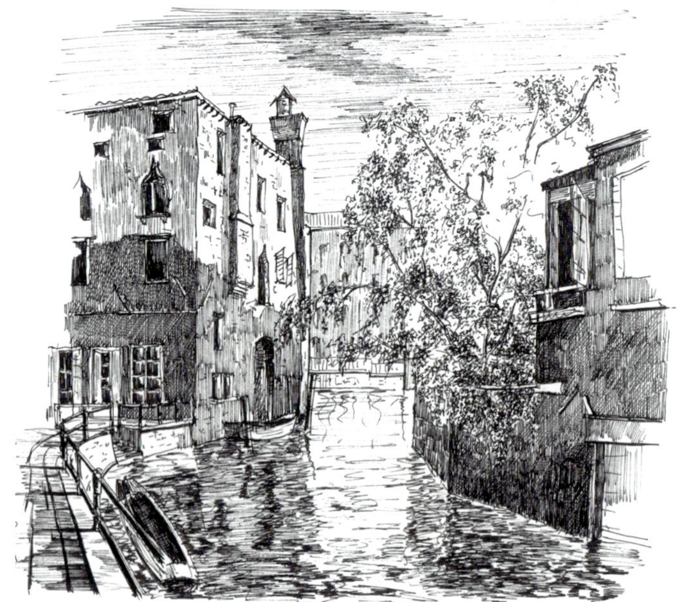

Campo S. Senero, Venice Ink
Completed during the 1961 Travelling Scholarship Tour.

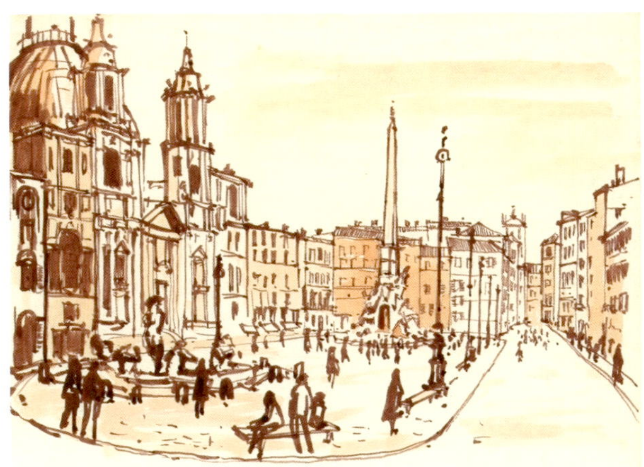

Piazza Navona, Rome
Ink & brush
250 x 345 mm.
Completed during the 1963 Rome Scholarship Easter Tour.

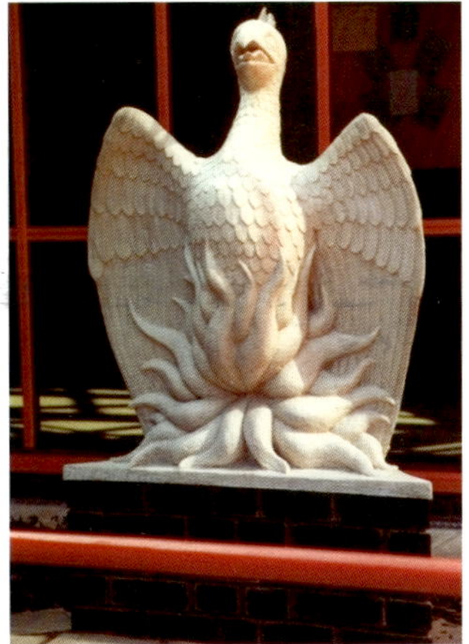

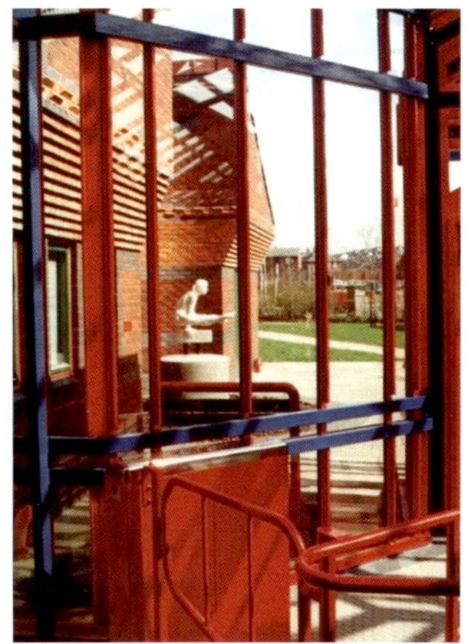

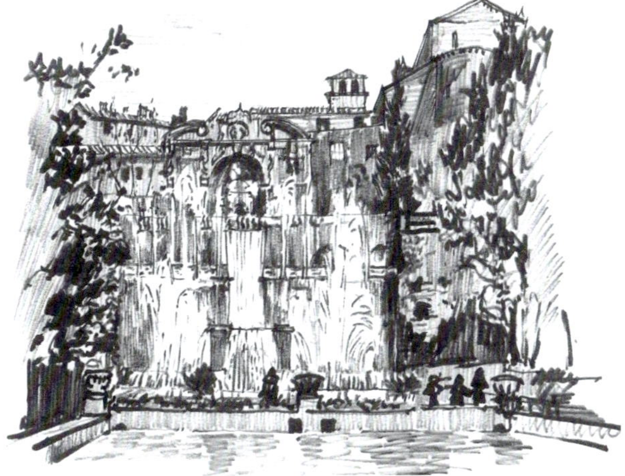

Villa D'Este, Tivoli
Fymo felt pen
230 x 300 mm.
Completed during the 1963 Rome Scholarship Easter Tour.

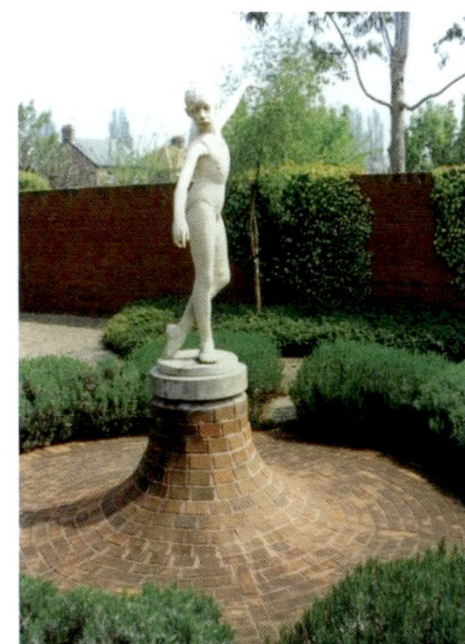

Above left & right: *Wonford Sports Centre, Exeter. Sculpture by Roger Dean.*

Left: *Housing Development, John Levers Way, Exeter. Sculpture by Marie Noelle Davies.*

Below left: *Housing Development, Wonford, Exeter. Sculpture by Roger Dean.*

Below right: *Exeter Quay, Conservation Scheme. Sculpture by Roger Dean.*

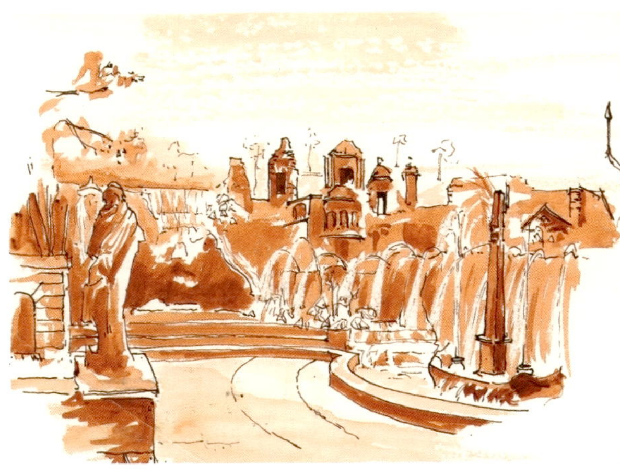

Villa D'Este, Tivoli
Ink, pen & brush
200 x 280 mm.
Completed during the 1963 Rome Scholarship Easter Tour.

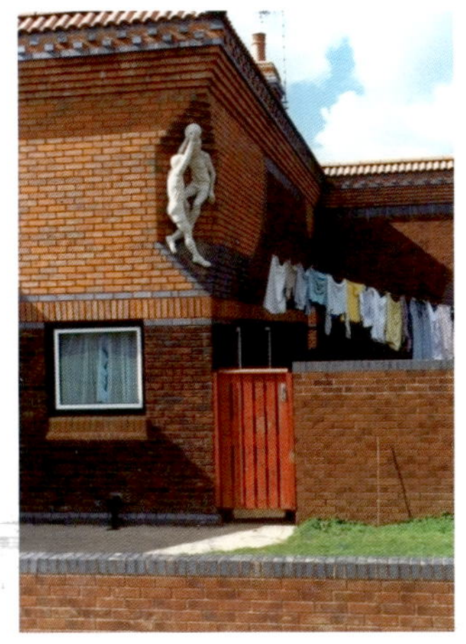

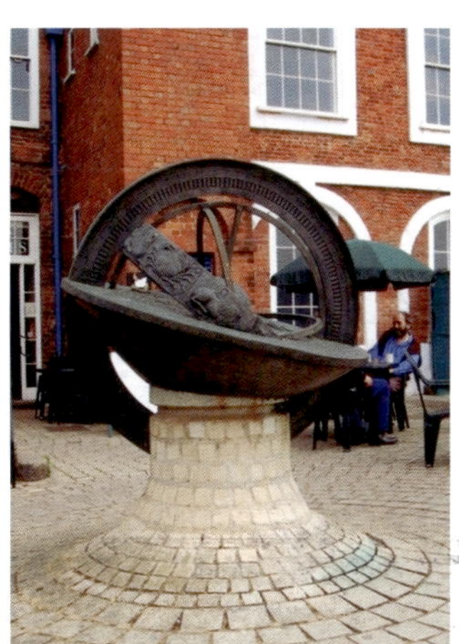

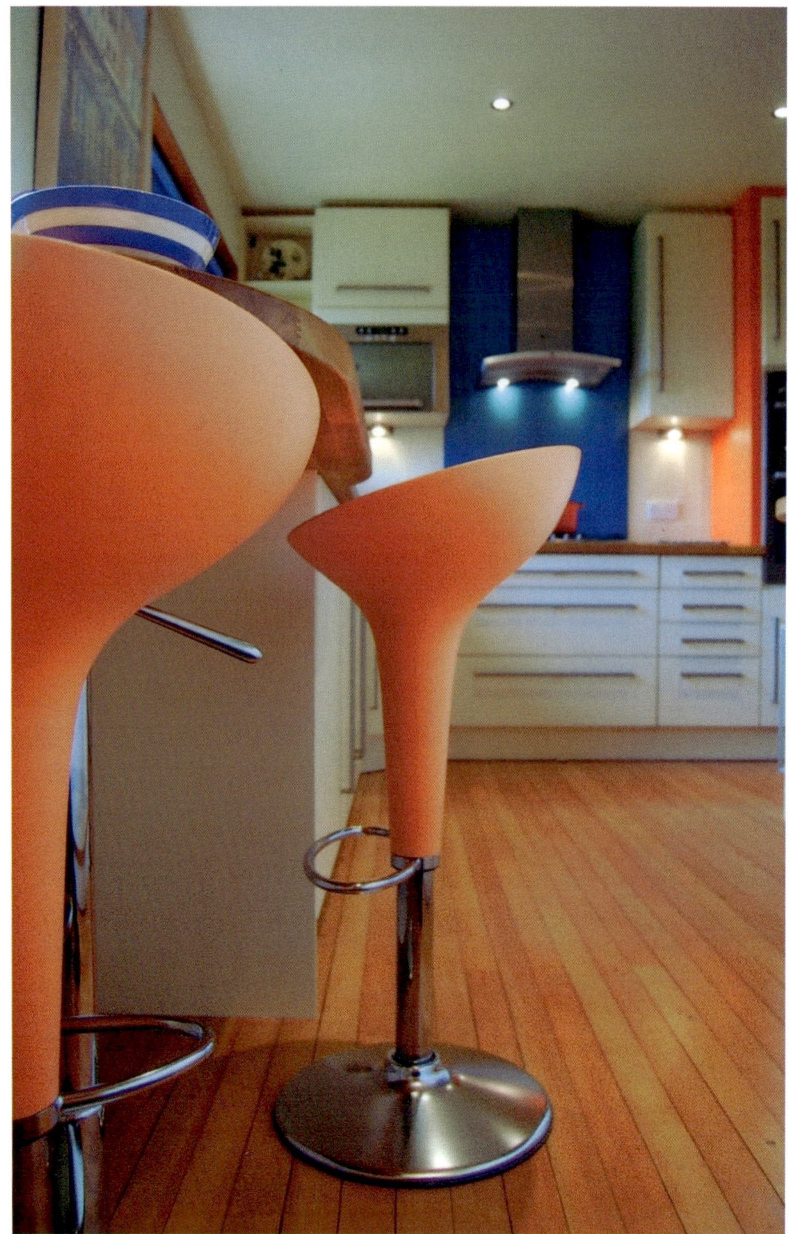

Lark Studio, Crediton. Bombo Stools by Magis, designed by Stefano Giovannoni.

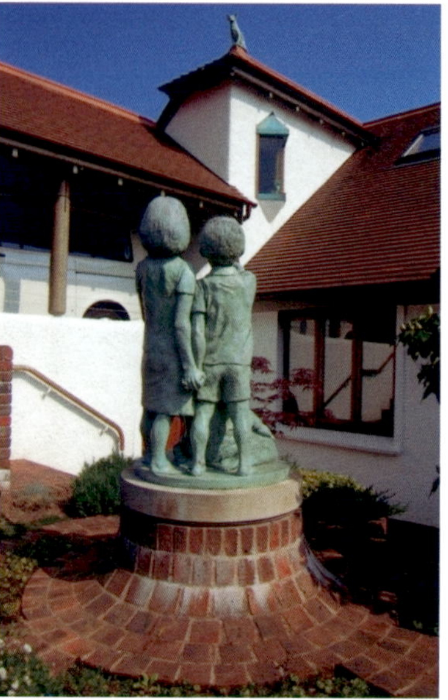

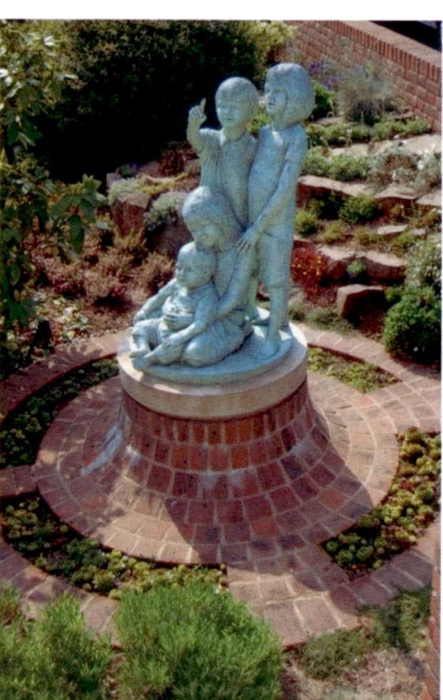

Lark Studio, Crediton. Sculpture by Roger Dean.

All of these early observations have influenced my modest architectural creations, particularly where sculpture has been introduced in specifically designed spaces, and where the surroundings are always taken into account. I am also not afraid of painting large scale "canvasses"! So these early excursions (apart from Rome, which I have yet to revisit, but will do so with Anne before long) laid the foundations for later working visits as a full-time artist.

The Italian Renaissance certainly had a profound affect on my approach to life. My introduction to it, occurring as it did, at a time when creative instincts were being stirred, initiated the will to at least strive for high standards in my chosen field i.e. art and architecture. Moreover it is essential for this endeavour to be balanced by a healthy interest in the general pursuit of culture, science, sport and outdoor activities. I was well versed in the latter disciplines, but it was high time a hitherto lacklustre academic career was kick-started into life through my own mini Renaissance.

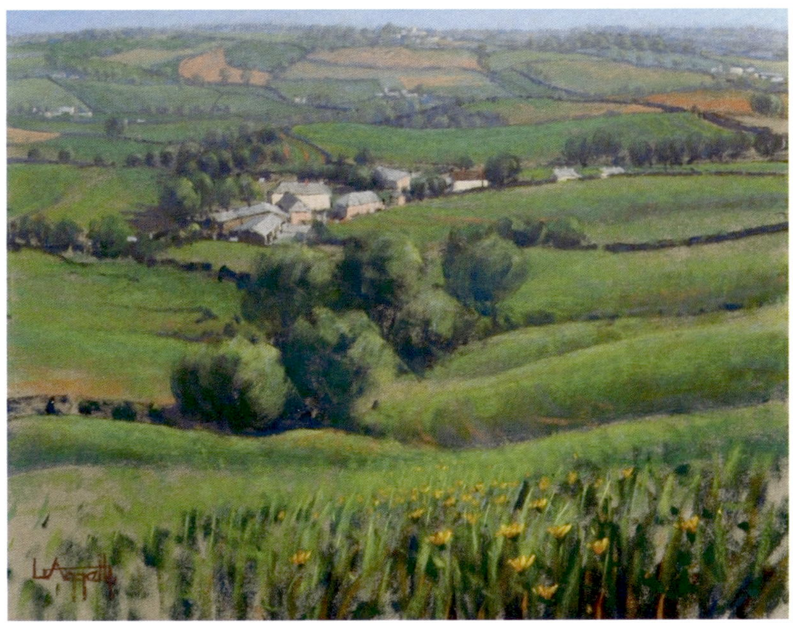

Mid Devon Landscape Pastel 250 x 325 mm

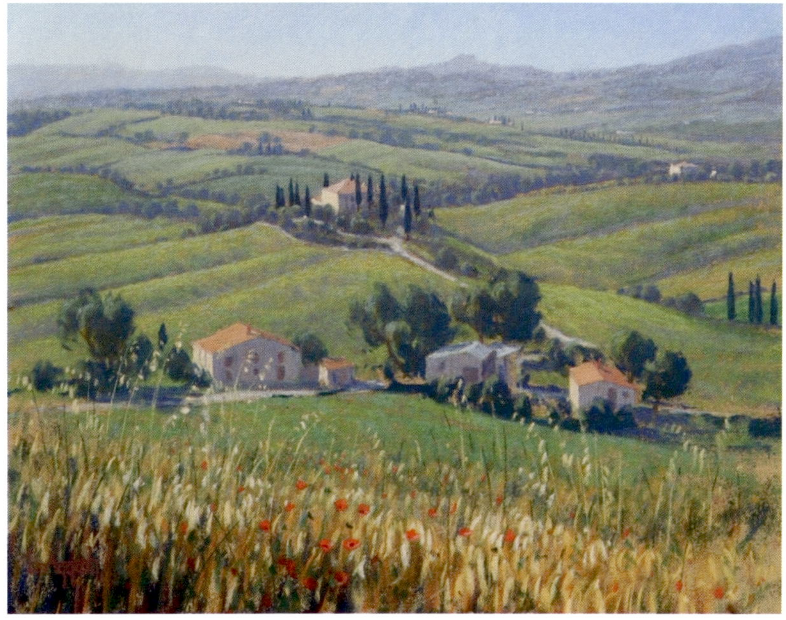

Tuscan Landscape Pastel 250 x 325 mm

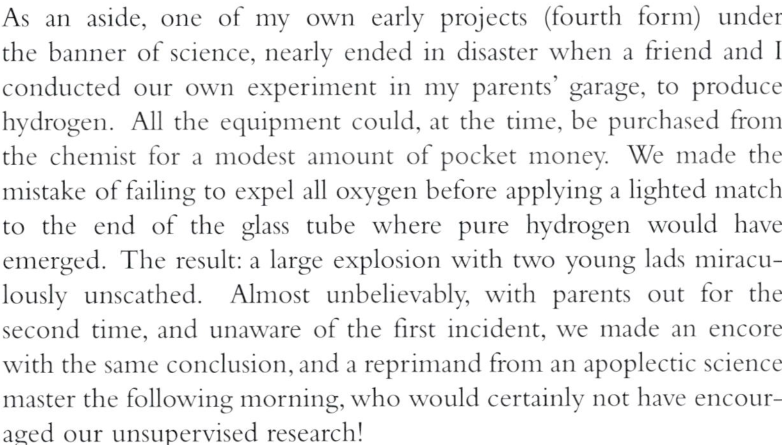

As an aside, one of my own early projects (fourth form) under the banner of science, nearly ended in disaster when a friend and I conducted our own experiment in my parents' garage, to produce hydrogen. All the equipment could, at the time, be purchased from the chemist for a modest amount of pocket money. We made the mistake of failing to expel all oxygen before applying a lighted match to the end of the glass tube where pure hydrogen would have emerged. The result: a large explosion with two young lads miraculously unscathed. Almost unbelievably, with parents out for the second time, and unaware of the first incident, we made an encore with the same conclusion, and a reprimand from an apoplectic science master the following morning, who would certainly not have encouraged our unsupervised research!

We Devonians, and the many welcome newcomers who choose to relocate in this part of the UK, are indeed most fortunate to reside in a most wonderfully varied county. The scenery and its making is not unlike the terrain encountered in Umbria and Tuscany. The deciduous woodland, and highly manicured rolling fields of our patch here in Mid Devon, referred to by chef Christopher Archambault as the "Tuscany of England", is very similar to the intensively farmed green heart of Italy. We are lacking those sentinel-like cypress trees, but the south-facing slopes do support increasing numbers of vineyards, and sunflower crops now compete on a modest scale with cereals in certain areas. We have hill top villages too, but above all, there is a common thread to both regions: an affinity and respect and a deep understanding for land management. Climate change may gradually herald more similarities.

Finally, my admiration for Italian design – Lambretta, Vespa, Pier Luigi Nervi, Gio Ponti, Renzo Piano – has been manifested recently by the purchase of two Magis Bombo stools designed by Stefano Giovannoni; the final piece of the jigsaw to phase three, and the last, of our redevelopment at Lark Studio, the kitchen!

Return Journey to the South

Our excursion to the South of Italy does not extend to the furthermost tip of the peninsula at Melito di Porto Salvo, in Calabria, or even Sicily, but as far as Taranto in Puglia. The journey nevertheless entails a fairly long drive, and by taking it in stages, sensibly paced, the opportunity is provided for capturing the gradual change in topography, and climatic conditions, through my diary sketches. This method of travel works best for me, as I arrive at the main destination primed and ready to paint. Flying is convenient and quick but time is then needed for acclimatization, thus cancelling out the advantage.

The basic decision to be made when driving to Italy, is how best to negotiate the Alps. We have tried several options with varying degrees of success. During one of my solo visits, I used the incredibly busy, but direct commercial Frejus tunnel, through to Susa, and on past Turin, with the return journey along the Valle d'Aosta and Mont Blanc tunnel. When the Mont Blanc tunnel was closed following the tragic fire, Anne and I used the San Gottard tunnel, only to discover as we encountered diversion signs, that one tunnel was closed for renovation. The experience of negotiating two way traffic in a normally one way tunnel was hairy to say the least. Anne, as passenger, in our right hand drive vehicle, was constantly facing huge articulated lorries, their lights blazing, hurtling towards her, and passing with inches to spare. We therefore decided for our most recent trip (2006) to by-pass the Alps, travelling down beside the Rhone and then along the Riviera. The route, which takes you through endless tunnels, is looking very tired, and several rest areas were being renovated. When fully restored, the road will once again revert to the engineering marvel it truly is.

I have also been over the top on a scooter, back in 1961, with my student pal David Rhys, riding pillion. Over the Simplon Pass on our

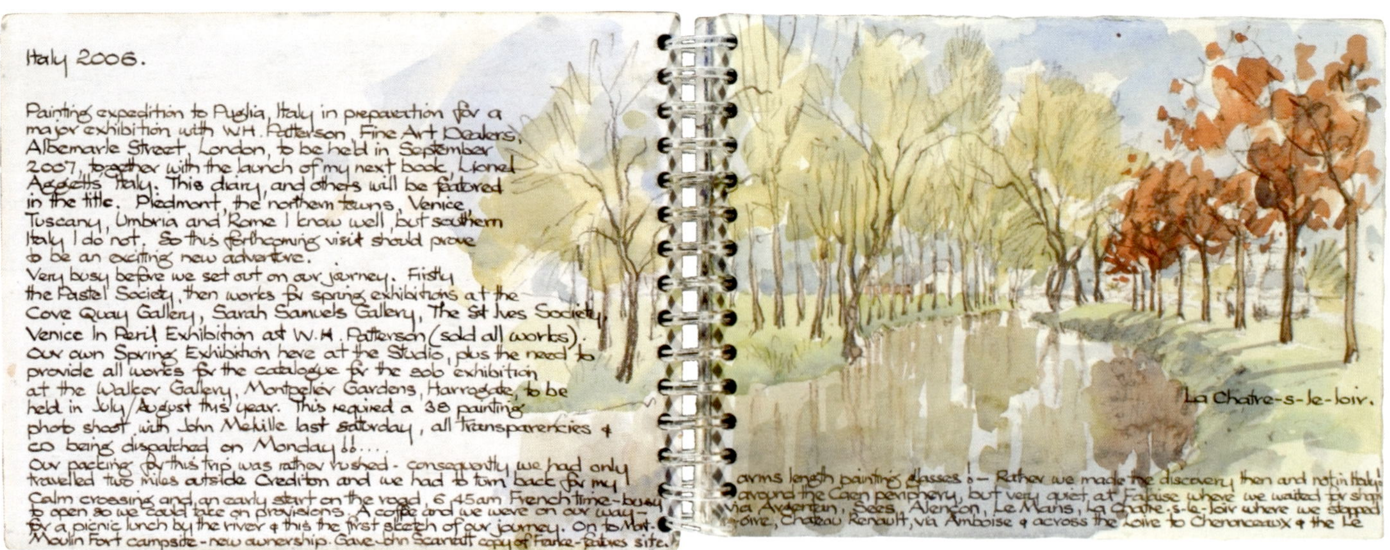

Diary Sketch 26th April, 2006 *La Chartre-s-le-Loir* Conté w/c

way down, and the San Gottard Pass, and Susten Pass on the return journey. Great fun around the wet cobbled hairpin bends, the small wheels spinning and slipping like tops! Many of the more recent trips have been made in the spring however, when these high altitude roads are closed.

Our journey south, although principally based on our visit last year (2006) to Puglia, will be an amalgam of the many undertaken. It will not include Venice, other than the logging of the 1961 scooter journey on the map. The delights of this magnificent city are described, and illustrated towards the end of this book.

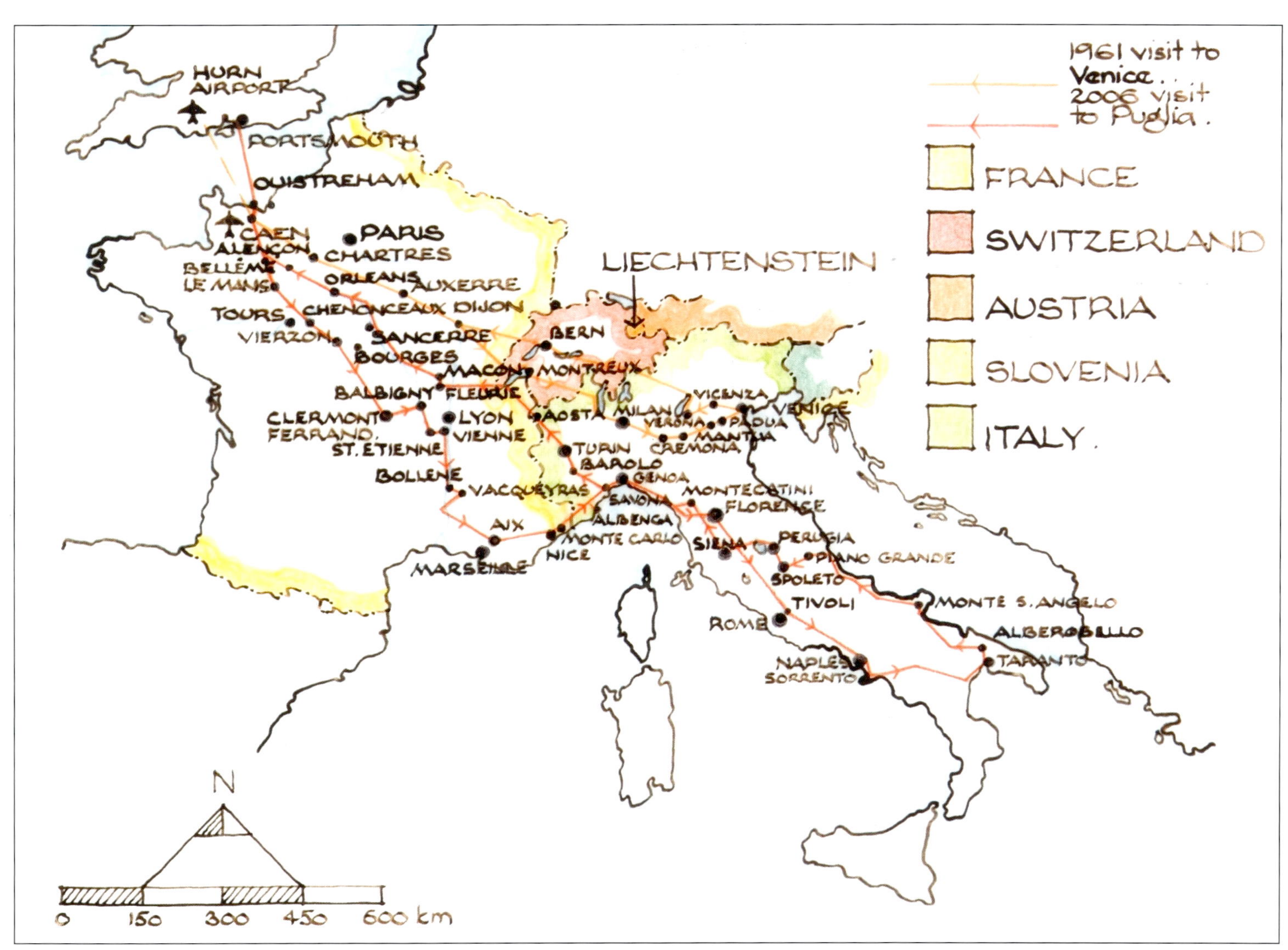

THE JOURNEY

When heading for the South we usually prefer to use the Portsmouth – Caen crossing. The overnight "voyage" deposits us and our VW on the French shore, in a convenient position for a bright and early start; the port at Ouistreham being approximately 100 miles further down into France than other points of disembarkation.

Heading for the Italian border near Ventimiglia on the Riviera, we took the option whereby the Alps are avoided, and the delights of the Rhône Valley, Provence and the Cote D'Azur are sampled.

Skirting Caen, as the city was stirring into life, we drove on to Falaise where we had coffee whilst waiting for the shops to open. Having taken on provisions, then down via Argentan, Sées, Le Mans, La Chartre-s-le-Loir (picnic lunch and sketch), across the Loire where we made our first stop beside the Cher at Chenonceux, a two night stay to recharge our batteries before the long drive. Our "At Home" studio exhibition finished just prior to our departure so we needed to "take five". The excellent Moulin Fort campsite, under new ownership is a wonderfully relaxing spot for both short and long stays.

The VW was repacked into some semblance of order following our hasty loading (usually more carefully done), and with Anne settled down to a good read, I decided to get into observation and painting mode by walking down beside the Cher to a spot beyond the bridge to the farmhouse I have sketched before, but from the opposite bank (*Lionel Aggett's France*). The late afternoon sun illuminated the fine building with a warm glow, and promised many exciting painting sorties to the South, in the weeks ahead.

As noted in my diary, we left Moulin Fort to the accompaniment of revving engines from across the river, where the Rallye National de Jardin de France was unleashing competitors upon the general public at one to two minute intervals. We were constantly buzzed as we made our way eastwards along the south bank of the Cher, until they made off to the south seeking rougher and more challenging terrain.

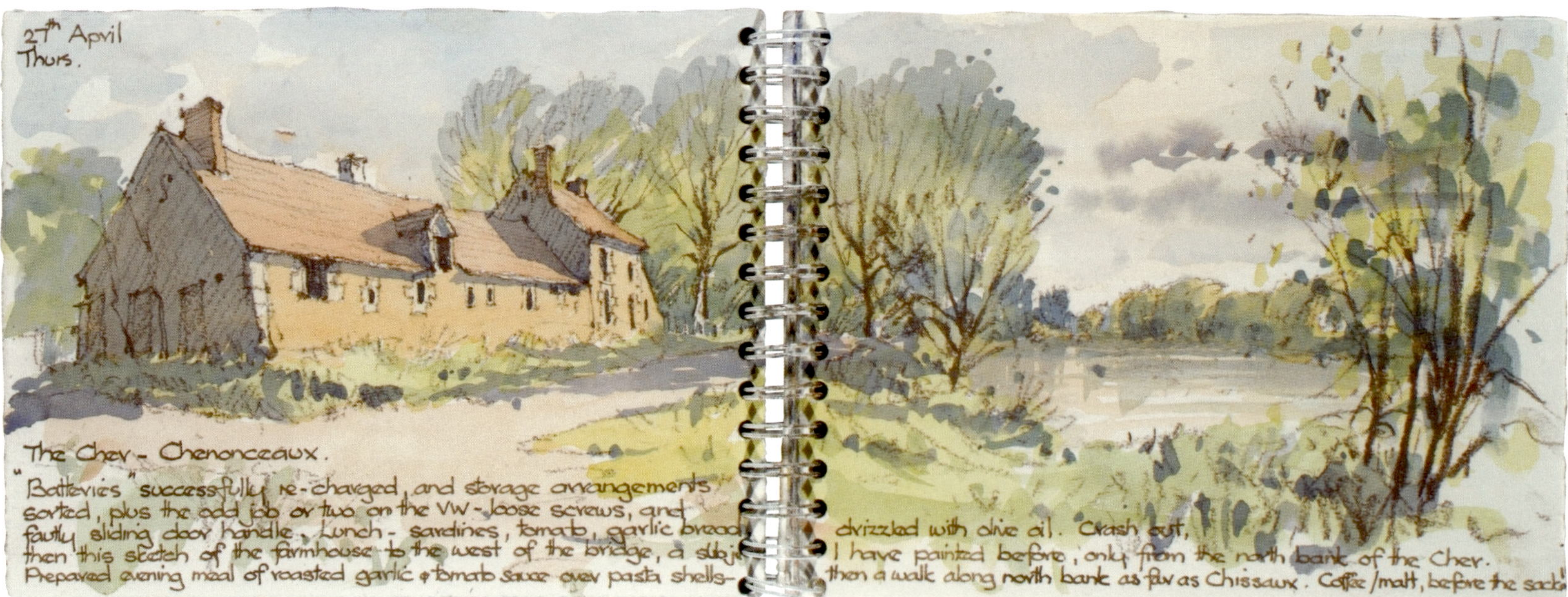

Diary Sketch 27th April, 2006 *The Cher, Chenonceaux* Conté w/c

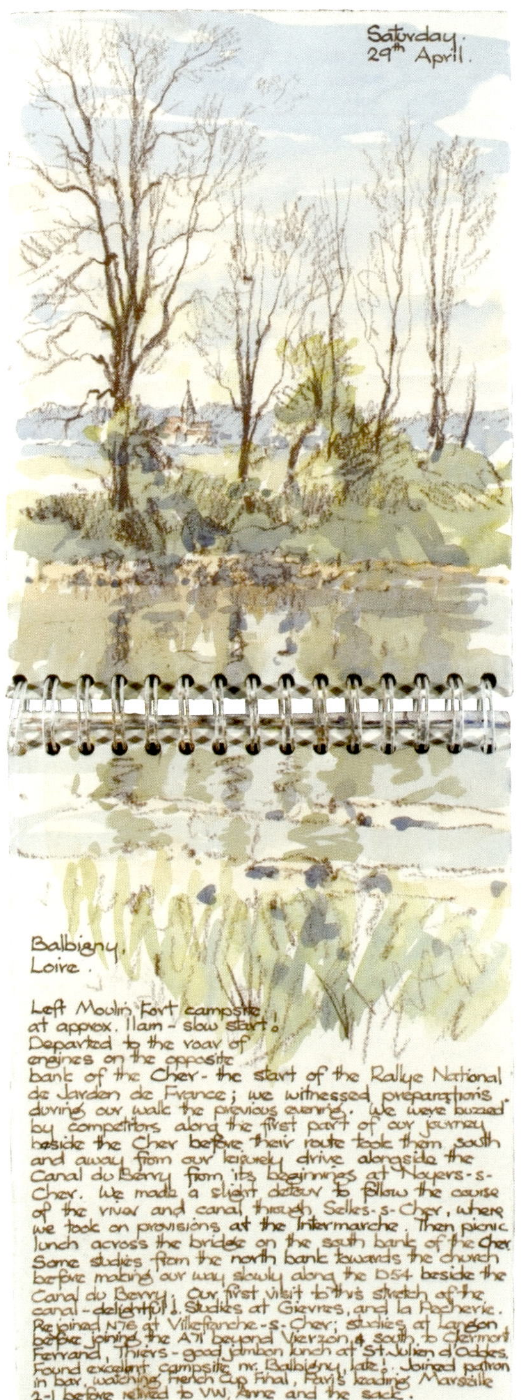

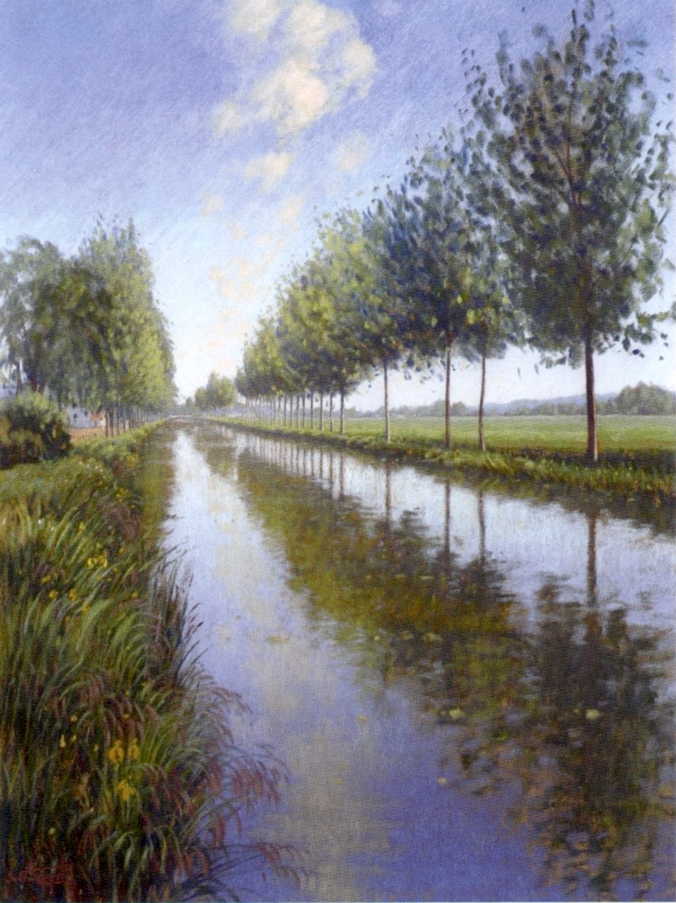

Left: *L'Eau Calme, Canal du Berry*
Pastel 650 x 500 mm.

Far left: Diary Sketch
29th April, 2006
Balbigny Conté w/c.

We lingered at Selles-s-Cher (lunch), and along the Canal du Berry for some more sketching, before heading down the A71 from Vierzon to Clermont Ferrand and across to Balbigny on the Loire. This move was in total contrast to our preferred comfortable pace, and working dawdle earlier in the day.

A quick diary sketch early the following morning down by the water's edge, outside this good Route Bleu, three star campsite. Then down the A72, via St Etienne to Vienne, and on down the Rhône Valley (A7) as far as Bollène, where we peeled off along the D8 for a leisurely doddle, past the vine covered slopes of Séguret, Sablet, Gigondas, and lastly, Vacqueyras, where we stayed at the superb municipal campsite, not for the first time, nor will it be the last. Superb wine, and beautiful scenery, worthy of a much longer stay (as we have experienced before), but onwards we must go.

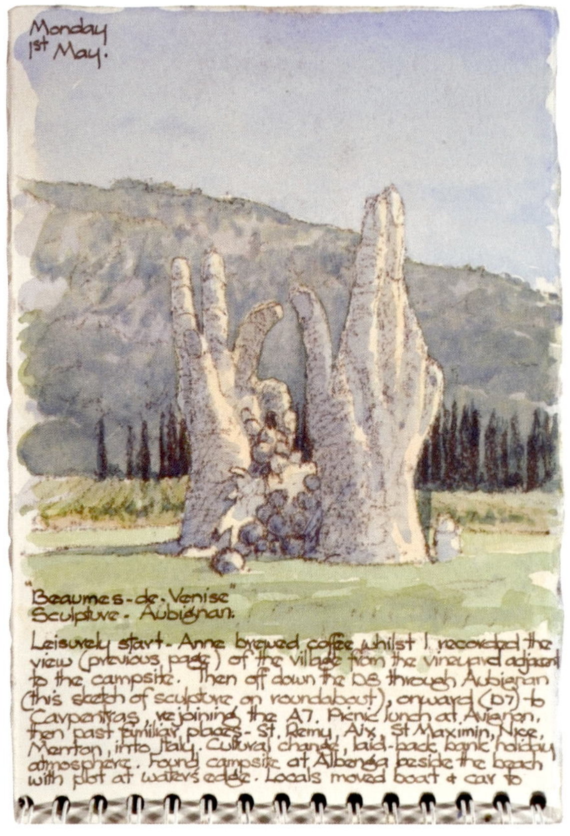

Past Carpentras to rejoin the A7 at Avignon, and then near haunts so very tantalisingly close, but which are not the focus of our attention this time; St Rémy-de-Provence, Aix-en-Provence, St Maximin-La-Ste-Baume, St Tropez and Vence, to the border between Menton and Ventimiglia, where our Italian adventure begins.

The frenetic, zippy driving experienced along the French Riviera was immediately exchanged for a more laid back, considerately driven, albeit more tired looking stretch of road (A10), shrouded by tunnel after tunnel, offering spectacular strobe-like, sunlit flashes of the coast and towns below.

Now we have arrived on Italian soil it would be appropriate perhaps to mention that this book does not purport to cover every aspect and corner of Italy. Many areas are omitted for the simple reason I have not been there. The Ligurian coastline is one such example. A better appreciation of this part of the region, where mountains tumble right down to the water's edge, would be achieved by dropping down to the Via Aurelia which winds through all the coastal towns and villages. We have yet to do this, and for now we are simply just passing through.

Left: Diary Sketch 1st May, 2006 *Beaumes-de-Venise. Sculpture, Aubignan* Conté w/c

Below: Diary Sketch 30th April, 2006 *Vacqueyras* Conté w/c

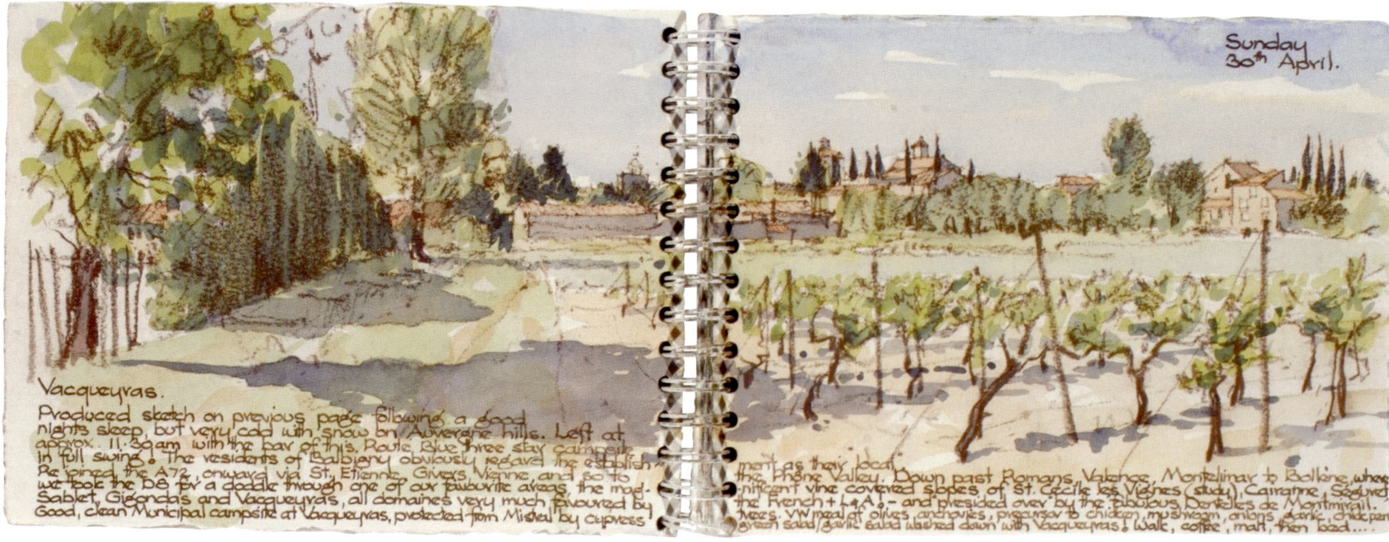

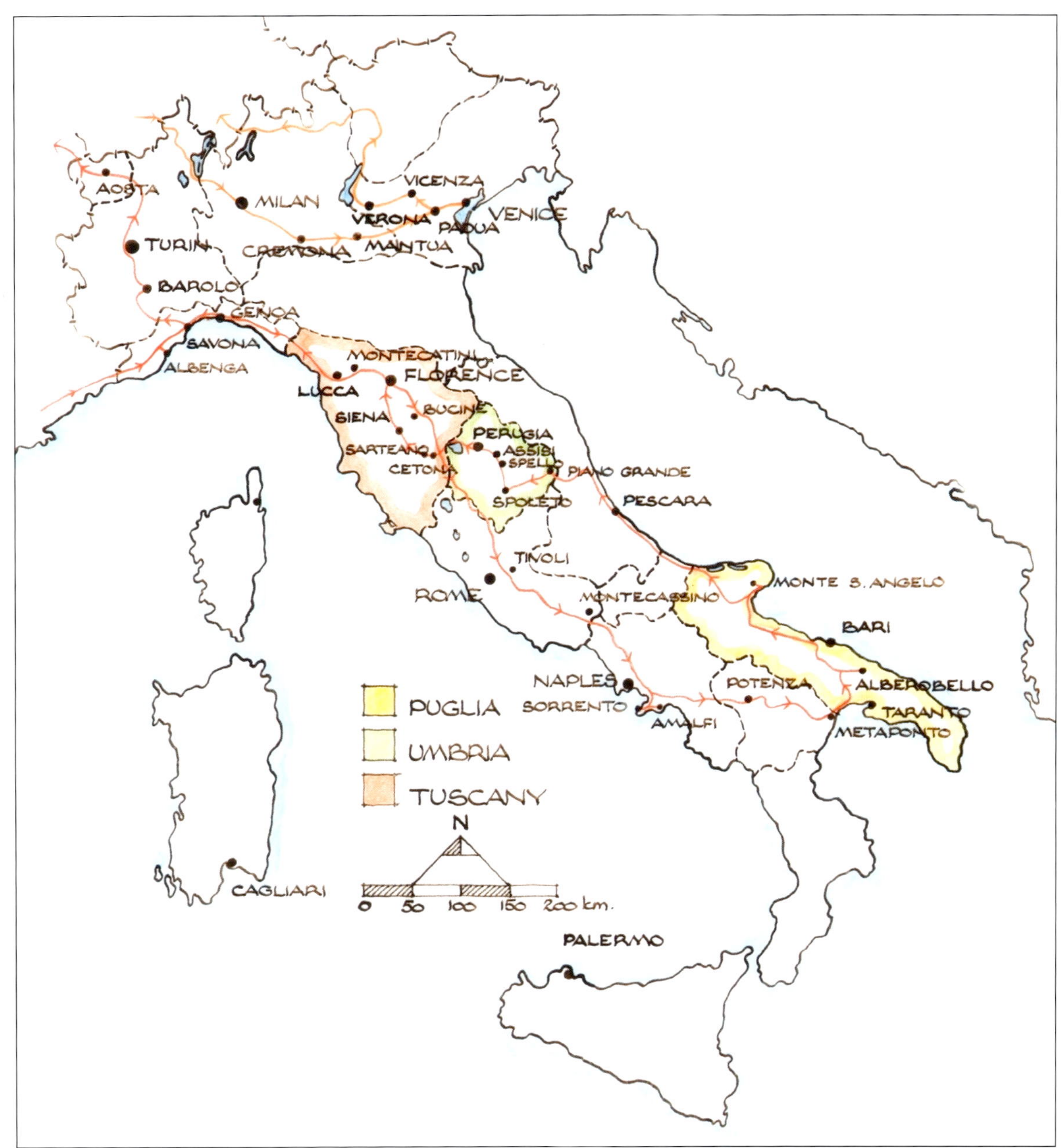
AOSTA
MILAN
VICENZA
VERONA
PADUA
VENICE
TURIN
CREMONA
MANTUA
BAROLO
GENOA
SAVONA
ALBENGA
MONTECATINI
FLORENCE
LUCCA
SIENA
BUCINE
PERUGIA
SARTEANO
ASSISI
CETONA
SPELLO
PIANO GRANDE
SPOLETO
PESCARA
TIVOLI
ROME
MONTECASSINO
MONTE S. ANGELO
BARI
NAPLES
POTENZA
ALBEROBELLO
SORRENTO
AMALFI
TARANTO
METAPONTO
PUGLIA
UMBRIA
TUSCANY
N
0 50 100 150 200 km.
CAGLIARI
PALERMO

LIGURIA – TUSCANY – UMBRIA – LAZIO

We did, however, wander down to the water's edge at Albenga beyond Alassio, for our first overnight stop in Italy. A friendly campsite; obviously a favourite with the Italians, many of whom possessed static wooden cabins or shacks. There was just one space remaining, albeit occupied by a car and boat, right next to the Mediterranean. The locals joyfully moved all obstacles, and kindly guided us to the spot that faced due east, and from where we experienced the most magnificent sunrise the following morning, followed by activities well documented in the diary excerpt below.

Refreshed once again, we drove along the extensively tunelled A12 through Genoa until eventually the mountainous coastal route opened out below the dramatic glistening white scarred peaks of Carrara, just over the border in Tuscany. Turning inland from Viareggio along the A11 past Lucca, Florence, the Duomo, with Brunelleschi's dome gloriously visible above this wondrous city; we skirted the northern edge of Chianti, down the A1 towards Rome.

We came off the motorway at Incisa in Val d'Arno to avoid roadworks and travelled along the R69 and P540 to Bucine, an absolute haven of a campsite after all the travelling. Olive groves, vineyards, cypress trees and deciduous woodland; we had arrived!

The following morning we set off, towards Arezzo before rejoining the A1 down through Southern Tuscany past Montepulciano, Chianciano, and Sarteano, an area to be considered in detail later.

A lunch stop at Fabro, just into Umbria, then on past Orvieto into Lazio and onward to Tivoli in the hills east of Rome. My batteries running down, I made a slight hash regarding the location of the campsite, which entailed a triple circumnavigation of the town before we engaged the correct road out to the campsite at La Cerra. An idyllic setting, just outside the town, our view from the VW is recorded in the diary excerpt, and the painting. The ink sketch of the Villa D'Este was produced in 1963 during the Rome

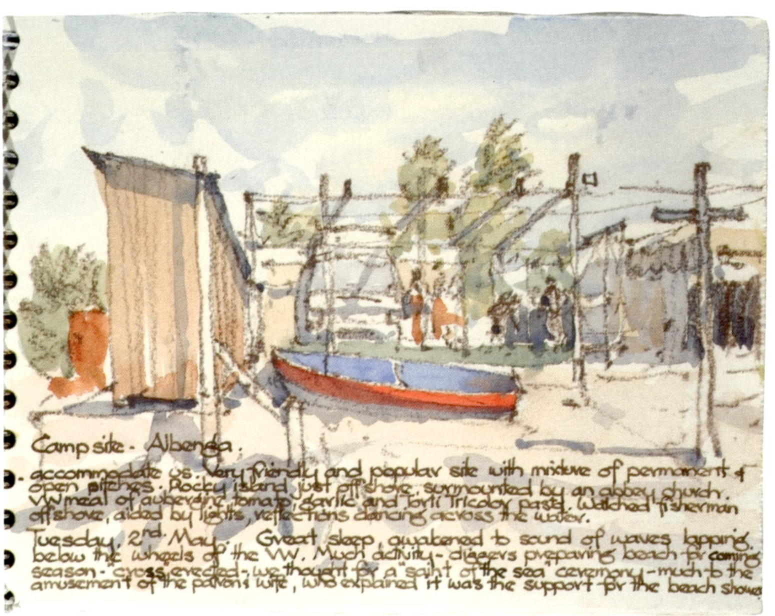

Diary Sketch 2nd May, 2006 *Albenga* Conté w/c.

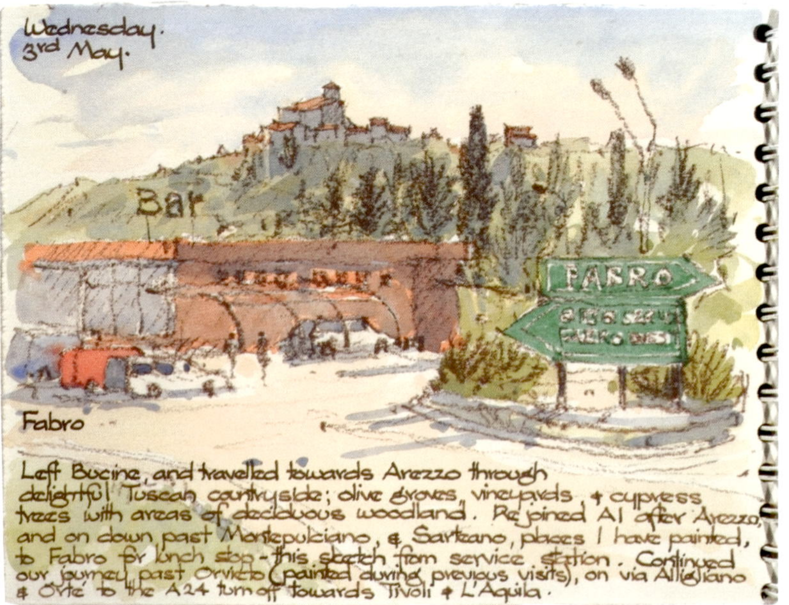

Diary Sketch 3rd May, 2006 *Fabro* Conté w/c

Scholarship Tour mentioned earlier. The crown jewel of the town, the garden is renowned for its magnificent fountains designed by the architect Pirro Ligorio, who utilised the water of the River Aniene to feed the water features. The location has provided the inspiration for many artists over the centuries including Liszt, D'Annunzio, Piranesi and Turner.

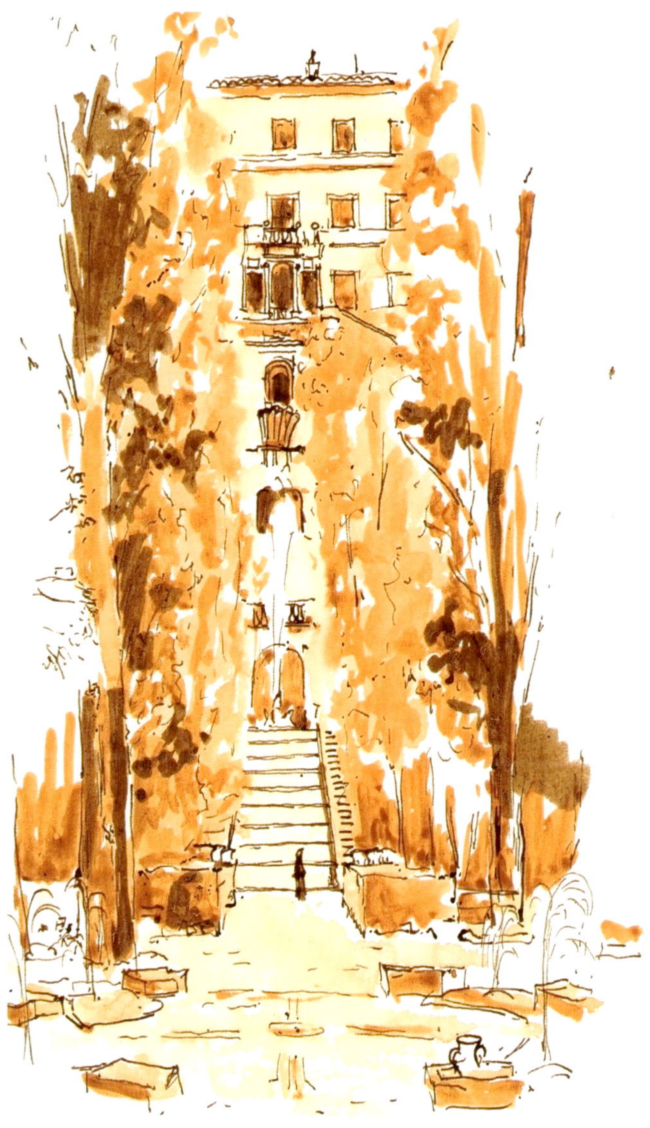

Villa D'Este, Tivoli Ink, pen & brush 310 x 83 mm. *Completed during 1963 Rome Scholarship Easter Tour.*

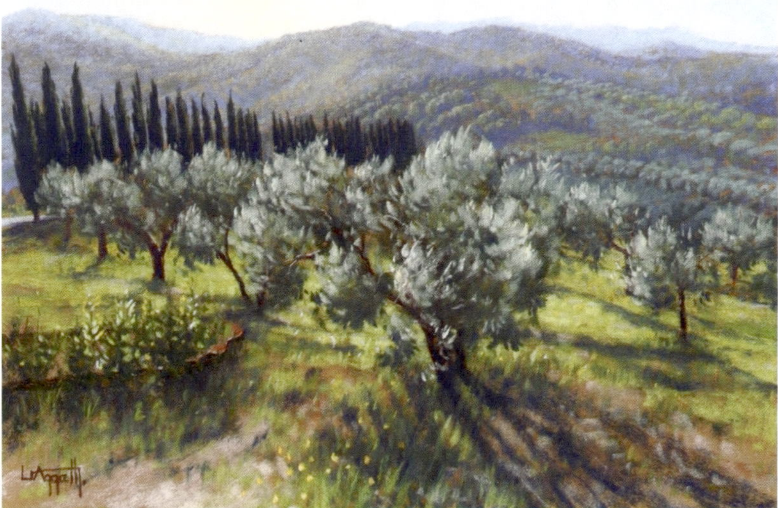

La Cerra, Tivoli Pastel 325 x 500 mm

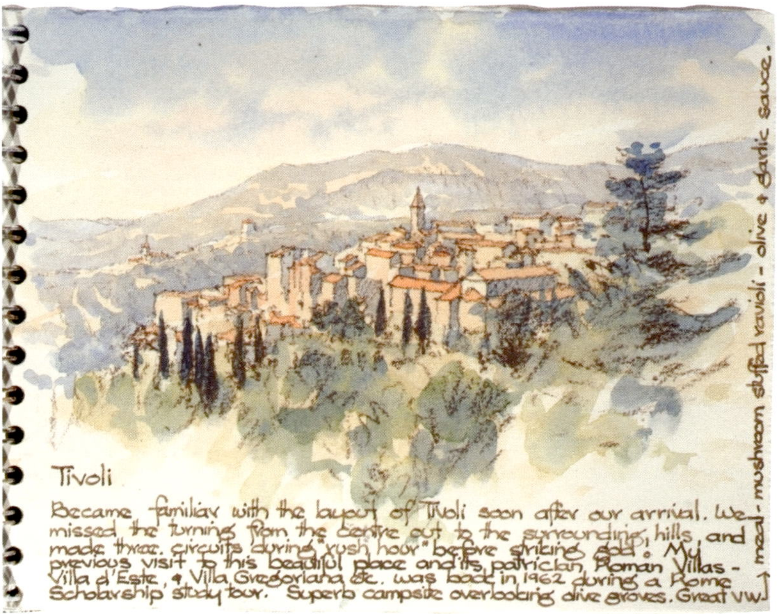

Diary Sketch 3rd May, 2006 *Tivoli* Conté w/c

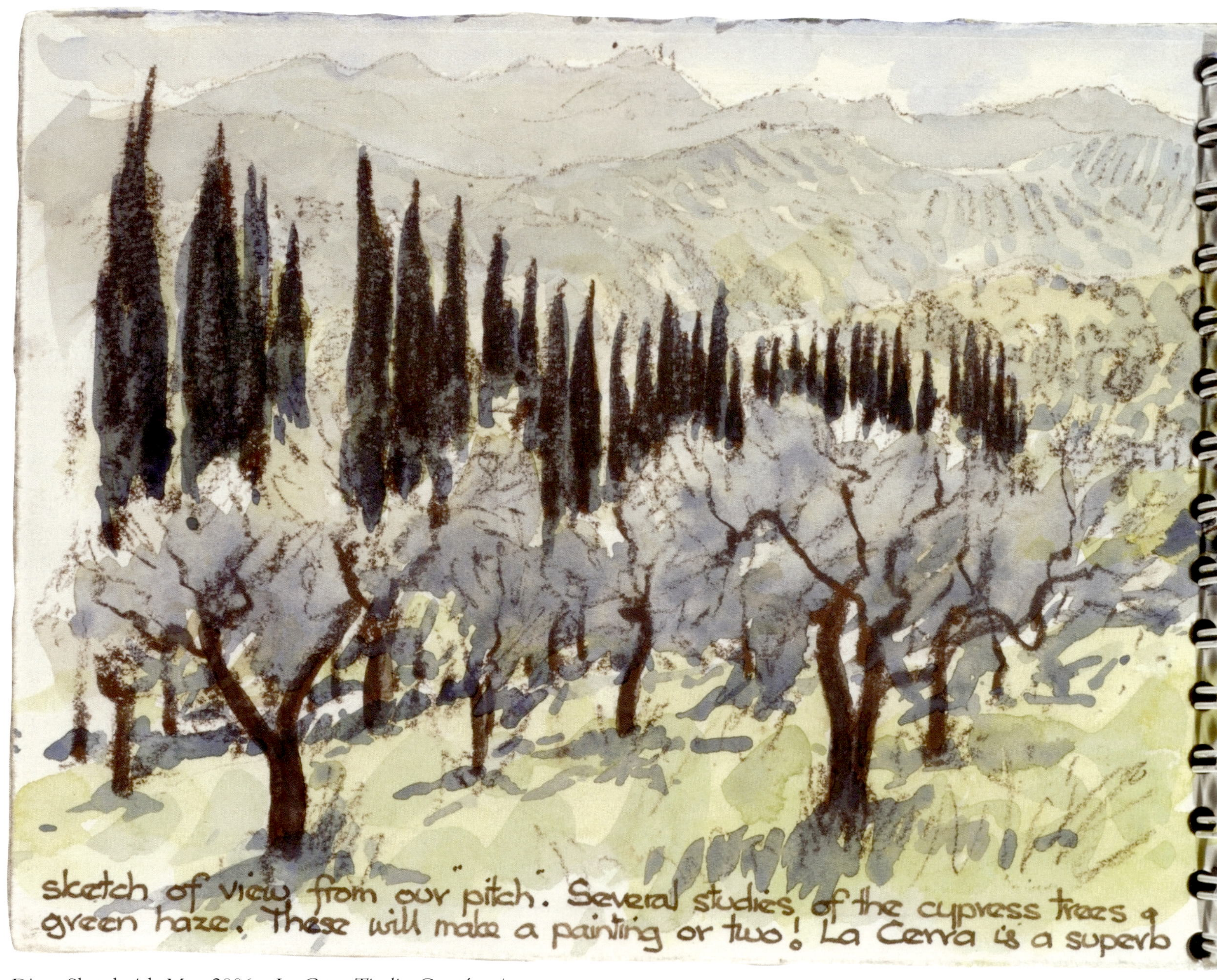

Diary Sketch 4th May, 2006 *La Cerra, Tivoli* Conté w/c

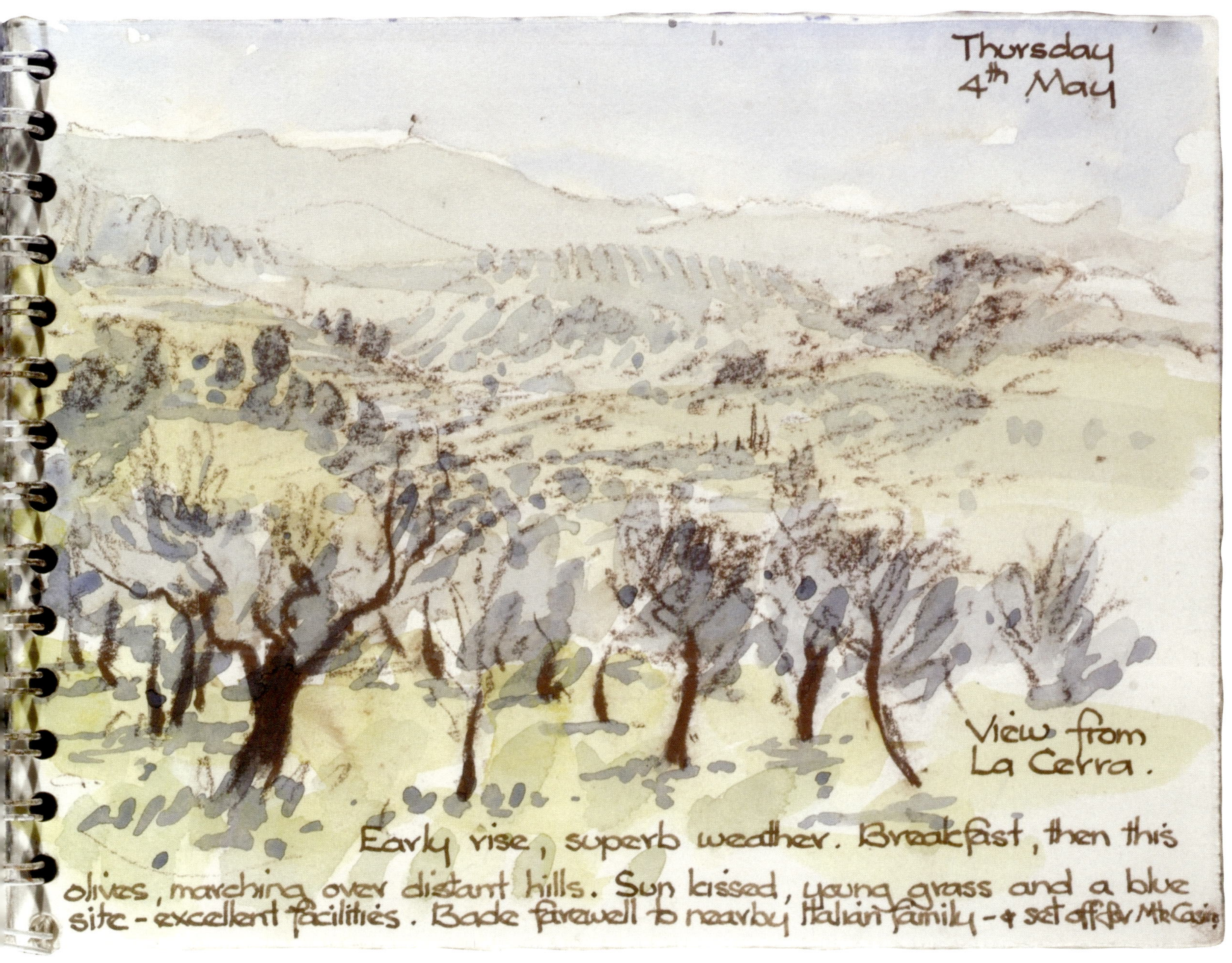
Thursday
4th May
View from
La Cerra.
Early rise, superb weather. Breakfast, then this
olives, marching over distant hills. Sun kissed, young grass and a blue
site - excellent facilities. Bade farewell to nearby Italian family - & set off for Mt Casin

CAMPANIA

Just one night's stay (we shall return), before we head on down the A1, destination Sorrento, with a stop for a picnic lunch, and sketch, at Montecassino. The monastery is situated above the plain on a spur of the mountains behind the town; a position of great strategic importance in 1944. We visited the Polish cemetery high on the mount to the north west of the Abbazia, an extremely moving memorial to those who carried the main offensive on foot.

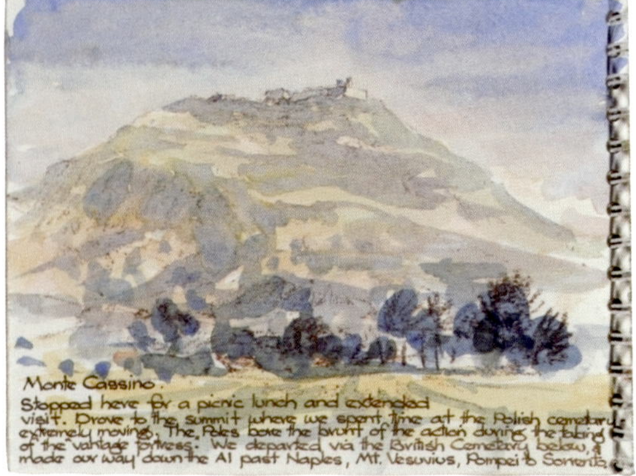

Diary Sketch
4th May, 2006
Montecassino
Conté w/c

The journey into Campania proved to be quite an experience, with the driving becoming more frenzied as we approached Naples. As we made our way around the south-east side of the city, and around the bay to Castellammare, I gradually appreciated that the southern Italians regard the automobile as an extension of the body, their combined movements akin to pedestrians weaving their way along a busy pedestrian thoroughfare. As long as you drive positively, you are fine, but show any sign of hesitation, and you are blared, honked and beeped at and, at worst, clobbered from behind. It is common to be overtaken on both sides, with scooters and motorbikes taking to the pavements in order to do so. We arrived in Sorrento unscathed, somewhat relieved, and rather elated! We found a very good campsite (there are many), the Santa Fortunata, with a terraced pitch and super view outside the sliding side door of the VW, as per the diary sketch.

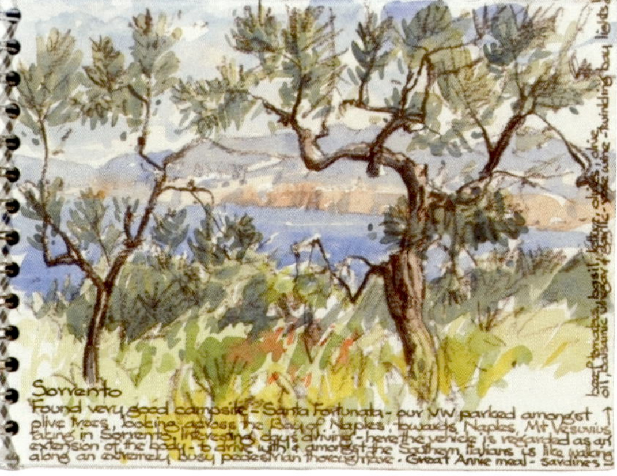

Diary Sketch
5th May, 2006
Sorrento
Conté w/c

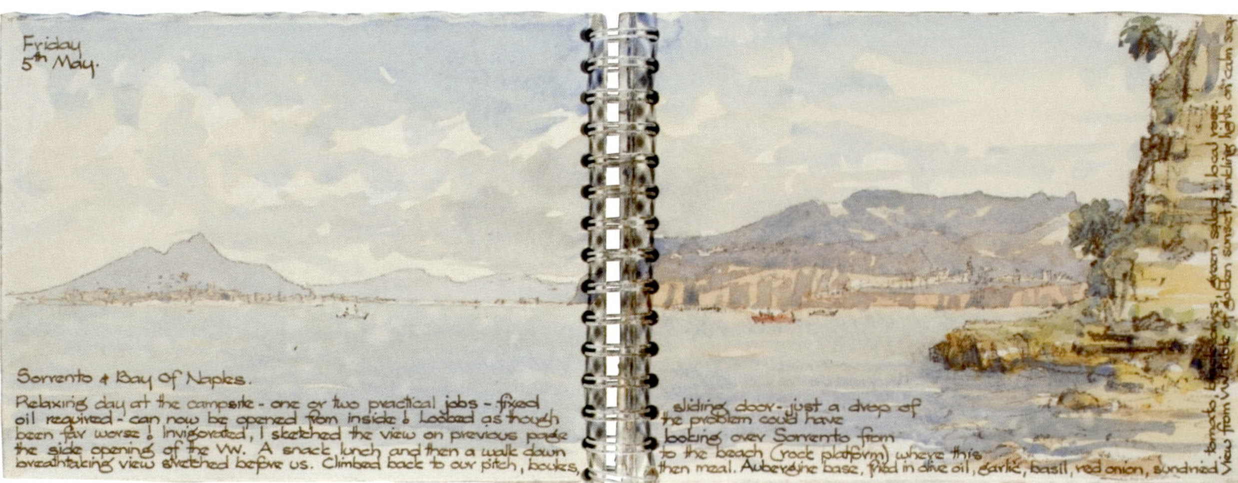

Diary Sketch 5th May, 2006 *Sorrento and Bay of Naples* Conté w/c

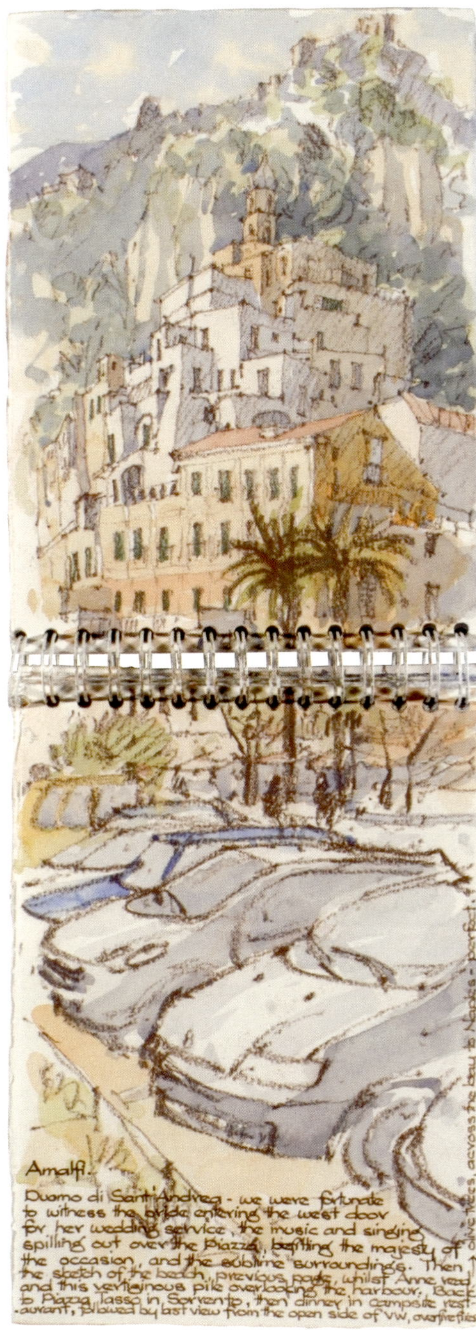

Diary Sketch 6th May, 2006 *Amalfi*
Conté w/c

We stayed here for three nights. The first day we spent relaxing and sketching, the next we caught the SITA bus to Amalfi, leaving the VW to recover. The Amalfi Drive, taking in Positano on the way, is beautiful, but for the painter, unless you have planned for a longer stay, also frustrating. Judging from the amount of traffic on the road, I am sure that, had we driven, most of the day would have been spent reversing, and with very few places to stop, that were not taken already. Although the coastline, densely populated in areas, is stunning, I prefer the more remote areas.

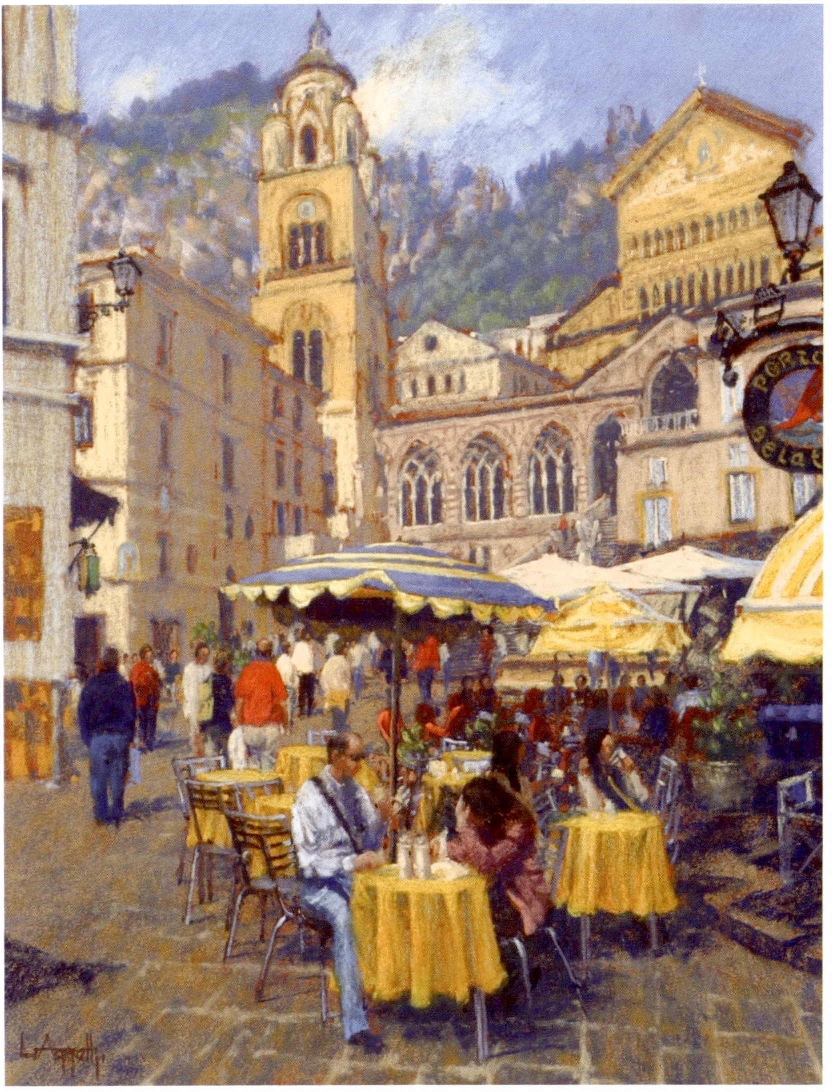

Blue & Gold, Amalfi Pastel 500 x 400 mm

BASILICATA – PUGLIA

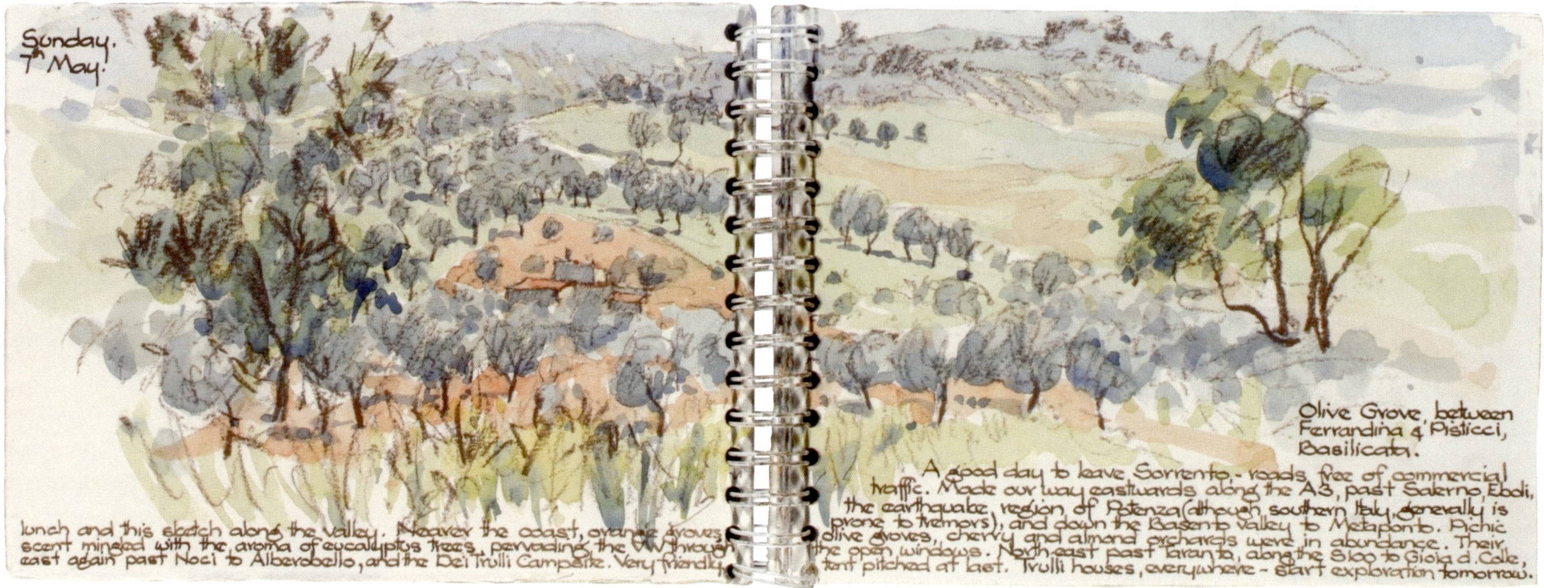

Diary Sketch 7th May, 2006 *Olive Grove between Ferrandina and Pisticci, Basilicata* Conté w/c

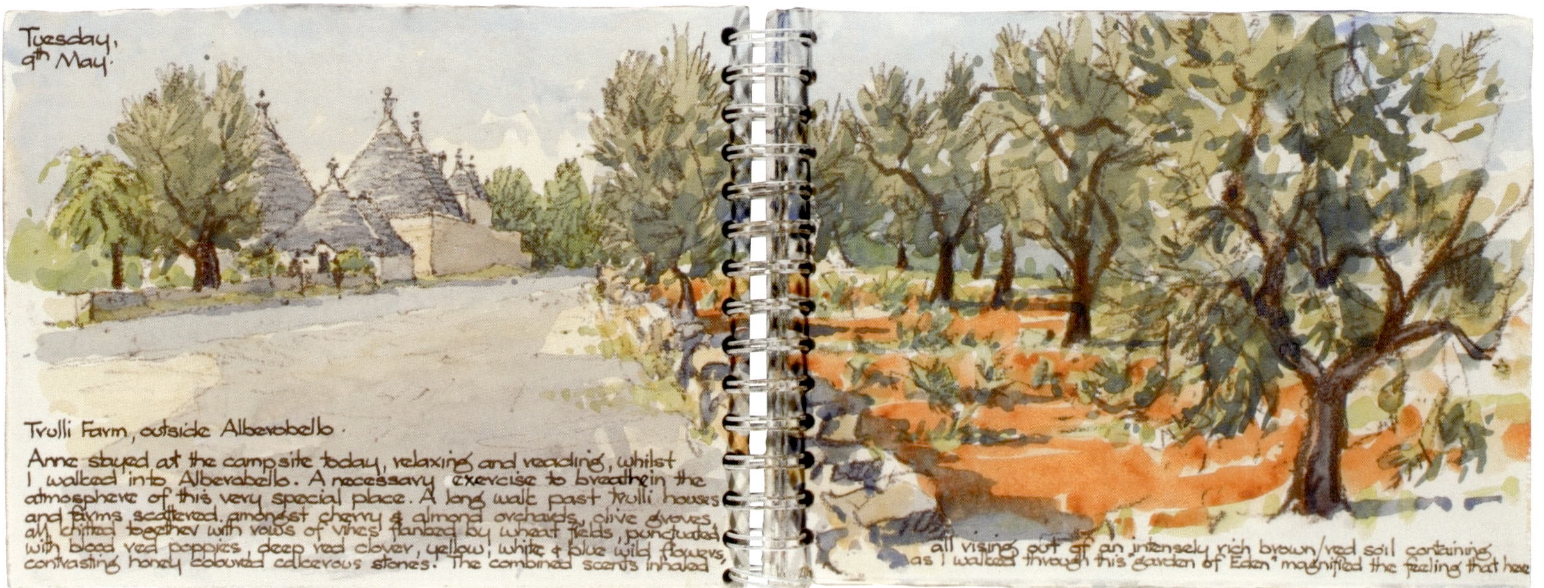

Diary Sketch 9th May, 2006 *Trulli Farm, Alberobello* Conté w/c

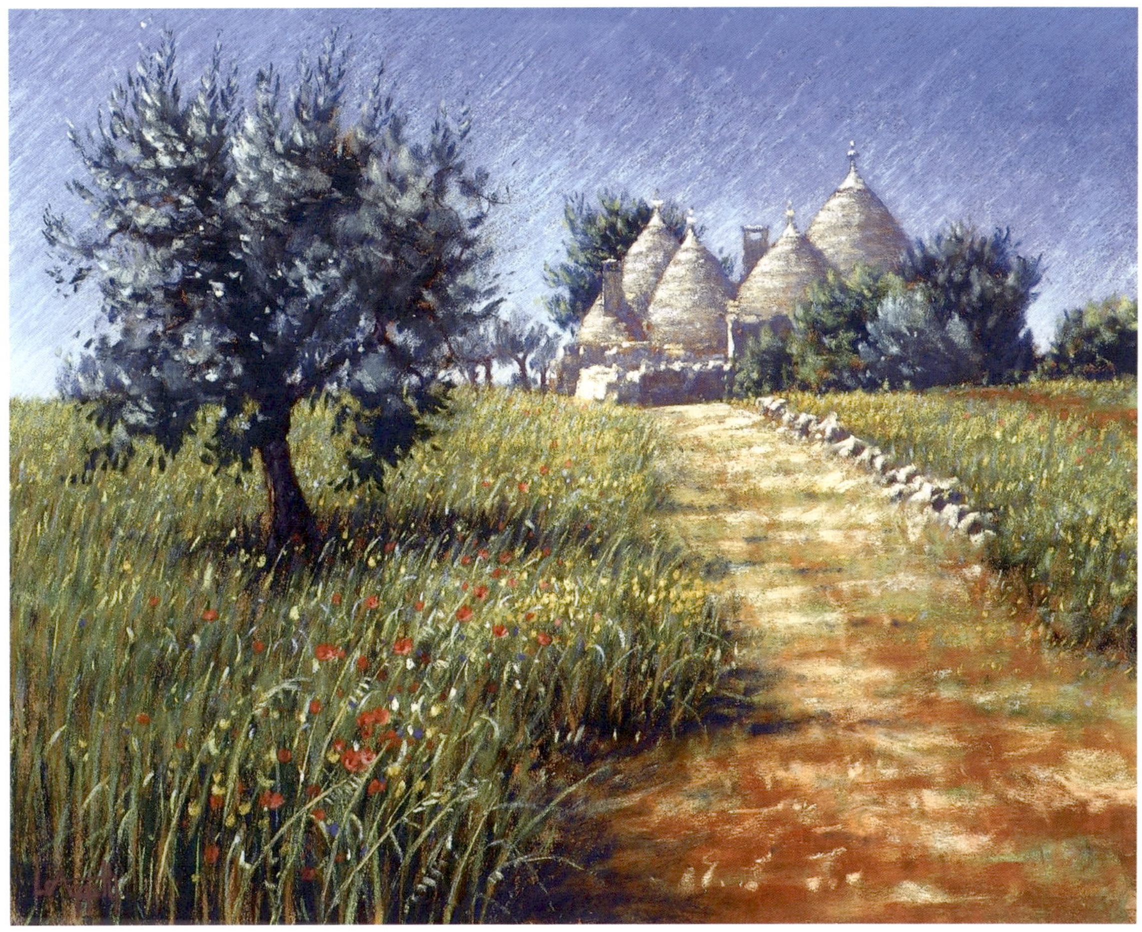

Olives and Trulli Pastel 400 x 500 mm

Our brief sojourn on the Sorrento Peninsula over, we rejoined the A3 beyond Castellammare and headed eastwards towards our ultimate destination, Puglia. Past Salerno and Eboli into Basilicata and around Potenza the capital, still recovering from the earthquakes of 1980. The whole area is prone to earth tremors, and coupled with the active volcanoes which erupt from time to time, one can understand why the Southern Italians adopt a laissez faire approach to life. Down the airy Bassento Valley to Metaponto on the coast of the Golfo di Taranto and the Ionian Sea. Then north through orange and olive groves, cherry and almond orchards, past heavily scented eucalyptus trees, by-passing Taranto, up to Gioia d. Colle and east to Noci and finally Alberobello.

To be explored in more depth later, this almost unbelievably strange and at times spooky town, with atmospheric outlying farms and villages, is what we have travelled all this way to see. A vast wood of millenary oaks called Silva Arboris Belli was located in the area where Aberobello now stands, in the hills of the Murgia region, the Murge. Throughout the Valle d'Itria the trulli houses predominate on the skyline, their amazing drystone construction testament to the immense skill of their masons. The trullo is unique in the world. The visual impact of these wonderful buildings, and the influence their inhabitants have on the surrounding landscape is discussed in the next chapter.

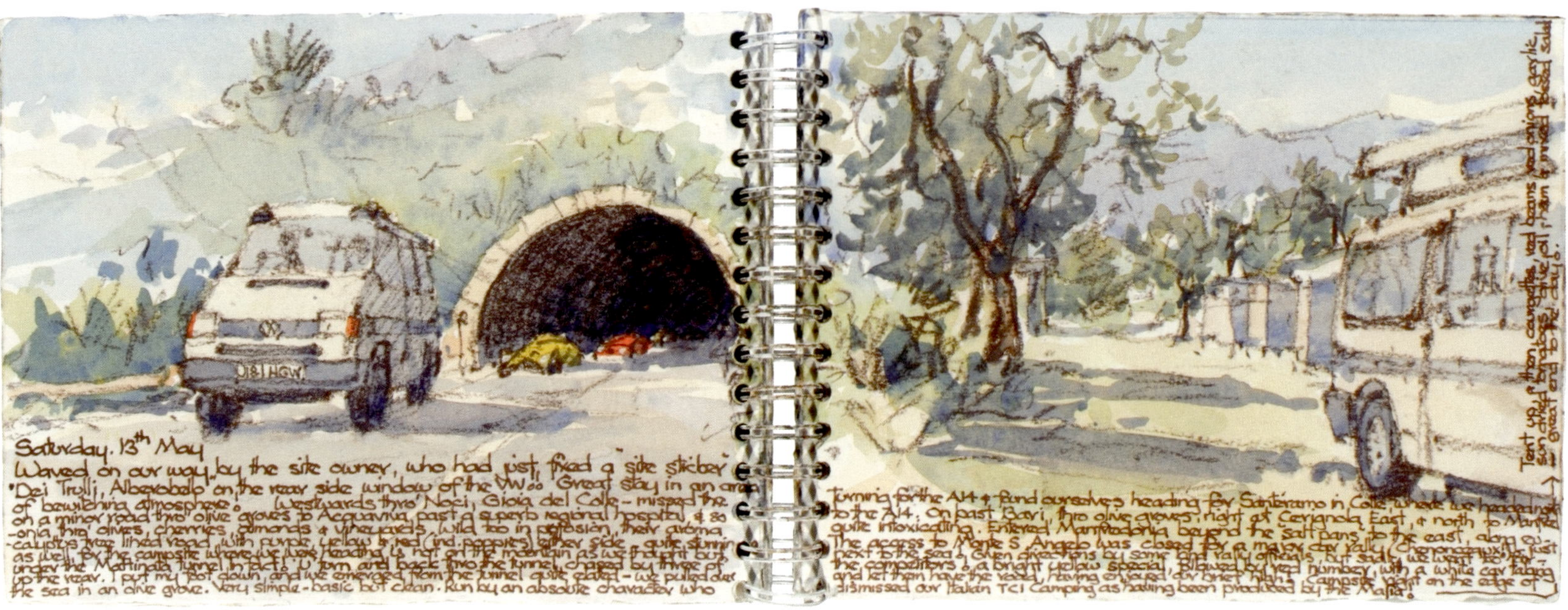

Diary Sketch 13th May, 2006 *Arrival in Gargano* Conté w/c

Camping Dei Trulli 1.5 km to the north east of the town is friendly, although in early May, the time of our stay, the owners were preparing for the coming season, as indeed are most of the sites in Italy.

Beginning our return journey, we headed north westwards to the Gargano Peninsula and one of the most spiritually uplifting sites in Europe and the world, Monte Sant'Angelo, where in AD 490 Michael the Archangel revealed himself to St Laurentius archbishop of Sipontium.

So westwards from Alberobello to Gioia de Colle and along minor roads, twisting through delightful rolling countryside, swathed in olive trees and vineyards to Acquaviva where we joined the A14 for fast-tracking to Cerignola and decantment on to the 545 northwards to Manfredonia where we were once again intoxicated with the combined scents of eucalyptus, cherries, almonds, olives and salty, warm, soft, breezes from the vast salt pans on the Adriatic Coast. The colours of the eucalyptus trees lining the road were breathtaking; purples, yellows and reds, heightened still further with bright splashes of poppies.

Whilst searching for the campsite we innocently and briefly participated in a major car rally taking place on Monte Sant'Angelo and the surrounding slopes. The memory of emerging from a long tunnel at speed, having completed a dodgy U-turn at the other end, and pursued by three roaring sports cars will remain with us for ever! See diary notes.

Our second base camp in Puglia, Camping Il Gelso at Macchia Libera, is right on the Adriatic coast, where olive groves run from the base of Monte Sant'Angelo right down to the sea. It is a wonderfully restful and quiet site, run by the welcoming and aptly named Michele and Madalene.

UMBRIA

The work produced from both areas, the Murge and Gargano, will, I'm sure, provide an interesting contrast with the subjects produced elsewhere in Italy, so different is the character of this region.

Although we prefer to travel the by-roads, thus ingesting the locale, there are situations where, in order to get from A to B within an overall working strategy, that you need to succumb to the convenience of motorway driving. So, joining the A14 at Foggia, we enter Molise, and by-passing all the Adriatic towns, we move into Abruzzo, past Termoli, Vasto, Ortona and Pescara, to beyond Alba Adriatica, where we head inland just inside Marche, onwards towards Ascoli Piceno, and on up the Tronto Valley to Arquata de Tronto and the Parco Nationale dei Monti Sibillini, just inside Umbria. The focus of our attention in this wild mountainous region is the Piano Grande, accessed along an unparapeted winding, climbing road. It is a unique, awe inspiring plain (a naturally drained lake) surrounded by mountain peaks, with an isolated village, Castelluccio, at the northern end. We camped au sauvage here, albeit in a special "corral" right in the centre of this natural amphitheatre; what subjects there were on offer – more later!

We then tumbled down via Norcia, and Triponzo, to the Valerina, the little valley of the Nera; wild beauty with striking upland villages like Castel San Felice and Sant'Anatolina di Narco. Through the new tunnel off the S209 to Spoleto, our next base stop. Much renovation work was in progress, repairing the latent damage caused by the earthquake which also damaged the Basilica di San Francesco, Assisi at the other end of the Vale of Spoleto. Several paintings were completed here, and in the surrounding areas, during this trip, and from nearby base camps at Bevagna and Assisi during other tours.

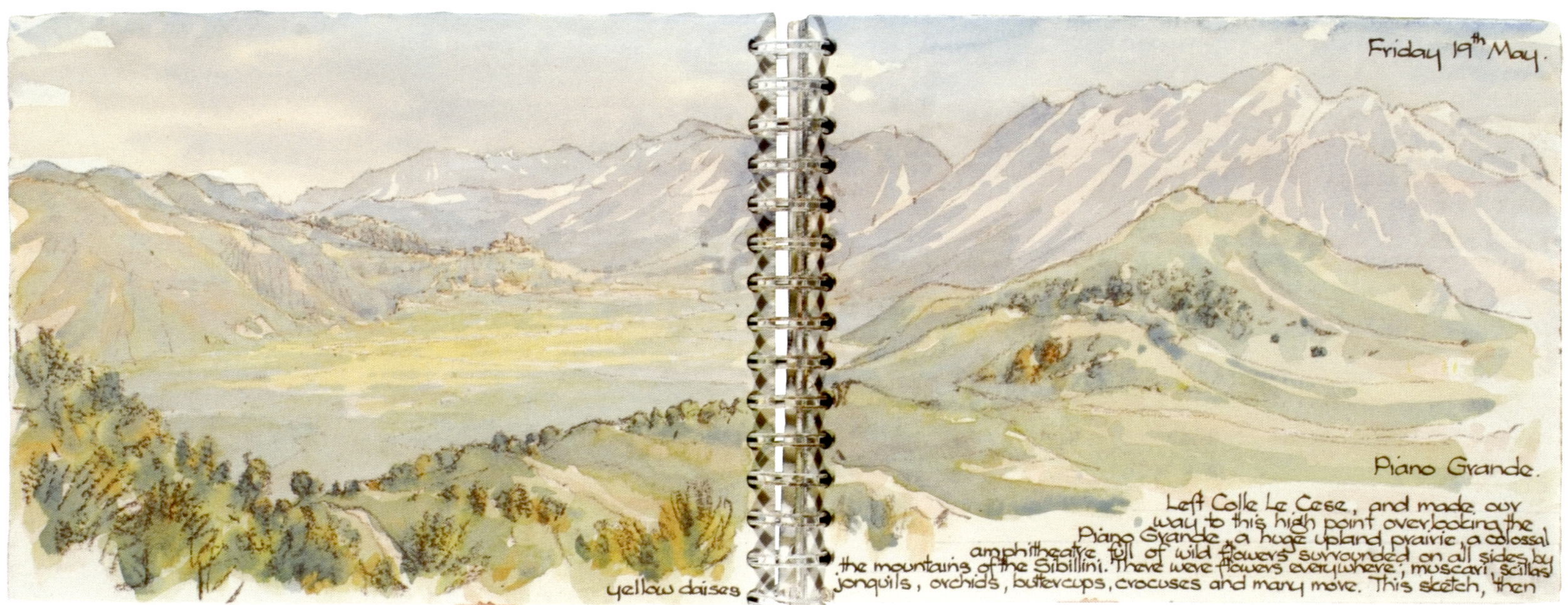

Diary Sketch 19th May, 2006 *Piano Grande, Umbria* Conté w/c

TUSCANY

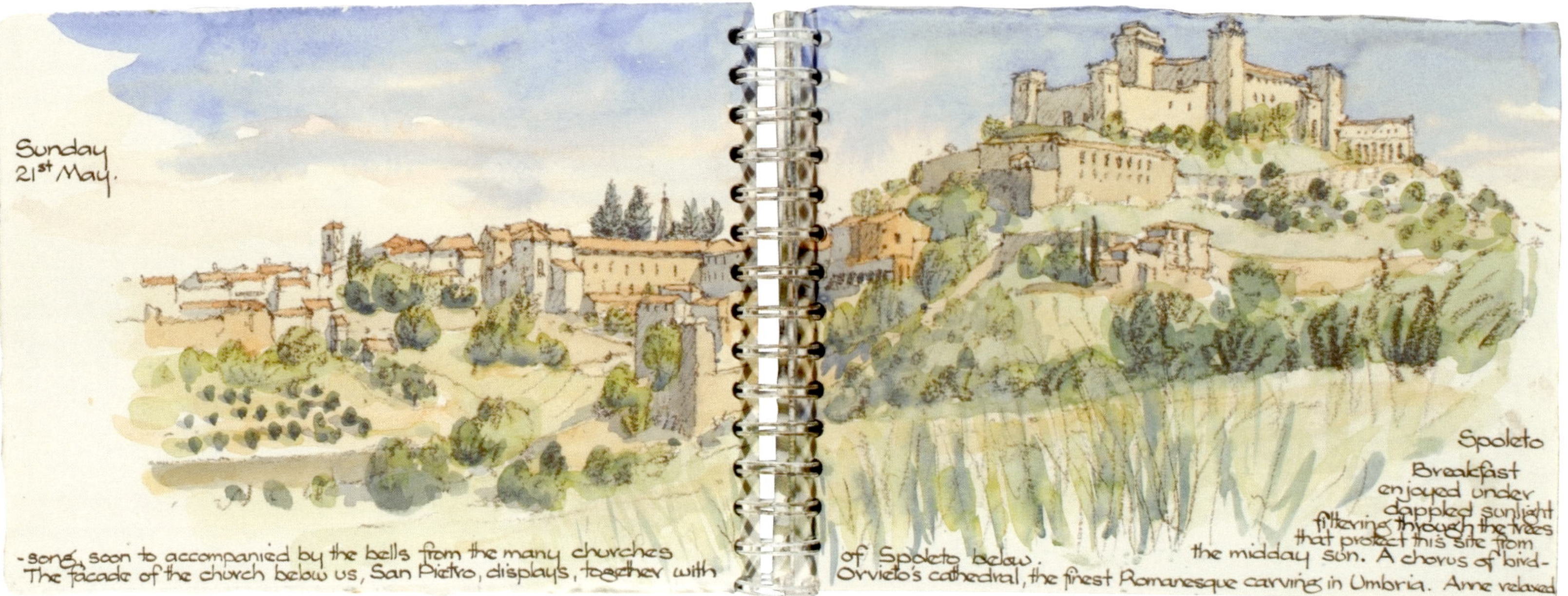

Diary Sketch 21st May, 2006 *Spoleto* Conté w/c

We left, taking the S3, heading north past several superb hill towns, all of which will be explored in the chapter on Umbria, past Montefalco, Trevi, Spello, on to the S75, the south side of Assisi (good base camp), and Perugia, around Lago Trasimeno, and then instead of immediately accessing the A1, for reasons of disruptive roadworks experienced on the way down, we negotiated minor roads towards Montepulciano and the delightful Val d'Orcia. Then along memory lane past Pienza, S. Quirico d'Orcia, Montalcino, Buonconvento, around Siena (another base camp), past Monteriggioni, and Colle di Val d'Elsa, all to be explored in the chapter on Tuscany; as will Florence which we passed by this time, on the rejoined A1. Then on to the A11 westwards to Montecatini-Terme, thus completing the lower loop of our journey.

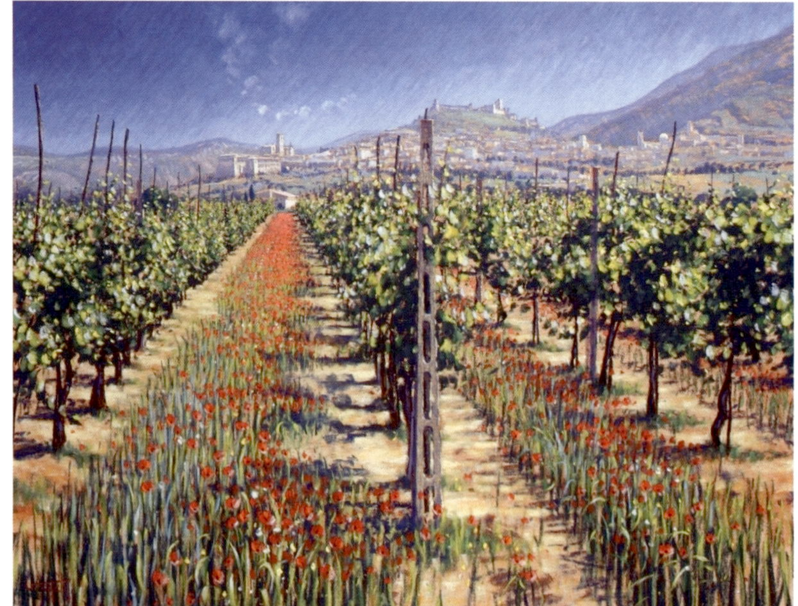

Vines and Poppies below Assisi Pastel 500 x 650 mm

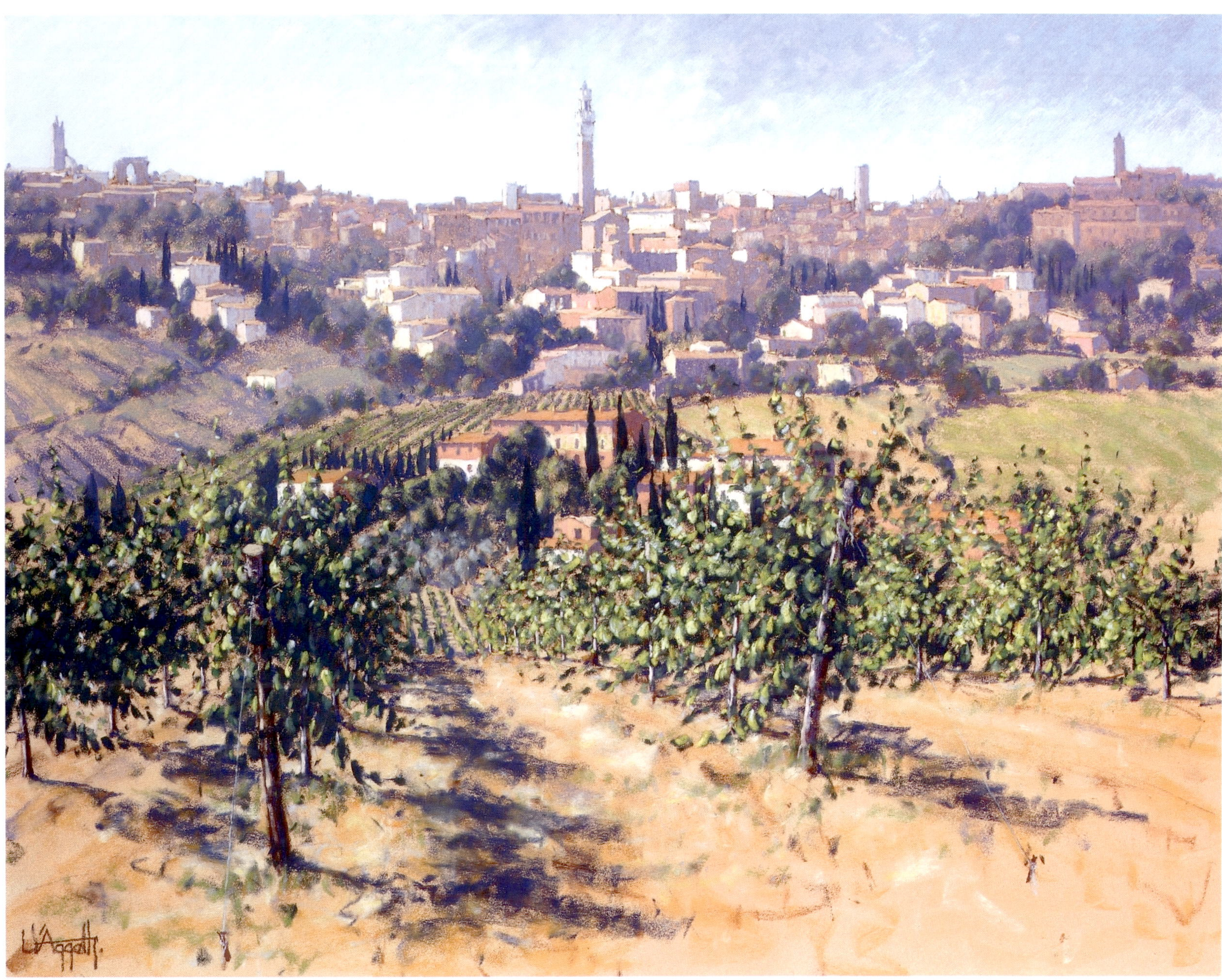

Siena Pastel 600 x 800 mm

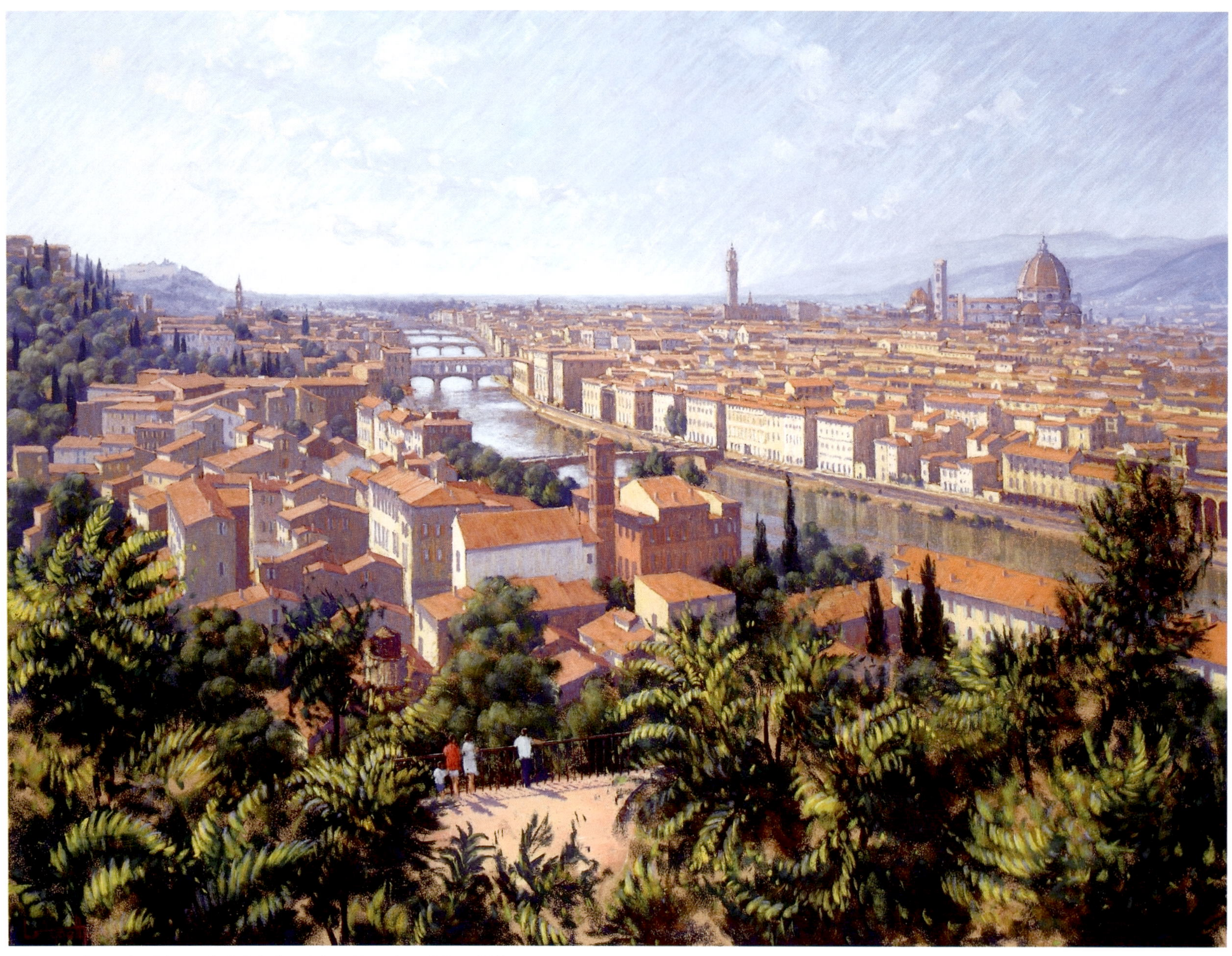

Florence, from the Piazzale Michelangiolo Pastel 600 x 800 mm

The most distinguished of all Italian spa towns, Montecatini, possesses many architecturally fine spas. The superb camp site, our home for two nights, is high up, midway between the main town and Montecatini Alto. Our planned visit to Lucca had to be aborted (see diary notes), but as we had been invited by our good friends Neil and Sue Ireson to stay in the city, in the near future, we were not too disappointed. Neil is an artist working in stained glass (he has completed several panels for us), and Sue is a classical pianist and teacher. Instead we explored Montecarlo, a lovely wine village perched on a hill top, overlooking the Valdinievole (Valley of Mists).

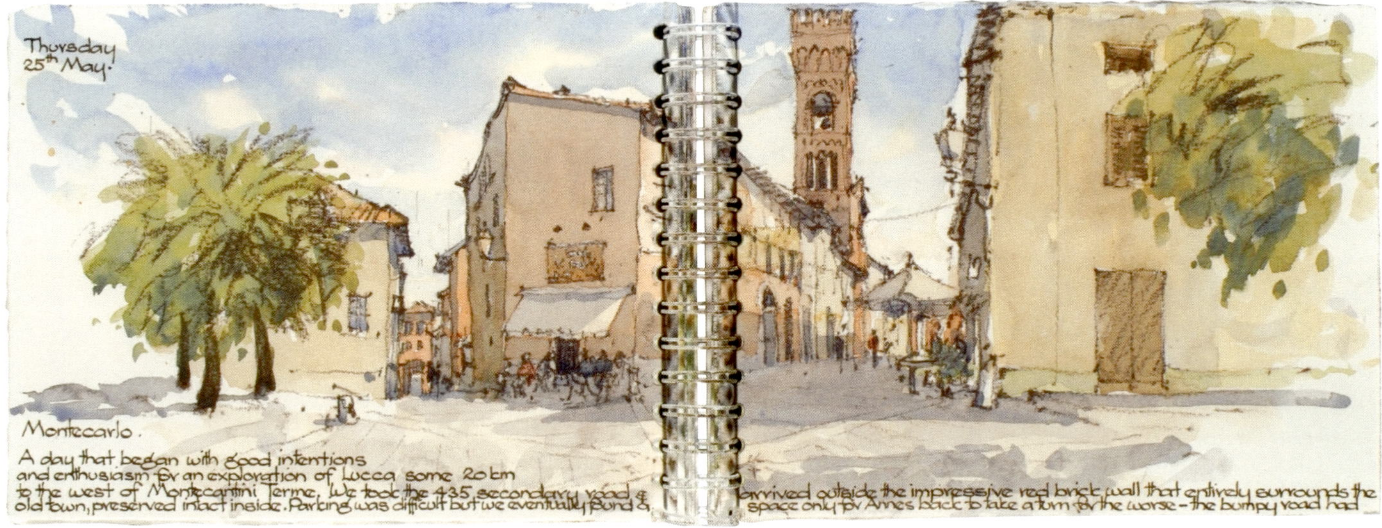

Diary Sketch 25th May, 2006 *Montecarlo* Conté w/c

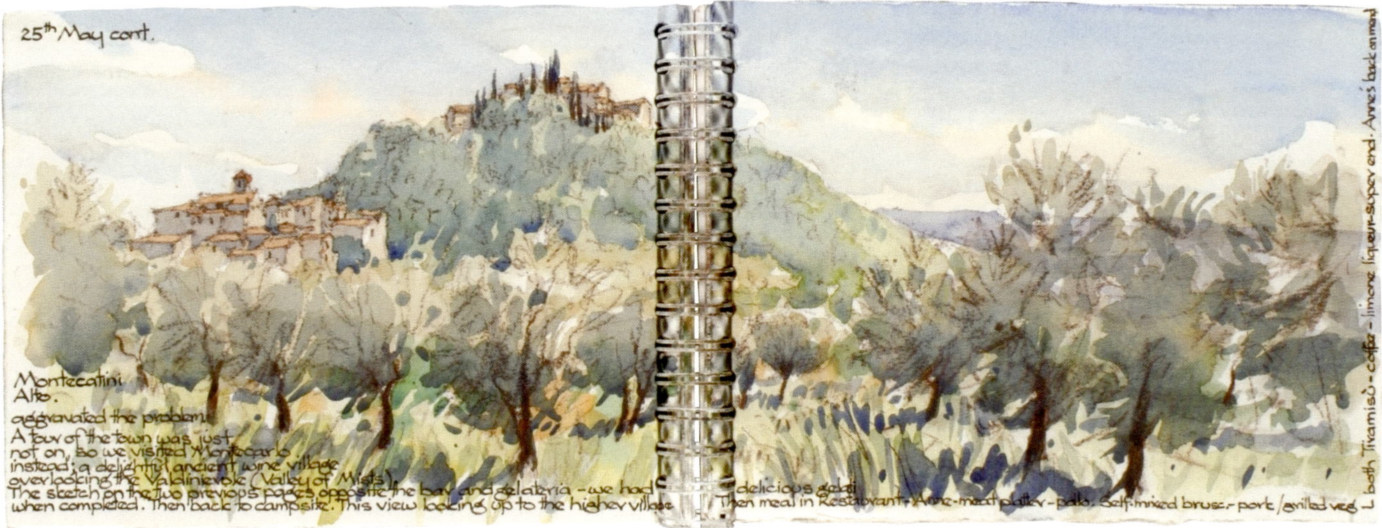

Diary Sketch 25th May, 2006 *Montecatini Alto* Conté w/c

PIEDMONT

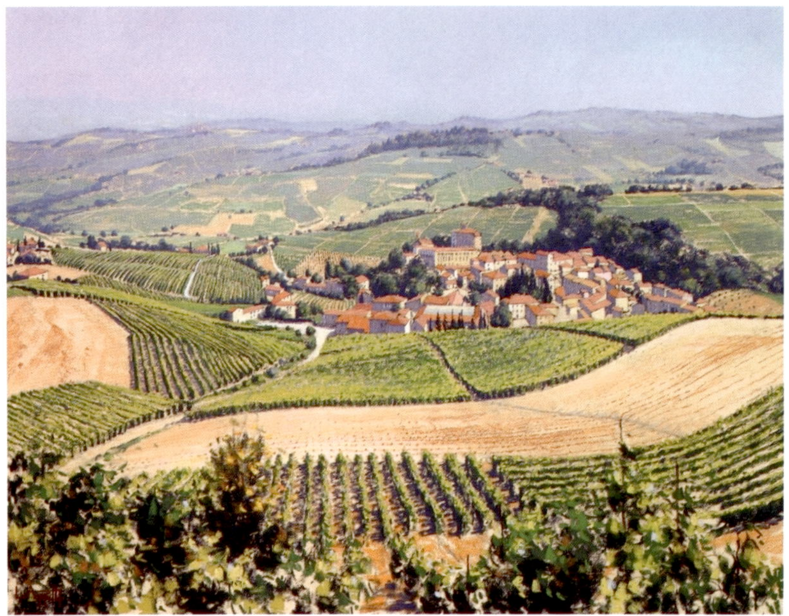

Barolo, Piedmont Pastel 500 x 650 mm

We retrace our steps away from northern Tuscany, back along the Ligurian coast on the A12 as far as Savona. Instead of continuing to our friends Alan and Jenny Rodd at Flayosc in the Var, as we did last year (2006), this is the point where we join the return route of an earlier working trip. Driving inland to the north west we enter Piedmont at Montezémolo, below the glorious vineyards of the Langhe. I was last here in 1993 working for a solo Italian exhibition at Llewellyn Alexander, London, which resulted in a 65-painting sell out. I stayed in the area famous for the king of Italian wines, the majestic Barolo red. I camped in the VW (our first, the rear engined water cooled model) right in the square at Barolo having sought permission, and came away with paintings, and bottles of the highly favoured nectar. All soon disappeared for different reasons!

Our journey continued northwards to the west of Turin, and on up through the Valle d'Aosta with an overnight au sauvage stop at Pont St Martin where I shared my whisky with a family who invited me in, after I had finished a typical VW nosh. Very sociable, and an excellent farewell to Italy following that particular tour with basecamps at Bevagna, Siena and Florence.

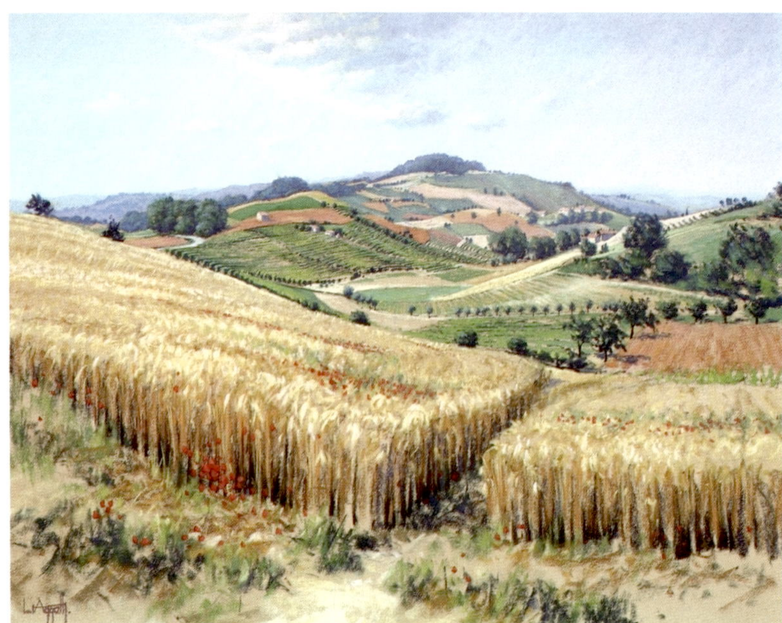

The Langhe, Piedmont Pastel 500 x 650 mm

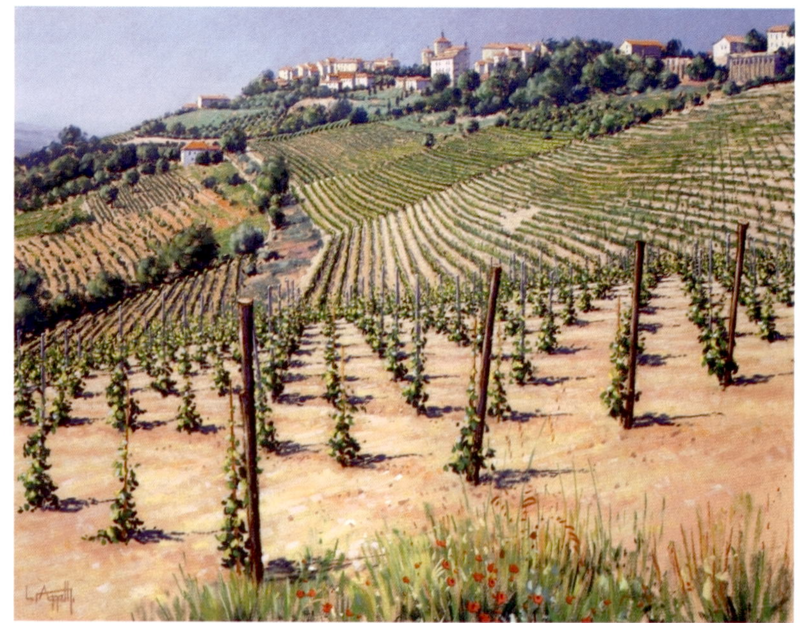

Novello, Piedmont Pastel 500 x 650 mm

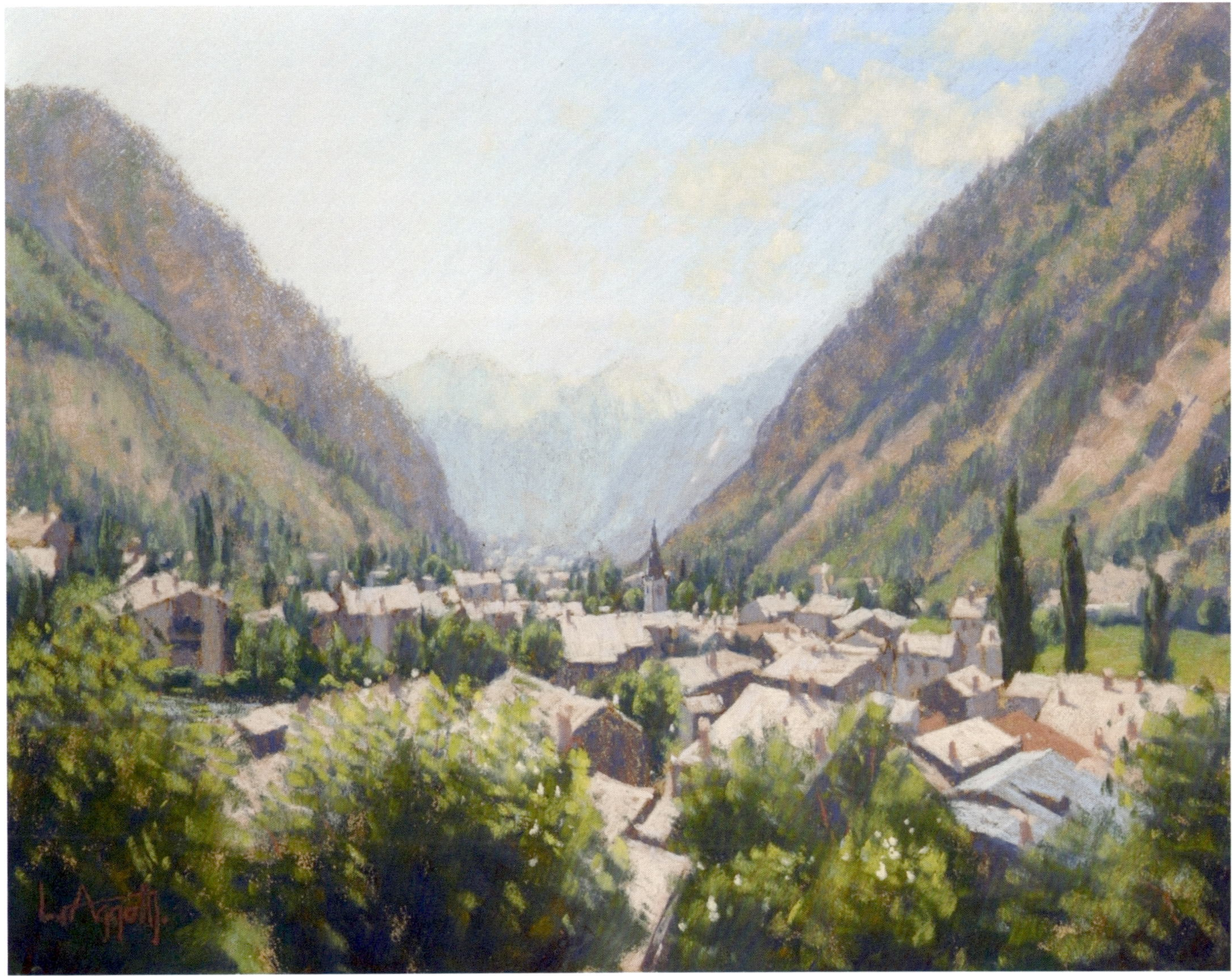

Valle d'Aosta Pastel 250 x 325 mm

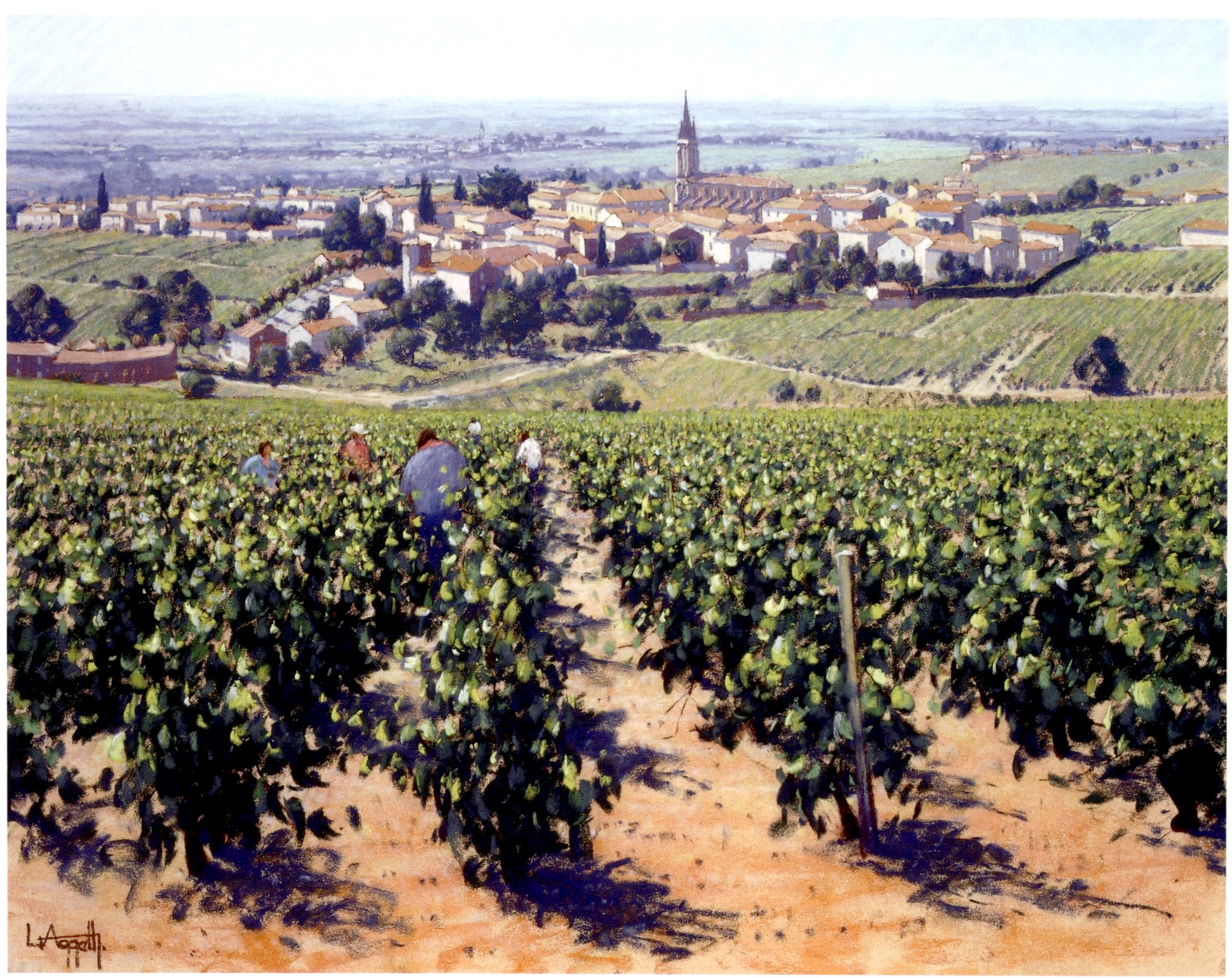

Grand Cru Fleurie, Beaujolais Pastel 500 x 650 mm

Through the Mont Blanc tunnel (pre the catastrophic fire) the following day, and on up via Geneva, across to Bourg-en-Bresse and over the River Saône to one of our favourite stop-overs, the Beaujolais village of Fleurie. Super campsite with the environs documented in my book on France. Always time for a sketch or painting here.

North through Mâcon, and west across to Charolles, Paray-le-Monial, to Digoin and Bourbon-Lancy alongside the Canal Lateral to Nevers. On down the Loire Valley via Sancerre, another favourite painting location of mine, and so to Beaulieu for the last overnight stop.

The following day, head down for Orleans, Chateaudon, and an enjoyable run through minor roads to Bellème for a lunch stop in the delightful square (diary sketch). Then a comfortable drive to Caen, thus completing the second loop of our figure of eight. Time for a browse through the Carrefour at St Hilaire and perhaps a bottle or two of Gigondas, and Vacqueyras, to add to our Italian collection!

Finally, to Ouistreham and a meal before embarkation …

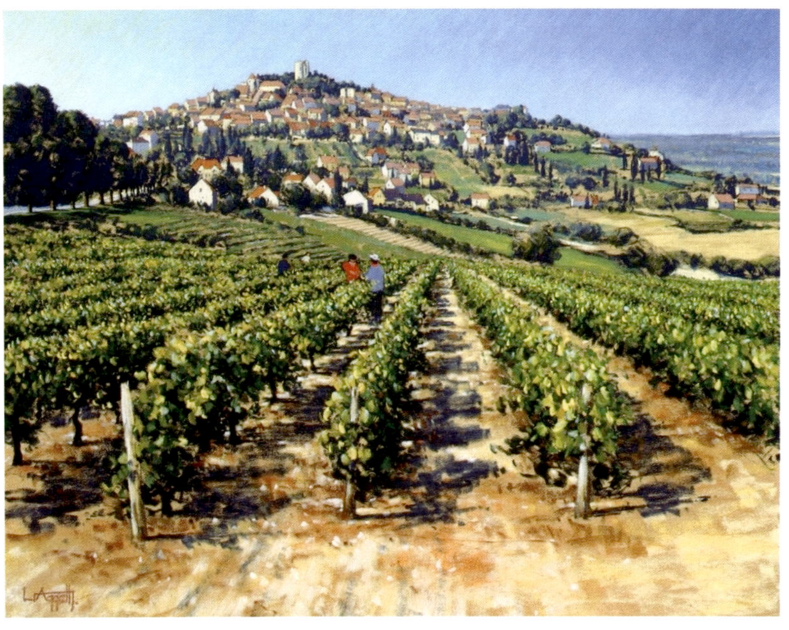

Sancerre Pastel 500 x 650 mm

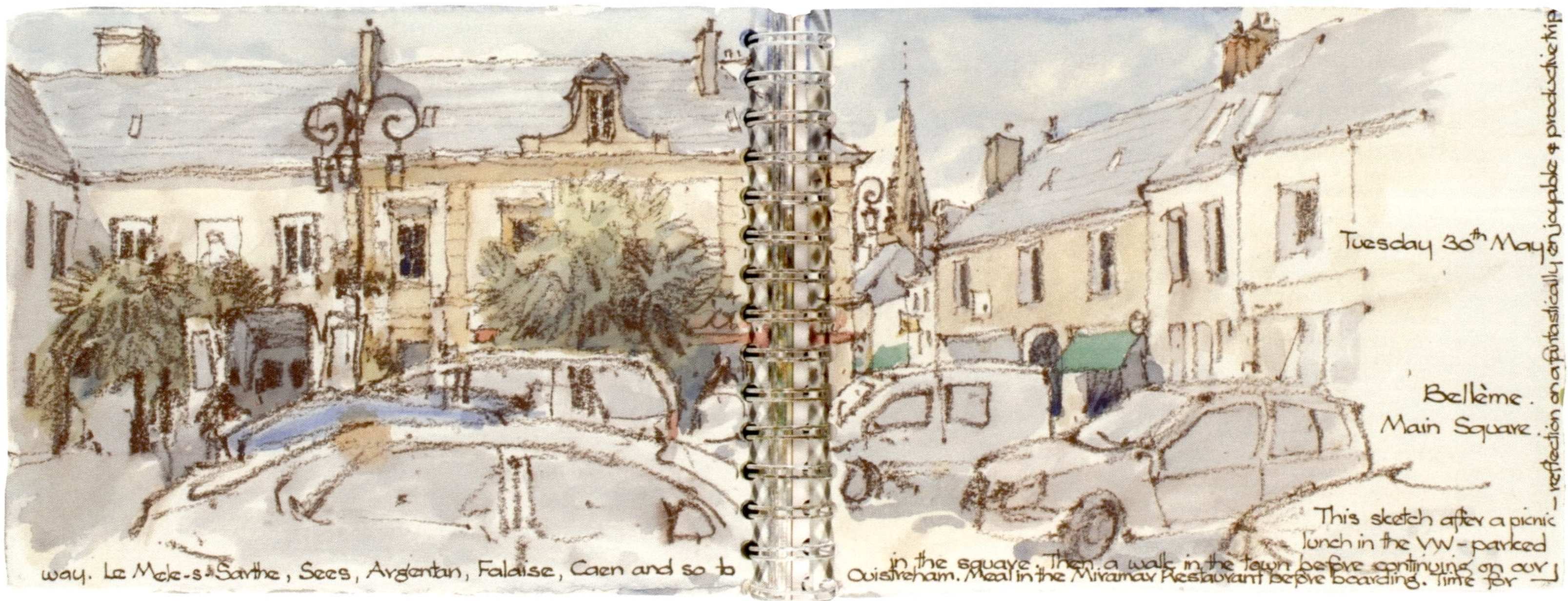

Diary Sketch 30th May, 2006 *The Square, Bellème* Conté w/c

Puglia

There is, of course, more to Puglia than trulli houses. The baroque city of Lecce on the Salentine Peninsula; ancient Taranto with its Mare Grande and Mare Piccolo; the mysterious Castel de Monte, high on a hill, overlooking the Puglian Tavoliere, and built by Emperor Frederick in the thirteenth century using endless repetitions of the Golden Section, with square and cubic roots, relations to the movements of the planets and the stars, plus the angles and proportions of the Pythagorean five-pointed star. Similar to the tower he built in Sicily, the palace seems to be at the centre of an enormous rectilinear network of alignments. The Gargano Peninsula to the north, with its rugged and beautiful coastline, with Monte Sant'Angelo, one of the most important pilgrimage sites in Europe, and the world, a truly wild and spiritual place. The nearby S. Giovanni Rotondo too, where Padro Pio received the stigmata. There are also the many traces of past civilizations including dolmens, menhirs and specchie from Bisceglie to Peuceti. All of these constituents have combined to produce an area of physical, mystical, mysterious and spiritual beauty.

We will be concentrating on two areas however; the Valle d'Itria and Murge, where trulli houses abound, and the Gargano Peninsula.

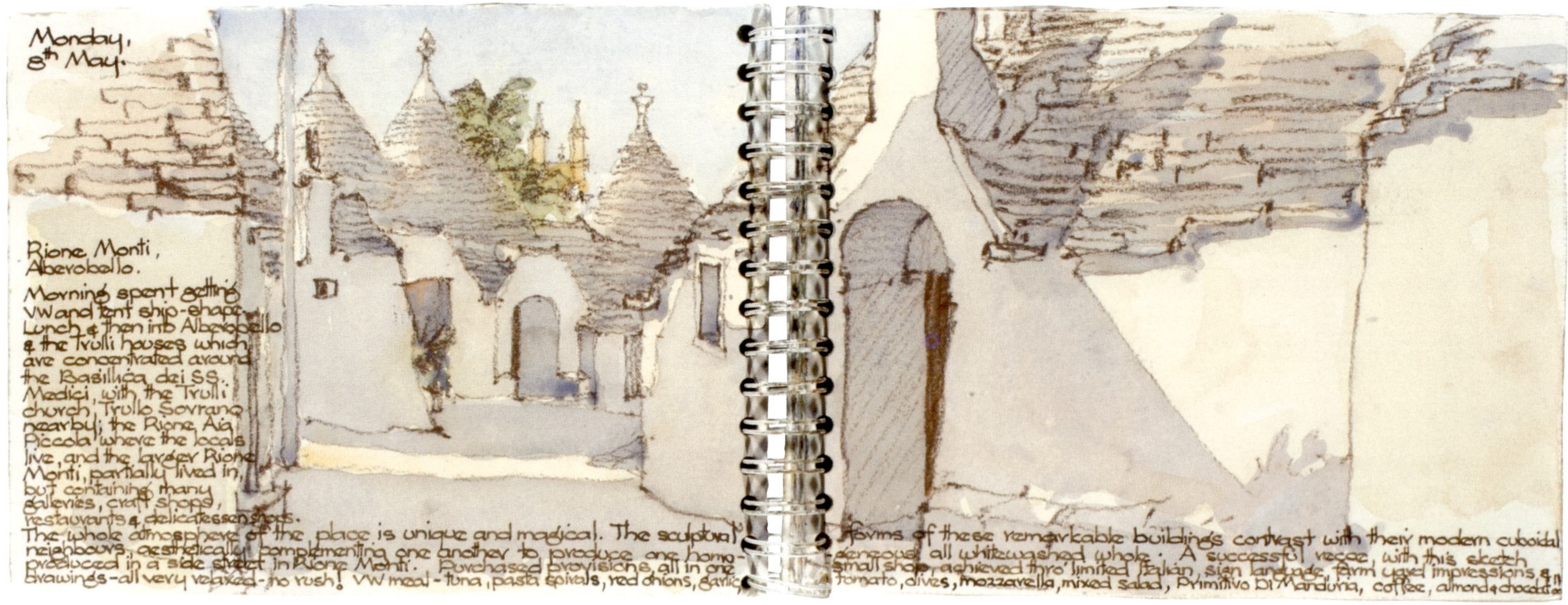

Diary Sketch 8th May, 2006 *Rione Monte, Alberobello* Conté w/c

MURGIA AND THE VALLE D'ITRIA

Alberobello is our first base, the trulli capital, with over 1500 of them still standing. These unique buildings are spread throughout the Valle d'Itria from Putignano to Martina Franca, and appear as far to the east as Ostuni. As you approach this area, characterised by the low hills of the Murge, you are acutely aware that the landscape is a wondrous expression of the inhabitants' hard labour over the centuries. Low stone walls divide parcels of land into a loosely patterned quilt, textured by cereals, vines propped up on arbours, covering the ground like roofs, olive groves, and vegetables, all growing out of a rich dark sienna earth, highlighted with calcareous stones. The farms (mas) are unique trulli buildings, rectangular or circular, and crowned with tall conical stone roofs, all of drystone construction. A plethora of subject matter at every turn.

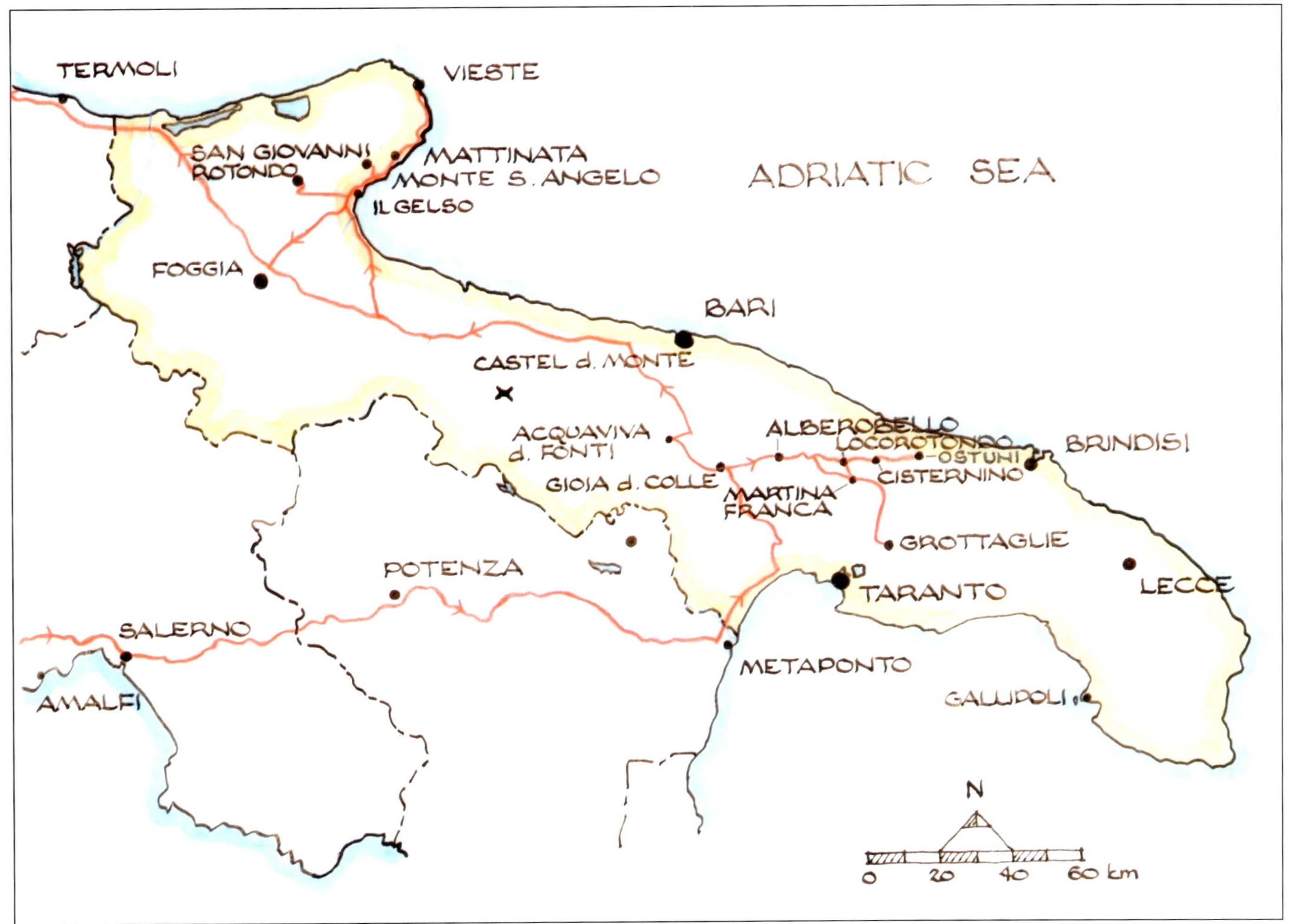

We pitched the tent at the Dei Trulli campsite, just 1.5 km to the north east of Alberobello, which was within walking distance for carrying easel and rucksack with materials etc. We also located a convenient parking area (always spaces available) to the north of the small group of trulli buildings gathered around the Basilica dei SS Medici, at the northern end of the Corso Vittoria Emanuele. Our logistical requirements thus sorted, the way was clear for a concerted study of the town, and what a delight. Although the larger of the two trulli areas, the Rione Monti has been commercially exploited, with the characterful houses converted to galleries and shops; the smaller Rione Aia Piccola opposite, on the other side of the dividing Largo Martellotta, is still principally a residential area.

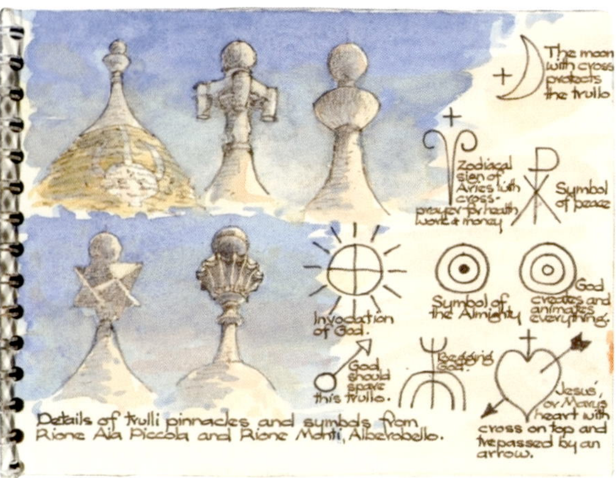

Diary Sketch 9th May, 2006
Trulli pinnacles and symbols Conté w/c

These remarkable buildings warrant further and more detailed consideration. They are found nowhere else in Italy or indeed the world. The word itself has no meaning, and even their origin is obscure, although they were probably inspired by eastern structures. A considered opinion is that these "dry construction" buildings, dating from the mid-fourteenth century evolved in such a form that enabled them to be quickly erected or dismantled in order to avoid the taxes which were liable regarding permanent homes. The concept of the trullo is quite "green", and the building is tailored to the needs of the self-sufficient family. It has a well, a cellar, and a very productive walled garden. Built in the time honoured technique of mortarless construction, using limestone blocks collected from surrounding fields, they are not large. Instead of constructing larger units when more space is required, other trulli are simply added on; hence the proliferation of domes as seen in Alberobello, villages and farms throughout the Valle d'Itria.

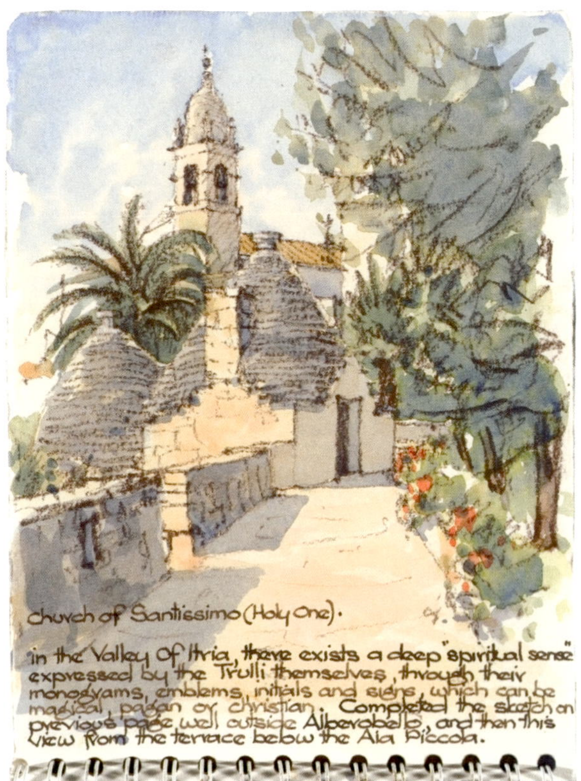

Diary Sketch 9th May, 2006
Church of Santissimo, Alberobello Conté w/c

The dome sits on the thick base walls, which are built square, or circular in form, between 1.50 m to 2.00 m high. In a quadrangular-based trullo, four stones (pieduccio) are placed in the corners upon the walls to support the spread of the dome's weight. The cone shaped dome is of limestone too; a single row of narrow slates (candle stones) wound in a gradually decreasing spiral up to the top. The rounded shape of the roof is formed when it reaches a height of 1.00 m from the top of the base wall. It takes approximately another 2.00 m to reach the apex. The exterior of the cone is then covered with "chiancarelle", thin trapezium-shaped stones, smooth faced and 7 cms thick, placed as a covering and to

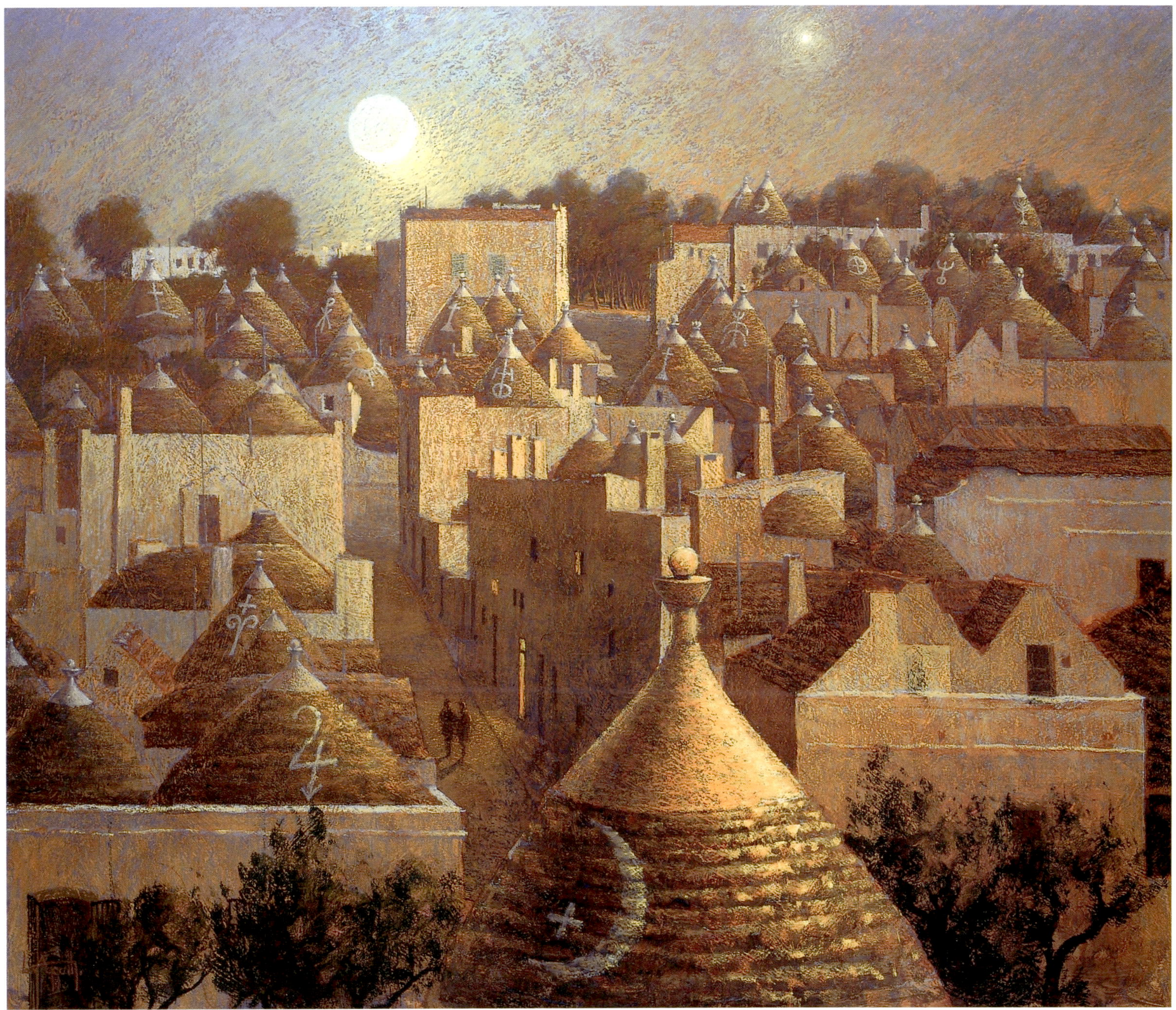

Waxing Moon, Alberobello Pastel 1016 x 1220 mm

the same spiral, but with an inclination of 3° to the horizontal, for shedding rainwater. Most base walls have now been mortared and whitewashed, thus increasing still further the tonal and textural contrast between roof and walls of these sculptural buildings.

The domes are capped by beautifully sculpted pinnacles, which, to begin with, were nothing more than a sign left by the master trullo-builder to distinguish his work from others. These developed from the simple forms of a circle, cross and cylinder surmounted by a horizontal disc, to the more complex sphere, star, tetrahedron, the sphere inside a hollow, priest hat and the sphere with cross on top.

Monograms, emblems, and initials, are often painted with lime on the roofs; signs which can be magical, pagan or Christian, and with a strong sense of mysticism are intended to protect home and family against evil.

Various examples can be seen right across the Valle d'Itria, and their designs add to the mythological and sometimes eerie presence of the trulli throughout this undulating landscape, particularly at dawn, sunrise, sunset and dusk.

I certainly fell under their "spell" after working amongst these strange edifices for only a day or so. This gradually intensified as we explored further into this fascinating region. At times the multi clusters of domes presented a rather comical hobbit-like appearance. Later, towards the end of the day, the atmosphere changed, and an air of intrigue, and mystery descended all around. Aesthetically I was moved by the textural and sculptural form of the domes, particularly when grouped together, and the manner in which they contrasted with the plain vertical areas of curved, and cubed walling. These presented complex compositions with abstract qualities, which could be developed further in the studio.

I did not have to venture far to experience the incredibly sincere and honest atmosphere of the Murge countryside, engineered and crafted by the custodians who use every square metre of ground to reap and maintain a true quality of life from the foundations of their heritage.

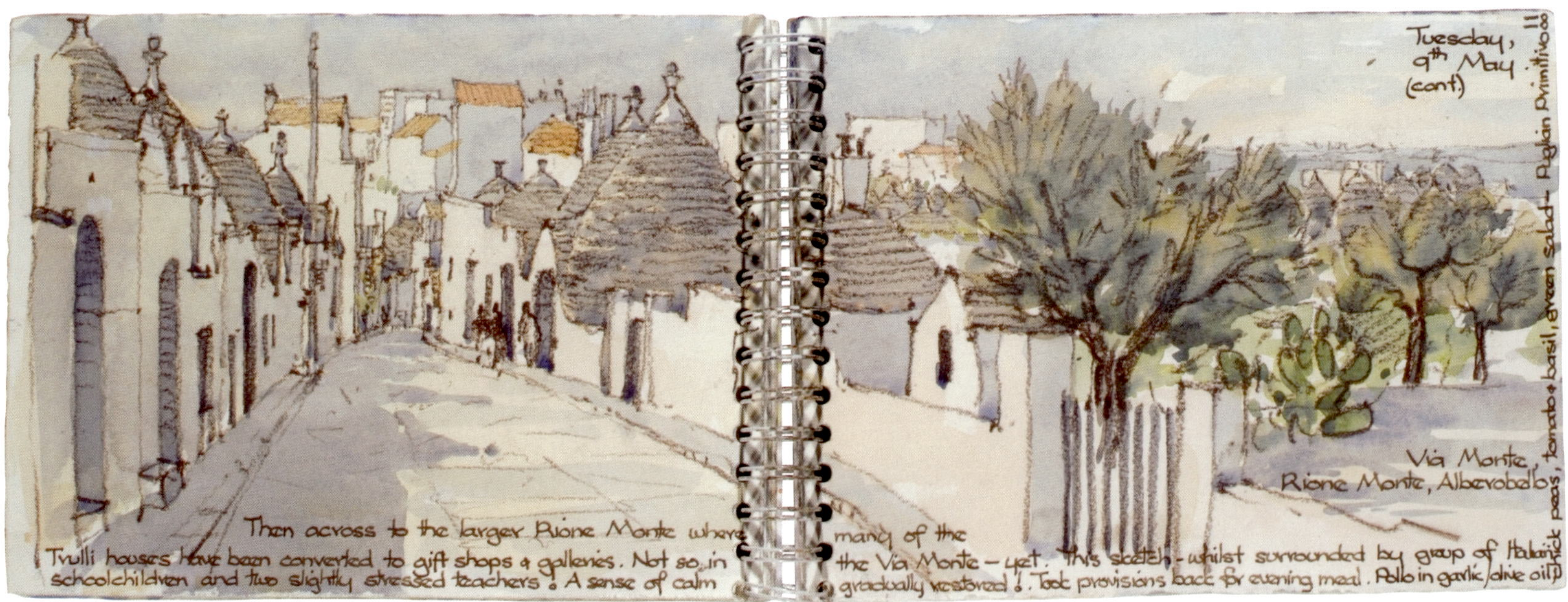

Diary Sketch 9th May, 2006 *Via Monte, Rione Monte, Alberobello* Conté w/c

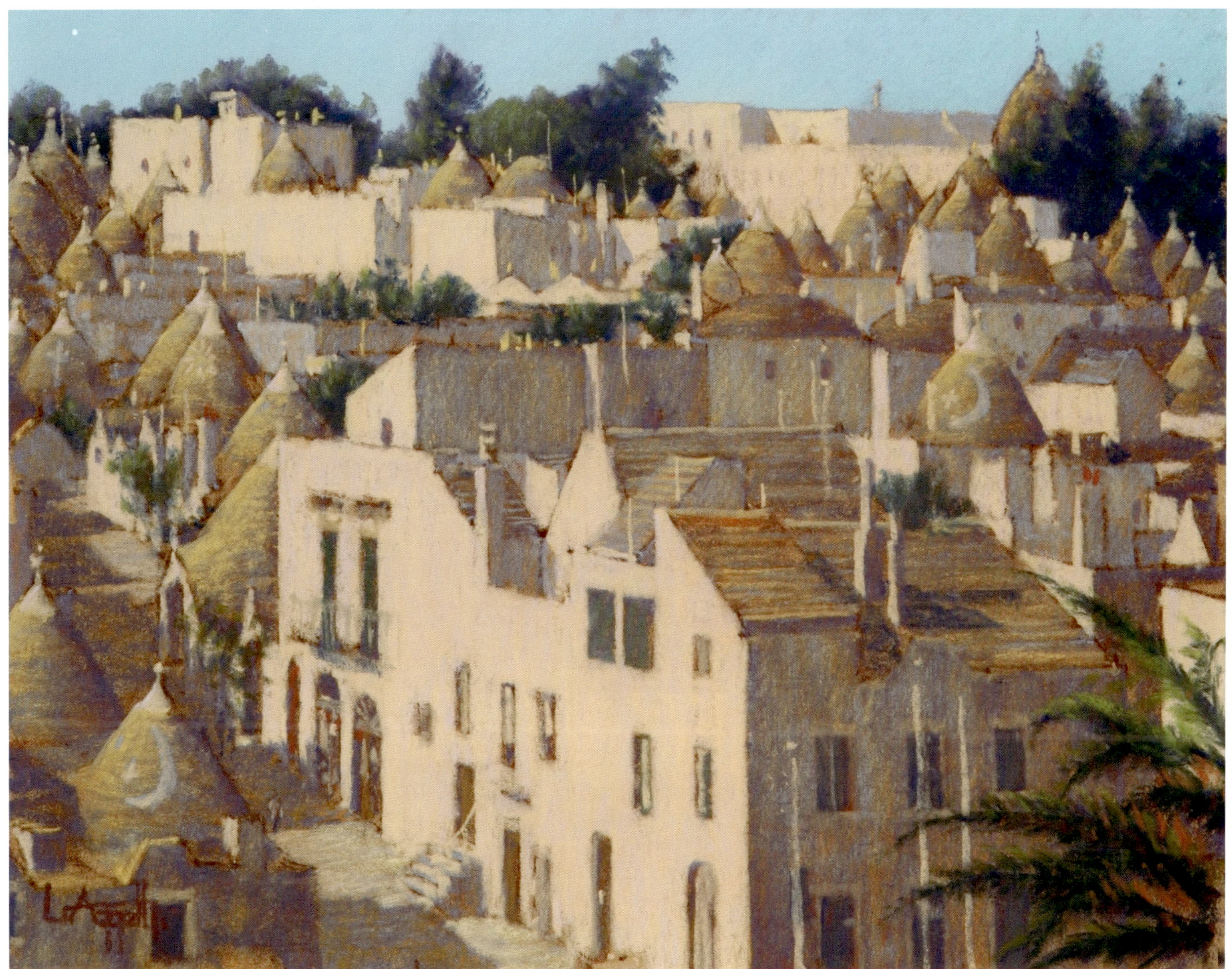

Rione Monte, Alberobello Pastel 250 x 325 mm

This view has a strange, contemporary feel about it, and an abstract portrayal is just one step away.

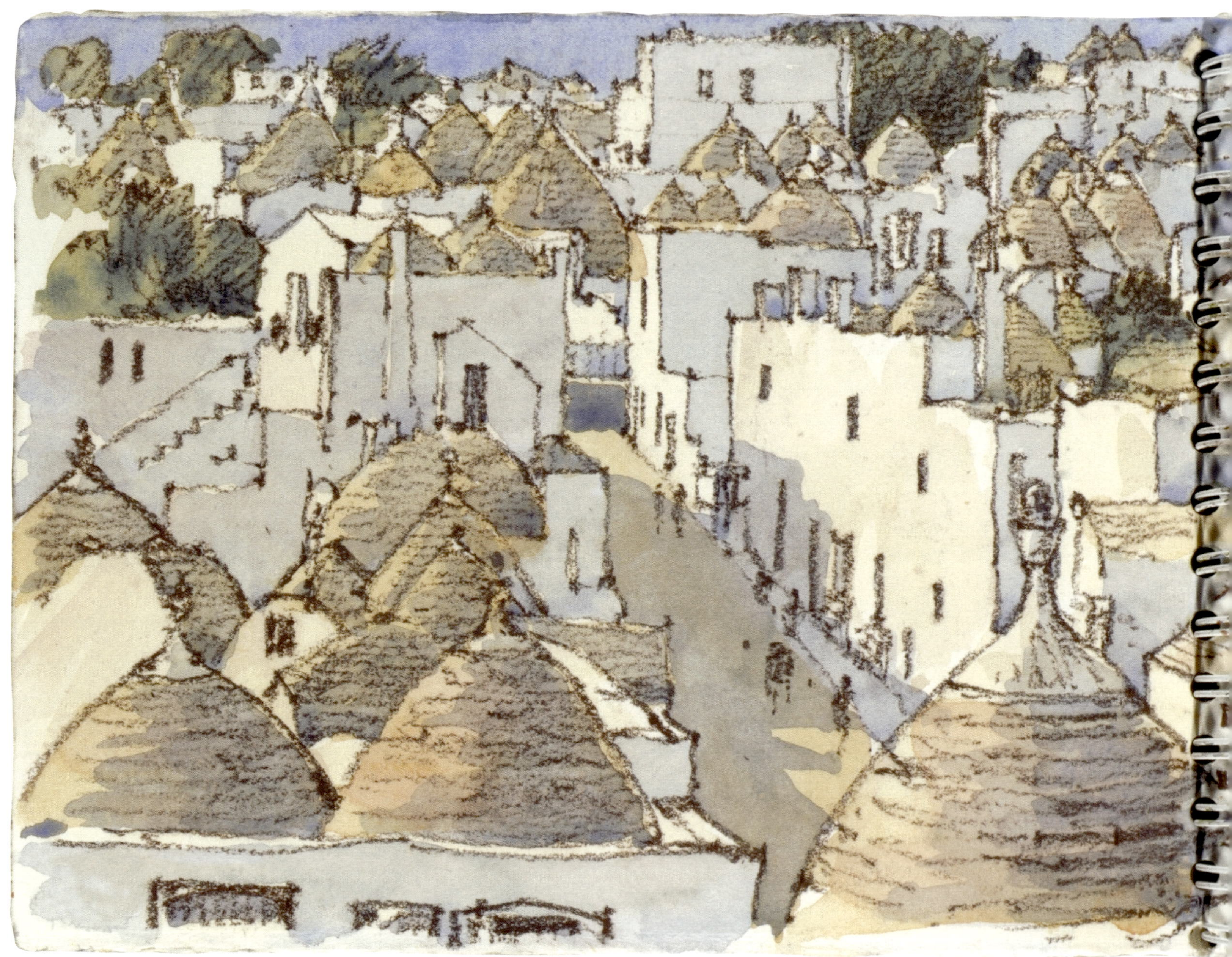

Diary Sketch 10th May, 2006 *Rione Monte from Rione Aia Piccola* Conté w/c

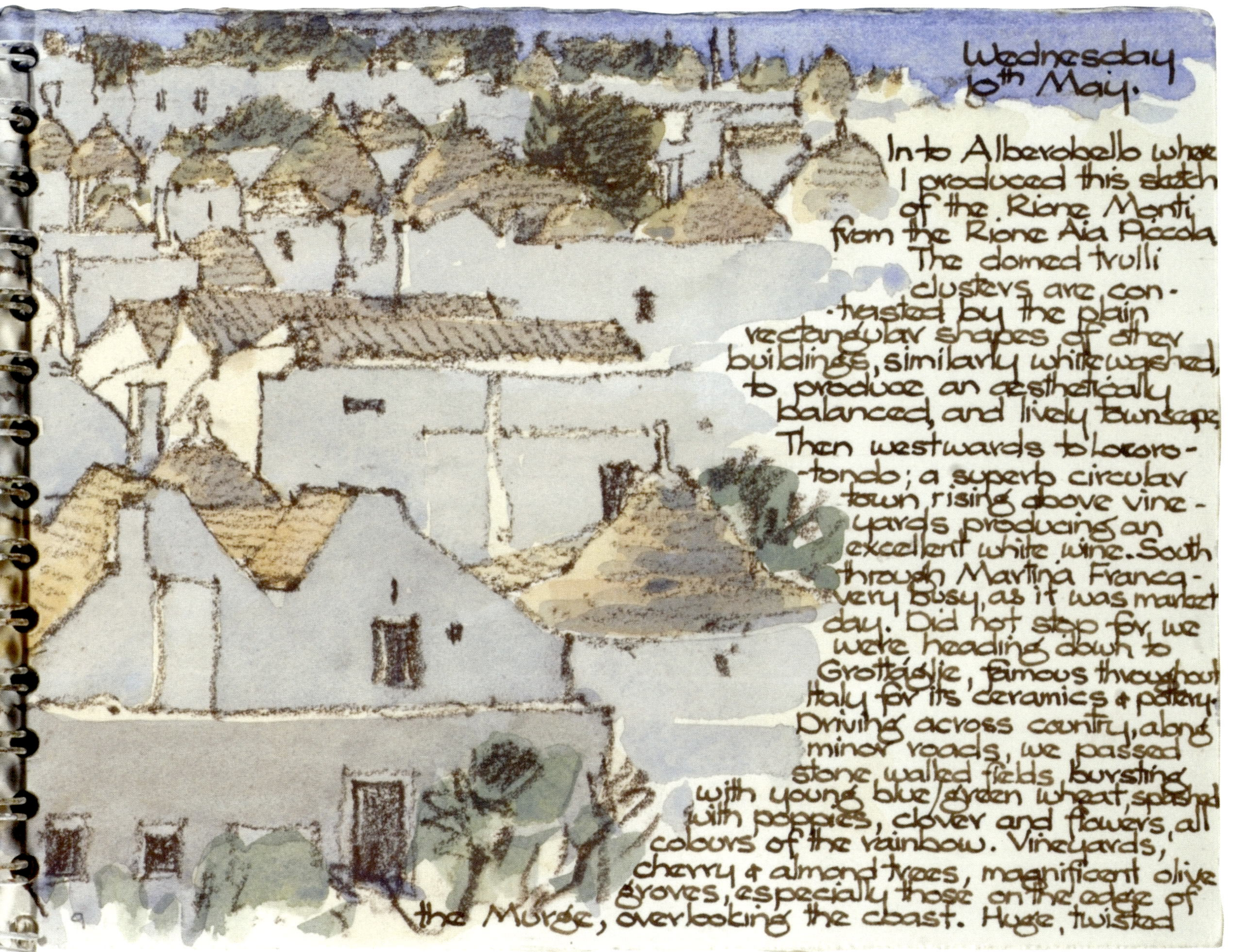

Wednesday
10th May.
Into Alberobello where
I produced this sketch
of the Rione Monti
from the Rione Aia Piccola.
The domed trulli
clusters are con-
-trasted by the plain
rectangular shapes of other
buildings, similarly whitewashed,
to produce an aesthetically
balanced, and lively townscape.
Then westwards to Locoro-
-tondo; a superb circular
town rising above vine-
-yards producing an
excellent white wine. South
through Martina Franca -
very busy, as it was market
day. Did not stop for, we
were heading down to
Grottaglie, famous throughout
Italy for its ceramics & pottery.
Driving across country, along
minor roads, we passed
stone walled fields bursting
with young blue/green wheat, splashed
with poppies, clover and flowers, all
colours of the rainbow. Vineyards,
cherry & almond trees, magnificent olive
groves, especially those on the edge of
the Murge, overlooking the coast. Huge, twisted

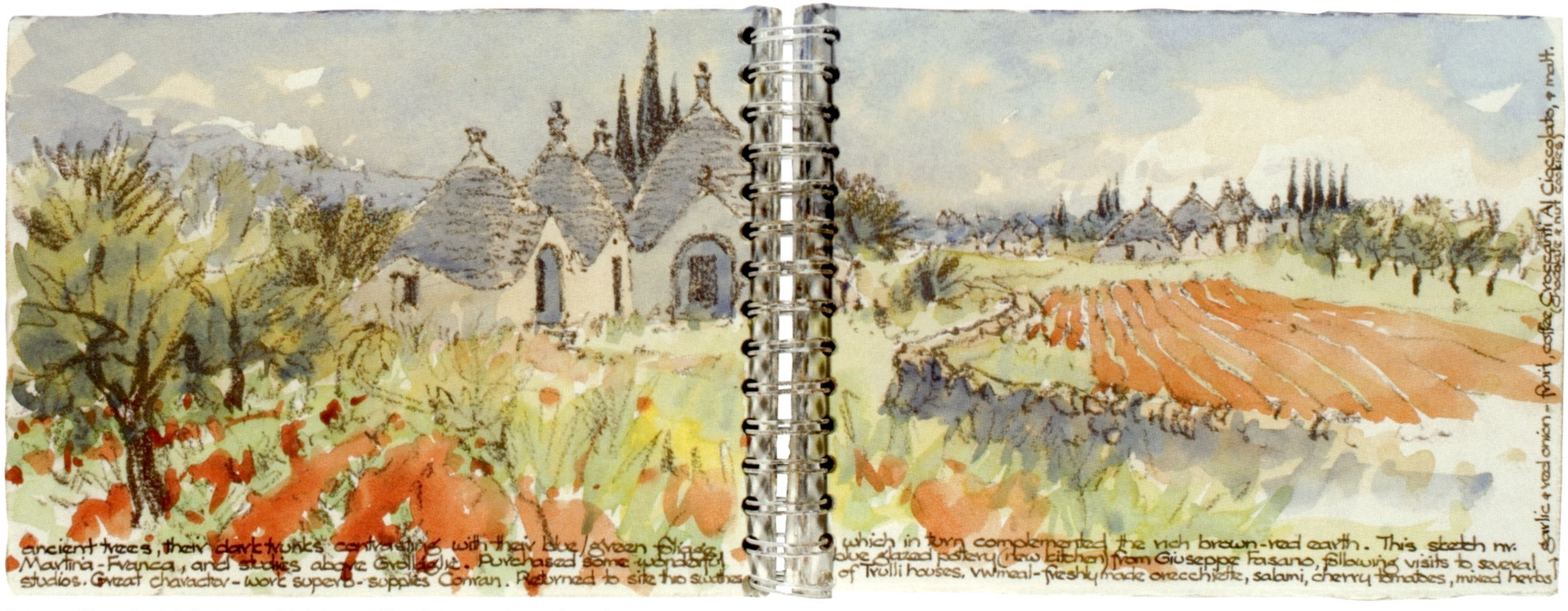

Diary Sketch 10th May, 2006 *Valle d'Itria* Conté w/c

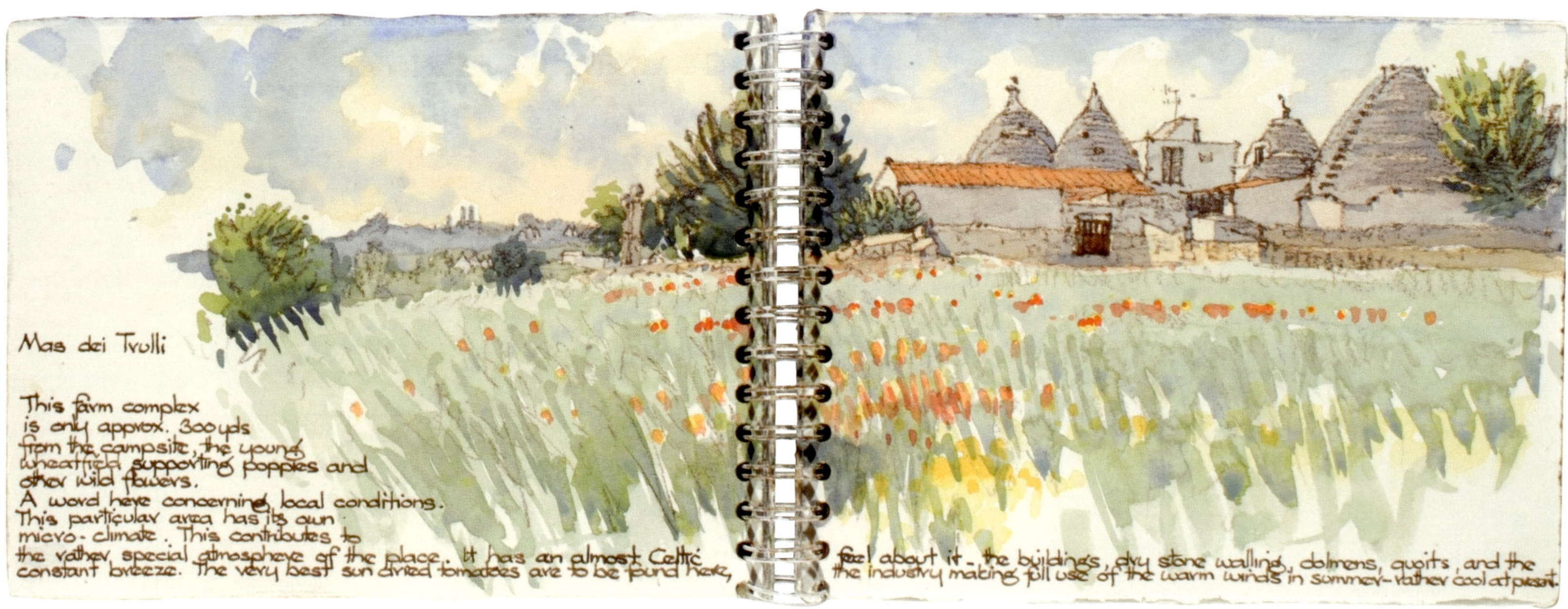

Diary Sketch 12th May, 2006 *Mas dei Trulli* Conté w/c

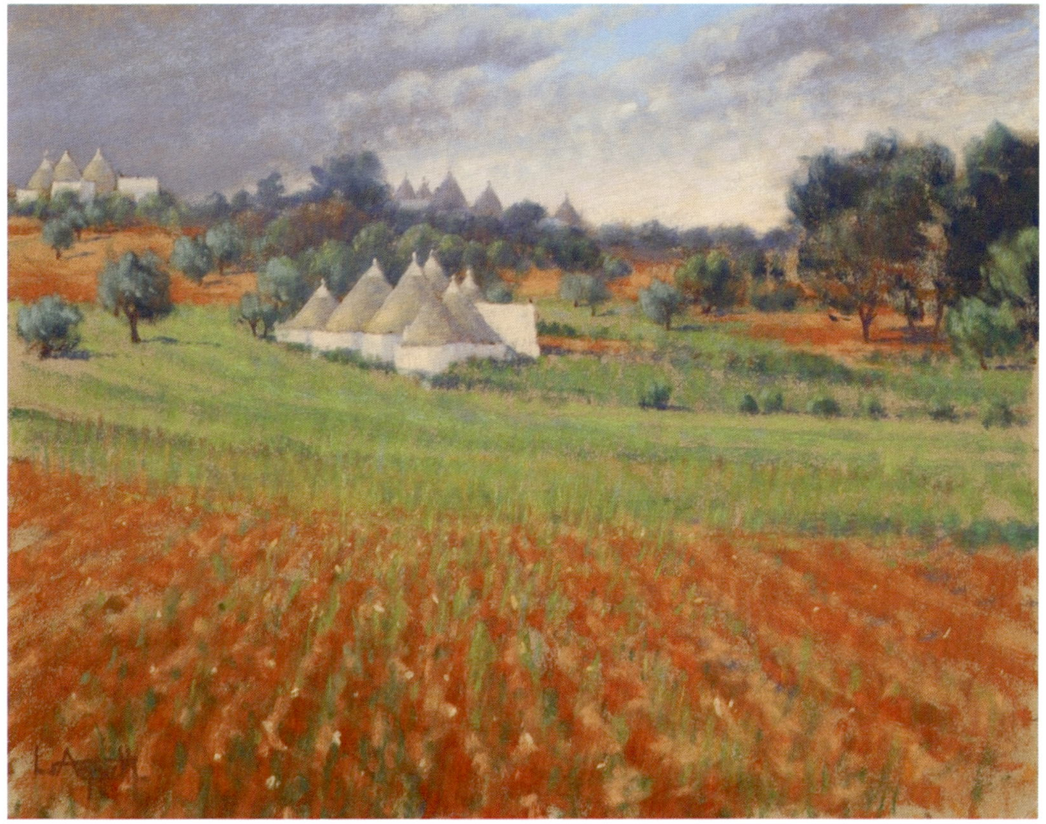

Mas Cristi, Valle d'Itria
Pastel 250 x 325 mm

Diary Sketches
11th May, 2006
Mas Zippo and Mas Cristi
Conté w/c

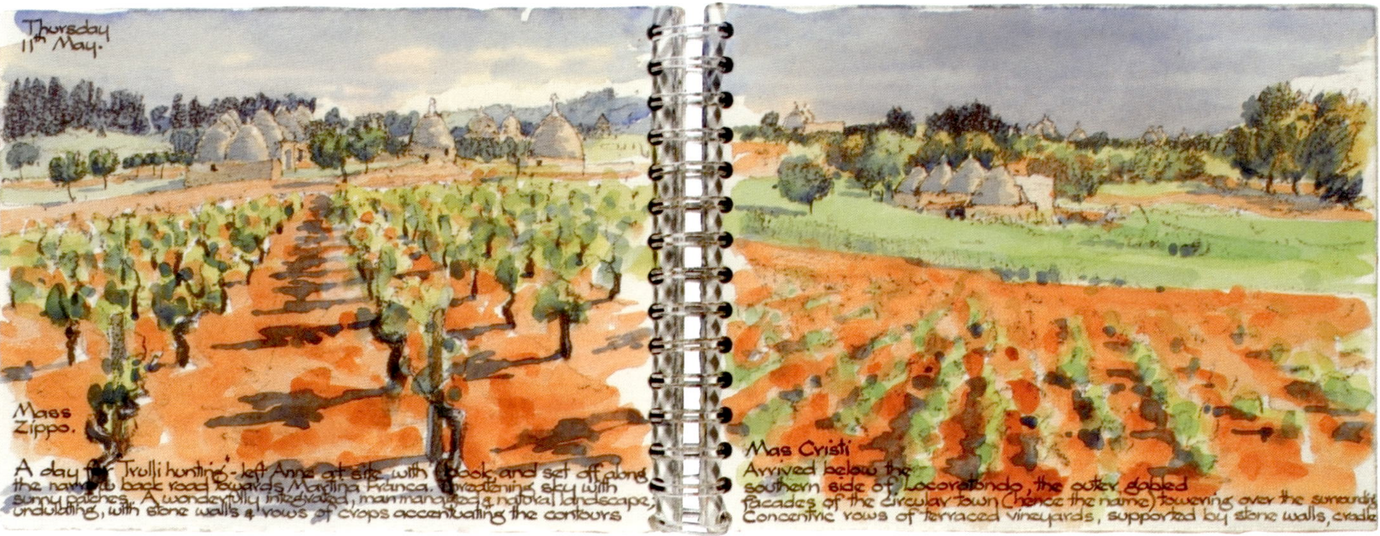

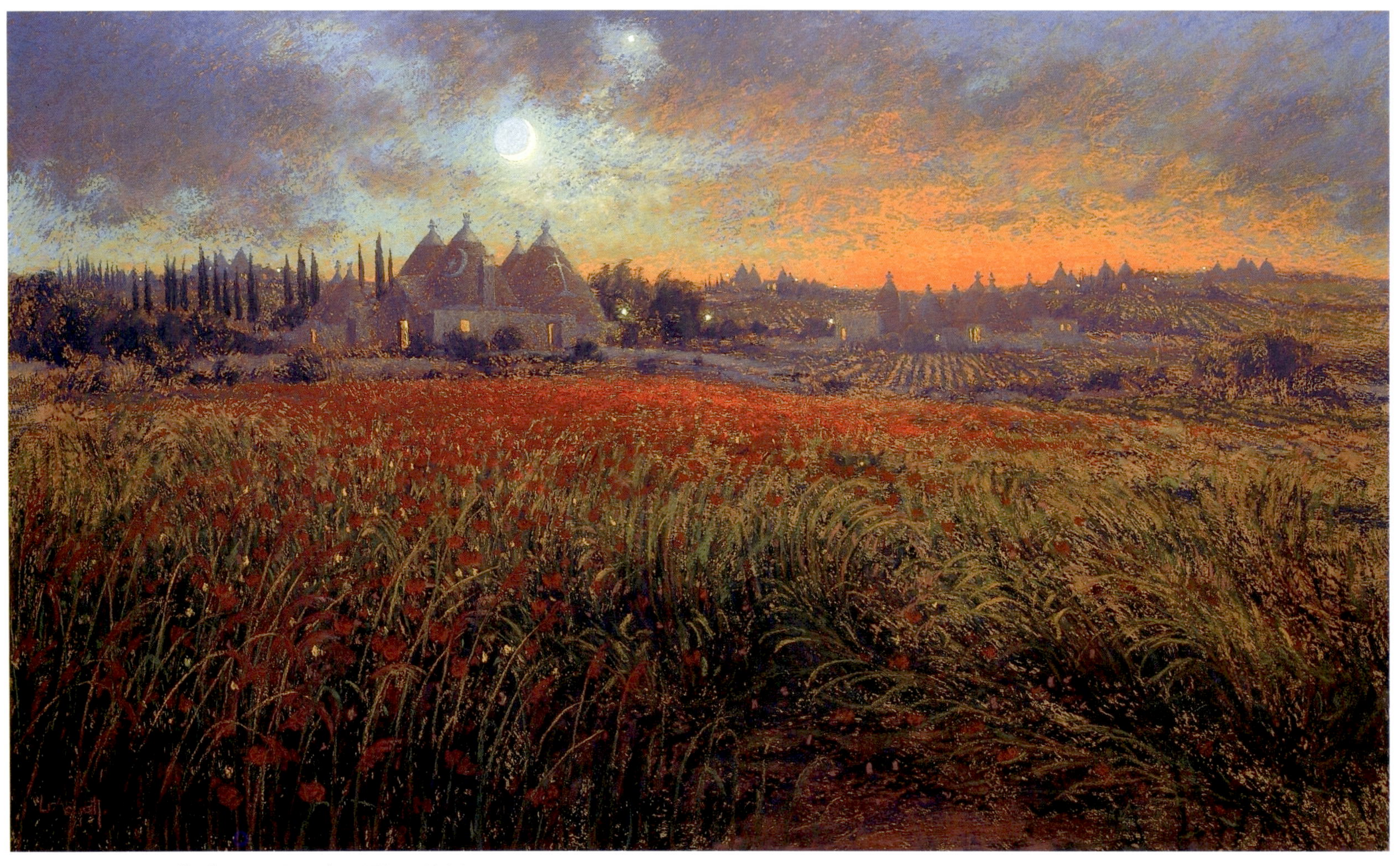

Crescent Moon, Valle d'Itria Pastel 650 x 1016 mm

It is out in the wider landscape that these unique buildings are somehow elevated to exude an even greater presence, particularly at dawn, or the close of day.

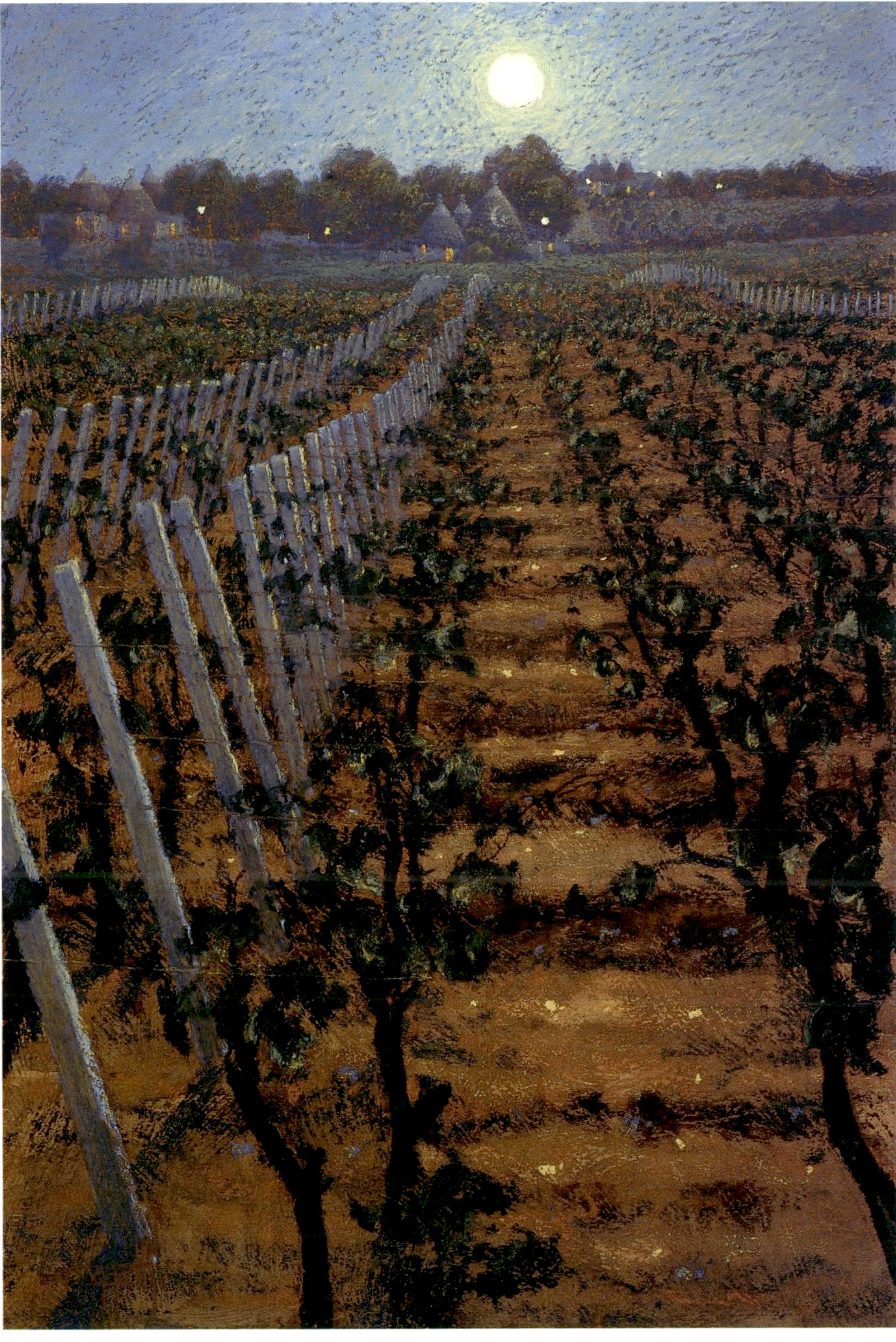

Lunar 15, Valle d'Itria
Pastel 500 x 325 mm

At nightime, interconnection with the universe seems a distinct possibility

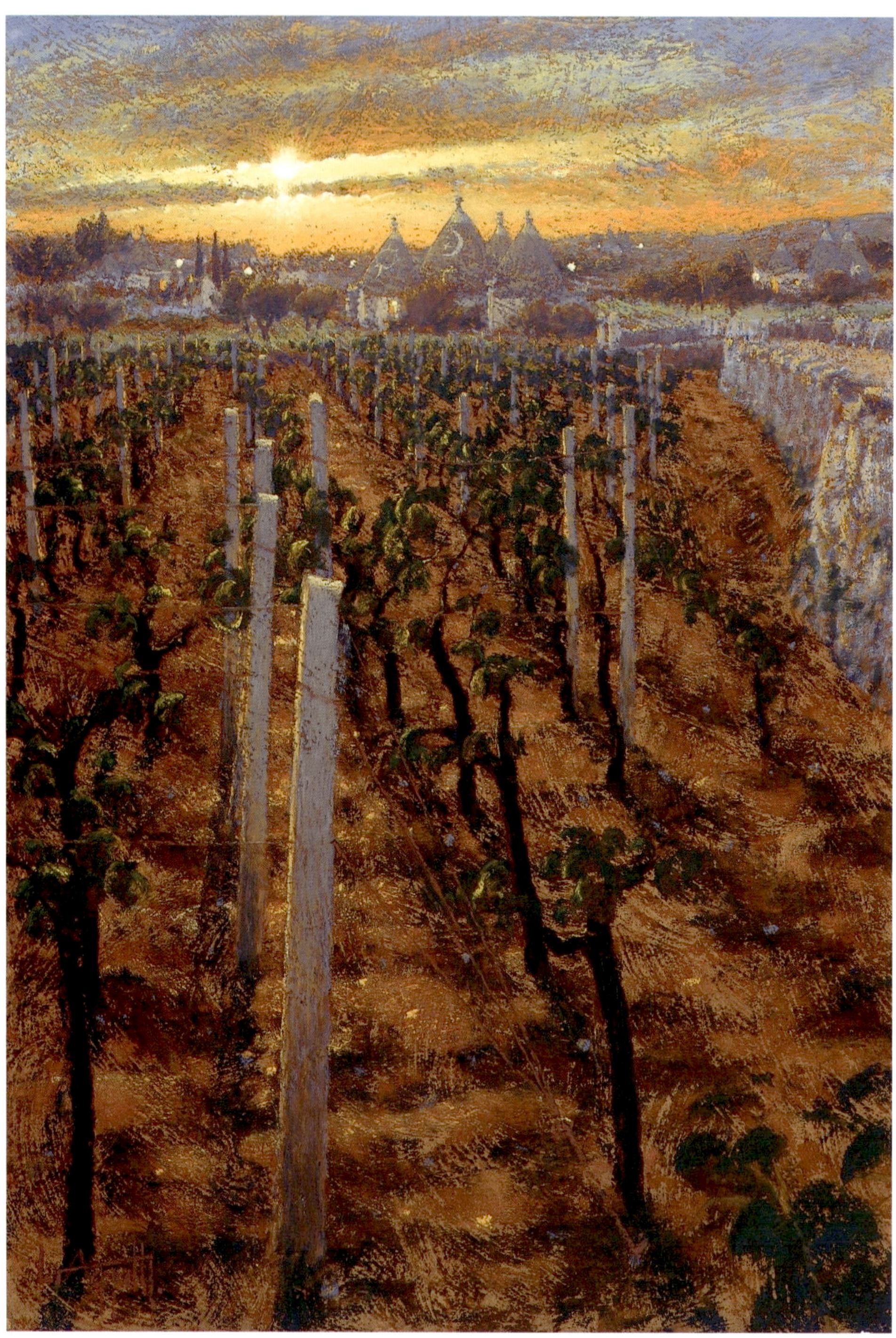

Failing Sun, Valle d'Itria
Pastel 500 x 325 mm

The way of life here is encapsulated in the proof of their labours, enabled by the vibrant light that shines upon the productive rich red/brown earth.

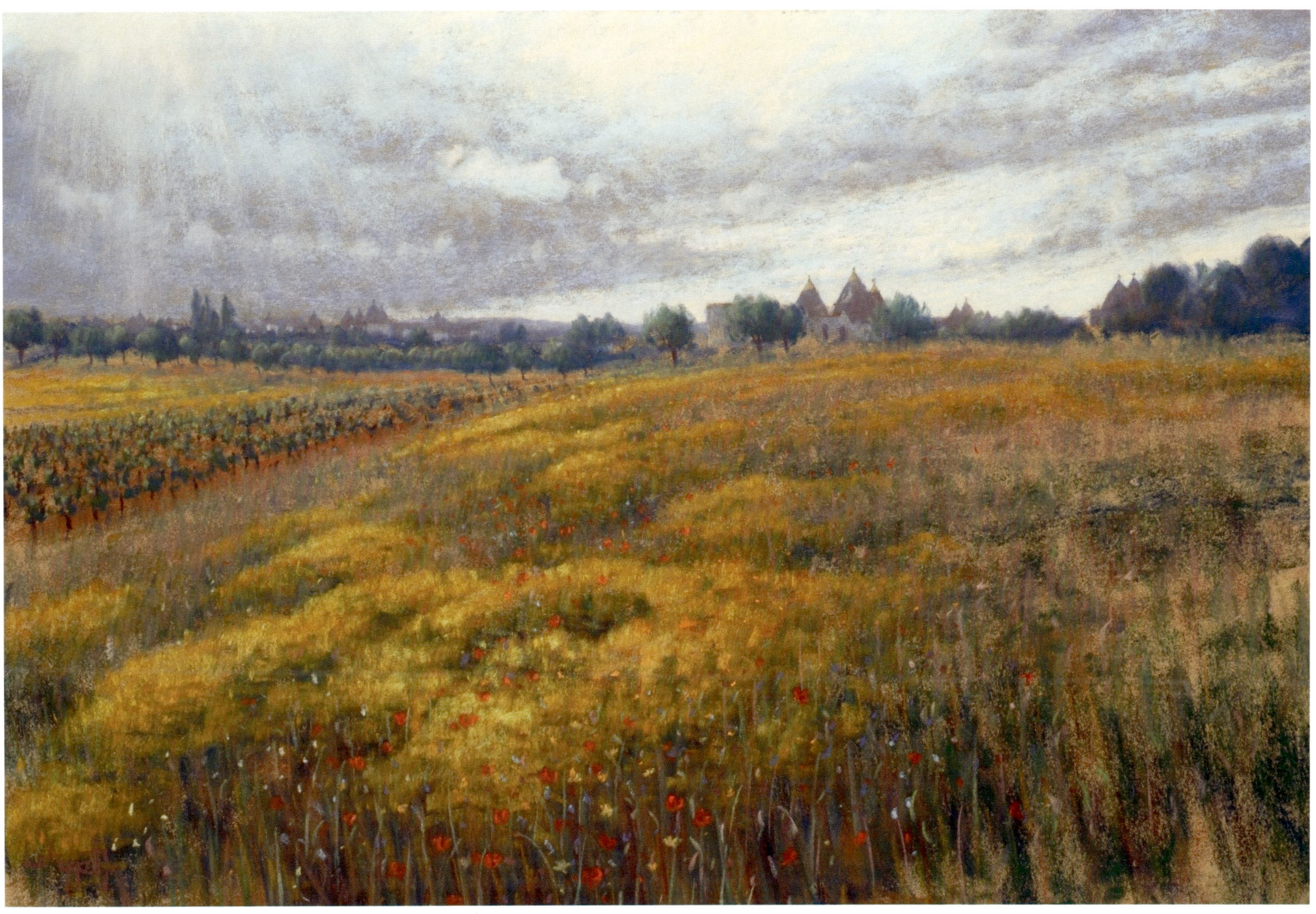

Valle d'Itria Pastel 400 x 600 mm

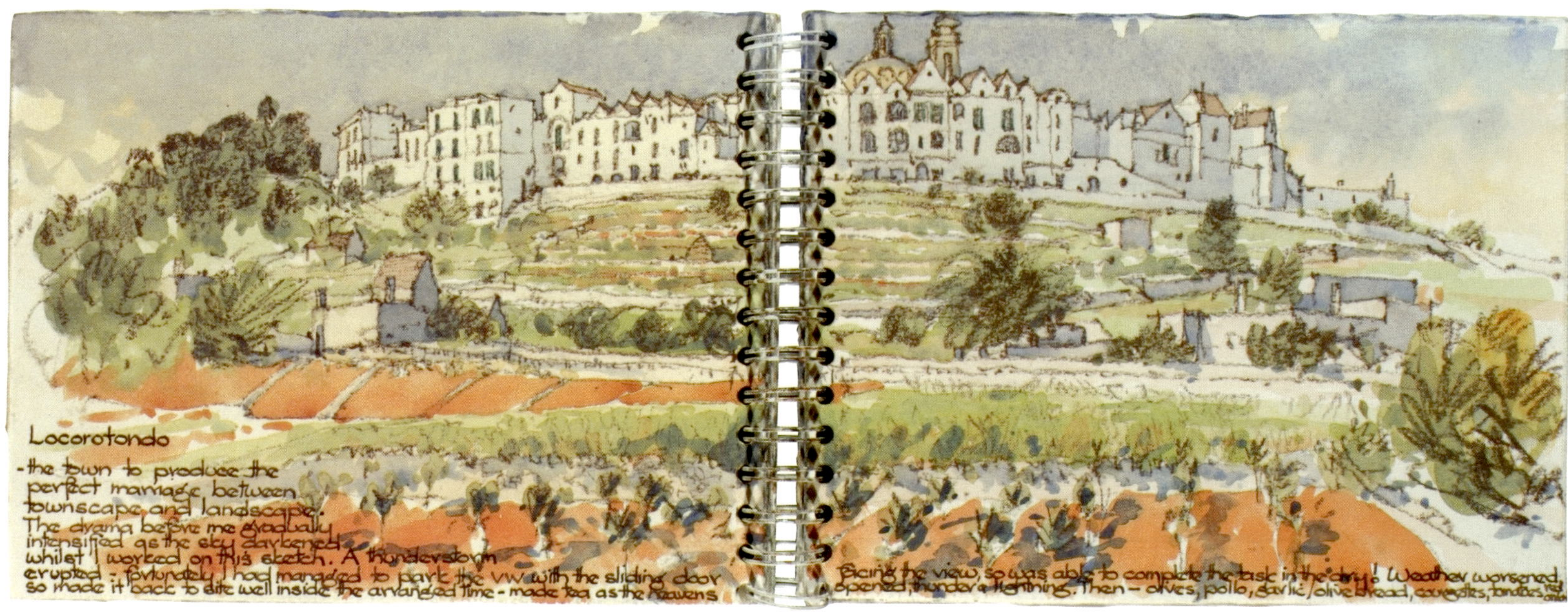

Diary Sketch 11th May, 2006 *Locorotondo* Conté w/c

Nearly 9 km to the east, the stunning hill town of Locorotondo looks out all around the Valle d'Itria. Surrounded by vineyards producing a favoured spumante wine, it takes its name "round place" from the fact that its streets radiate from its centre, where there is a well dedicated to St George, like water ripples. The vineyards tumble down in terracing from the rows of white distinctive gables, most dramatically to the south, with trulli farmhouses punctuating the olive groves below. These hobbit-like dwellings spread even further eastwards through Cisternino over to beautiful Ostuni where white façades contrast with Renaissance and Baroque buildings honestly expressed in their natural stone envelopes.

The paintings of olive trees were produced during our visit to Grottáglie to the south, below the magnificent escarpment of the Murge, overlooking the Golfo di Taranto. The town is renowned for its pottery, and ceramics evolving from the age of Magna Graecia. After a tour of the different studios, we bought some ware for our "new" kitchen from Giuseppe Fasano, who supplies Conran.

Whilst working on an olive grove painting outside Grottáglie, a lone cyclist pulled over in some state of dehydration. He explained that he required aqua (no English, we very little Italian), pointing to the rack where his water bottle had once lodged. We gave him a bottle of the precious nectar from the fridge. Restored, off he went with a refill. It was later in the afternoon that he sped past on his return journey, with the no doubt well rehearsed words, "thank you, and good morning"!

The olive groves in this area consist of huge, majestic and wise ancient trees, with massive dark twisted trunks bearing huge canopies. What a harvest they must provide.

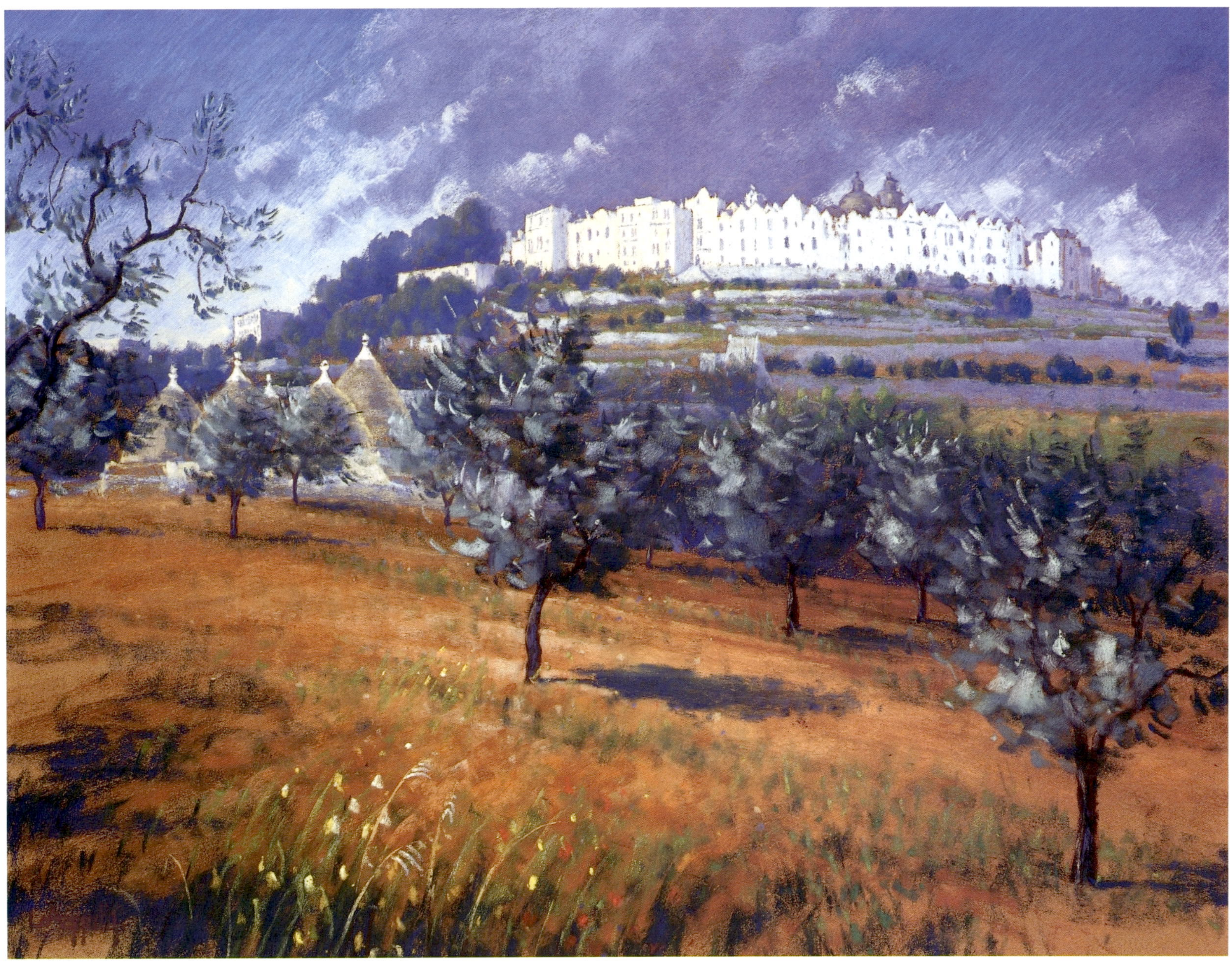

Locorotondo Pastel 500 x 650 mm

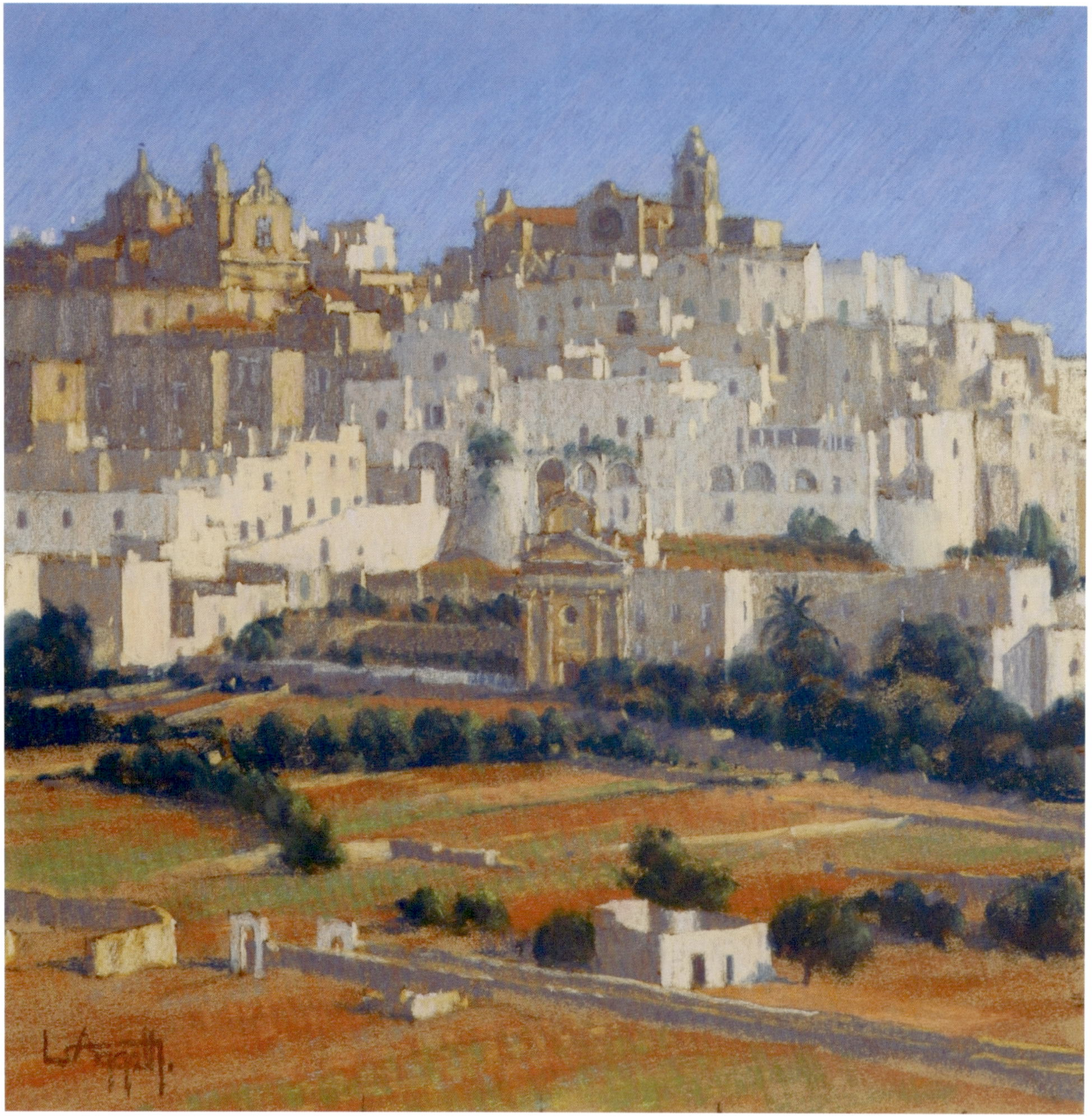

Ostuni Pastel 325 x 325 mm

Renaissance and Baroque stone buildings contrast with the white-washed façades, lining the streets.

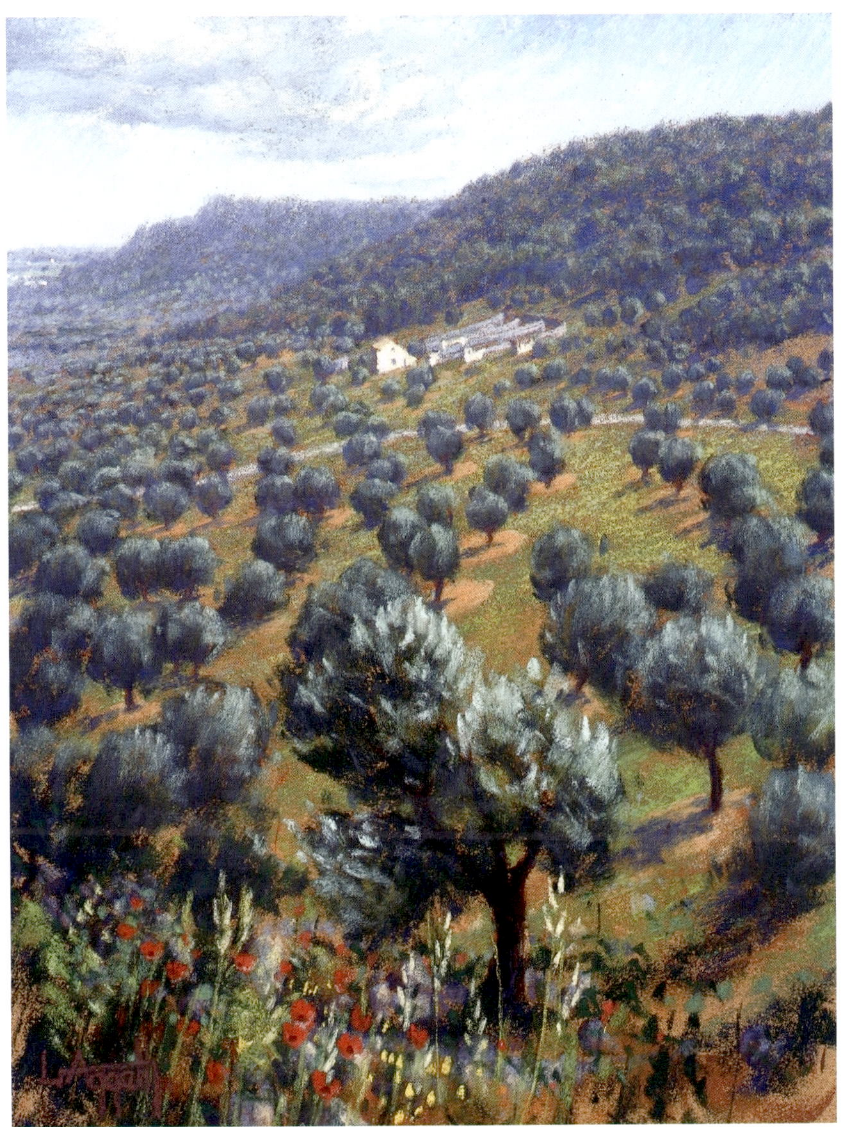

Olives near Grottáglie Pastel 325 x 250 mm

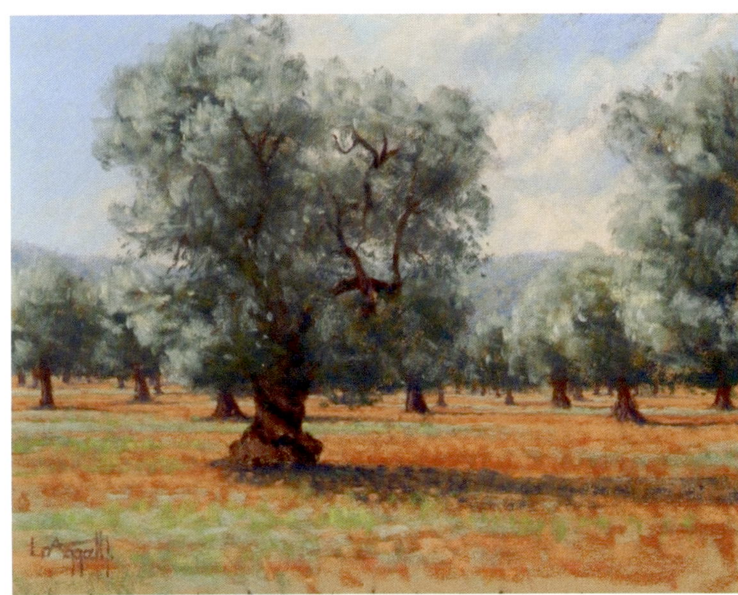

Ancient Olives, Grottáglie Pastel 250 x 325 mm

THE GARGANO

"Different" would be a gross over simplification when considering the contrast between the two regions of Puglia that we explored during this trip. It would be true to say, however, that they triggered a similar emotional response. Monte Sant'Angelo at the southern end of the Gargano Peninsula stands high and proud overlooking the plain of Sipontia, and the lost, great city of nearby Sipontium, spiritually nestling far below in an olive blue haze. Before silt, washed down by the rivers, gradually joined it to the mainland, thus creating this vast plain, the Gargano was an island. It could still be regarded as such, for this region is as different from the adjoining lands in attitude as it is in its landscapes.

The cult of Michael the Archangel is described in my diary notes, so I will here just simply try to explain the deep inspirational and spiritual influence this place and the people we met had on our well being. Our campsite, Il Gelso, right on the Adriatic shore, and surrounded by olive groves, is run by Michele and Madelene. You will receive the friendliest of welcomes from this sincere and warm-hearted couple, who produce their own heavenly red wine which they decant into plastic bottles at 2 Euros each. They grow lemons, oranges, almonds, olives, and a variety of vegetables. These they also preserve for their own use and retail, together with their own version of Limoncello, a lemon flavoured liqueur with cream and egg; very smooth, and with a delayed kick. Michele and Madelene will also prepare a sumptuous dayfresh seafood meal. His brother is a local fisherman. Indeed, one of the abiding memories of this wonderful site was watching, near to midnight, the fishing fleet chugging up and down just offshore in the moonlight, their twinkling lights too, reflected in the almost still waters.

The whole area, stretching from the water's edge of this rather "off the wall" campsite, through the olive groves which run right up to the lower slopes of Monte Sant'Angelo and up to the lofty Mount itself, has a uniquely and rather uncanny spiritual feel about it. There is most definitely a presence here, which equates with the stunningly beautiful and rugged topography.

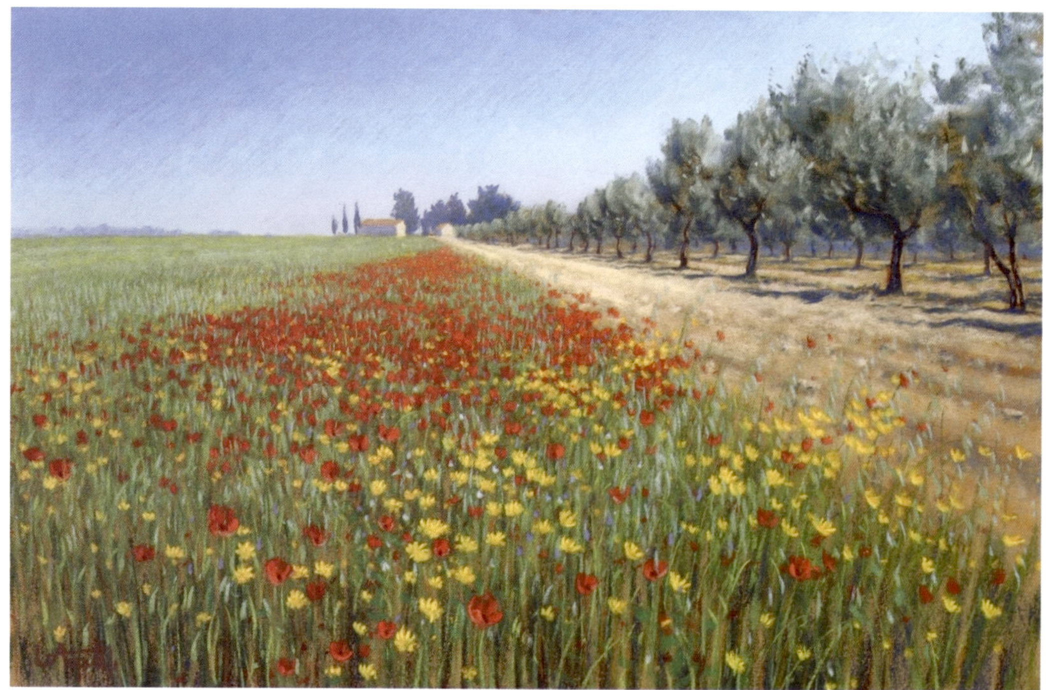

Poppies and Olives, Plain of Sipontia Pastel 325 x 500 mm

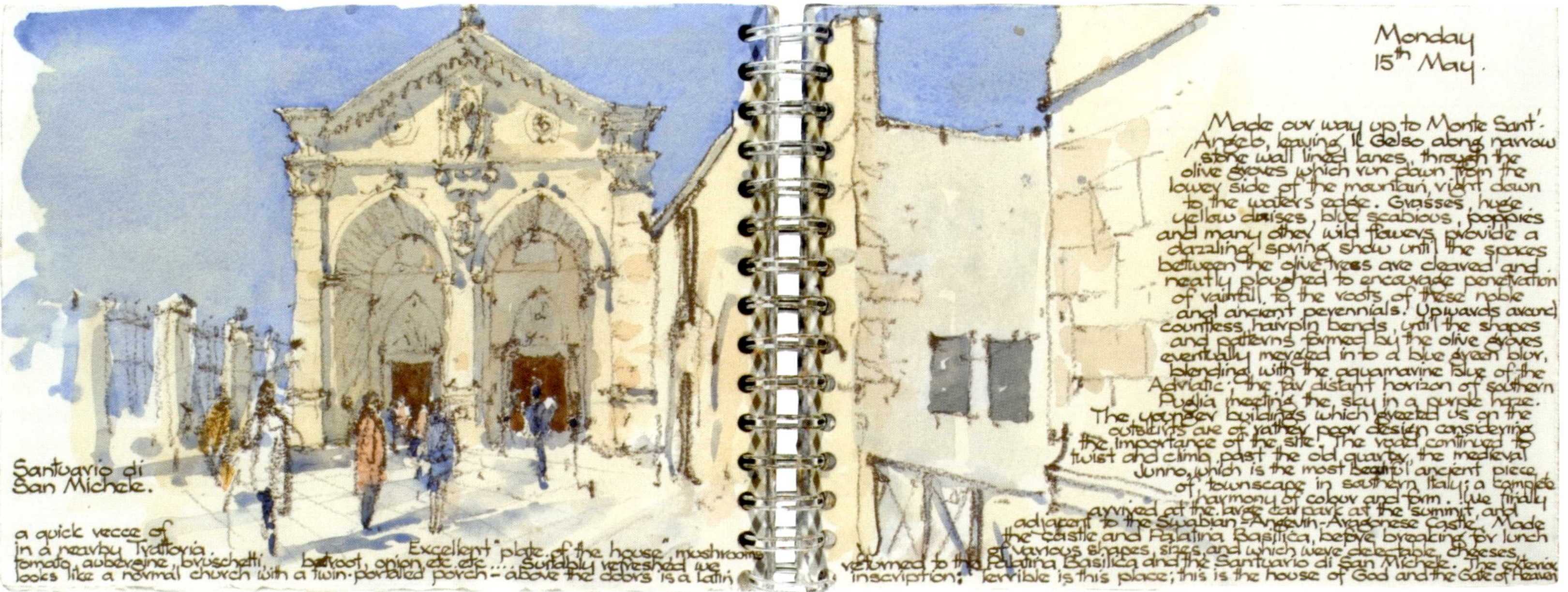

Diary Sketch 15th May, 2006 *Santurio di San Michele Monte Sant' Angelo* Conté w/c

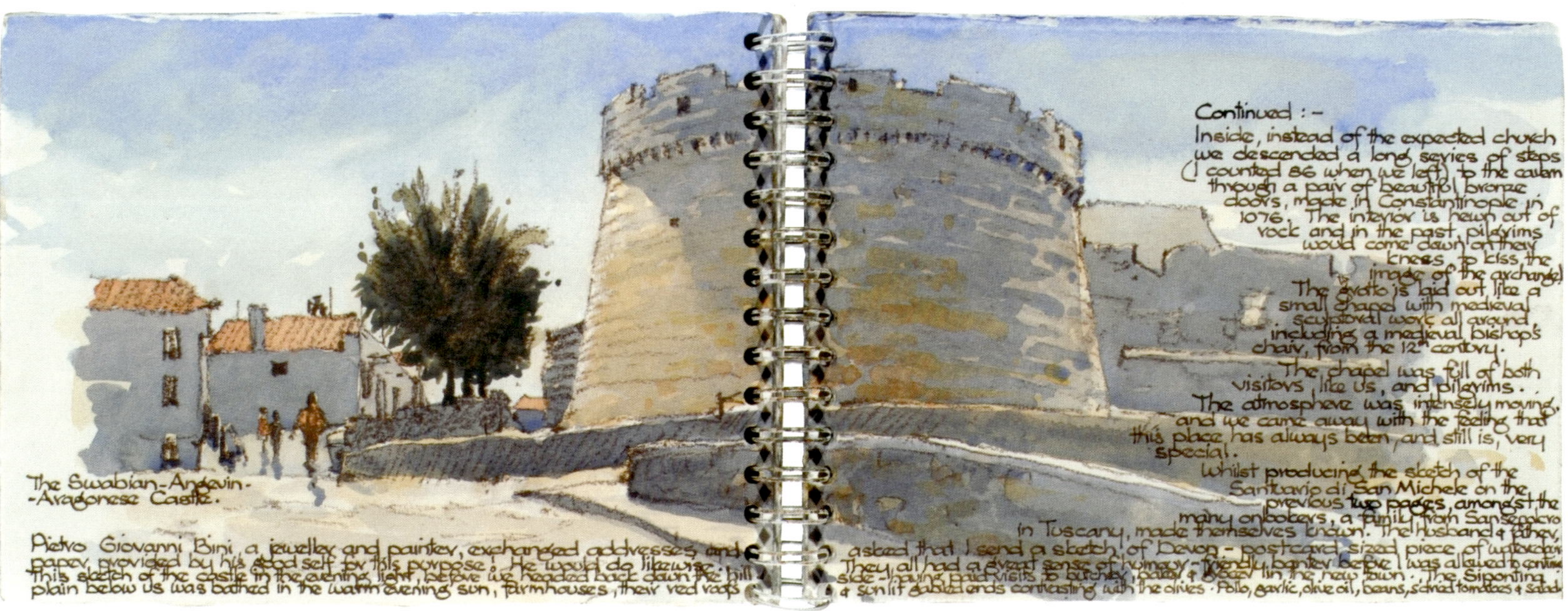

Diary Sketch 15th May, 2006 *Swabian Angevin Aragonese Castle Monte Sant' Angelo* Conté w/c

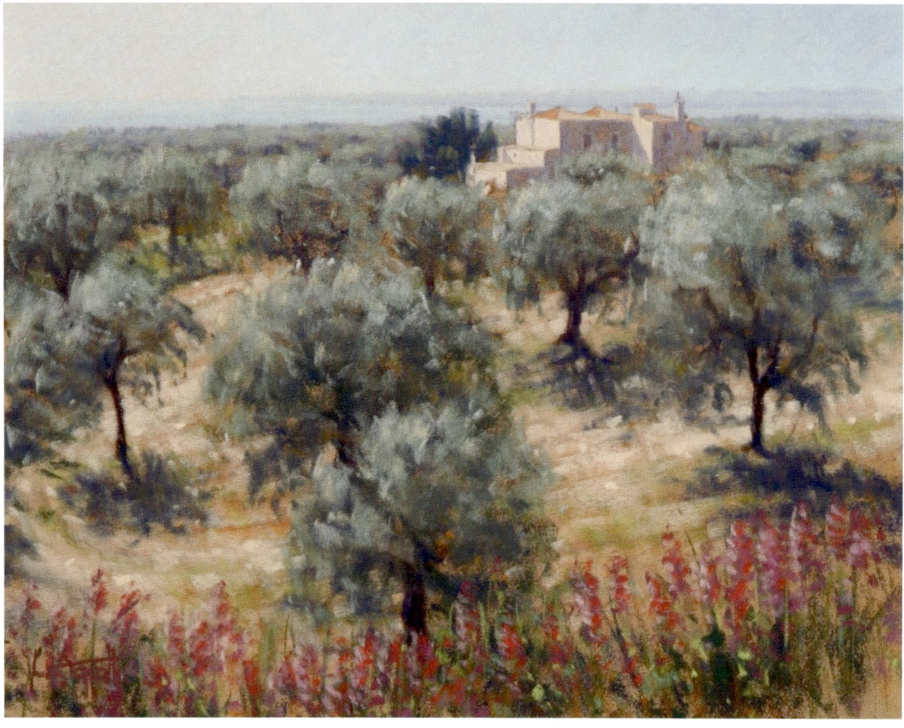

Olive Groves, Il Gelso
Pastel 250 x 325 mm

Diary Sketch 14th May, 2006
Olive Grove below Monte Sant'Angelo
Conté w/c.

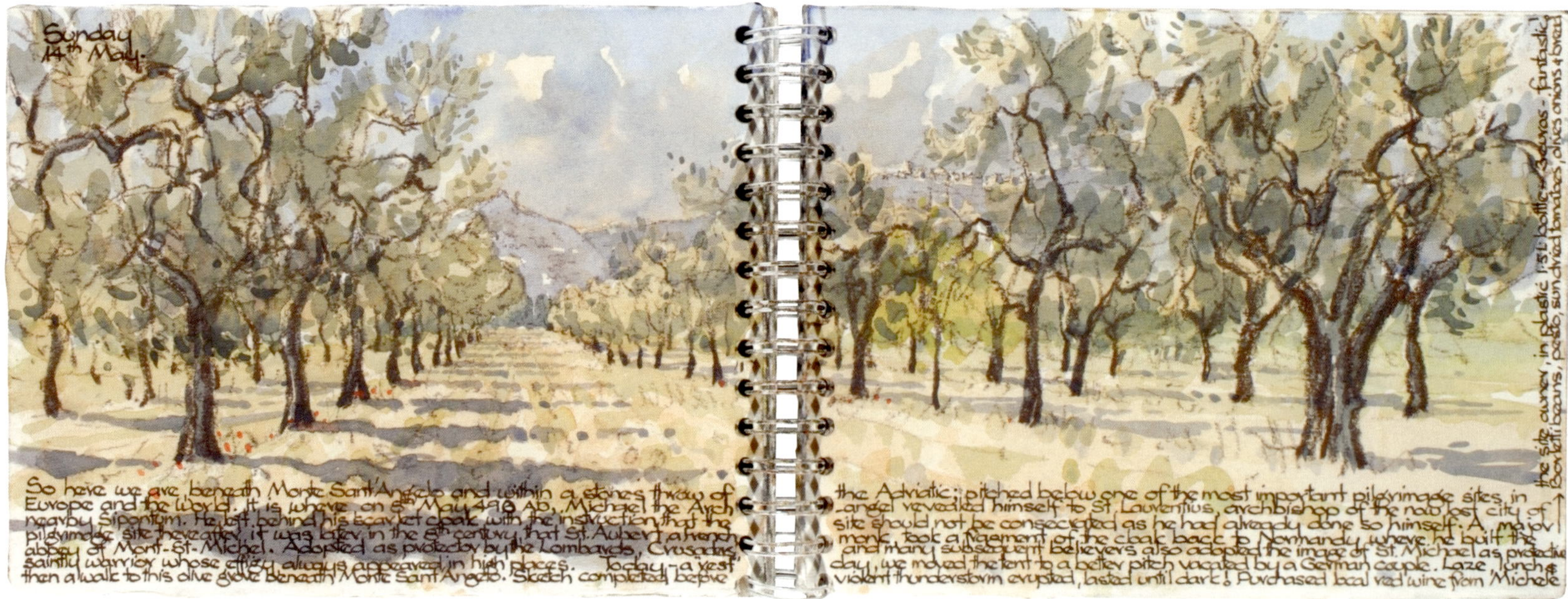

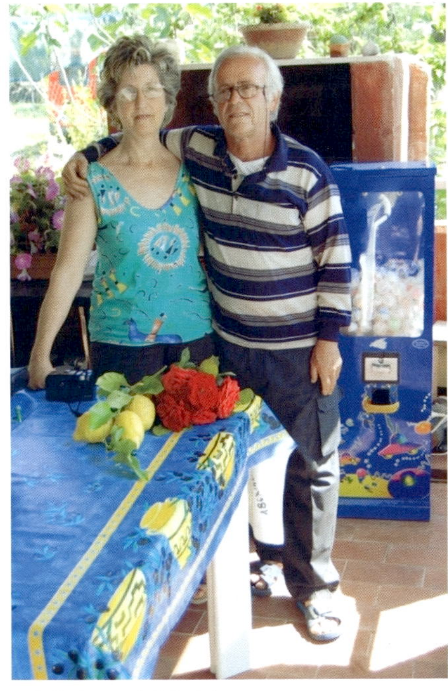

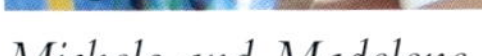

Michele and Madelene.

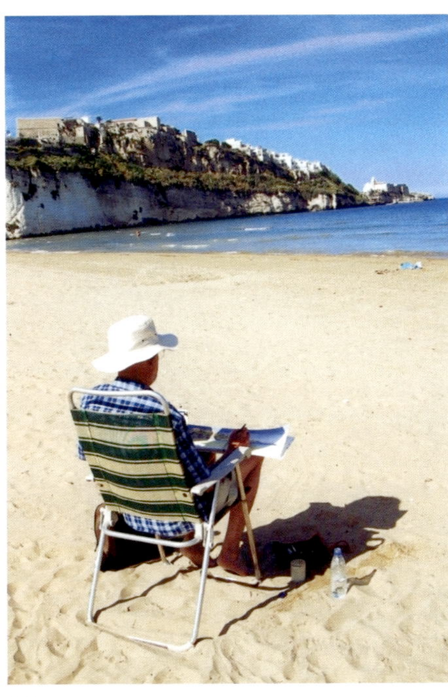

Vieste.

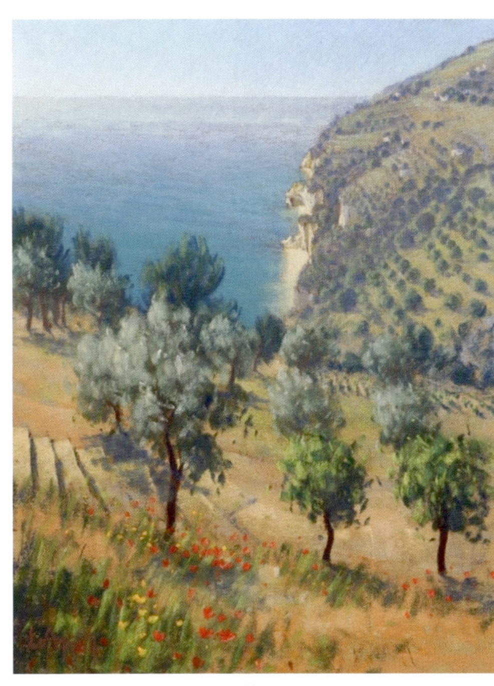

Gargano Coast Pastel 325 x 250 mm

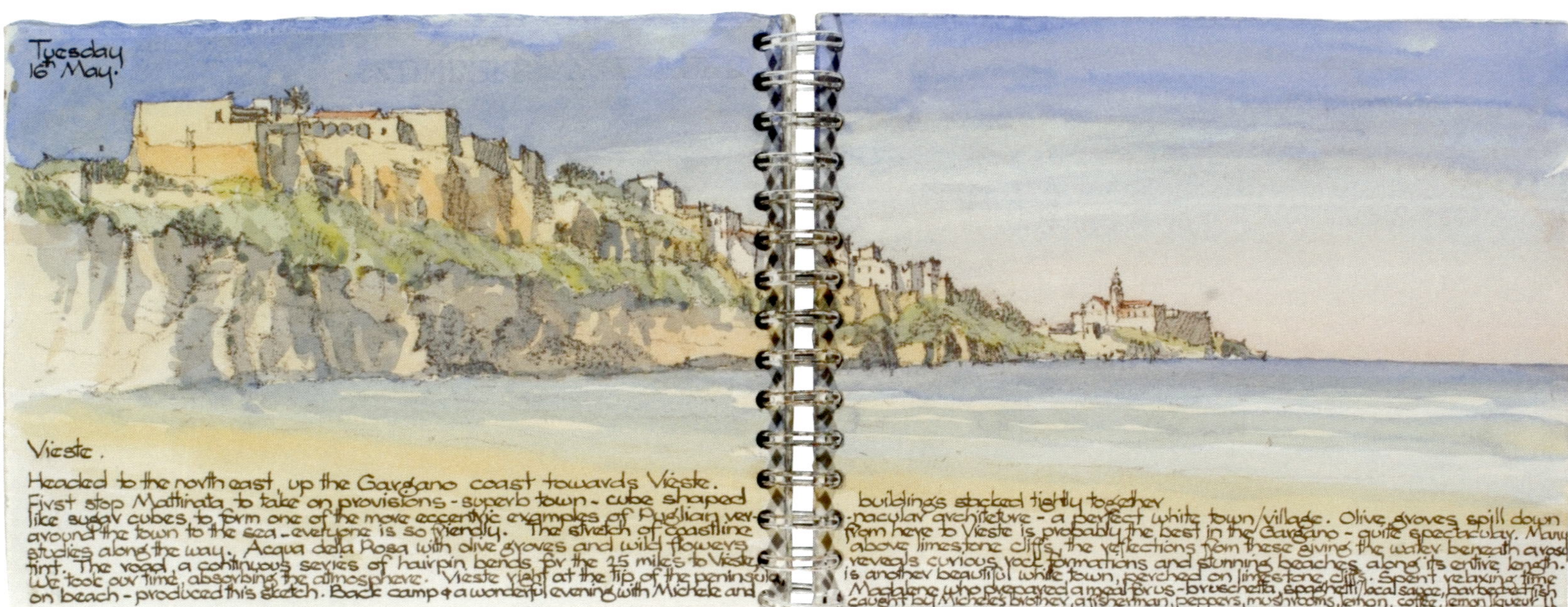

Diary Sketch 16th May, 2006 *Vieste* Conté w/c

Our exploration along the south-eastern coastline from Monte Sant'Angelo to the tip of the peninsula at Vieste, and recognised as being the most beautiful stretch, revealed superb subject matter. Beyond Vieste, the area has become rather spoiled by the tourist sprawl, but southwards the limestone cliffs, aquamarine blue sea and fine beaches, overlooked by old watchtowers, present an exceptionally fine coastline.

Just 7 km up the coast from Il Gelso lies Mattinata at the foot of Monte Sant'Angelo, with its olive groves seemingly marching into the sea. One of the more eccentric examples of Puglian vernacular architecture, and quite different from the trulli to the south, the gleaming white village looks like a neatly arranged stack of sugar cubes. Beautifully kept stepped alleys connect the contoured streets, such as illustrated by the diary sketch of the Vittoria Emanuel III flight.

Our last afternoon was spent to the west, at San Giovanni Rotondo, where Padre Pio de Pietralcina received the stigmata in 1918. This place of pilgrimage, the event and consequent beatification in 1999, was described to us following an excellent meal of barbecued fish, by Michele, who knew him well.

The event and his miracles have always aroused suspicions within the church, although his honesty and endeavour have always been recognised. Popular devotion there has always been however, and when expressed, as we witnessed by a constant stream of pilgrims touching items he possessed in the Sanctuary of Santa Maria della Grazia, it can seem a little too intense.

The new Chiesa San Pio da Pietrelcina, designed by top Italian architect Renzo Piano, is a revelation however. Restraint in the use of simple but beautiful materials, i.e. stone, timber, glass and copper, has resulted in a building which is successfully dedicated to a person whom some regard as the "embodiment of the living god".

The following morning we departed from Il Gelso laden with gifts from Michele and Madelene including a huge bouquet of roses for Anne, picked from their garden.

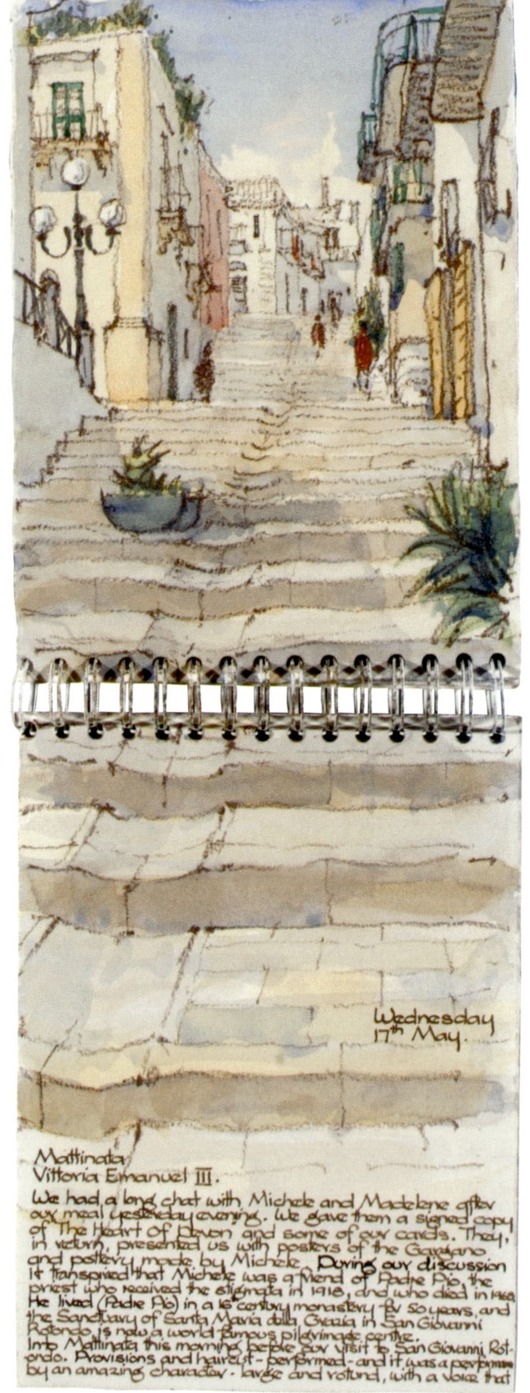

Diary Sketch 17th May, 2006
Mattinata, Vittoria Emanuel III Conté w/c

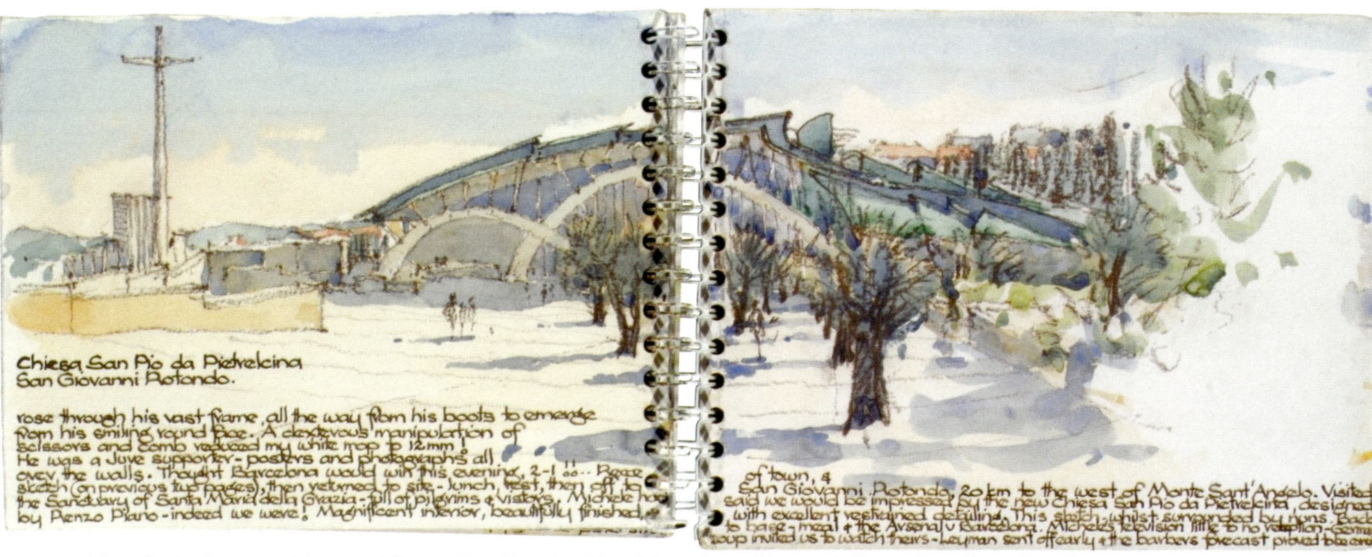

Diary Sketch 17th May, 2006 *Chiesa San Pio da Pietrelcina, San Giovanni Rotondo* Conté w/c

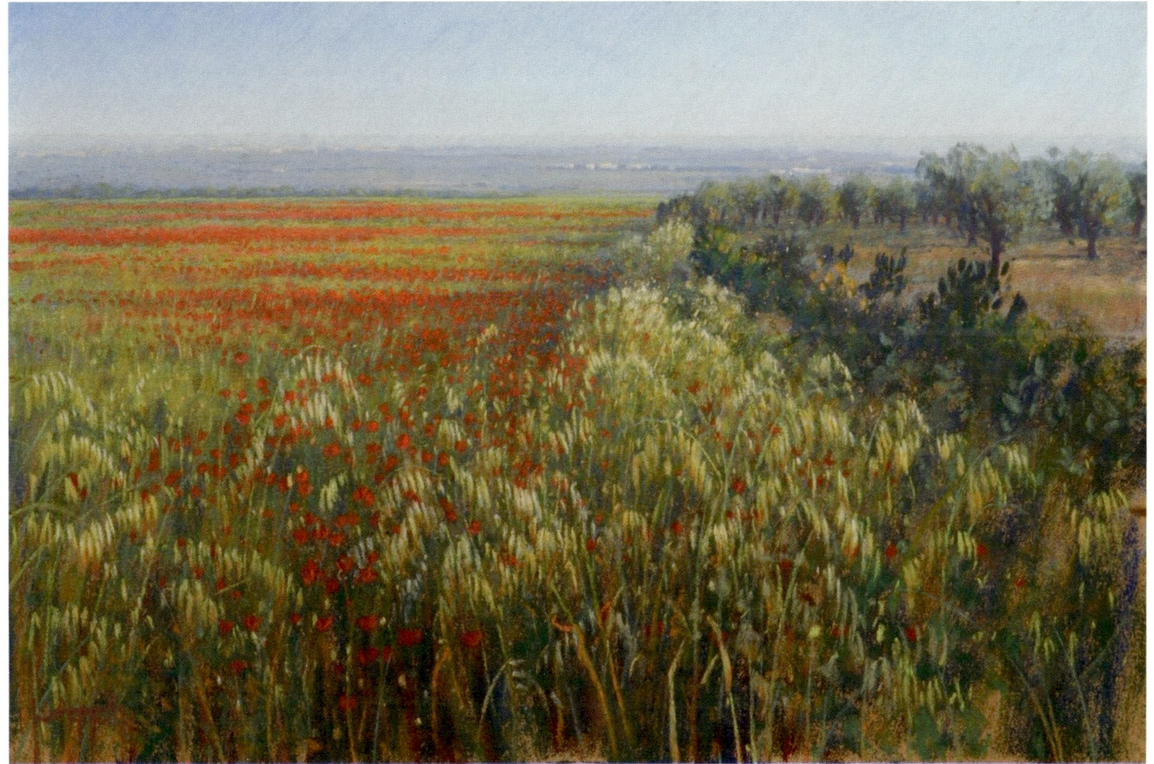

Poppies, Poppies, Plain of Sipontia Pastel 325 x 500 mm

Umbria

Situated in the middle of the country and without coastal areas, Umbria is known as "the green heart of Italy". The Apennines run north to south on the eastern side, spawning gently rolling hills and green valleys which emerge to provide a soft and undulating landscape, freshened by the lightness and purity of the air, illuminated by a sky of changeable limpidity. It is also renowned for its splendid hill towns of such concentration as to be unique in the world. These artistic gems of comparatively unspoiled medieval origin are all located within a short distance of one another: Gubbio, Perugia, Assisi, Spello, Trevi, Montefalco, Spoleto, Norcia, Todi and Orvieto …

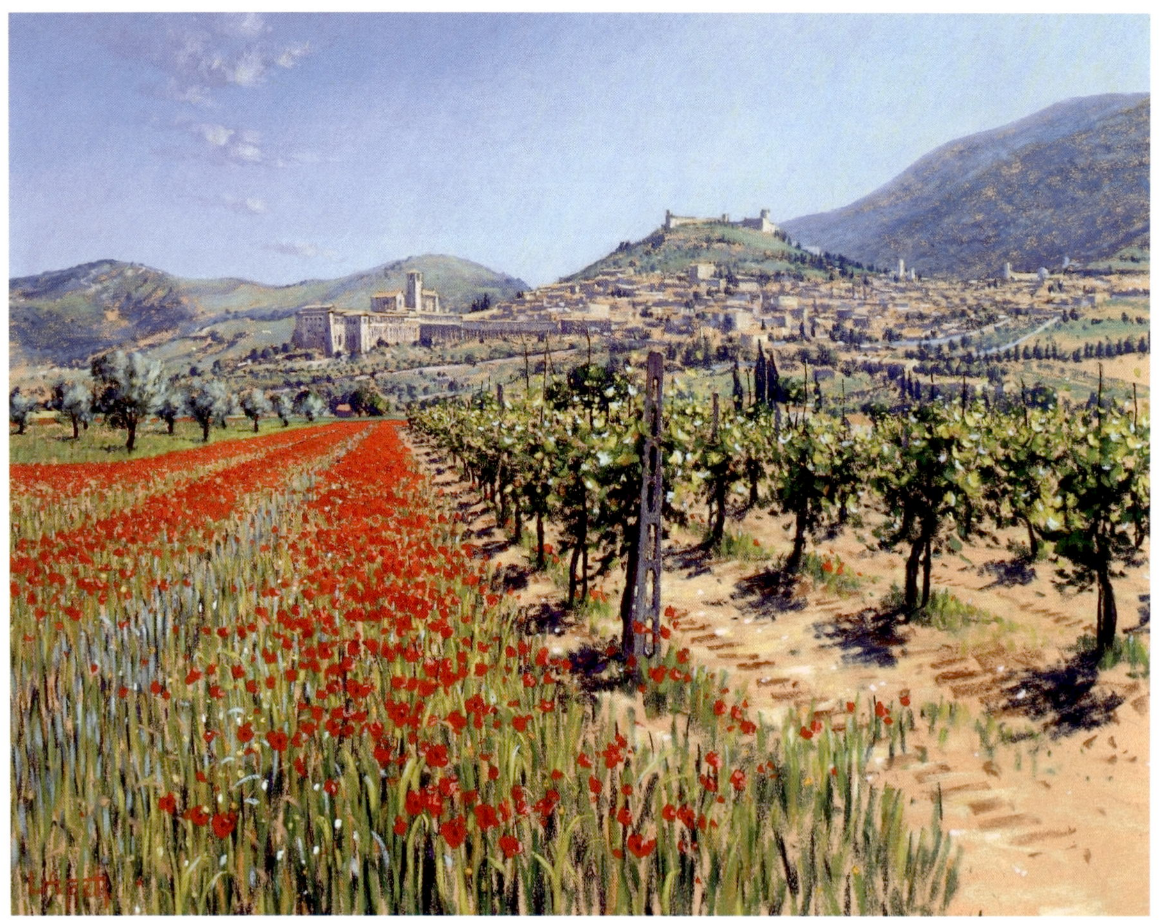

Poppies and Vines below Assisi Pastel 500 x 650 mm

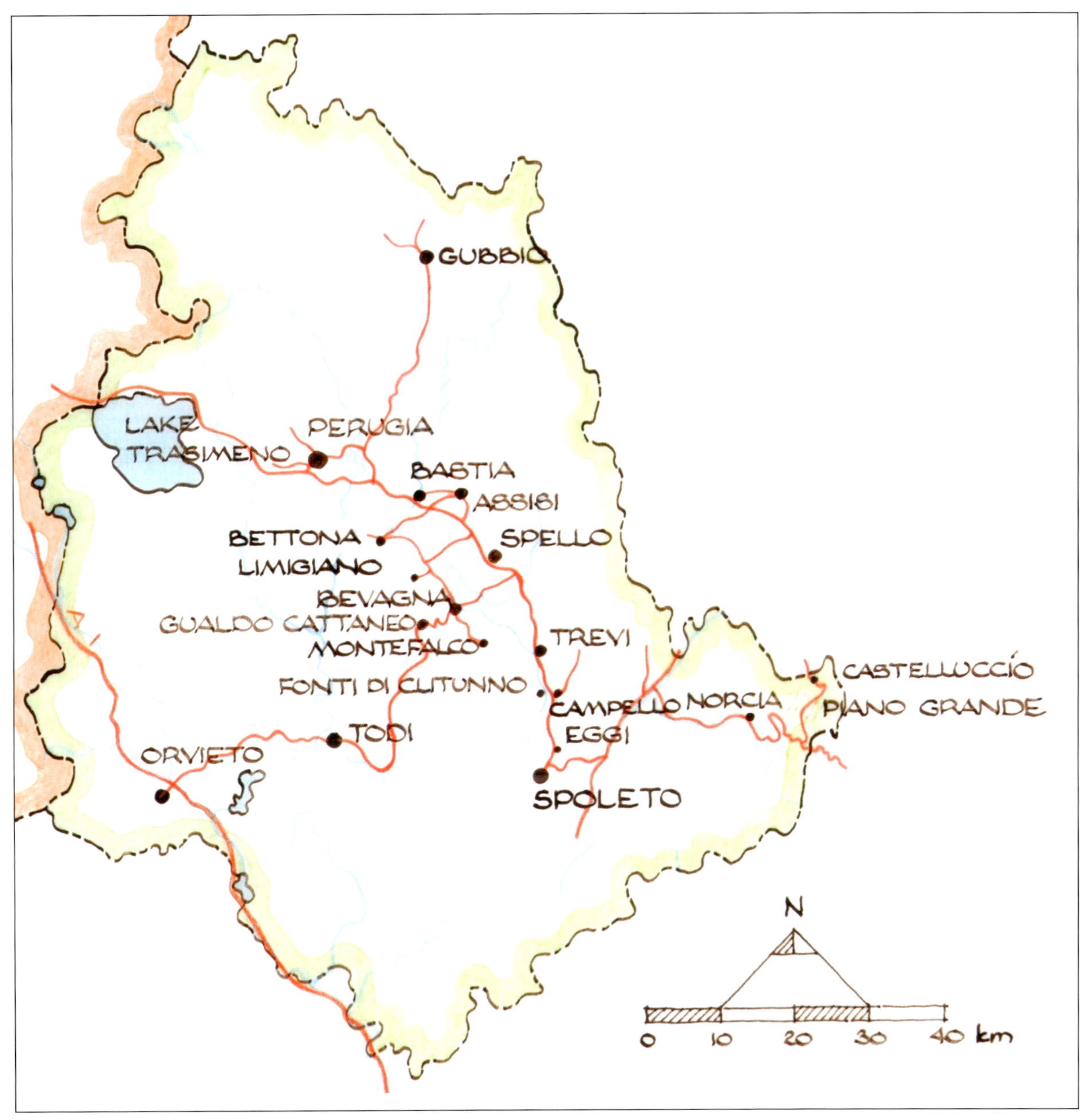
GUBBIO
LAKE TRASIMENO
PERUGIA
BASTIA
ASSISI
BETTONA
SPELLO
LIMIGIANO
BEVAGNA
GUALDO CATTANEO
MONTEFALCO
TREVI
FONTI DI CLITUNNO
CAMPELLO
NORCIA
CASTELLUCCIO
PIANO GRANDE
EGGI
TODI
ORVIETO
SPOLETO
N
0 10 20 30 40 km

PARCO NAZIONALE DEI MONTI SIBILLINI

The region high up in the Parco Nazionale dei Monti Sibillini, in the south-east corner is, however, quite different, being one of the most distinctive in all Italy. This is where our exploration of Umbria begins.

The principal reason for visiting this remote area, was to visit and paint its centrepiece, the magnificent and sometimes eerie Piano Grande. We finally made it up to this vast upland prairie in May last year (2006), the itineraries of previous excursions not quite stretching this far. The mountains of the Sibillini surrounding the plain on all sides were covered with gradually melting snow which, in ghostlike fingers, extended downwards, towards the peripheral slopes, to where the patchwork of lentil fields, for which the area is famous, reach up to meet them.

Spring is undoubtedly one of the best times to experience the grandeur of the Piano, when this huge level area is ablaze with an extraordinary profusion of wild flowers. One month there are butter-cups, the next poppies and narcissi. Rare Alpine flora such as the unique Carex buxbaumi are woven into this colourful carpet. On the mountains around, and the higher slopes near the Rifugio Colle Le Cese, where we camped au sauvage on the way here, there are tulips, fritillaries and peonies, as well as Apennine edelweiss, the martagon lily, bears grape, Apennine potentilla, and the Alpine buckthorne.

Castelluccio at the northern end of the Piano, is an isolated farming settlement, which has made a few concessions to tourism with a couple of renovated bars and a hang gliding school (no trees here). The overall atmosphere of the place is bleak, although friendly, and the general appearance of the village is what one would expect from an uncompromising and hard-working community.

We camped in the middle of the huge arena, in a confined space adjoining the horse corral, the campervans thus prevented from spoil-ing the feeling of remoteness; the very reason why visitors drive up the vertiginous narrow unparapeted road to see it. One of the lasting memories from this amazing place will be of standing at night time in the middle of the vast amphitheatre, in total darkness, apart from the few twinkling lights in Castelluccio at the far end; with the canopy of the universe overhead, spectacularly illuminated, even right down to the smallest and most distant stars.

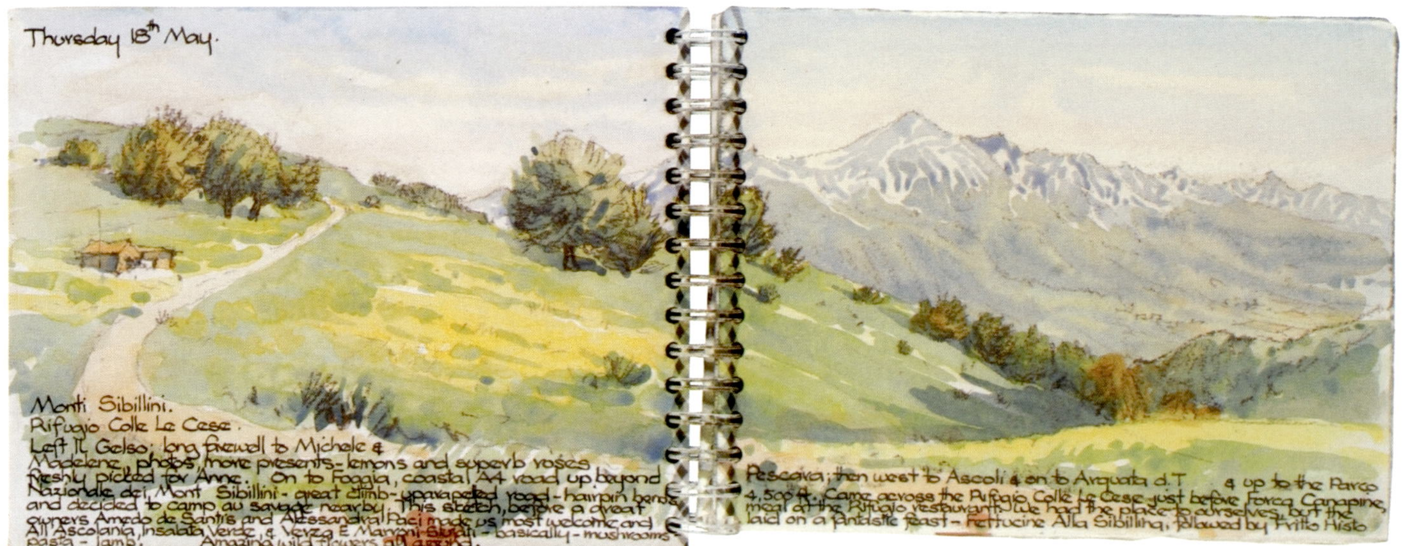

Diary Sketch 18th May, 2006 *Monti Sibillini* Conté w/c

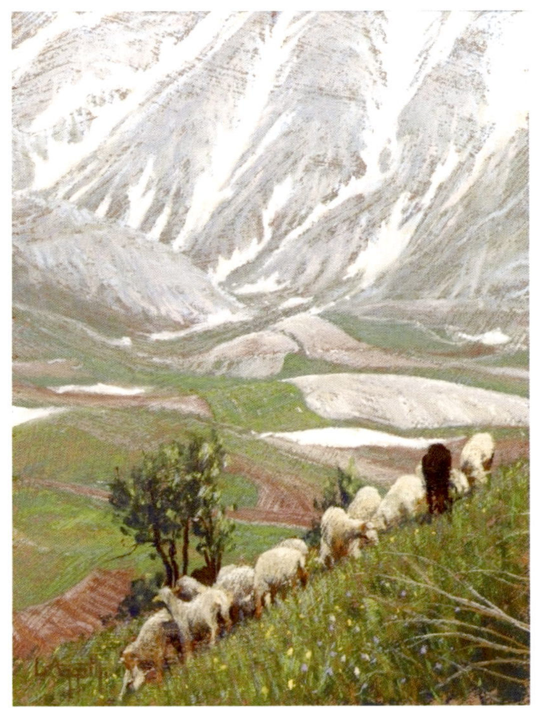

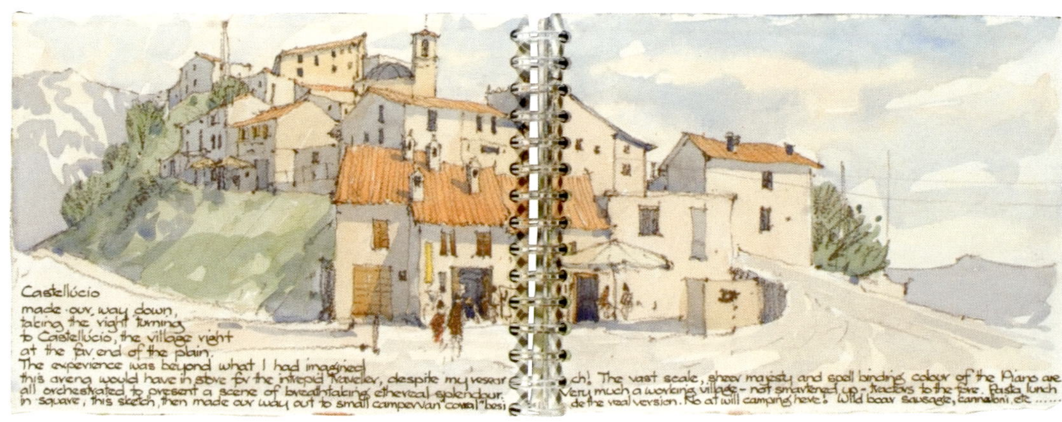

Diary Sketch 19th May, 2006 *Castelluccio* Conté w/c

Piano Grande Pastel 325 x 250 mm

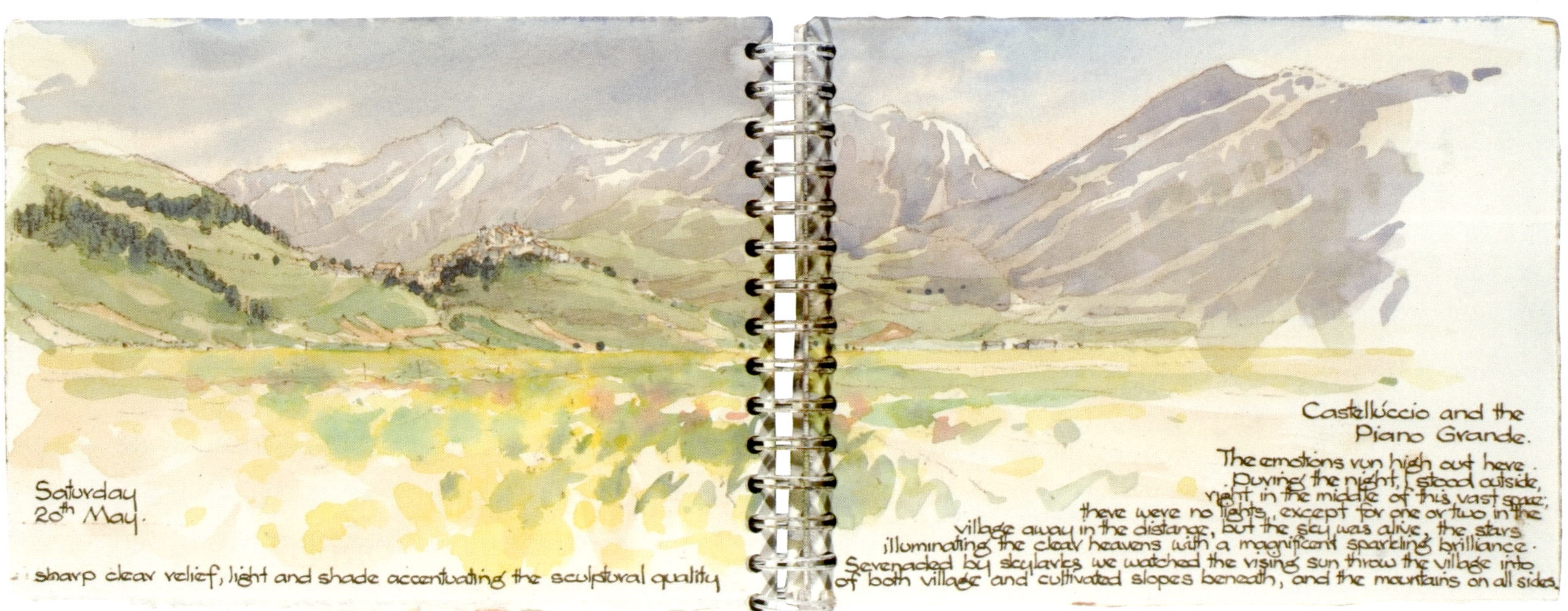

Diary Sketch 20th May, 2006 *Piano Grande and Castelluccio* Conté w/c

The views from the western side of the Sibillini across Norcia way below, towards the Vallerina are simply stunning. A long descent brings you to one of the lowest east to west routes across the Apennines, where Norcia occupies a commanding position midst superb agricultural land, watered by abundant springs. A constant threat of earthquakes has resulted in thick walled and heavily buttressed buildings with a ban on the erection of buildings over 12.5 m high since 1859. This, together with an intact fortified wall, gives the feel of a frontier town (especially when viewed from the western side), which indeed it was for five centuries before Italian Unification between the Papal States and the Kingdom of Naples. It is now one of the country's great culinary capitals, possessing many food-processing concerns.

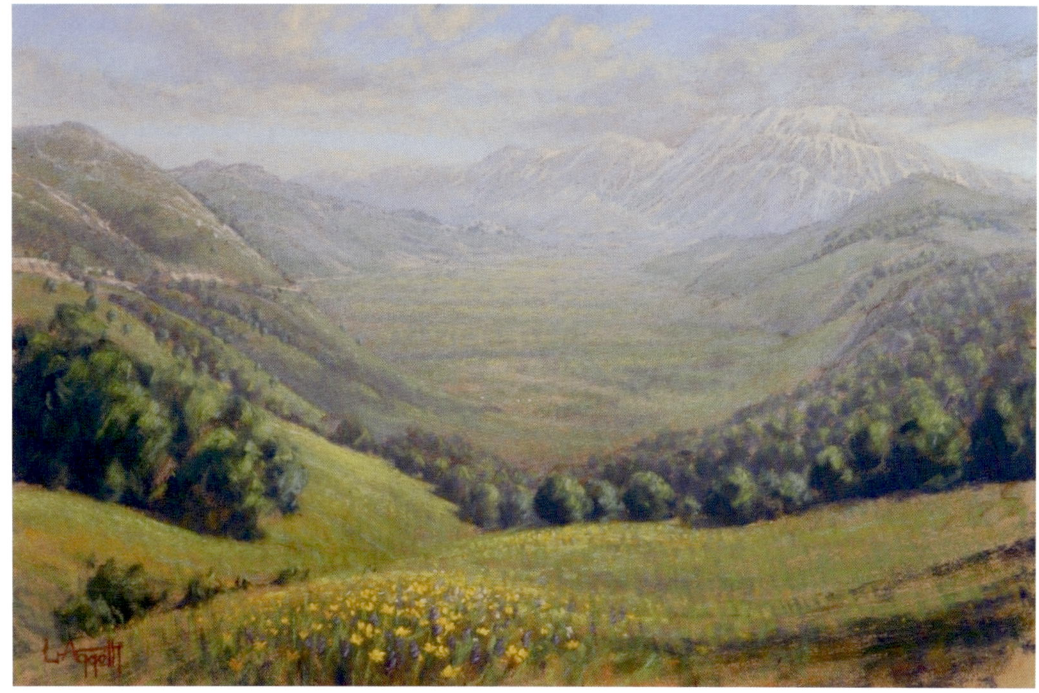

Piano Grande Pastel 325 x 500 mm

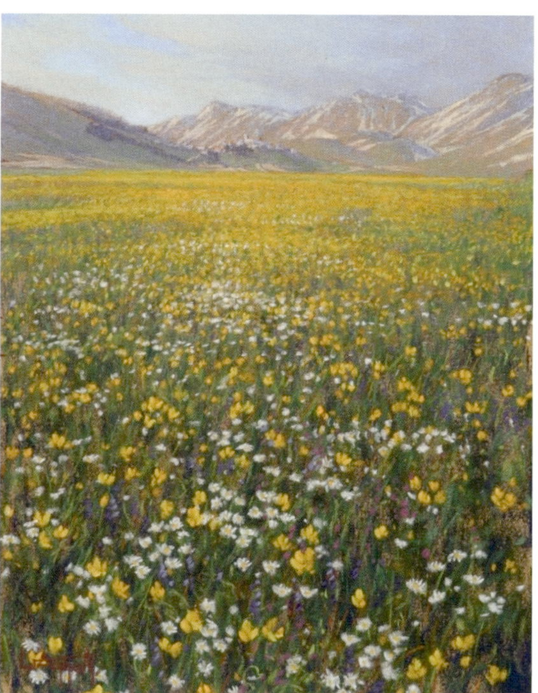

Buttercups, Piano Grande Pastel 325 x 250 mm

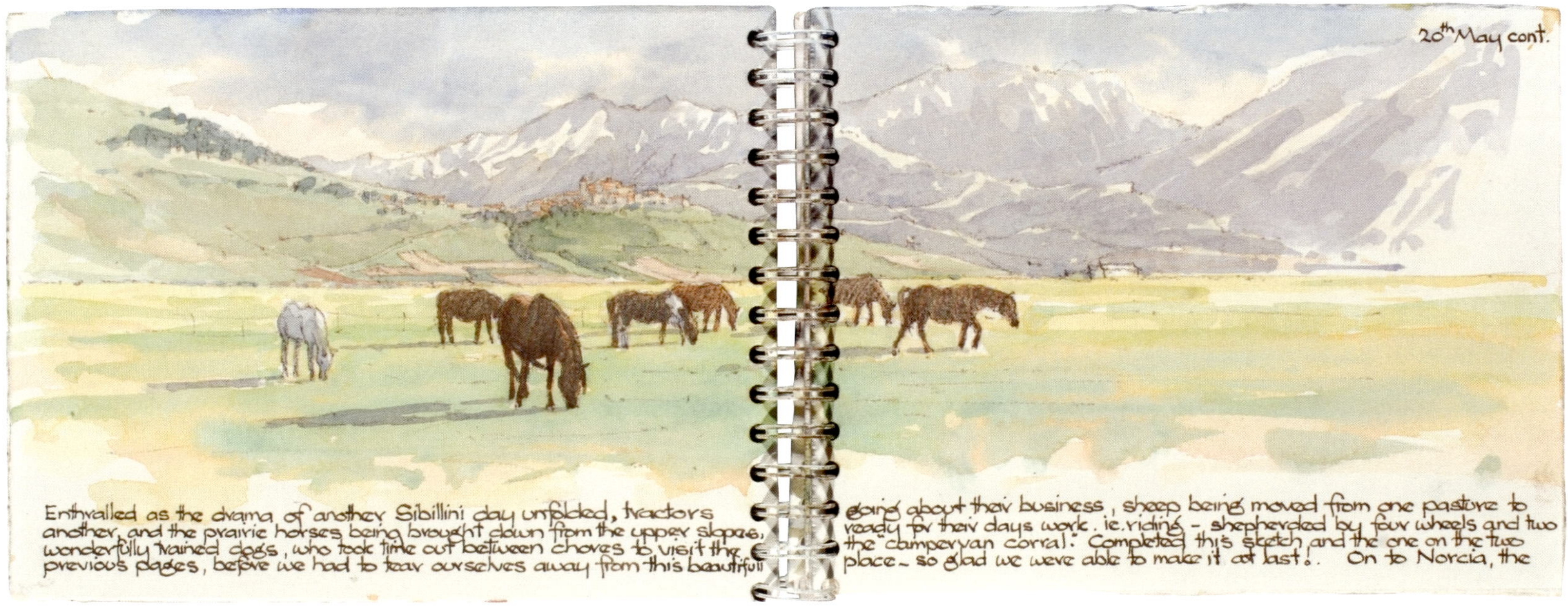

Diary Sketch 20th May, 2006 *Piano Grande Horses* Conté w/c

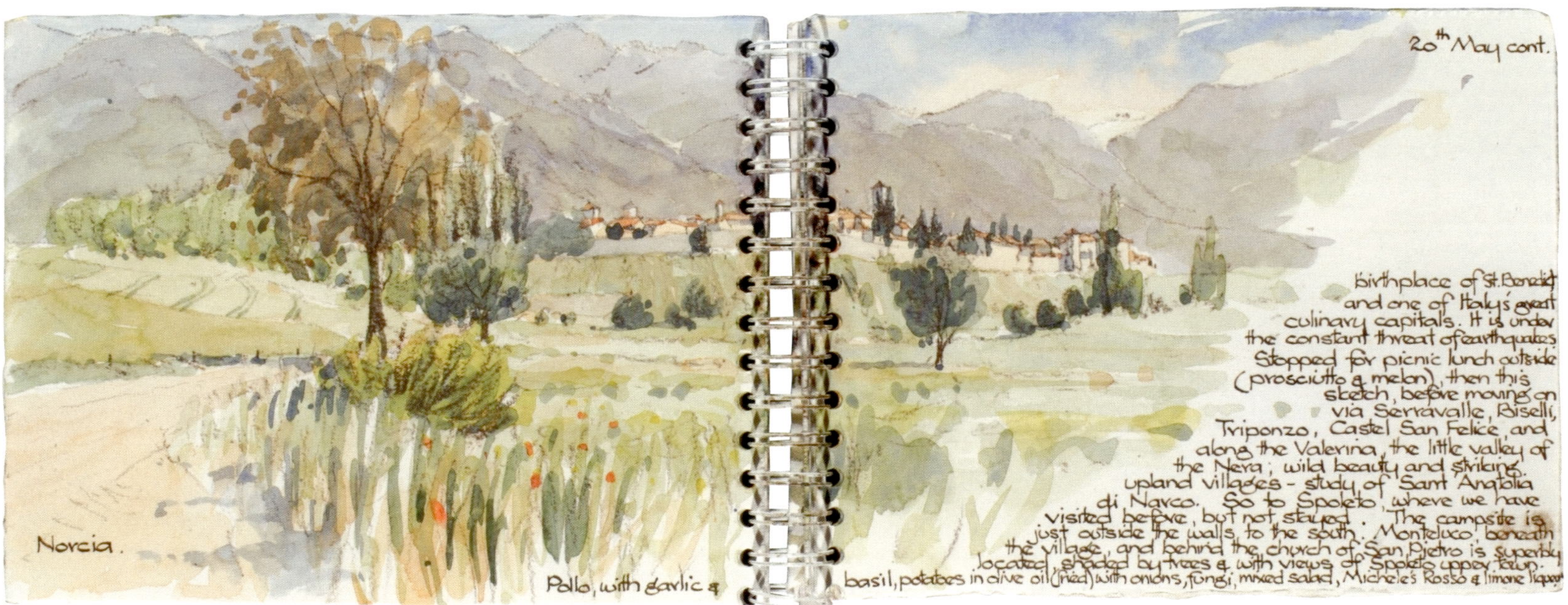

Diary Sketch 20th May, 2006 *Norcia* Conté w/c

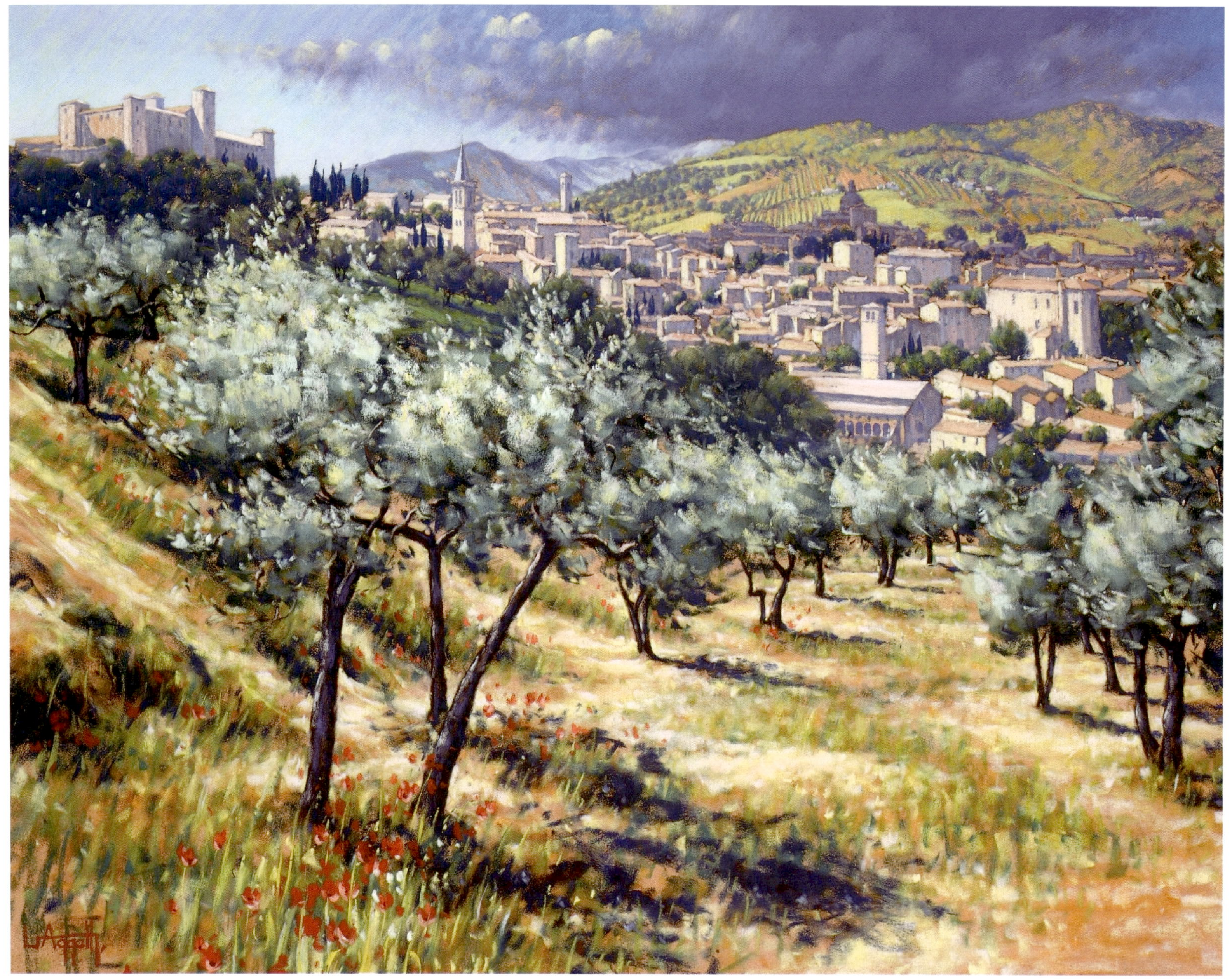

Olive Grove, Spoleto Pastel 500 x 650 mm

Apparently the most romantic city that Percy Bysshe Shelley ever saw and, particularly when viewed from this spot, where in 1994 I produced this en plein air *painting near San Salvatore, I would concur with those sentiments.*

SPOLETO

Further to the west beyond the Valerina, and at the southern end of the Vale of Spoleto, Spoleto itself will become our base camp for a painterly study of the city and surrounding countryside. The campsite, Monteluco, is superb, and situated on the south-east side of the city behind the church of San Pietro, on the slopes of Monteluco. Very friendly, and with an excellent restaurant (San Pietro) well patronised by locals, which is usually a sign of good reasonably priced fare.

There is an excellent 2 km walk from the campsite along and above the Tessino gorge to the 240 m span Ponte delle Tori, an astonishing piece of medieval engineering built originally as an aqueduct. There are good views of the Upper Town along this route which gains access to the Rocca, a castle standing proud above the city and which is featured in the olive grove painting from the north, taking in both Lower and Upper Towns.

A lively city, especially so in and around the Piazza del Mercato, the old forum, where you get a real sense of Spoleto's market town roots. There is much local banter and gossip, both in and outside the bars; alimentari selling the renowned olive oil, its top producer Mononi, a favourite all over Italy; truffles, dried porcini, and famous (in Italy) Montefalco Sagrantino Passito red wine, too good for the export market!

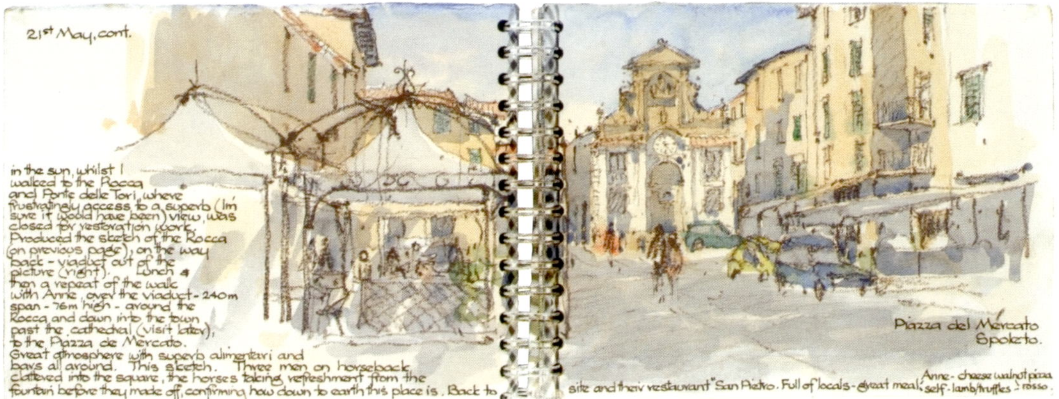

Diary Sketch 21st May, 2006 *Piazza del Mercato, Spoleto* Conté w/c

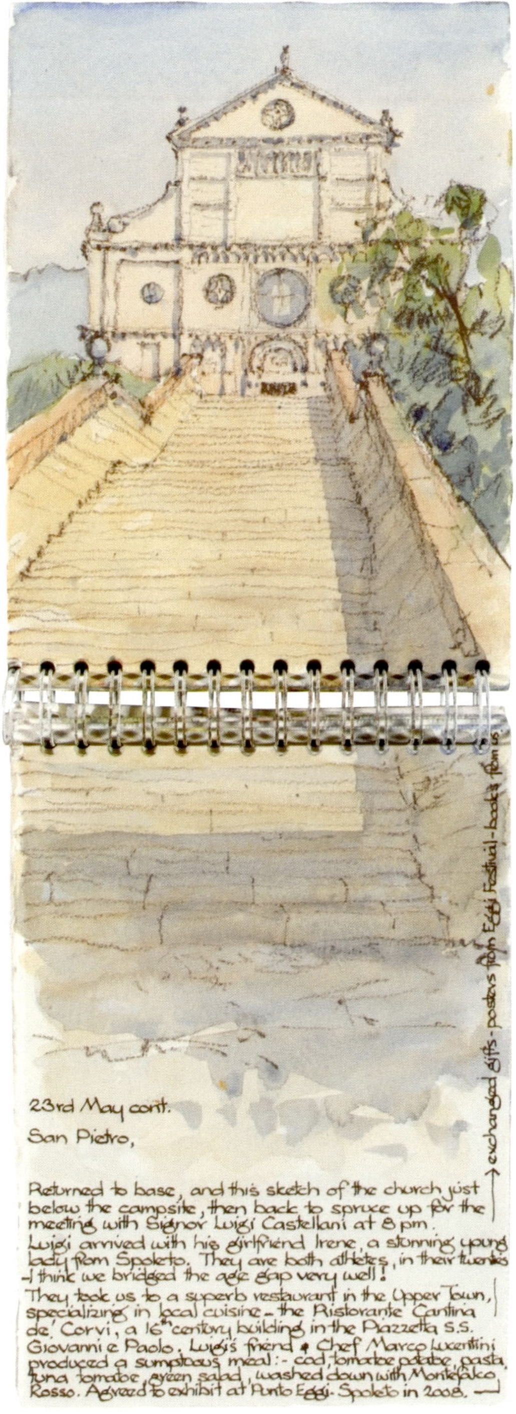

Diary Sketch 23rd May, 2006 *San Pietro, Spoleto* Conté w/c

Monday, 22nd May.

Decided to make the ascent to Monteluco way above the campsite - very pleasant & well managed woodland with ancient holm oaks. We expected to find a fortified village, but scattered buildings, a Franciscan Priory, around a peaceful open space, occupied by sunbathers from nearby hotels provided the sum total.

Some studies of Spoleto on the way down, then on to Eggi, where I have been invited to exhibit at the Punto Eggi Festival, held during April/May each year.

A Mr. Luigi Castellani, whilst surfing the net (the festival President) found the Llewellyn Alexander web site, which showed my painting of Eggi (now sold), the product of a previous visit. We corresponded by e-mail, and our visit to Spoleto - Eggi was planned partly to discuss details. We have arranged to meet him tomorrow over dinner to chat further.

Eggi is delightful - not too touristy - if at all. Positioned on a spur, it is well kept - standing proud in the farming community. Took on provisio

Diary Sketch 22nd May, 2006 *Eggi, Spoleto* Conté w/c

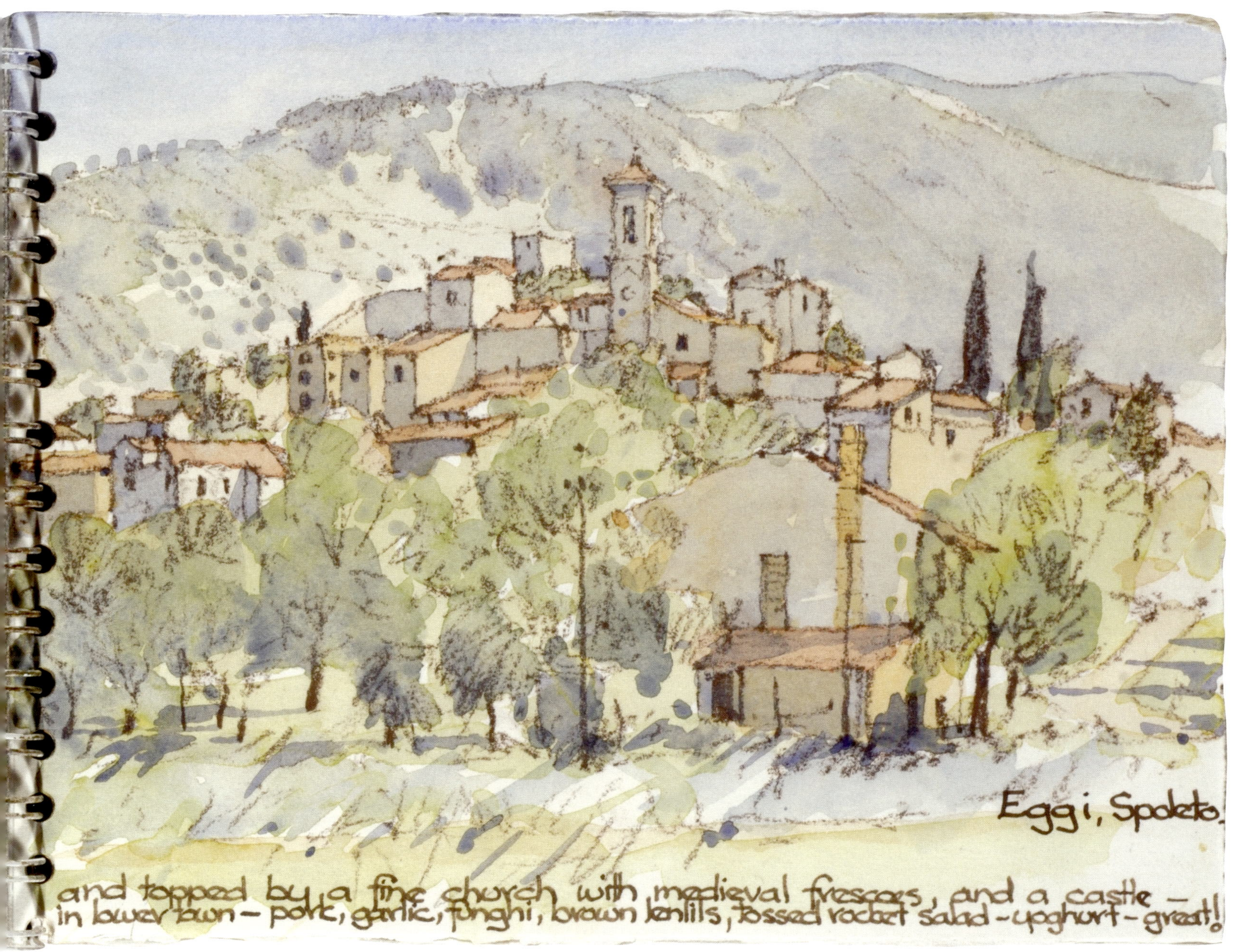
Eggi, Spoleto.
and topped by a fine church with medieval frescoes, and a castle –
in lower town – pork, garlic, funghi, brown lentils, tossed rocket salad – yoghurt – great!

Prior to making this trip, we were contacted by a Mr Luigi Castellani, who lives in Eggi just 3km to the north of Spoleto. He saw my painting, "Poppies and Vines, Eggi", on the Llewellyn Alexander website whilst surfing the net, and asked if I would like to exhibit at the Punto Eggi Festival in April/May. Organised by L'Associazione Amici di Eggi of which he is President, the festival draws several thousand visitors. We arranged to meet in Spoleto during last year's (2006) visit. He and his girlfriend Irene came to the campsite prior to taking us to his friend's restaurant in the Upper Town. I had somehow, and perhaps naturally, visualised a middle-aged gentleman, and we were surprised to be greeted by two youngsters in their twenties, both studying, and extremely fit. Luigi is a pole vaulter, and Irene a champion 400 m runner. We had a most enjoyable evening at the Ristorante Cantina de'Corvi, a sixteenth-century building in the Piazzetta S.S. Giovanni e Paolo, where Luigi's good friend and Chef, Marco Lucentini produced a wonderful meal, accompanied by some exceptional Montefalco

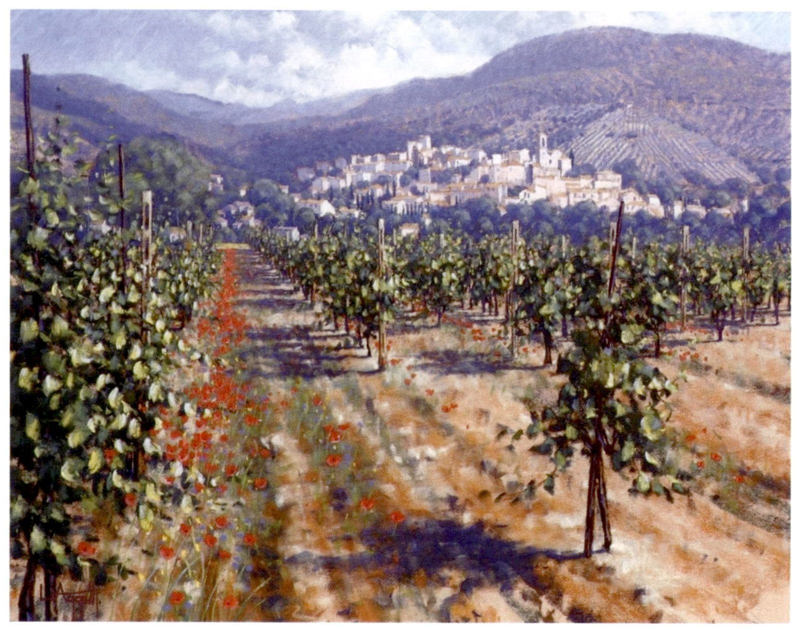

Poppies and Vines, Eggi, Spoleto
Pastel 500 x 650 mm

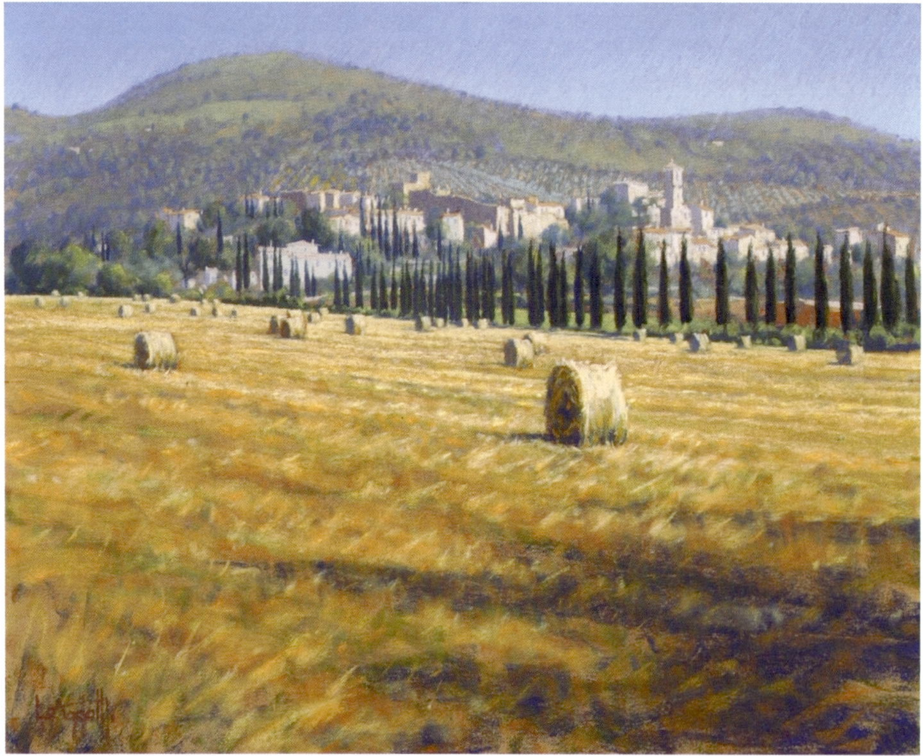

Summer Gold, Eggi, Spoleto
Pastel 400 x 500 mm

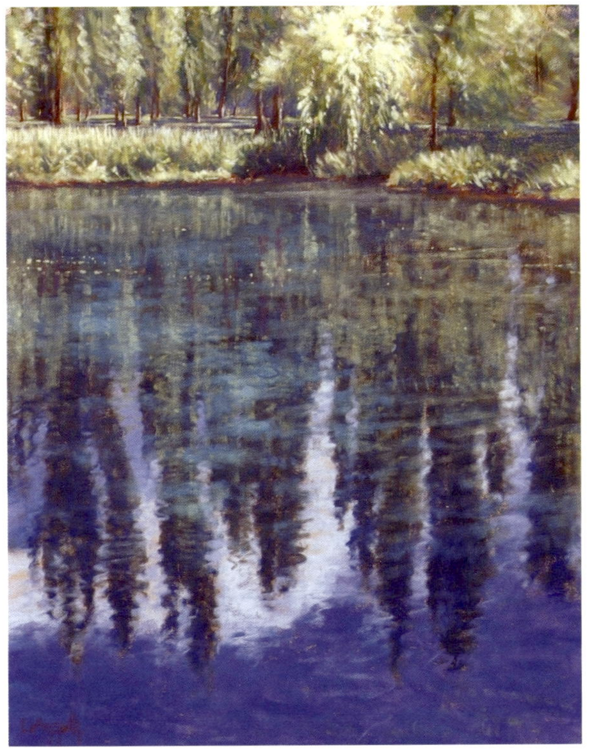

Fonti di Clitunno Pastel 650 x 500 mm

Rosso. We were made to feel most welcome, and the whole evening proved to be a wonderfully memorable occasion, with gifts exchanged, and a provisional arrangement made to exhibit at the Festival in April/May 2008.

Eggi, is the most painterly of hill villages, and I have produced works from several aspects here. Topped by a small castle and church, it is a working, farming community, surrounded by cereals, vineyards and olives.

A further 9 km up the Vale of Spoleto, on the west side of the S3, the sacred and magical Fonti di Clitunno has provided inspiration to poets from Virgil to Byron. The translucent spring waters were originally dedicated to the oracular god Clitunnus, and were often used by the likes of Caligula and Claudius. They are still as limpid as they were when Byron extolled "the sweetest wave of the most living crystal ... the purest god of gentle waters". The colours emerging from the depths through the clear liquid blend with the reflections of the willows and the shimmering sky to present a harmony of colour destined to be metamorphosed on canvas.

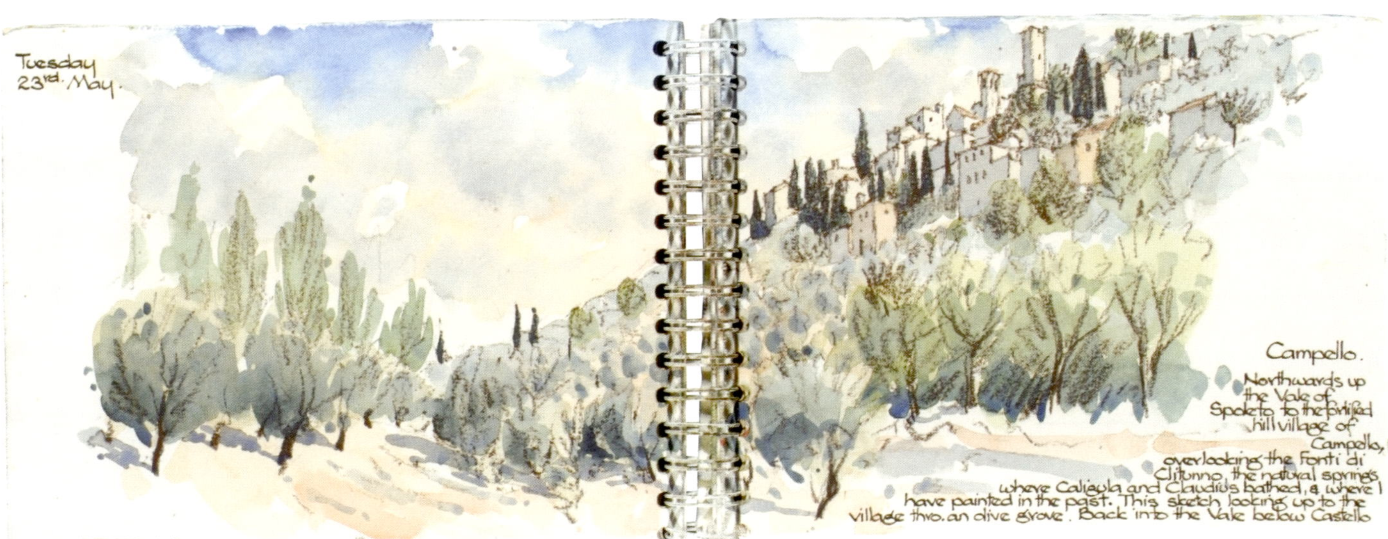

Diary Sketch 23rd May, 2006 *Campello* Conté w/c

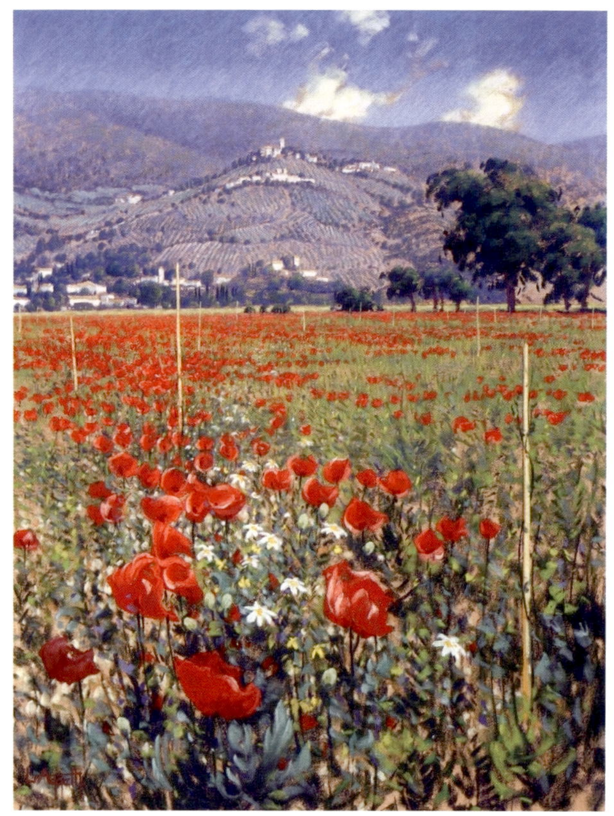

Poppies, Vale of Spoleto Pastel 650 x 500 mm

The fortified village of Campello overlooks this part of the Vale from a commanding position high on the hill to the east. Below and stretching back towards Eggi, fields of poppies produce a blaze of complementary reds and fresh young greens during May. This vivid and sometimes overpowering contrasting delight is not countenanced by all, but my senses are always aroused by the spectacle. At this particular time of the year, they are an integral part of the landscape and you just can't avoid them, and so I record them.

Diary Sketch 23rd May, 2006 *Poppies near La Bianca* Conté w/c

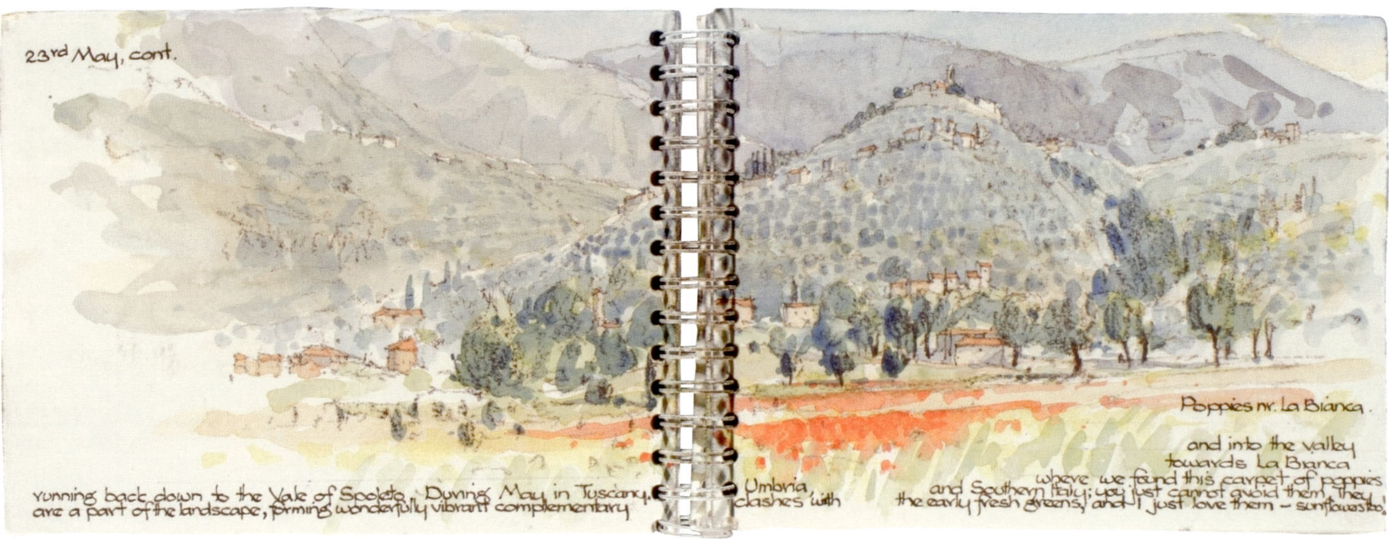

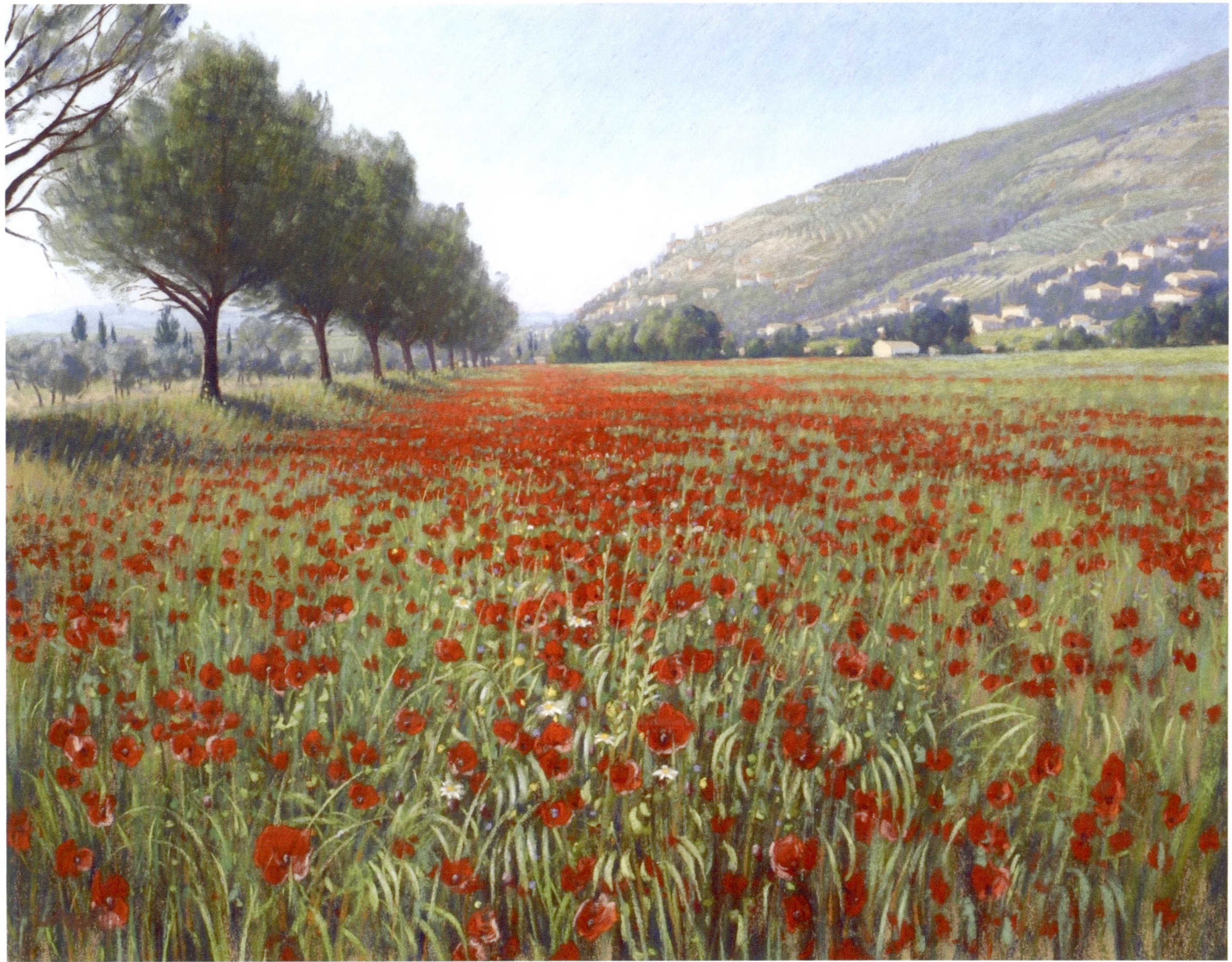

Poppies, Poppies, Vale of Spoleto Pastel 500 x 650 mm

BEVAGNA

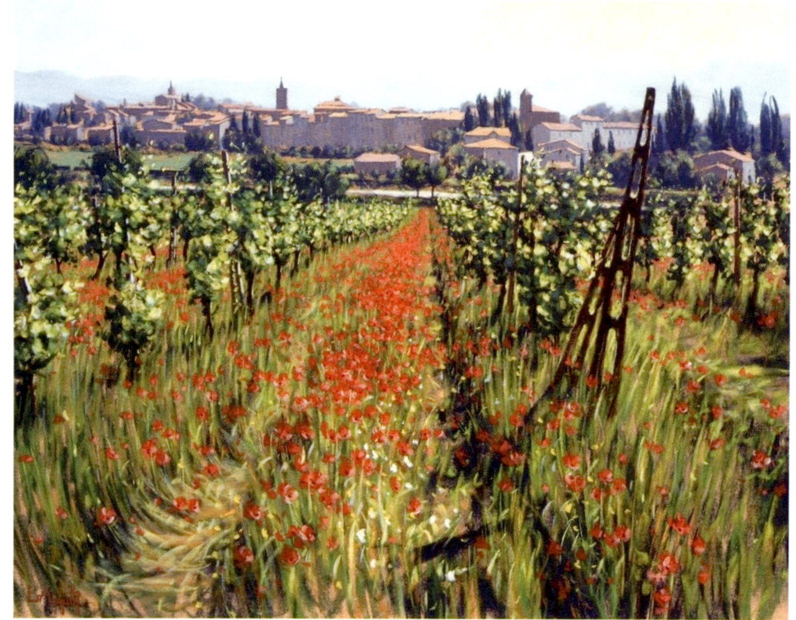

Poppies and Vines, Bevagna Pastel 500 x 650 mm

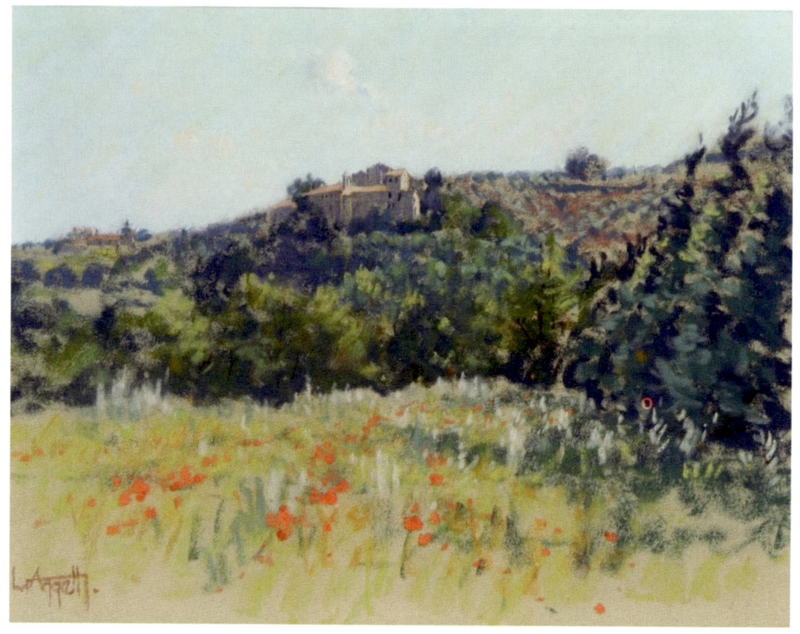

Pian di Boccio, Bevagna Pastel 250 x 325 mm

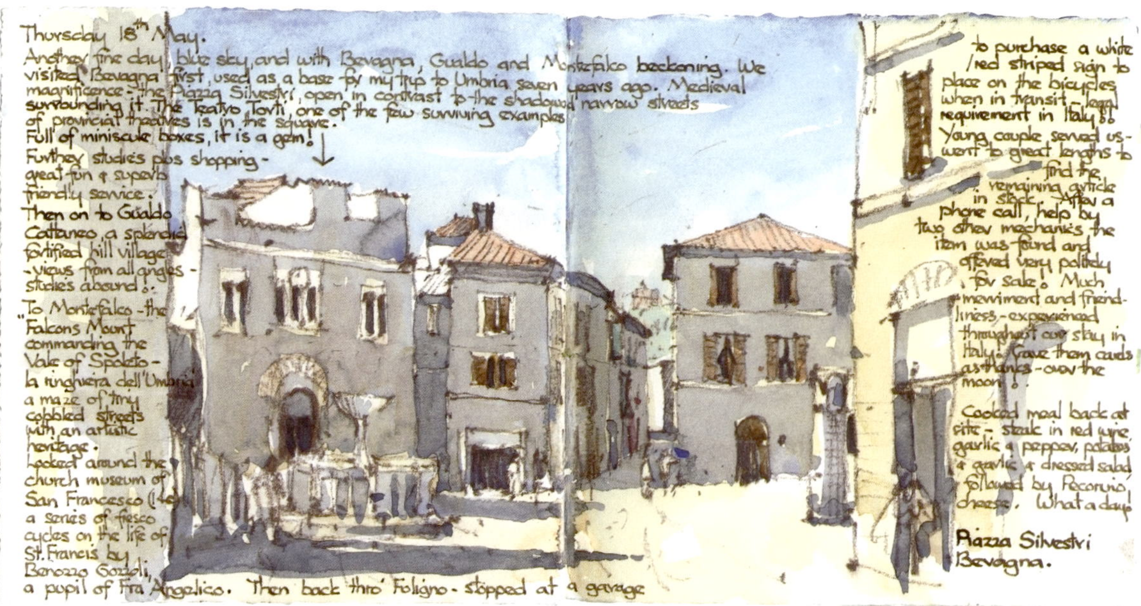

Diary Sketch 18th May, 2000 *Piazza Silvestri, Bevagna* Conté w/c

I chose the Pian Di Boccio campsite, located in a wooded area outside Bevagna, almost in the centre of Umbria, for one solo working visit. An excellent centre for exploring the many nearby fabulous hill towns, and their surrounding topography, this town is a serene medieval backwater. Whereas some towns suffer from urban blight, Bevagna has scarcely spread beyond its intact walls and perfect interior. The pedestrianized main square, Piazza Silvestri, contrasts with the narrow shaded streets of its surroundings. The town lies in a rich agricultural plain, not on a hill, and supports cereals, olives, vegetables, and vines. It was originally an Umbrian, then an Etruscan settlement; later as Mevania, under the Romans, it became a staging post on the Via Faminia (220 BC).

My painting excursions from this site took me northwards to Limigiano and Assisi, and the delightful countryside surrounding Montefalco and Gualdo Cattaneo (south), also Todi and Orvieto to the south west. As fine as these towns are, I spent more time outside, sketching and painting the wonderfully organic relationship they have with their surroundings, than I did inside their walls.

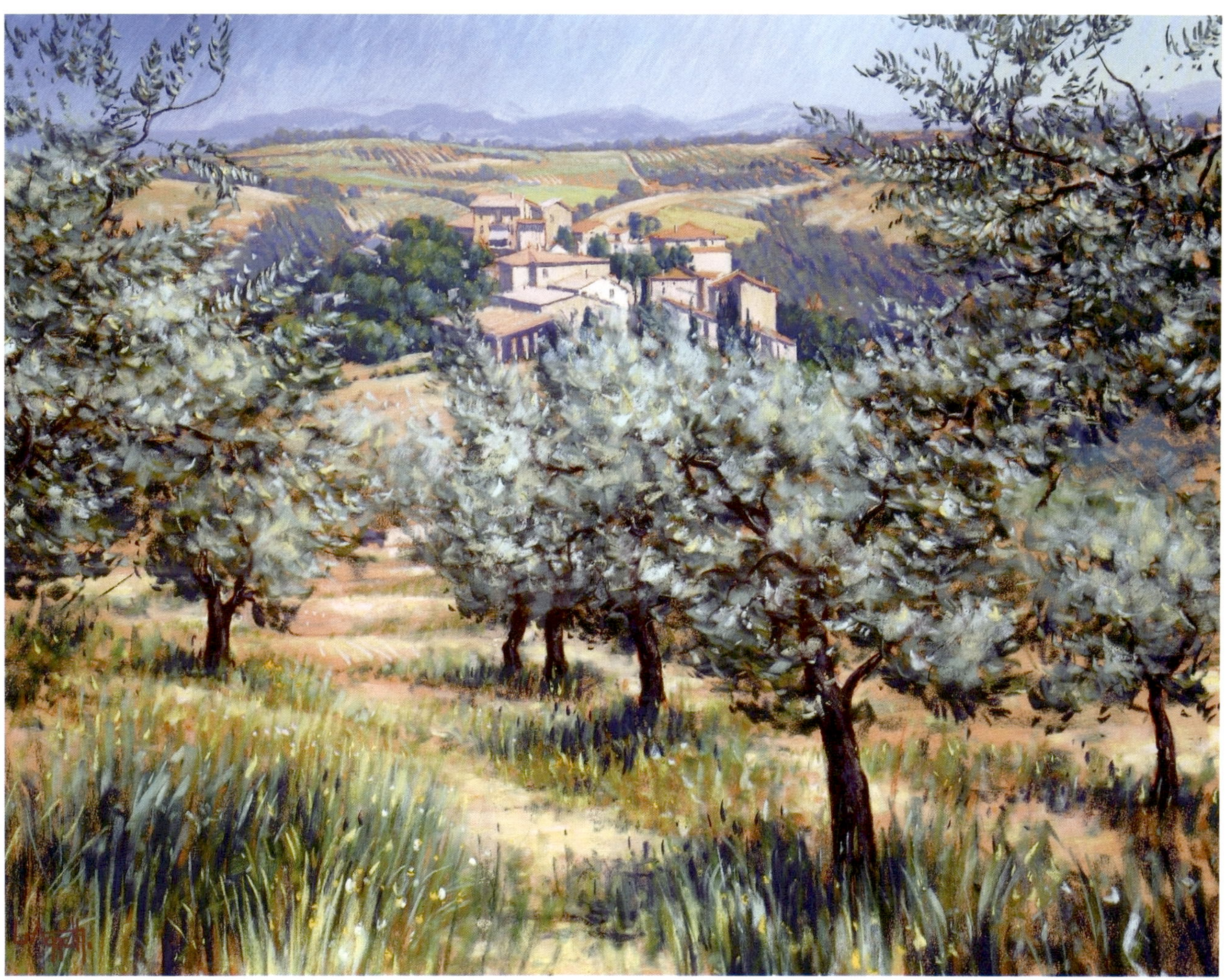

Olive Grove near Bevagna Pastel 500 x 650 mm

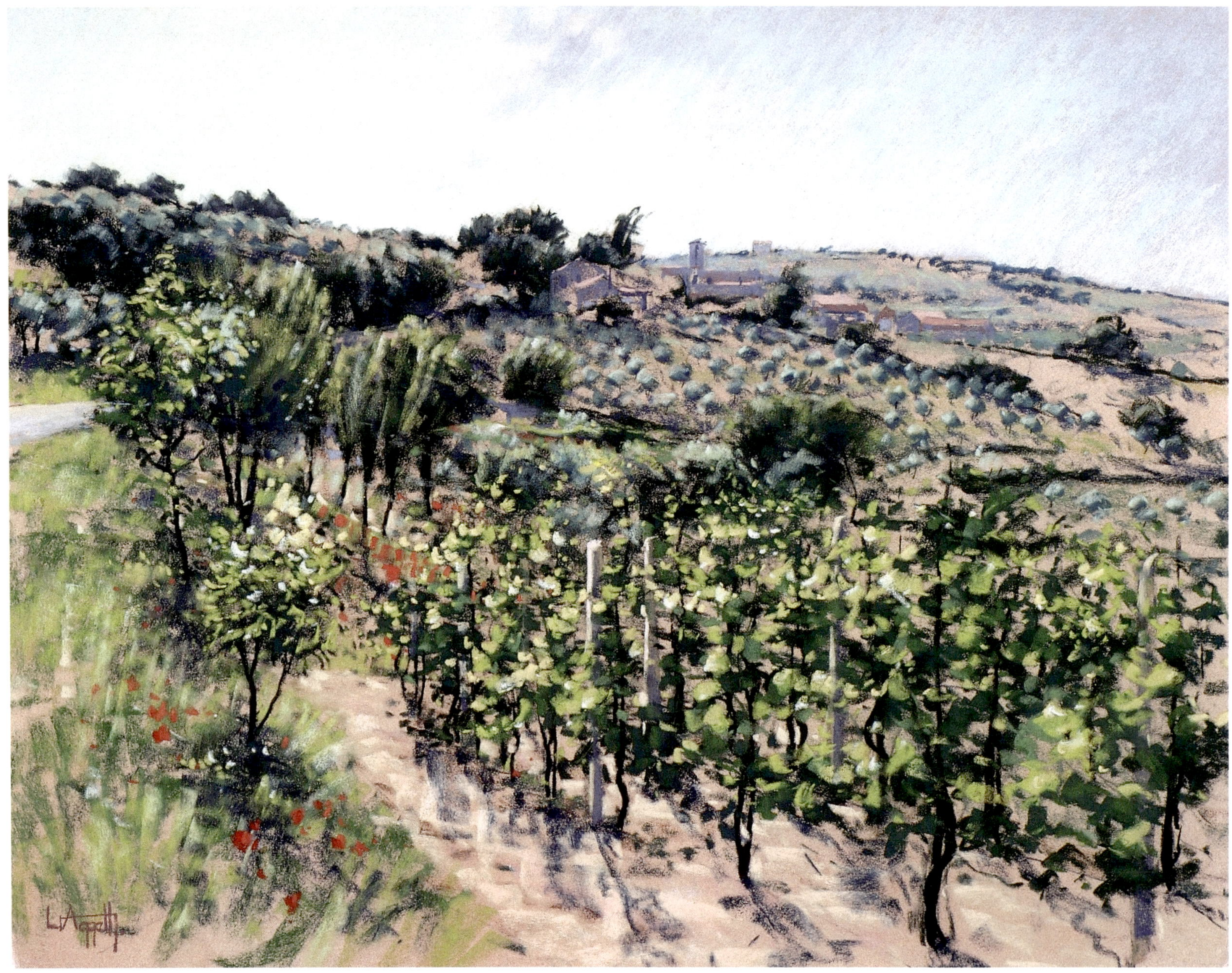

Limigiano Pastel 500 x 650 mm

This en plein air *work was painted less than a kilometre from the spot on the road between Bevagna and Cannara where St Francis preached his famous sermon to the birds.*

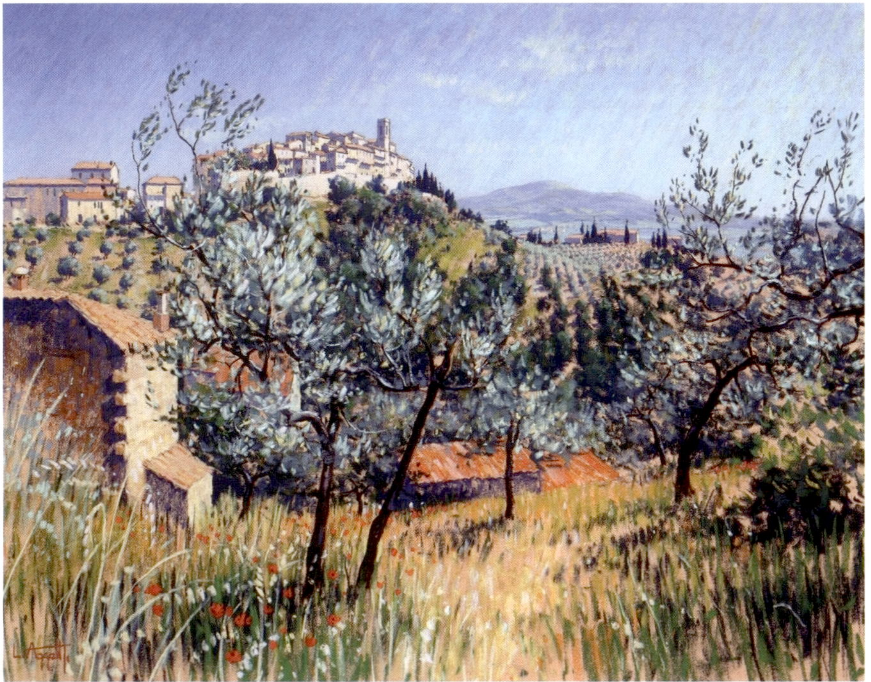

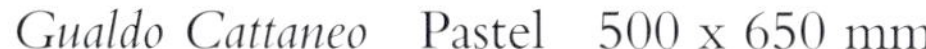

Gualdo Cattaneo Pastel 500 x 650 mm

This view of the small fortress town high on an outcrop near Bevagna was obtained through scrambling up the vertiginous olive terraces opposite.

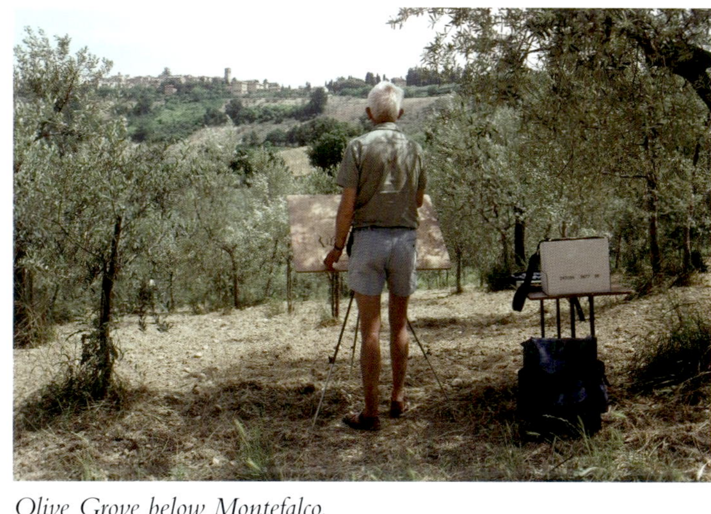

Olive Grove below Montefalco.

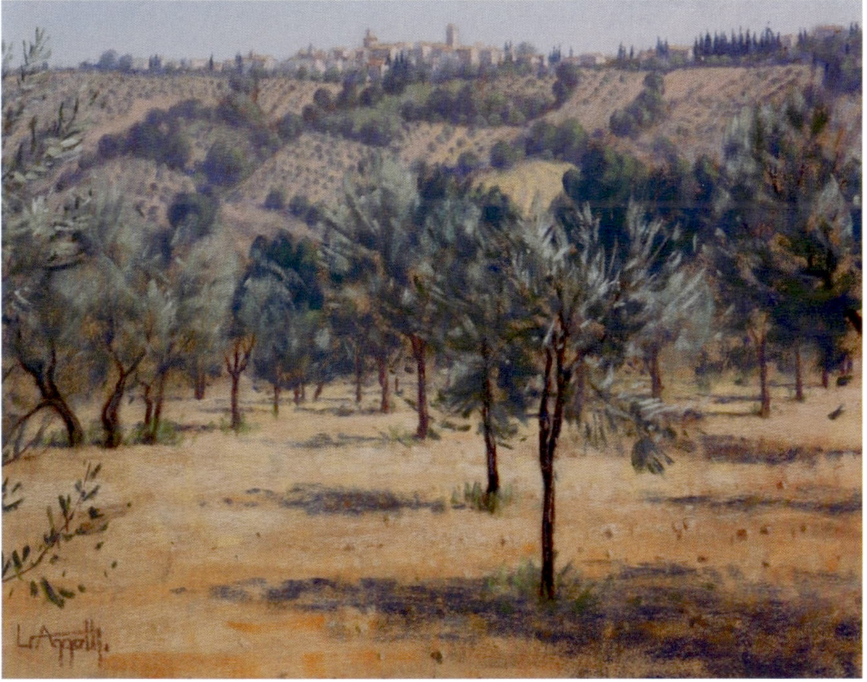

Montefalco Pastel 250 x 650 mm

View of the Falcons' Mount from the olive groves below; a number of paintings were completed from here.

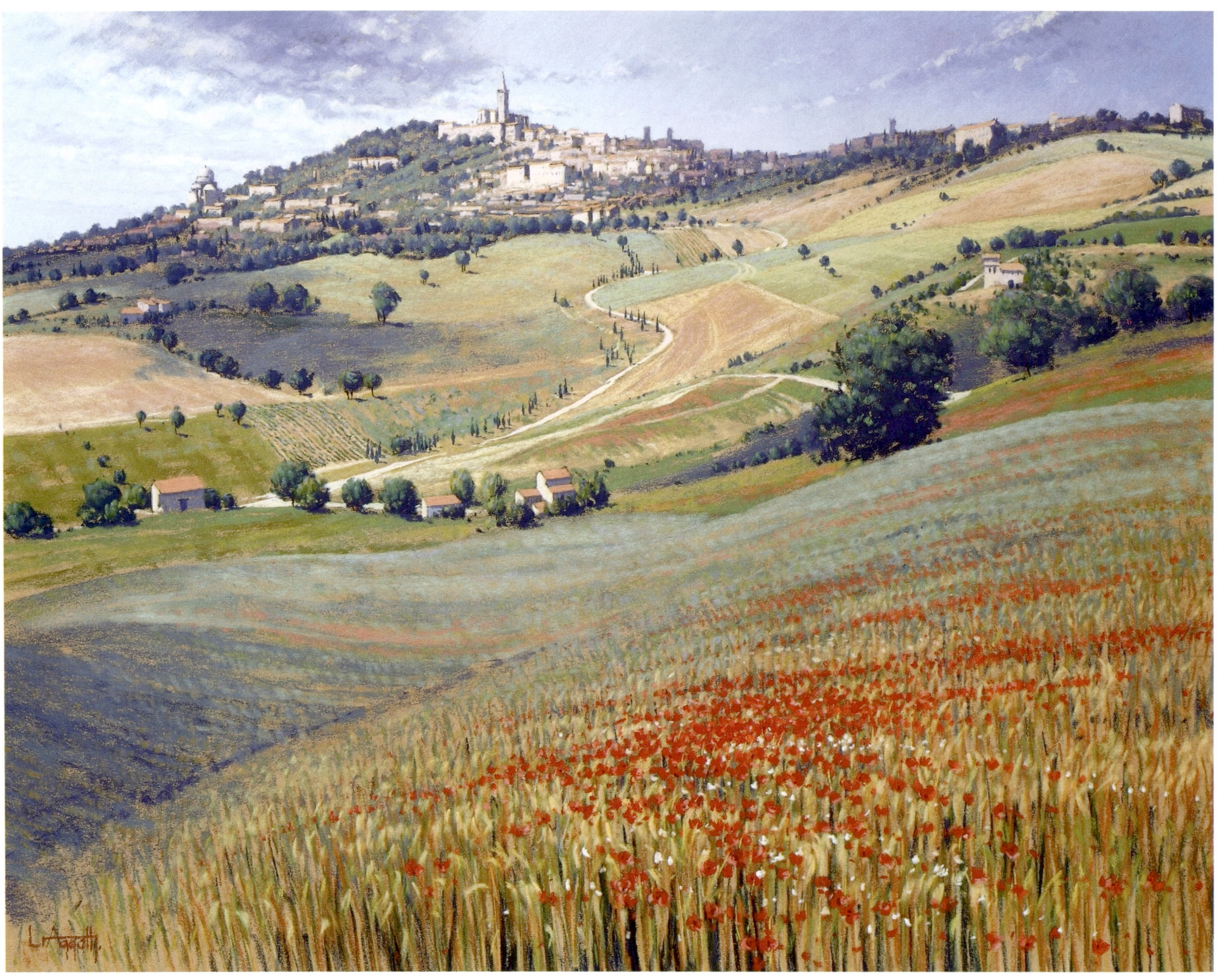

Todi Pastel 500 x 650 mm

My paintings here have all been completed outside the town, so stunning is its location at the heart of an agricultural area. I have yet to discover the interior.

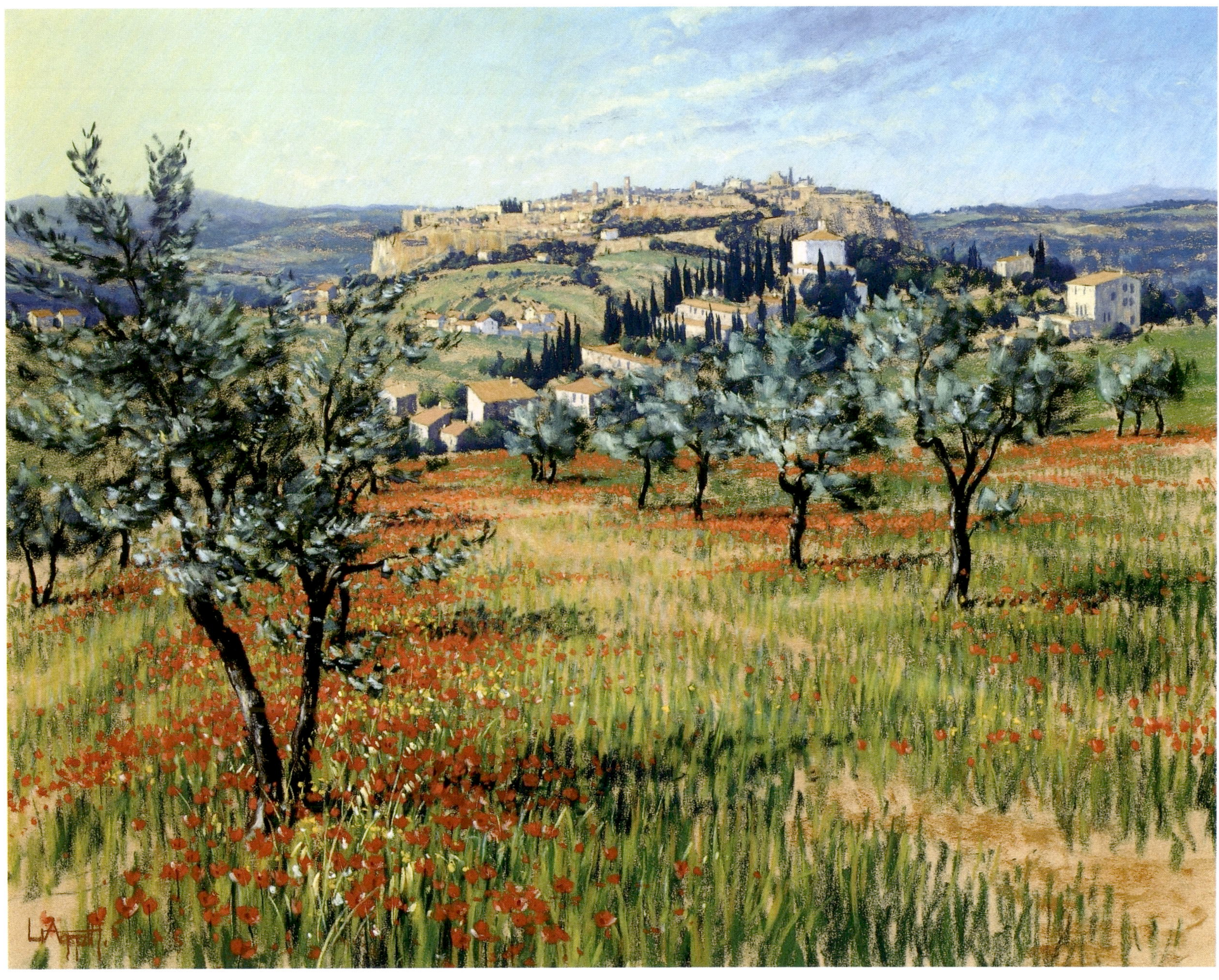

Orvieto Pastel 500 x 650 mm

Although I have visited the cathedral and precinct, the same applies to this walled city, perched dramatically on a volcanic tufa table top, spectacularly visible from the celebrated vineyards and olive groves below.

ASSISI

Assisi, the northern focus of the Vale, is busier now than when I first came here in 1959. The town makes a good base for working down the Vale and northwards to Gubbio. It has two campsites, and we opted for the Internazionale Assisi, to the west between the town and Bastia. The site is ideally placed for exploring the delightful area between Assisi and Santa Maria Degli Angeli, either cycling or on foot. We were once caught in a violent thunderstorm beneath the town whilst on our bikes. It was like cycling through a continuous warm power shower, to be efficiently warm air dried afterwards, by the time we returned to the site.

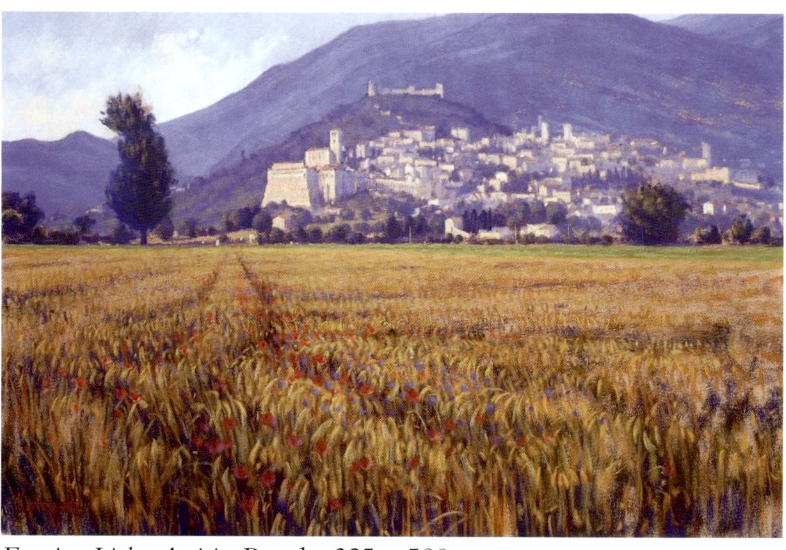

Evening Light, Assisi Pastel 325 x 500 mm

The views of Assisi from the Vale are spectacular, the castle, town and the Basilica di San Francesco straddling a spur of the whaleback lower slopes of Monte Subásio. The dynamic composition is accentuated by the linear perspective of the surrounding olive groves, vineyards, cereals, fruit and vegetables.

A major pilgrimage site, Assisi attracts a staggering five million visitors each year, which is a very good reason for staying here. The evenings are much quieter when the coach parties have departed and the town becomes peacefully enjoyable for locals and visitors alike. The whole magnificent setting also becomes even more eminently paintable when bathed in the warm evening light.

Diary Sketch 17th May, 2000 *Santa Maria Degli Angeli* Conté

Wednesday, 17th May.

Crash out day, spent at the site, studying maps and generally working out an itinerary for our stay at Assisi. Following an afternoon kip and whilst Anne did some reading I cycled towards Santa Maria degli Angeli, the huge domed basilica rising above the new town clustered around the new station.

Magnificent views of Assisi through vineyards, olive trees, vegetables, cereals, and poppies. Several studies and then back to site.

Used our phone for the first time to contact Russell & Lynne - everything okay - Russell watching the UEFA Cup Final, Galatassary v Arsenal. Anne cooked the meal - vegetable and tomato sauce & sphagetti - super & energy restoring.

Then a walk which culminated in a visit to the bar - guess what! UEFA Cup final on the television!. Watched the game - Anne retired at half-time - said I wouldn't be long - one second half, extra time and penalty shoot out later I rejoined her. Arsenal lost on penalties after a 0-0 draw.

Santa Maria degli Angeli.

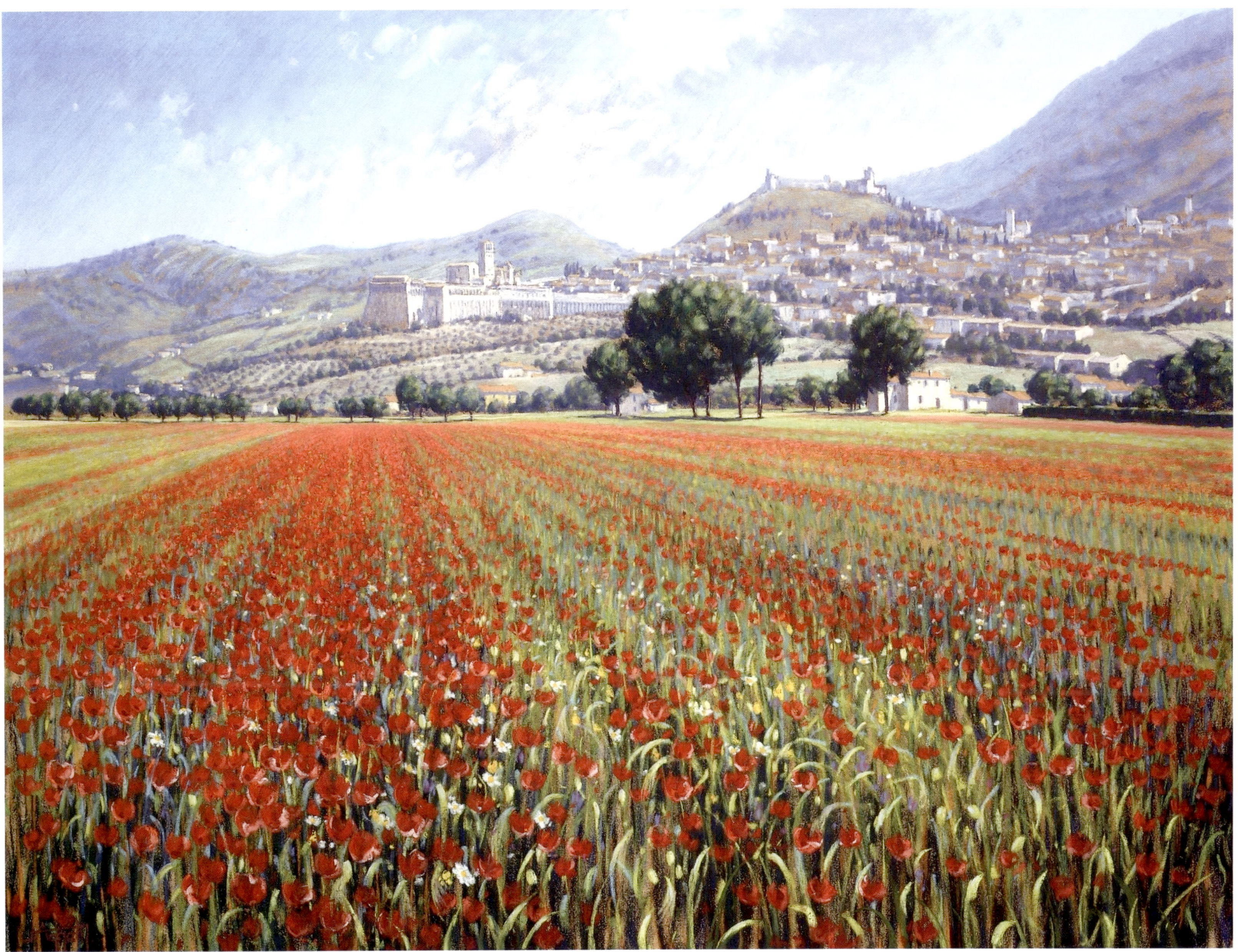

Poppies below Assisi Pastel 600 x 800 mm

The reason for choosing our camp site location; the views of Assisi from the Vale are stunning.

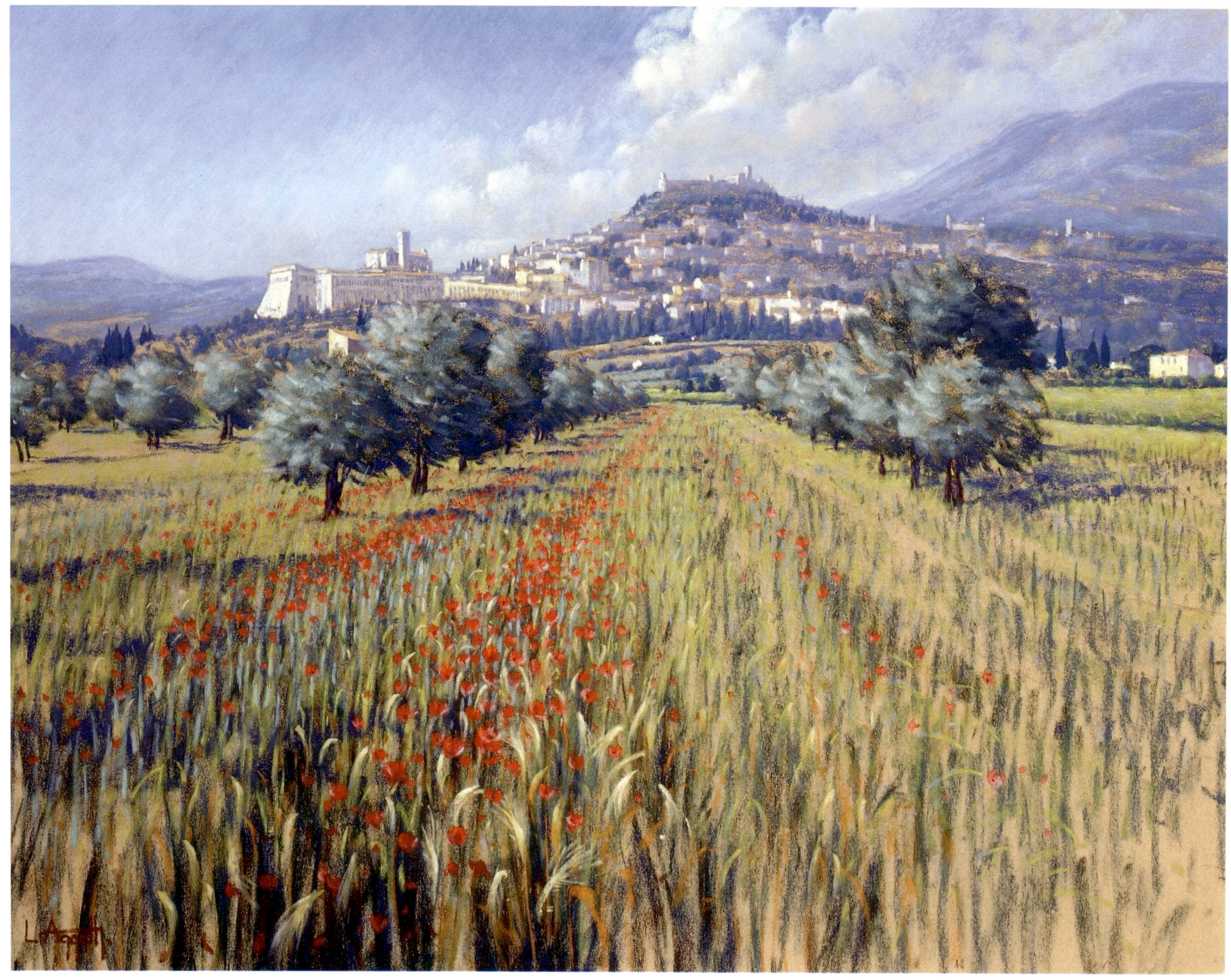

Poppies and Olives, Assisi Pastel 500 x 650 mm

Olive groves, vineyards, vegetables, fruit and flora all lead the eye to this irresistible assemblage of architecture on the slopes of Monte Subásio.

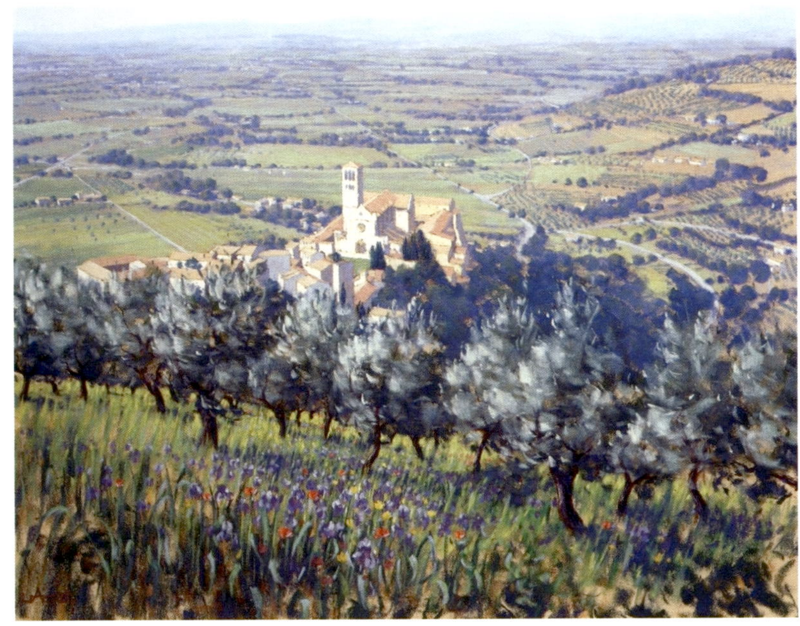

The experience which has to be on everyone's itinerary is a visit to the Basilica. The lower church with frescoes by Giotto, Simone Martini, Pietro Lorenzetti and Cimabue, and the tomb of St Francis (crypt), provides a contemplative aesthetic and emotional experience, whereas a study of Giotto's Life of St Francis in the Upper Church inspires celebration. So one emerges elated, if somewhat exhausted. What better, after some refreshment in the form of a gelato perhaps, than a climb up above the town to the Rocca Maggiore. From here there are stupendous views across Assisi, and particularly to the west over the Basilica, and the Vale of Spoleto beyond. A series of sketches and paintings were produced from this spot.

Irises and Olives, Basilica di San Francesco, Assisi
Pastel 500 x 650 mm

Diary Sketch 19th May, 2000
Basilica di San Francesco, Assisi Conté w/c

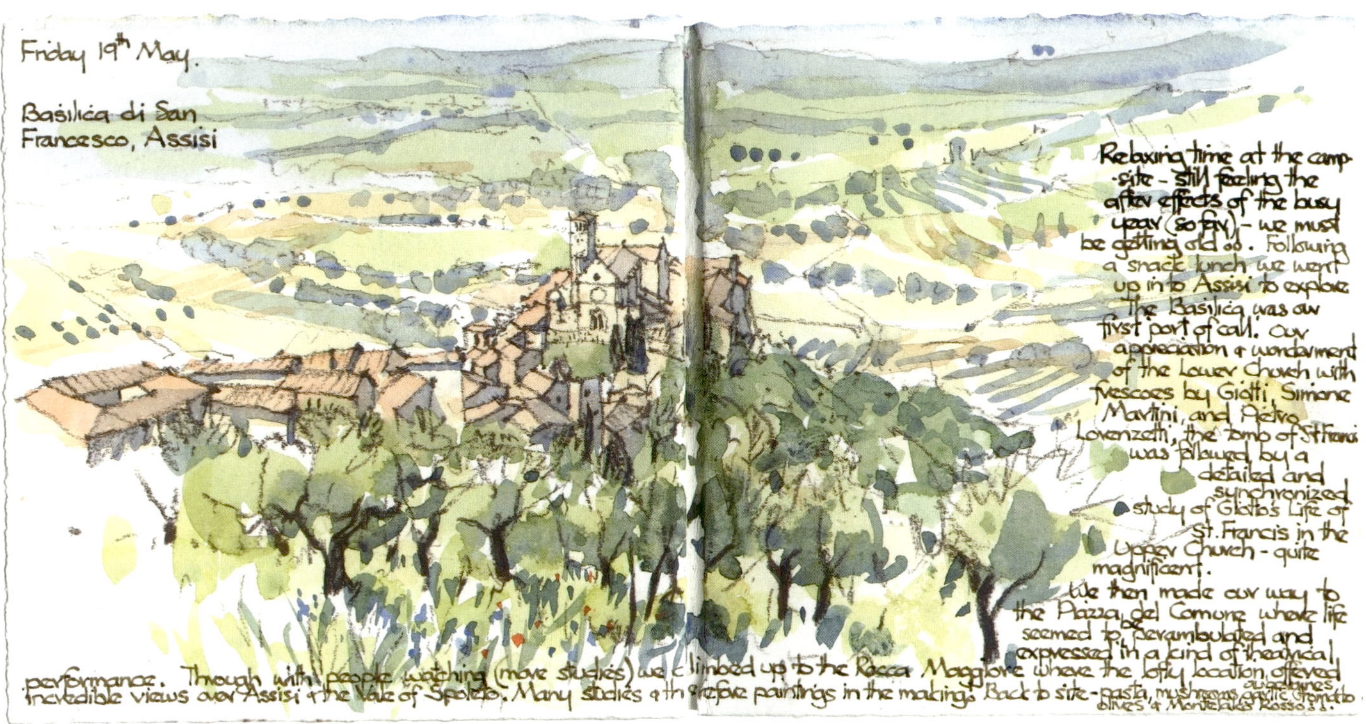

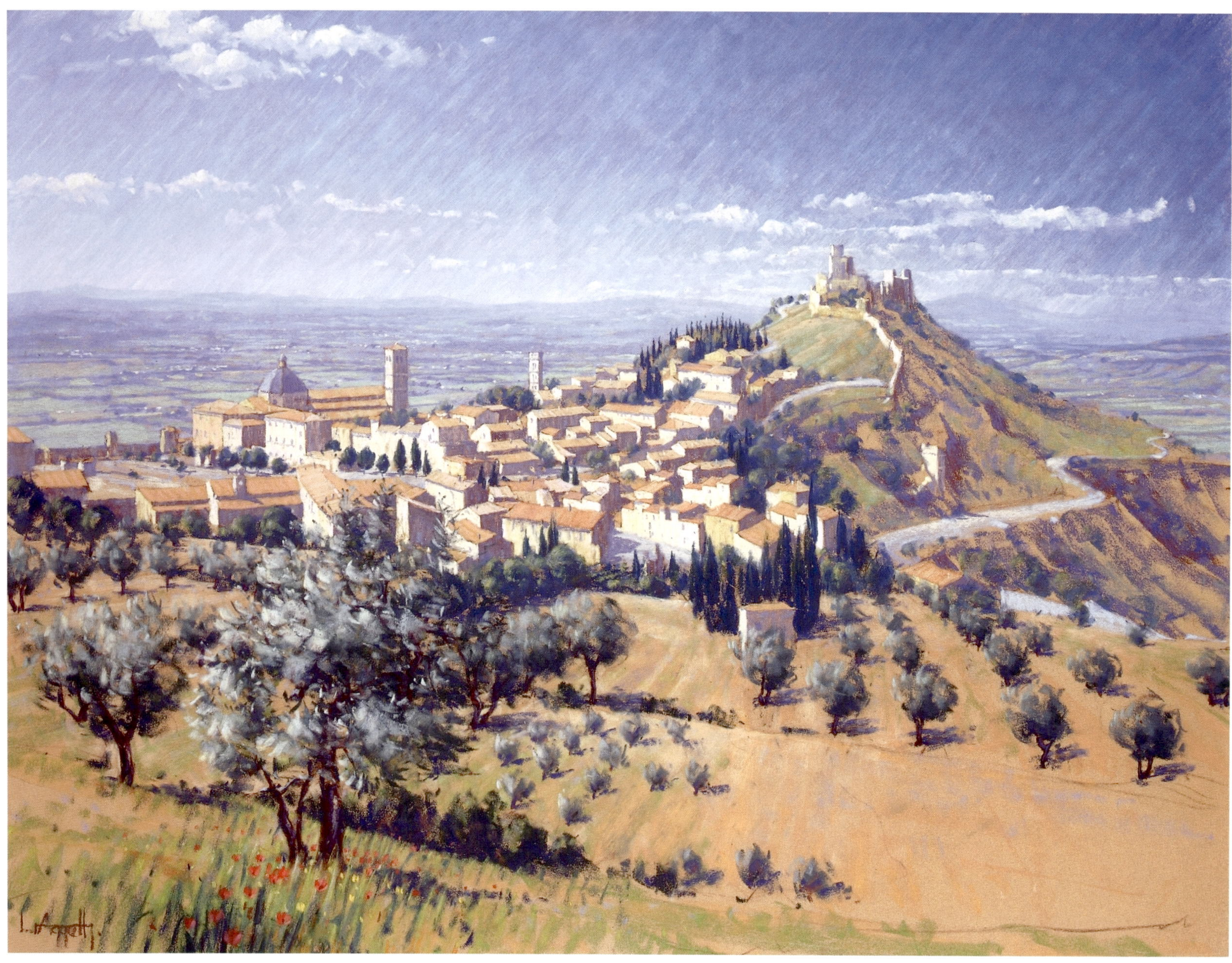

Olive Grove above Assisi Pastel 600 x 800 mm

Worth the long climb.

Spello, just 10 km further down the Vale, is situated on a spur at the southern end of Monte Subásio. The town retains much of its medieval charm, with narrow streets and courtyards leading off the main street which climbs from Vale level to the Rocca, and Santa Maria di Vallegloria at the top. Subjects abound, but I particularly enjoy the views of the lower portion, seen through the vineyards at the bottom.

On our way up, the superlative Pinturicchio frescoes in the church of Santa Maria Maggiore, for which the town is renowned, prime all creative instincts for the wonderful views which lie ahead. Beyond the Porta Montanara the road climbs up through olive groves towards the summit of Monte Subásio. The topography looking back through the olives, over Spello to the Vale of Spoleto beyond is absolutely stunning. I have produced several paintings from these heights, the view constantly and subtly changing as the route winds its way upwards. It is very peaceful up here too, for very few visitors seem to make the effort.

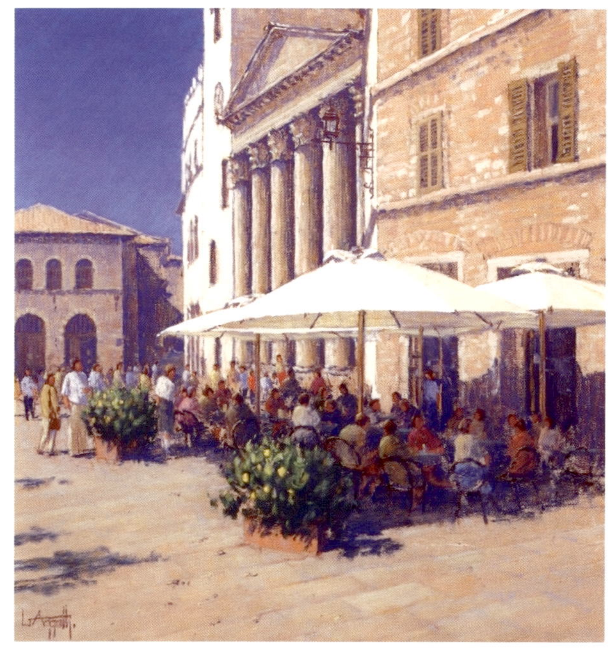

Tempio di Minerva, Assisi Pastel 500 x 400 mm, cropped to 400 x 400 mm

Diary Sketch 20th May, 2000 *Vineyard below Spello* Conté w/c

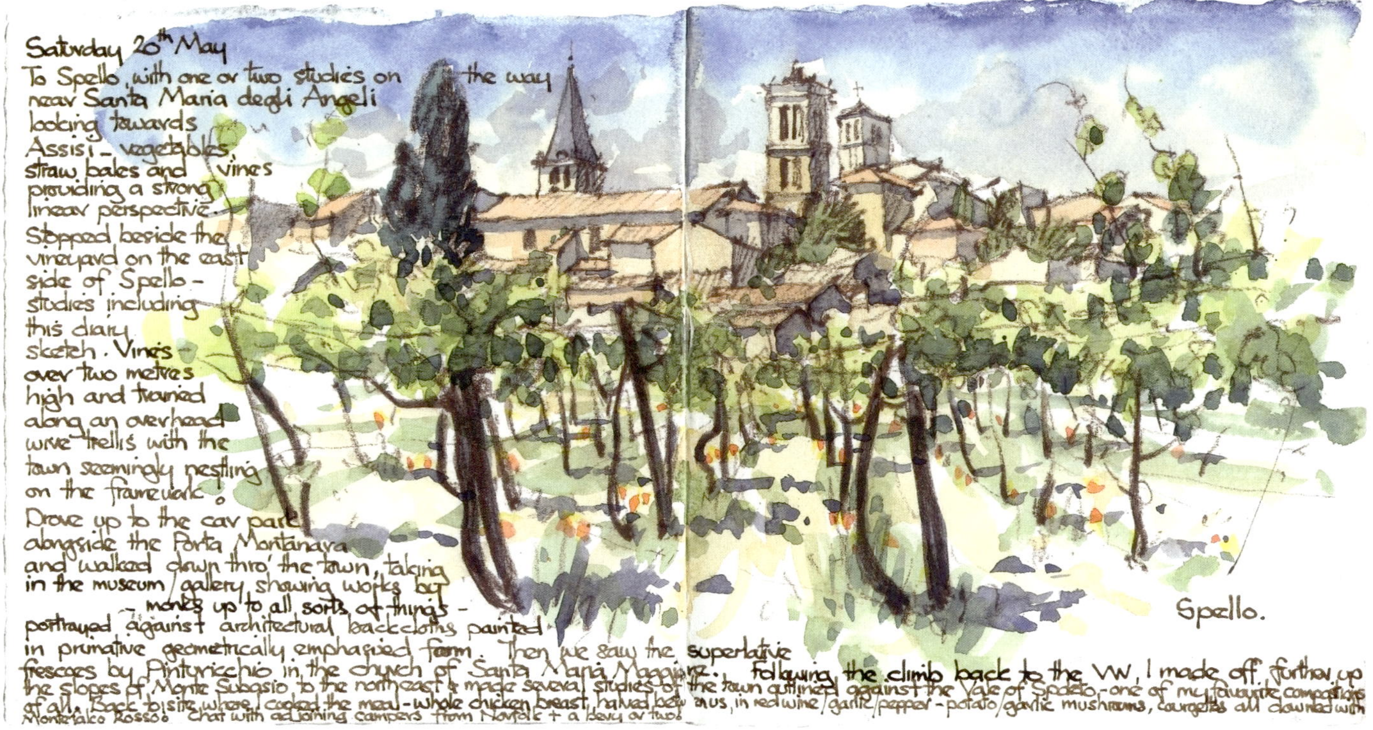

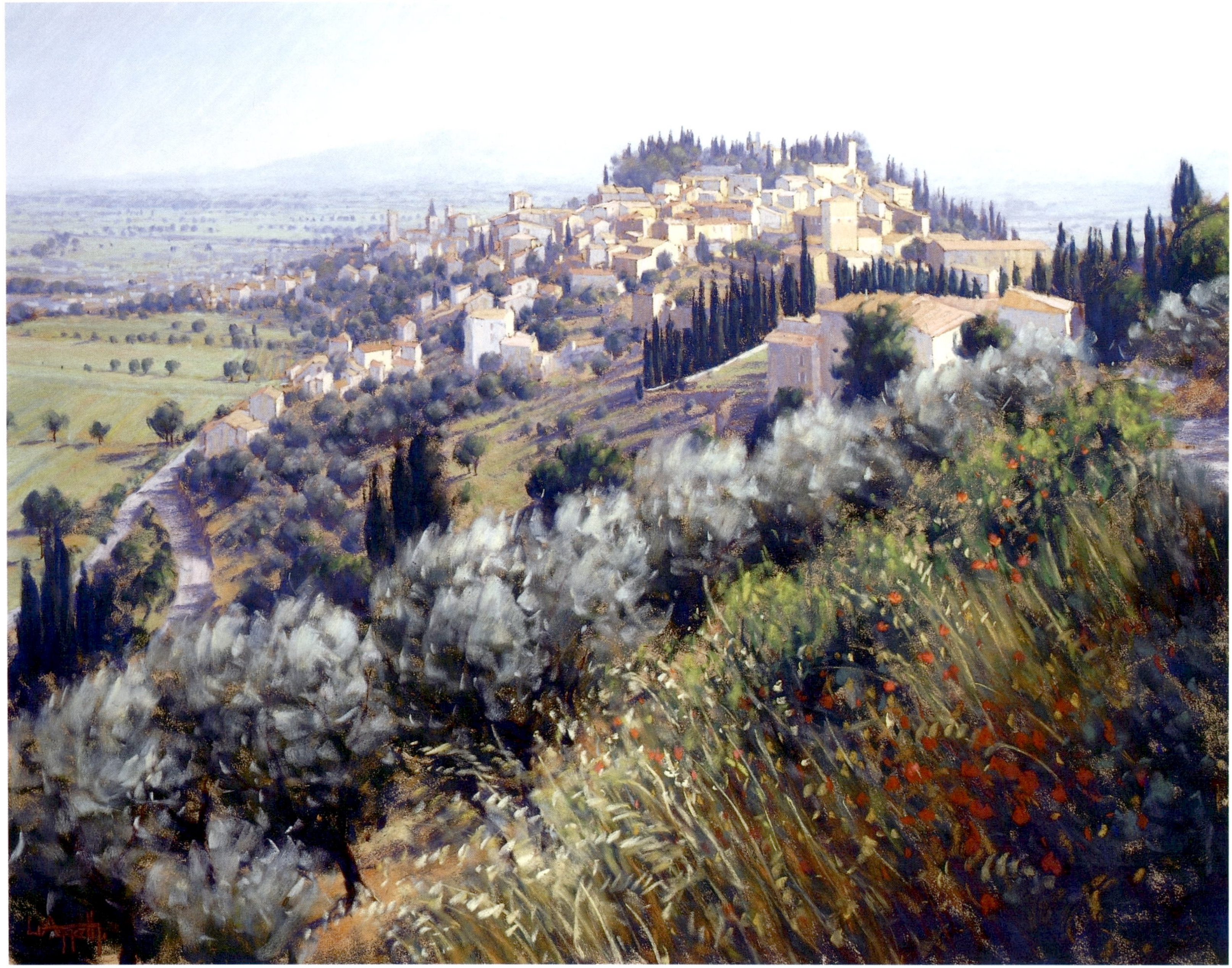

Spello, Vale of Spoleto Pastel 500 x 650 mm

To paint up here in comparative solitude is absolute heaven.

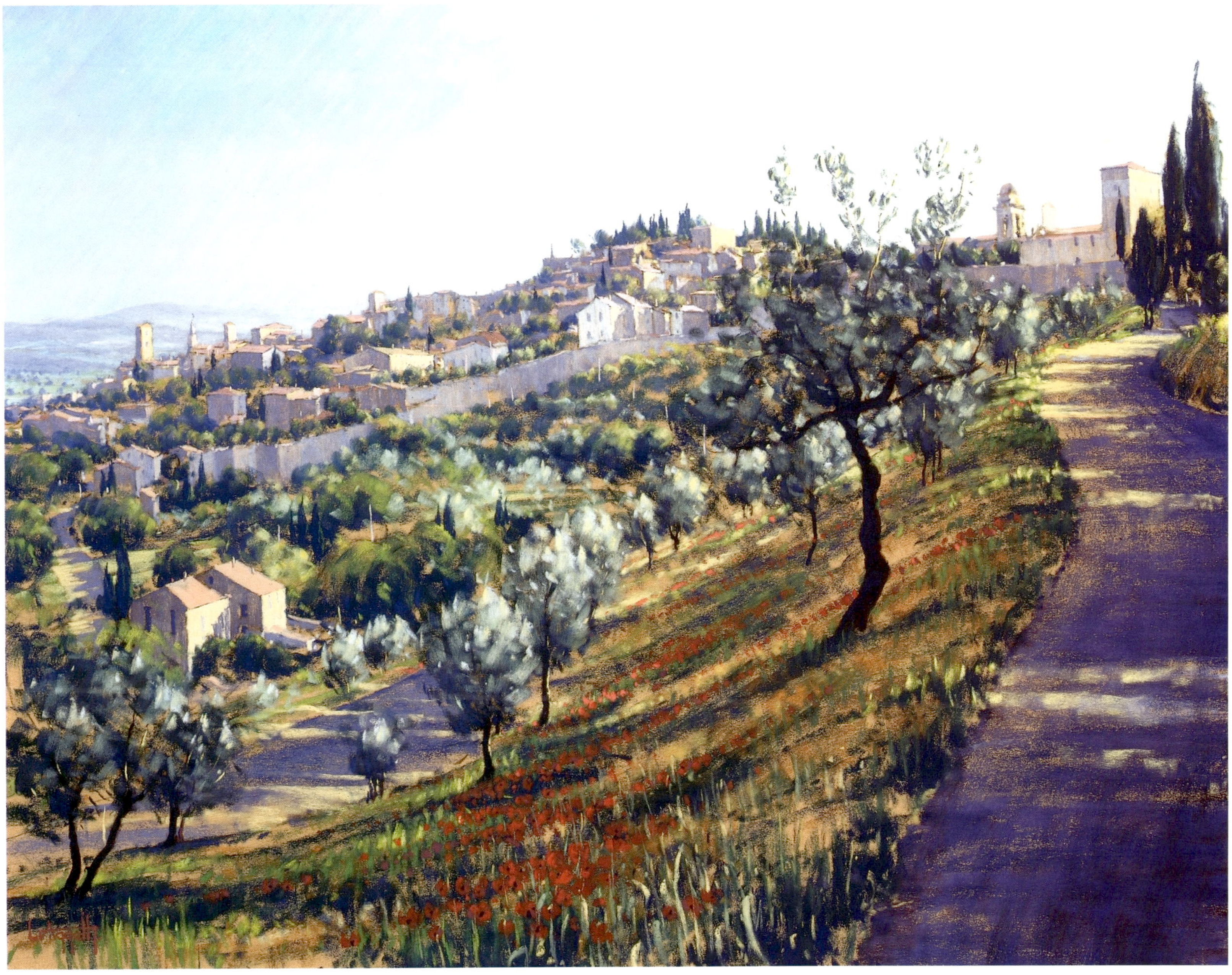

Evening Light, Spello Pastel 500 x 650 mm

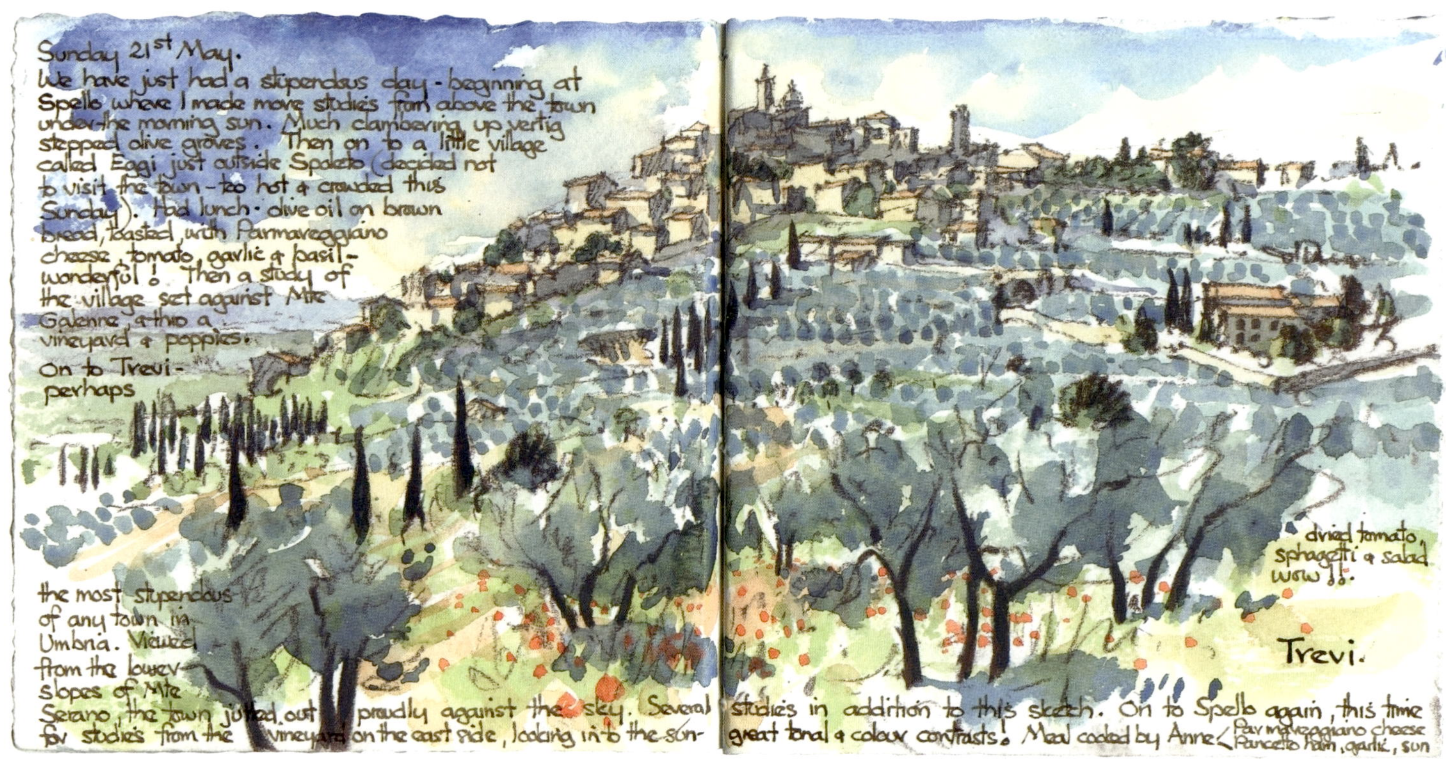

Diary Sketch 21st May, 2000 *Trevi* Conté w/c

Trevi, a further 18 km down the Vale past Foligno is the archetypal Umbrian hill town, possessing the most perfect appearance of any. A pyramidal hill at the end of a spur, jutting out from Monte Brunette, supports terraces of medieval houses encircling its slopes. This handsome pile of buildings, surmounted by the Romanesque Sant'Emiliano is surrounded by endless swathes of olive groves, pierced by strings of cypress trees.

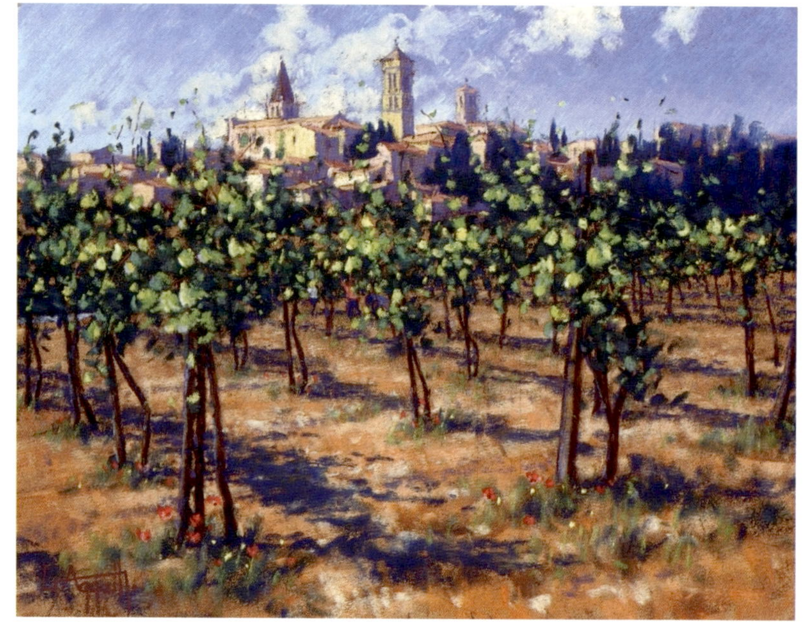

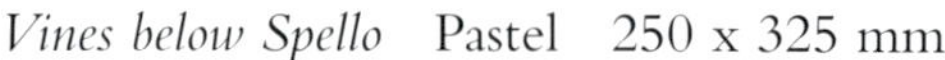

Vines below Spello Pastel 250 x 325 mm

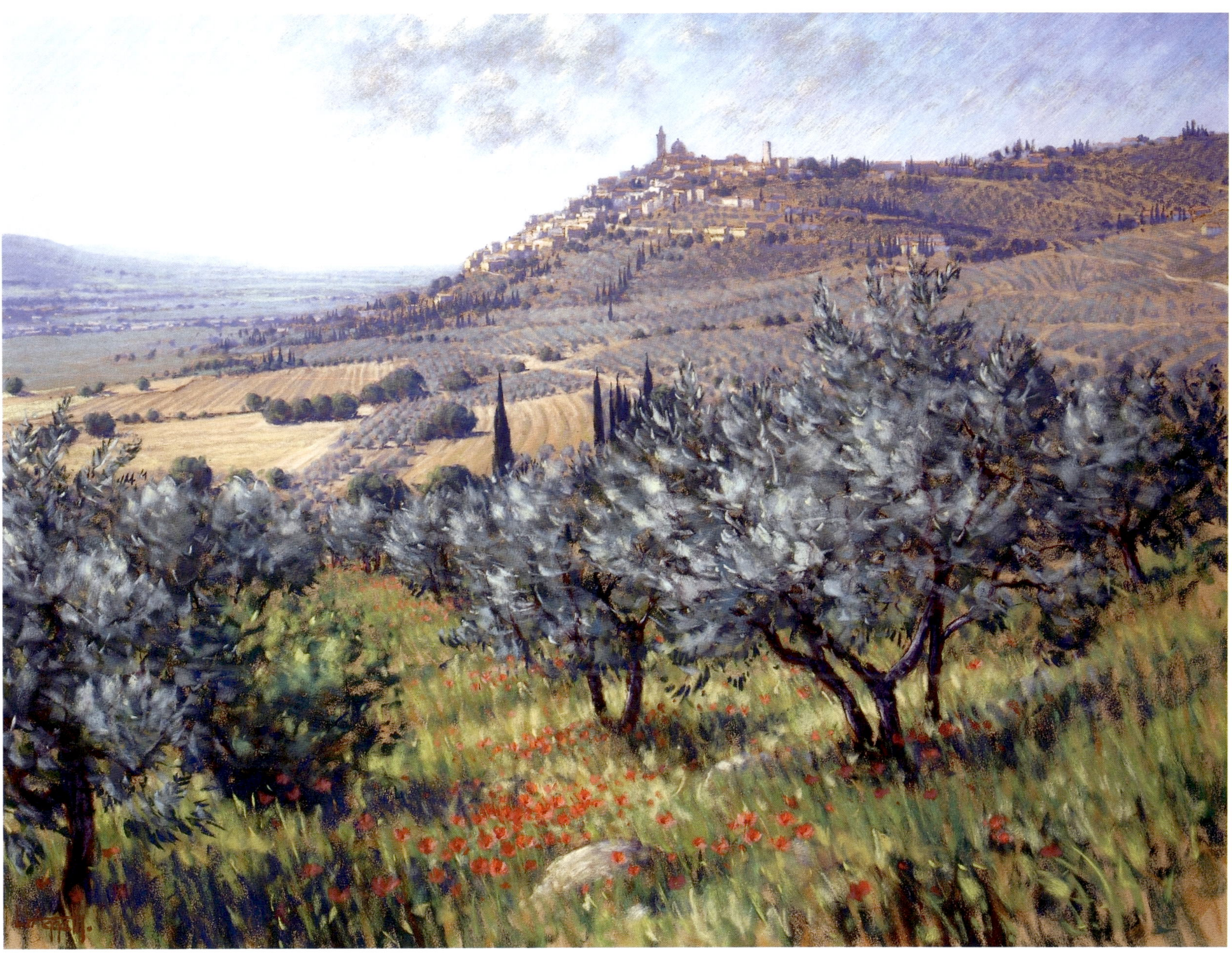

Trevi, Vale of Spoleto Pastel 600 x 800 mm

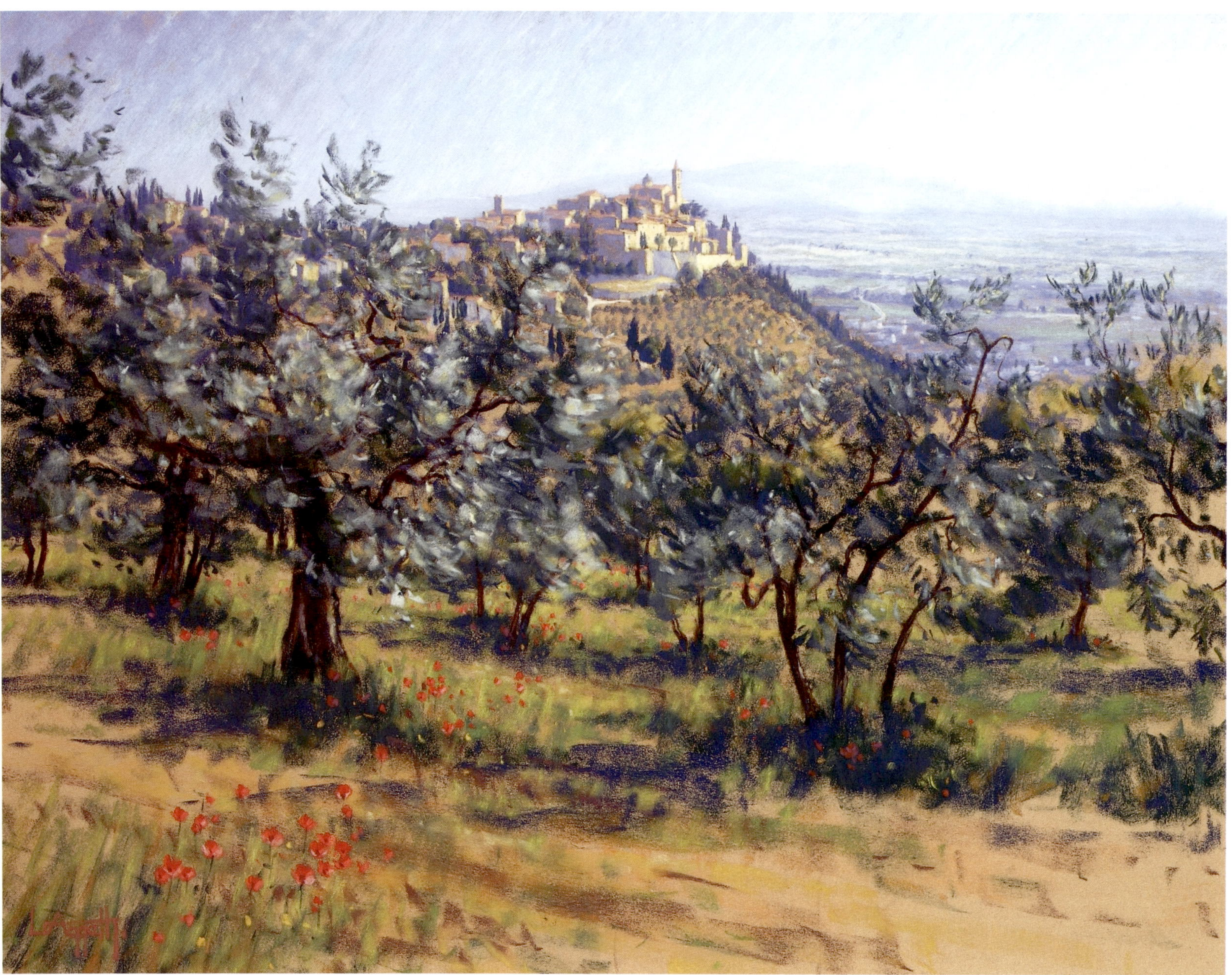

Trevi, Vale of Spoleto Pastel 500 x 650 mm

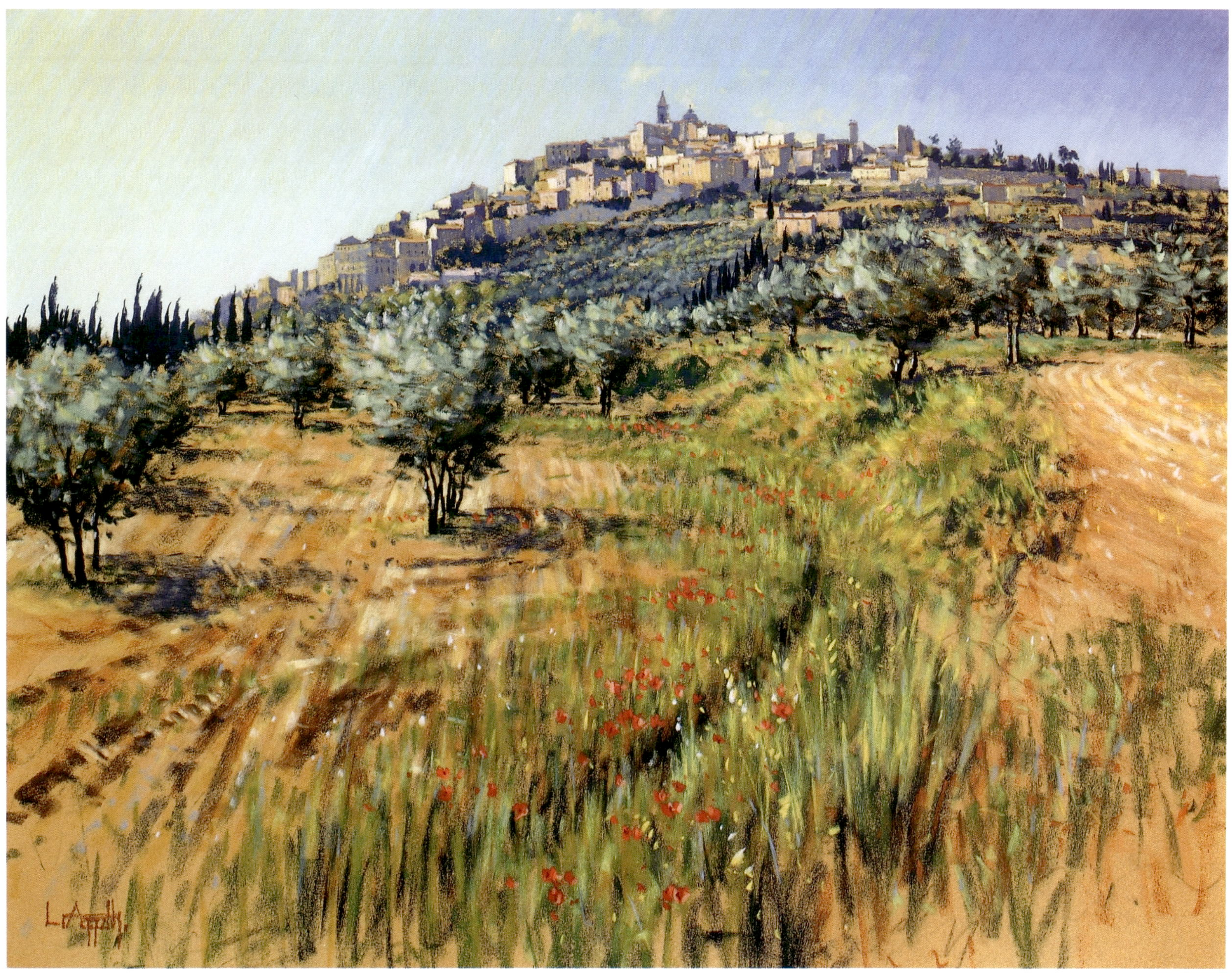

Olive Grove below Trevi Pastel 500 x 650 mm

A plein air *painting completed in 1994, as was the painting of Gubbio on the next page, both sites visited from the base at Bevagna.*

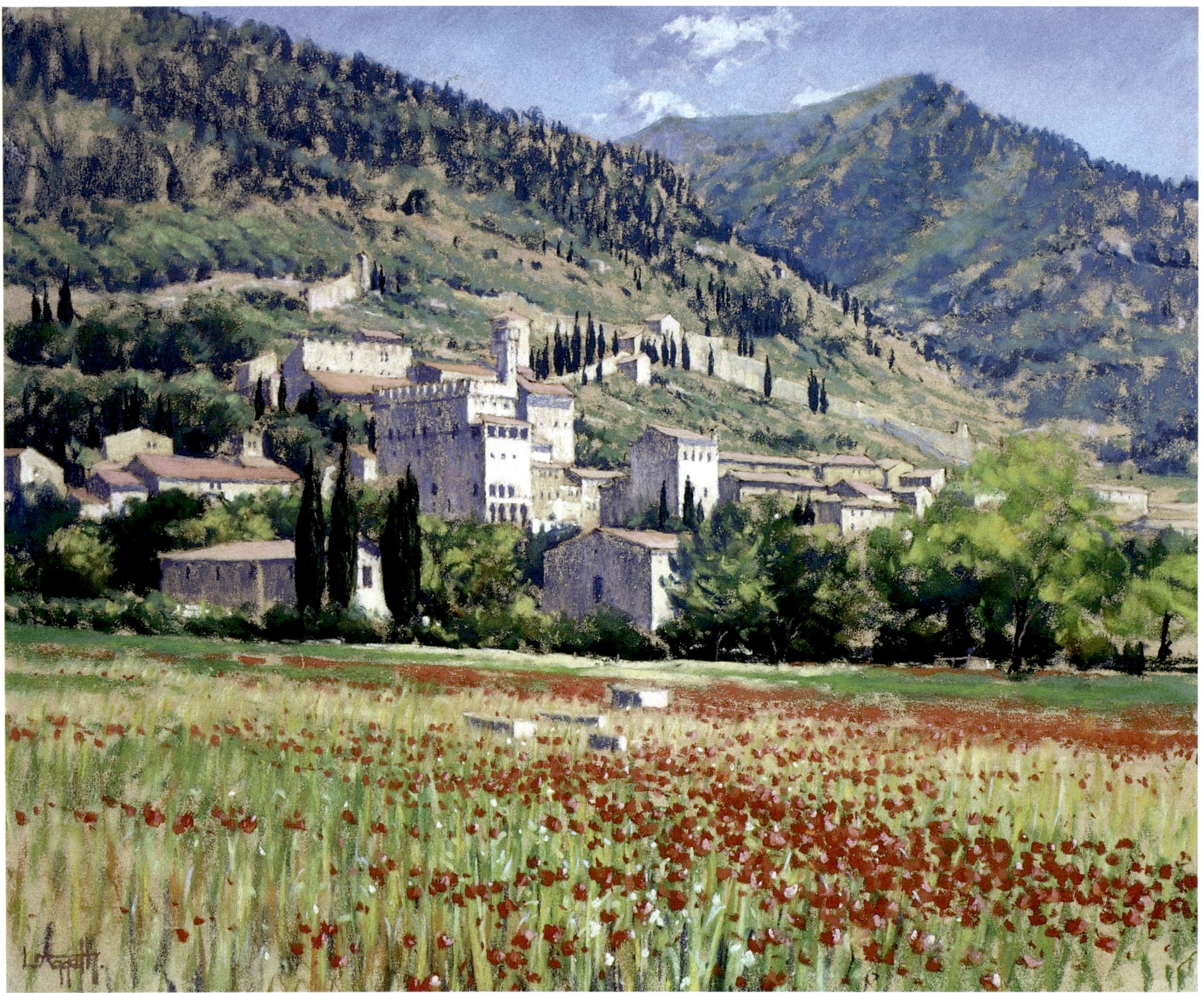

Poppies below Gubbio Pastel 400 x 500 mm

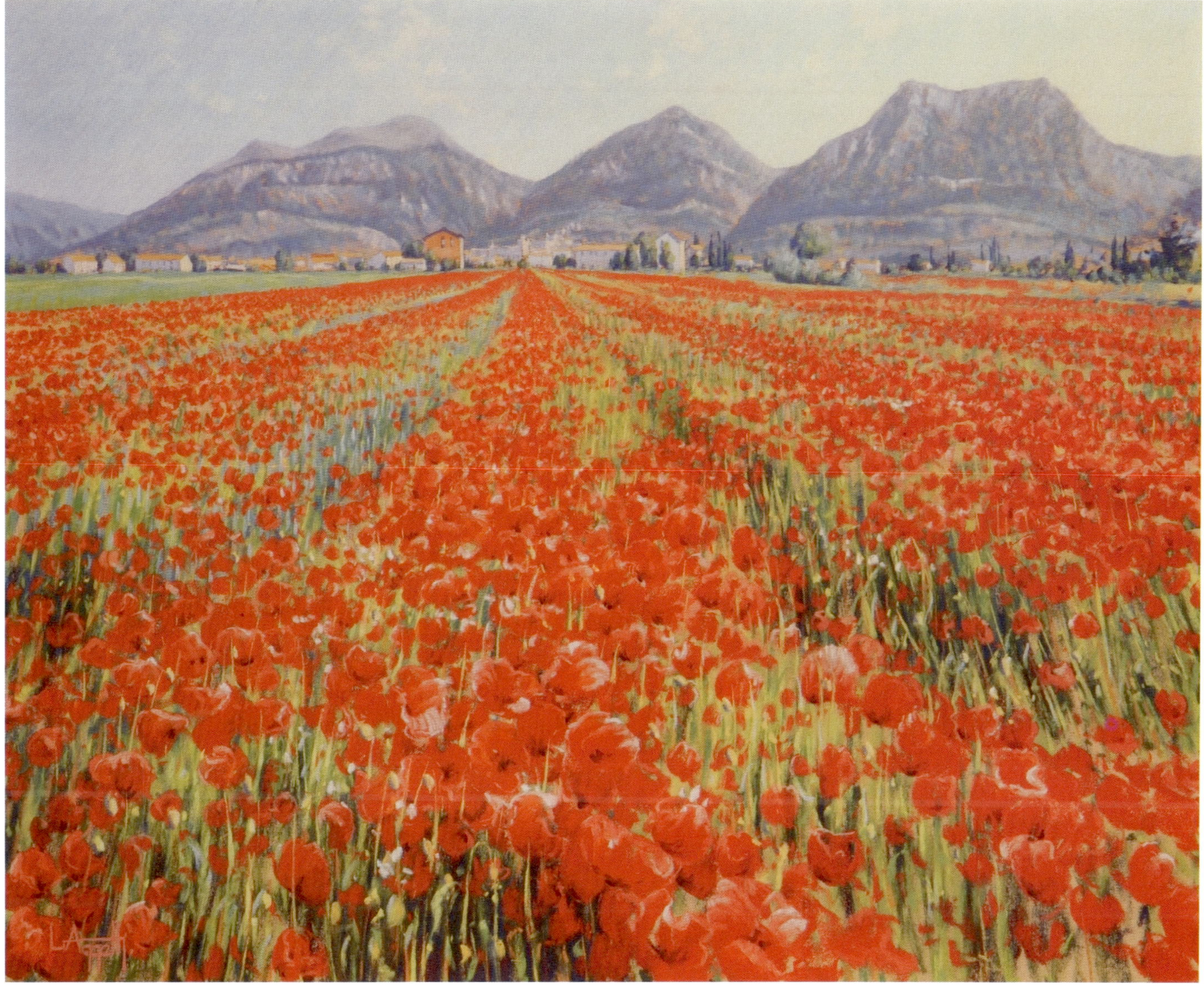

Poppies outside Gubbio Pastel 500 x 650 mm

To the north of Assisi, the beautifully-maintained medieval town of Gubbio is attractively situated at the end of a plain, with the forested mountains of the Apennines rising up behind from which flow the waters of the Camignano Gorge through the town. When viewed from across the fertile poppy-covered plain, the town has all the appearance of a resolute mountain outpost, which indeed it is.

Tuscany

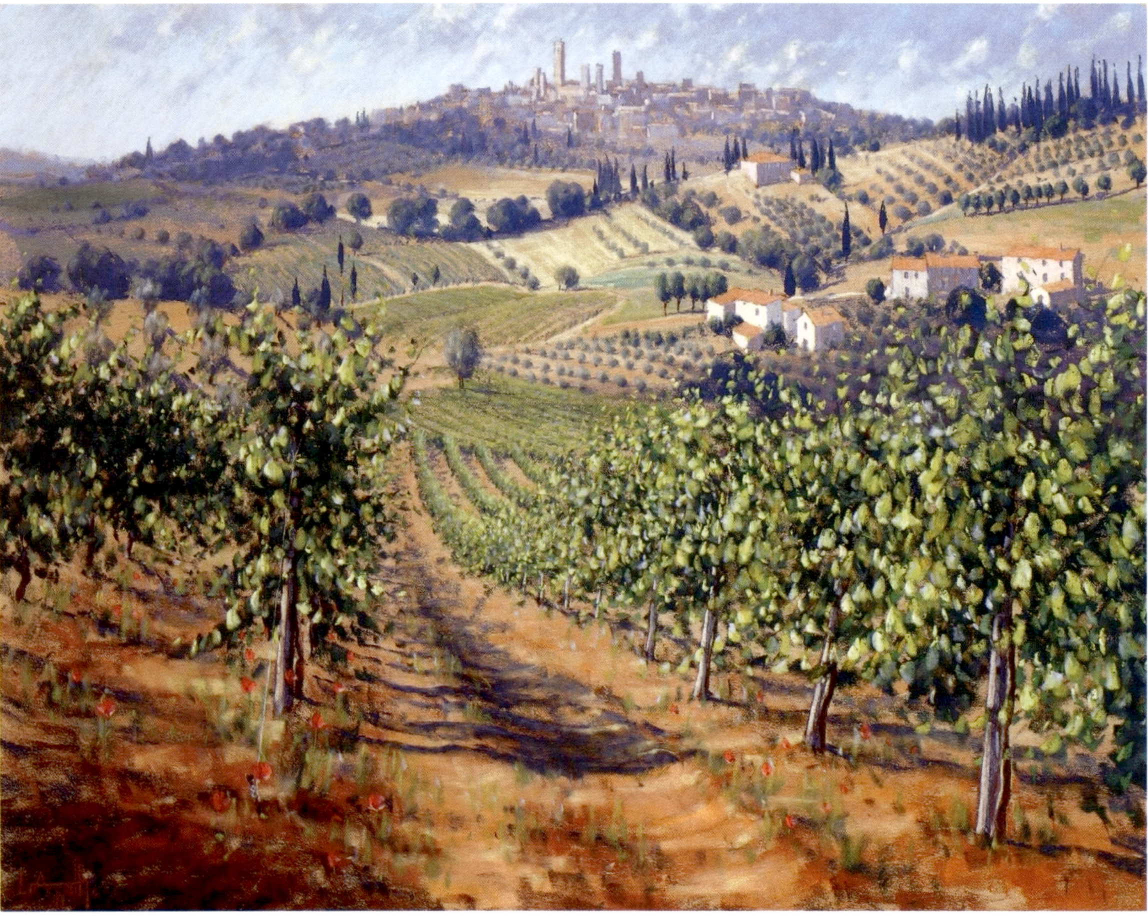

Vernaccia di San Gimignano Pastel 500 x 650 mm

Tuscany, Umbria's more illustrious neighbour, is renowned throughout the world for its architecture, art, history, and beautiful landscape. Its people are immensely proud of their Etruscan heritage, and consequently the past merges with the present to a remarkable degree. Independent and resolute for centuries, they have preserved their traditions and surroundings, which is the reason why many of us are so fascinated with the region, and its wonderfully varied landscape.

The Garfagnana, in the north-western corner, consists of deep valleys and mountain spurs, with a narrow coastal strip known as the Versilia.

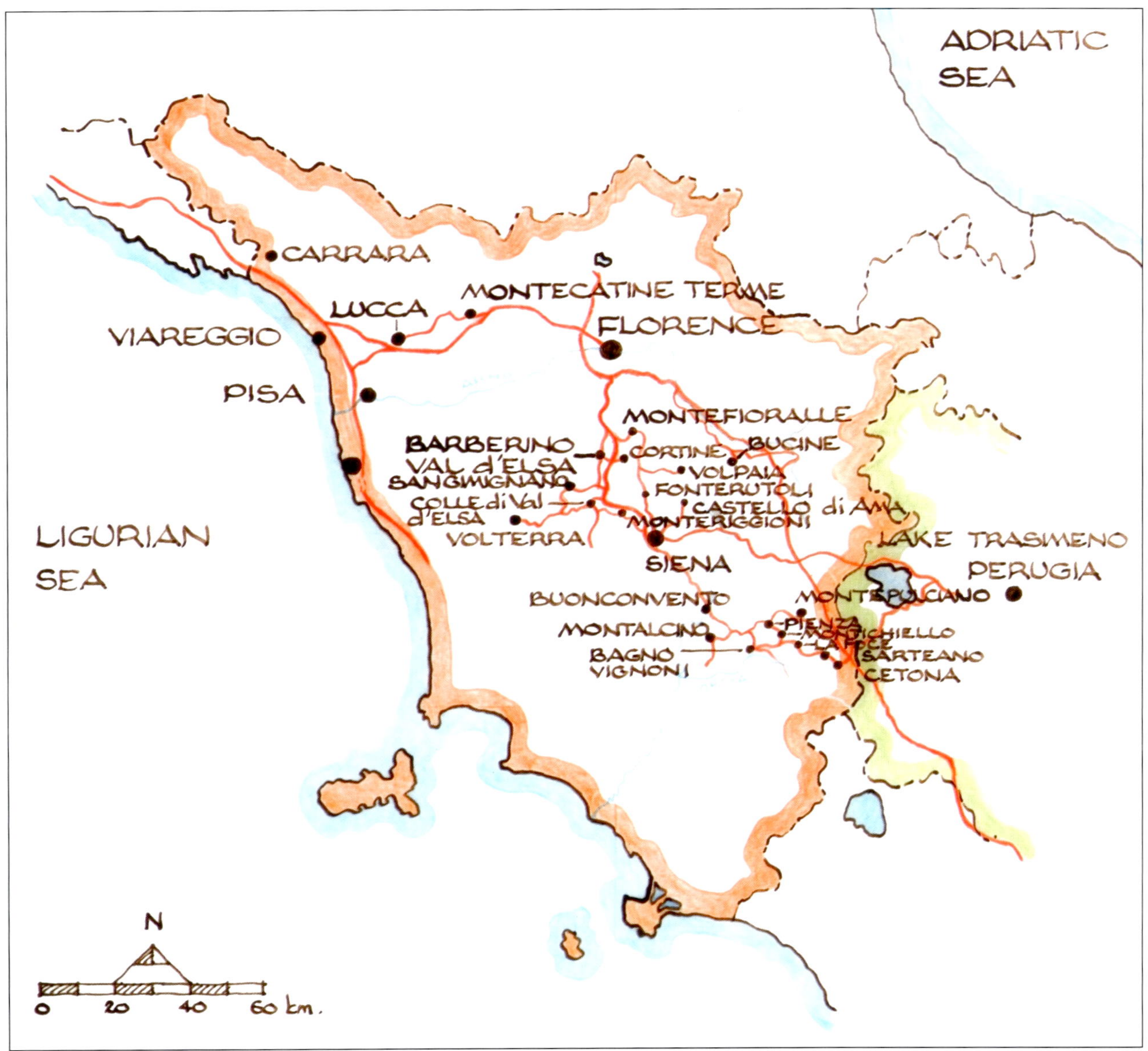
ADRIATIC
SEA
CARRARA
MONTECATINE TERME
LUCCA
VIAREGGIO
FLORENCE
PISA
MONTEFIORALLE
BARBERINO
VAL d'ELSA
CORTINE
BUCINE
VOLPAIA
SANGIMIGNANO
FONTERUTOLI
COLLE di Val
d'ELSA
CASTELLO di AMA
MONTERIGGIONI
VOLTERRA
LIGURIAN
SEA
LAKE TRASIMENO
SIENA
PERUGIA
BUONCONVENTO
MONTEPULCIANO
PIENZA
MONTALCINO
MONTICHIELLO
LA FOCE
BAGNO
VIGNONI
SARTEANO
CETONA
N
0
20
40
60 km.

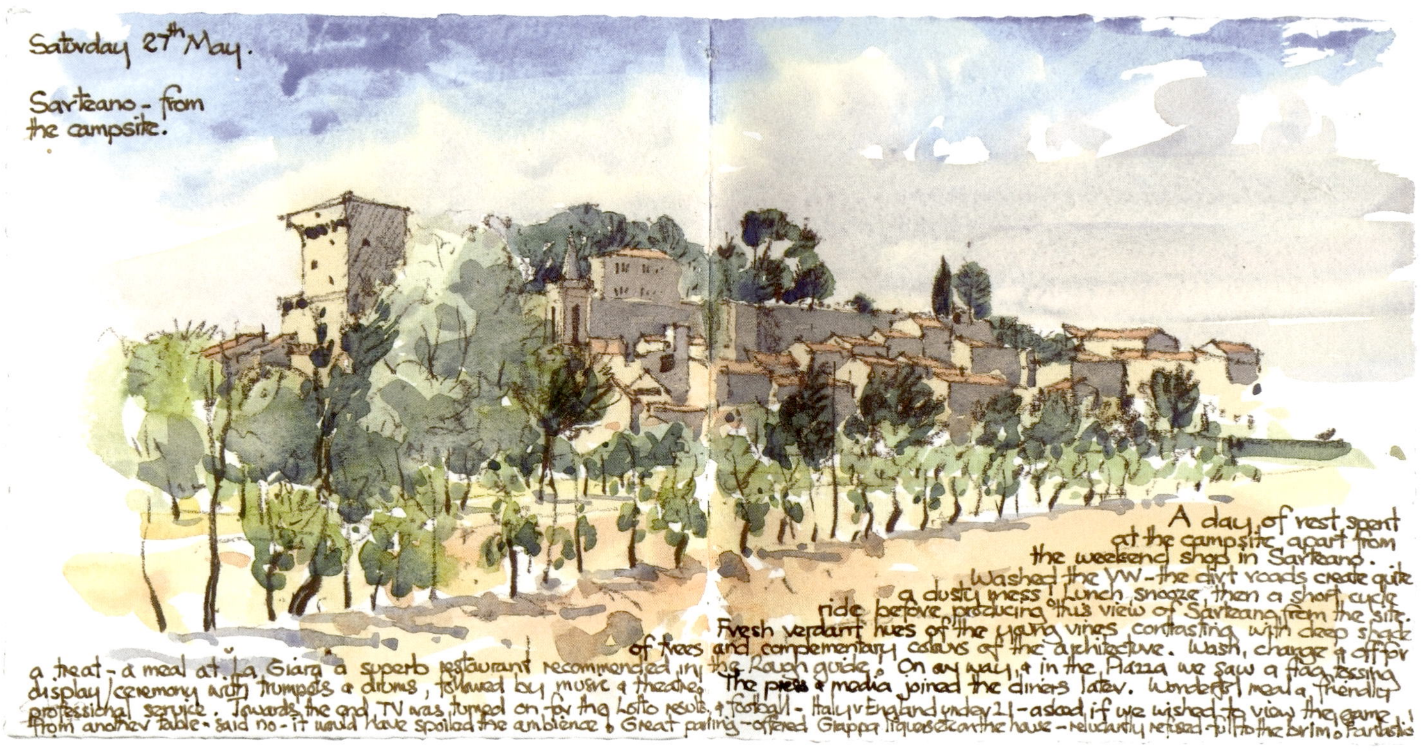

Diary Sketch 27th May, 2000 *Sarteano* Conté w/c

Continuing south beyond Pisa, lies the Maremma, a series of plateaux, scrubby heathlands and bald hills. To the east, the Val d'Orcia, and further north, the Crete Senese are both characterized by rolling hills, surmounted by jagged peaks, supporting lone farmsteads, protected by clumps of cypress trees, a magical timeless landscape. Siena, still gloriously trapped in its medieval cloak, from the time its arch rival Florence prospered under the burgeoning Renaissance, and the Sienese hill towns, Volterra, San Gimignano, Colle di Val d'Elsa and Monteriggioni, surrounded by intensively farmed land, producing olives, grapes, almonds, cereals and vegetables, could all pictorially form the background of a Fra Angelico panel, a Giotto fresco, or a Sienese quattrocento altarpiece. The deciduous woodland, olive groves, vineyards, hill villages and towns of the Chianti region below Florence present an even more ordered canvas, where every aspect of life seems in perfect balance, producing a sublimely crafted landscape nurtured by the balmy climate. Then there is Florence itself, often celebrated as the most beautiful city in Italy. Of this there is no doubt, when considering the wealth of architecture, art and sculpture the city has produced. But permit me to make the following observation. Beyond Brunelleschi's stupendous dome, the duomo itself and baptistery, the Ponte Vecchio, Piazza della Signoria, San Miniato and the Palazzo Vecchio; the streets and squares away from the immediate city do not compare with those of Siena, Rome, Spoleto, Perugia, Venice, Verona and the northern towns. The true beauty of Florence is to be witnessed in the interiors and their contents, viz the Uffizi, Bargello, Santa Croce, Santa Maria Novella, San Lorenzo, Santo Spirito, Palazzo Pitti and the Accademia etc … Much of my time in this incredible city, which I adore, has been spent viewing works of art and architecture, both externally and internally, whilst most of my painting activities have been confined to the views down and across the Arno.

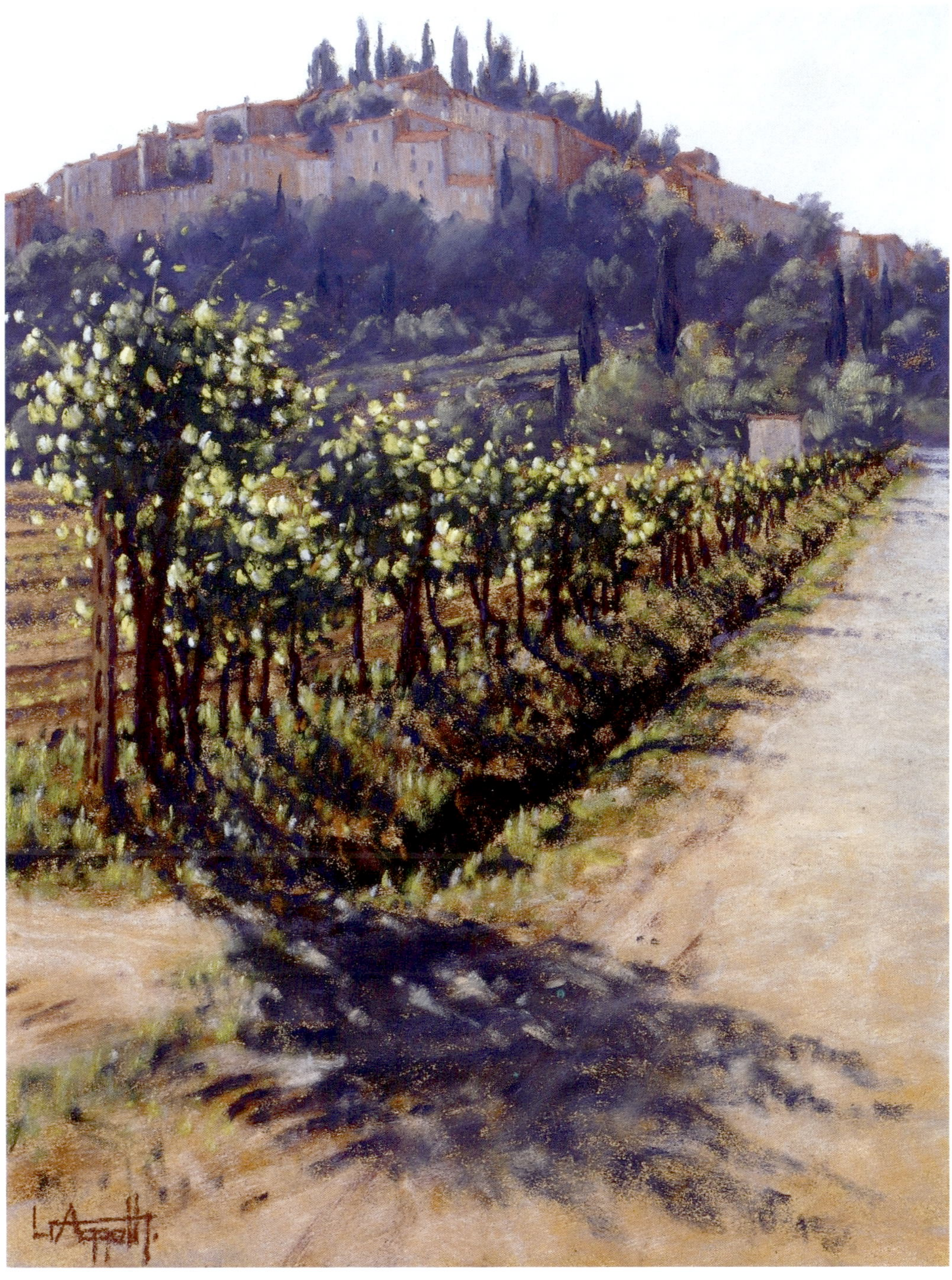

SARTEANO AND THE VAL D'ORCIA

We enter Tuscany from Umbria at the southern end, via Cetona, an ancient Etruscan town, where I produced a watercolour painting and this small pastel, looking up at the settlement and directly into sunlight. Our destination, Sarteano, is one of the five locations I have used as a base for exploring the Tuscany I have so far become acquainted with. The campsite, Parco delle Piscine, is a well run, four star complex, conveniently situated for working in the Val d'Orcia area. Whilst there during our last visit we were entertained each evening by the sound of drums and trumpets, accompanying the Medieval flag waving, drifting across to the site from the town square.

Cetona Pastel 325 x 250 mm

To the north east in the Val d'Orcia, Bagno Vignoni possesses one of Tuscany's most memorable sights. The square is occupied by an arcaded Renaissance piscine, built by the Medici who took the sulphur cure here. The hot springs still bubble away in the bath, and hot streams emerge down the hillside below the village, where we paddled and bathed our feet. Chiropodists were also treating the feet of several locals, obviously a regular occurrence and most hygienically practical.

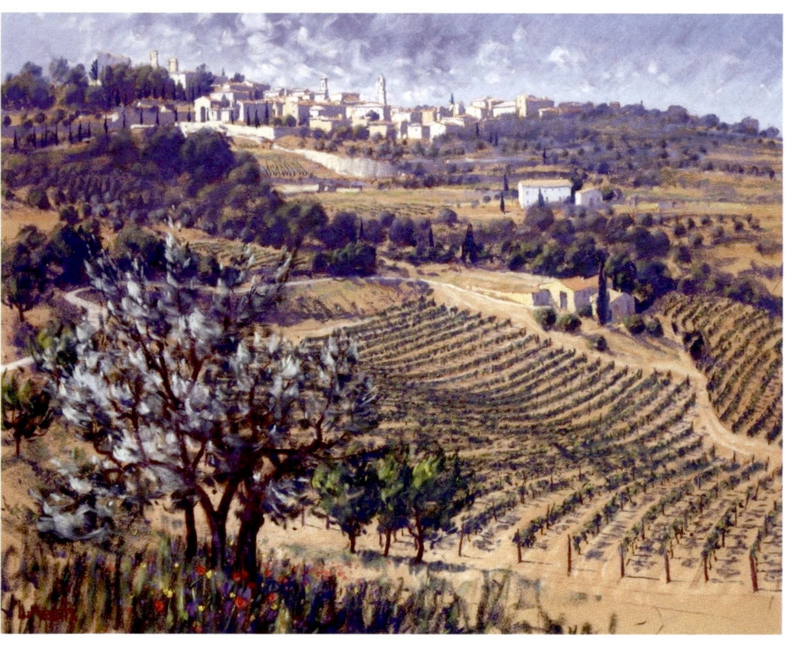

Montalcino Pastel 500 x 650 mm

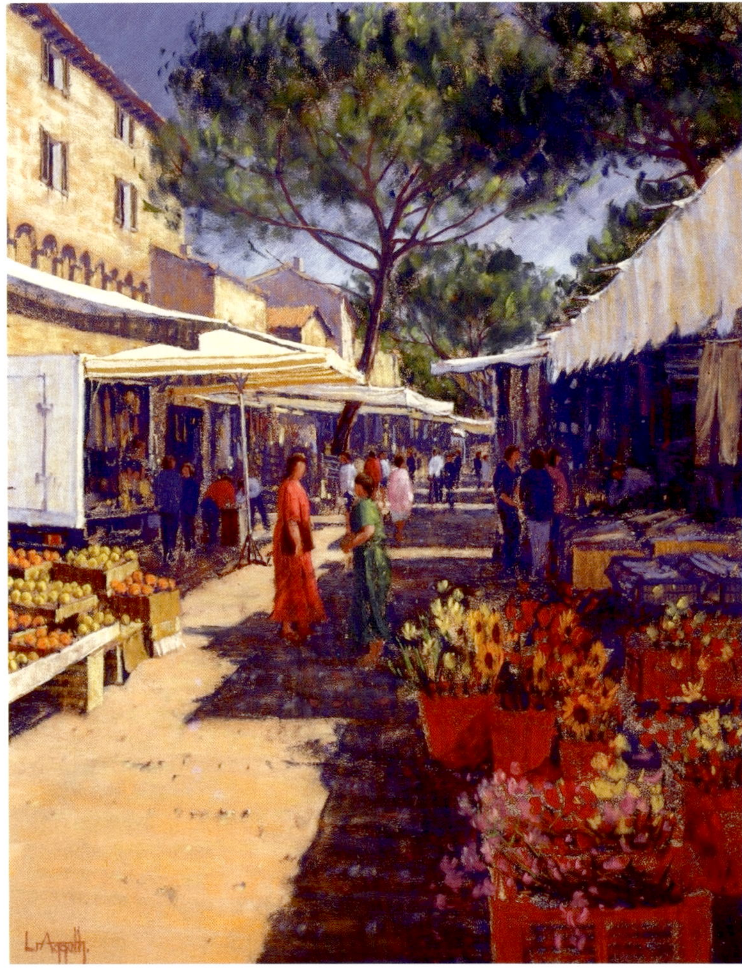

Market, Buonconvento Pastel 500 x 400 mm

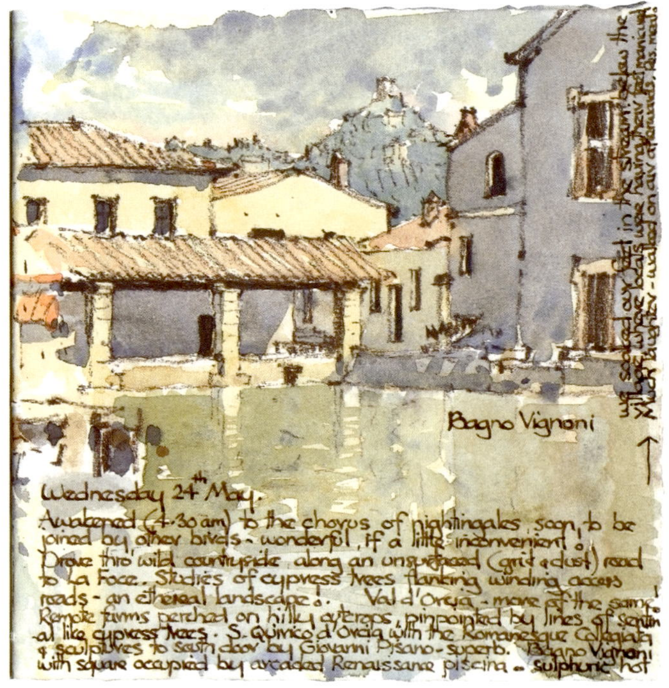

Right: Diary Sketch 24th May, 2000 *Bagno Vignoni* Conté w/c

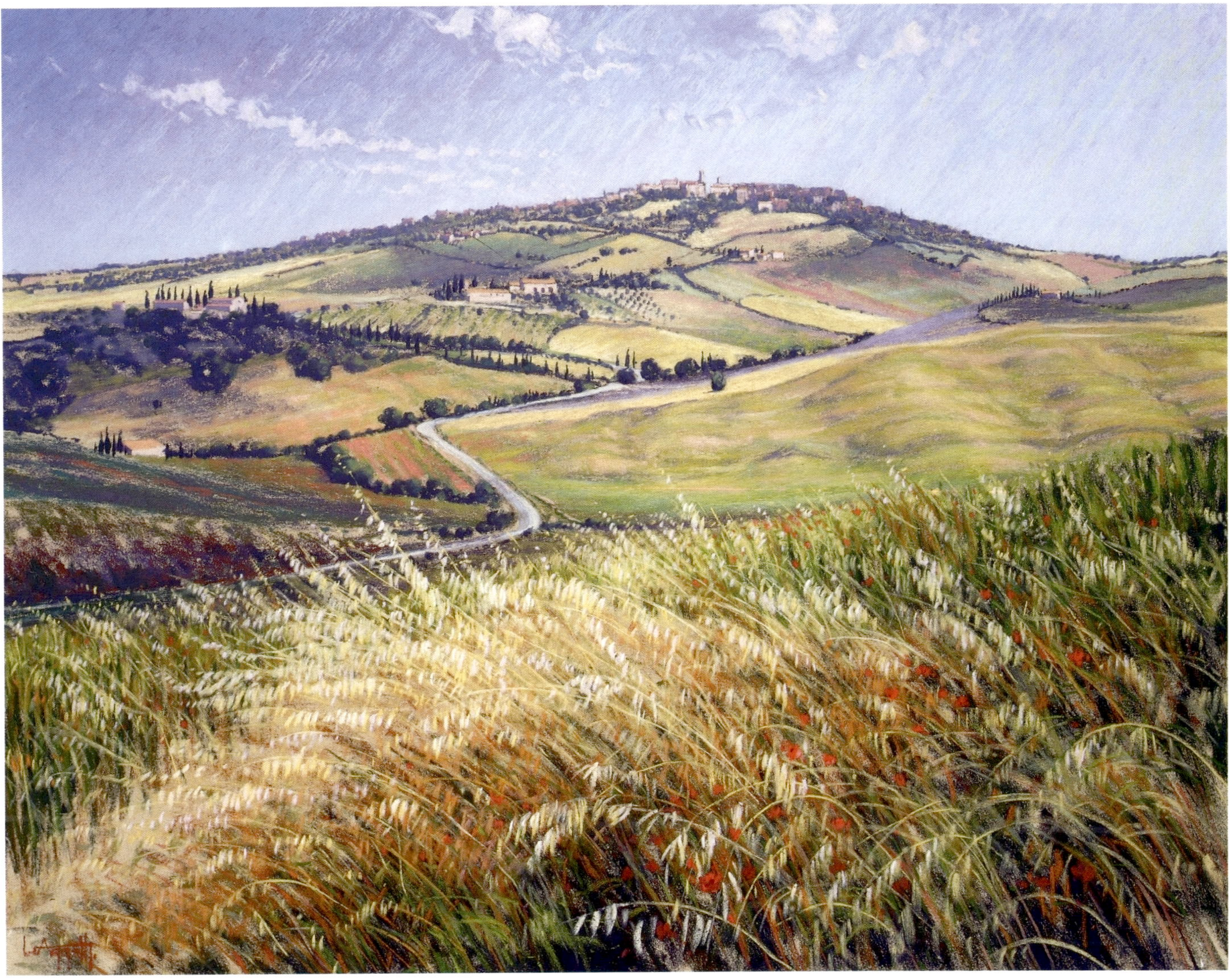

Pienza, Val d'Orcia Pastel 500 x 650 mm

Tuscany is renowned for its wine, and Montalcino, further to the west produces an exceptional red, using a superior clone of the Tuscan sangiovese grape, Brunello di Montalcino. The small fortified hill town was the final bastion of the Sienese Republic when Siena fell to the Medicis. It is most paintable, with fabulous views through vineyards, up to the town, and down towards the Val d'Orcia.

To the north lies the perfect walled medieval Sienese village of Buonconvento. We have stopped here on more than one occasion to enjoy the colourful market outside the wall. It is, however, the Val d'Orcia which has provided most of my subject matter in this region, down the river valley itself, and running in an arc from S. Quirico d'Orcia, to Pienza, Montichiello and Montepulciano.

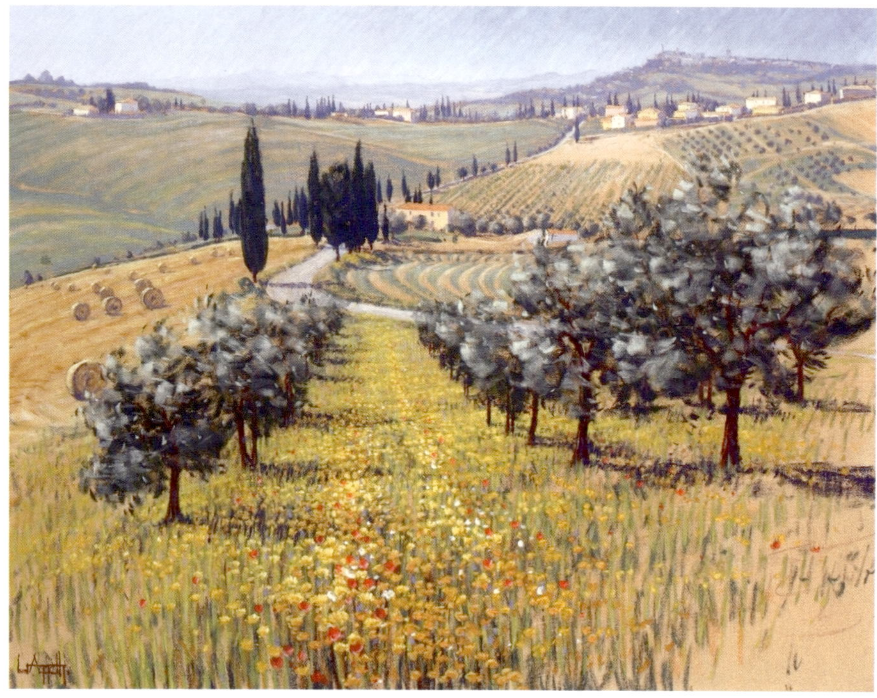

Strada di Montichiello
Pastel 500 x 650 mm

A typically Tuscan cypress-lined thoroughfare leads the eye into the glorious Val d'Orcia landscape. La Foce is another example.

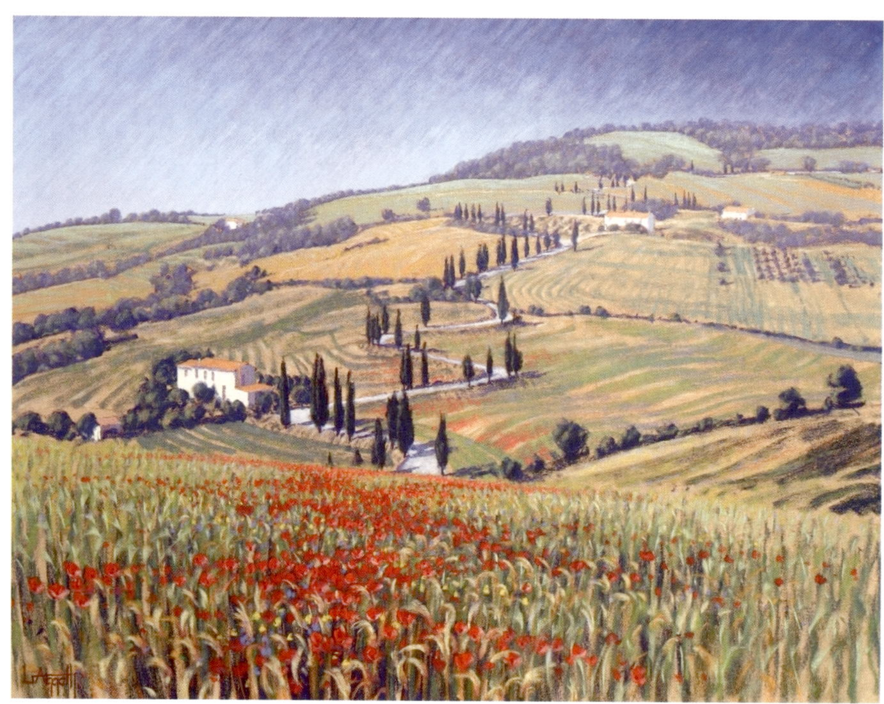

Strada di Montichiello
Pastel 500 x 650 mm

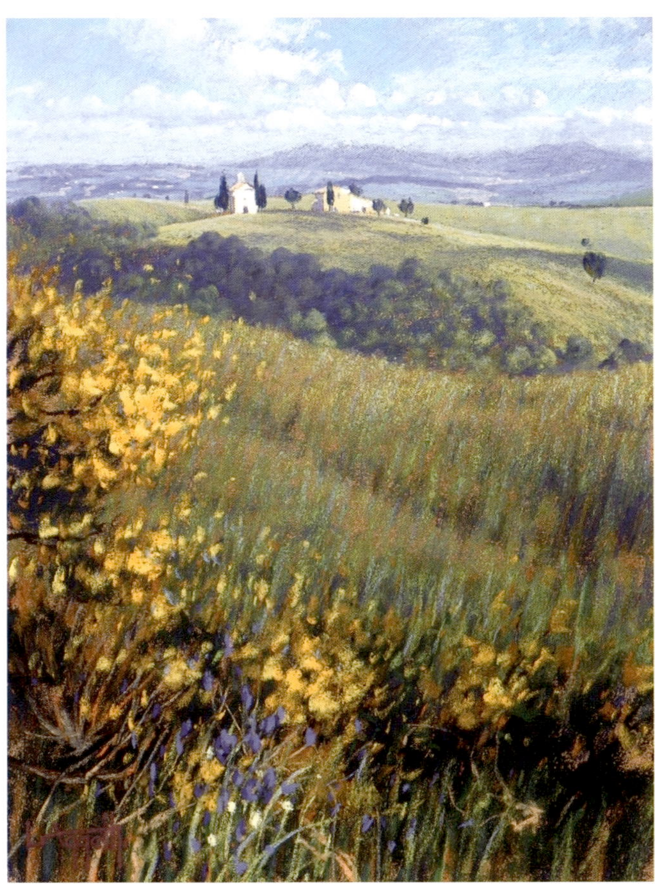

Chiesina di Vitaleta Pastel 325 x 250 mm
One of the most moving sights in the Val d'Orcia, this small remote church, accompanied by cypress trees, presents a simple and sublime composition.

La Foce Pastel 150 x 200 mm
These ancient Tuscan sentinels have witnessed remarkable deeds of heroism accomplished during our more recent history. The estate of La Foce was the home for many years of the Anglo-American writer Iris Origo, author of the classic Merchant of Prato. *It was here as the Marchesa Origo that she hid partisans and allied troops during the German occupation of Italy following Mussolini's fall in 1943. These events are recorded in her autobiography* War in Val d'Orcia.

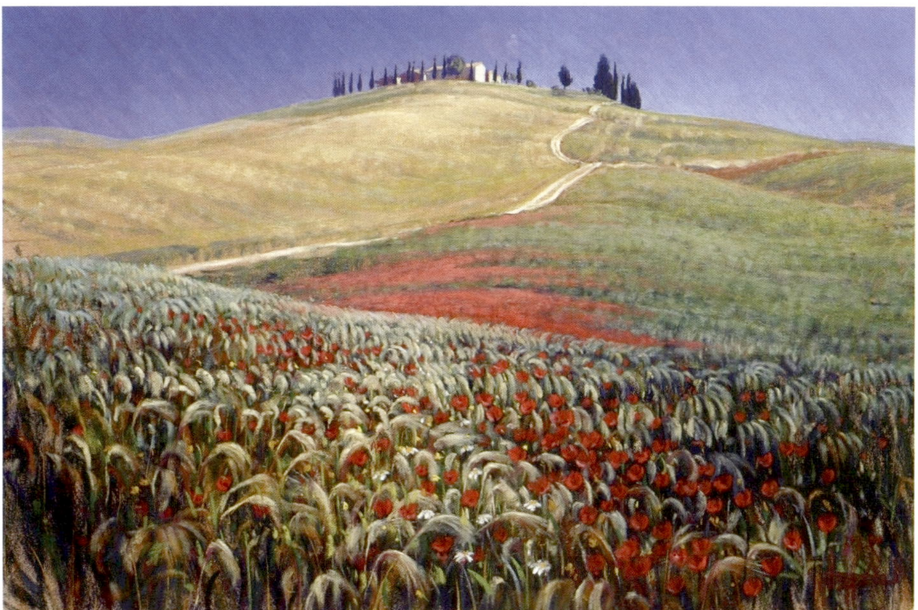

Val d'Orcia Pastel 325 x 500 mm
A typical Val d'Orcia landscape with a remote farmstead perched on a hillock and flanked by cypress trees.

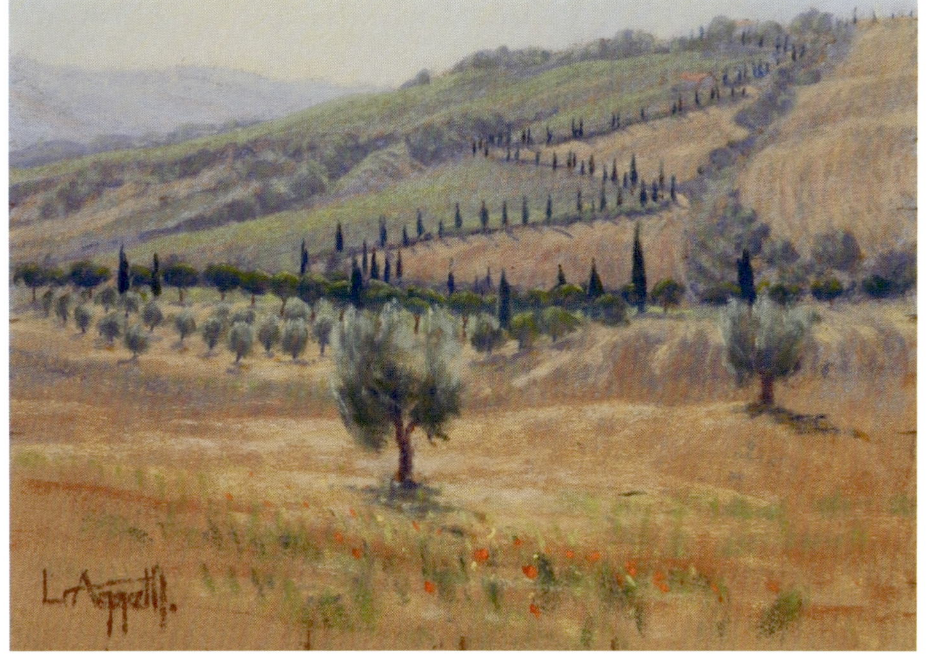

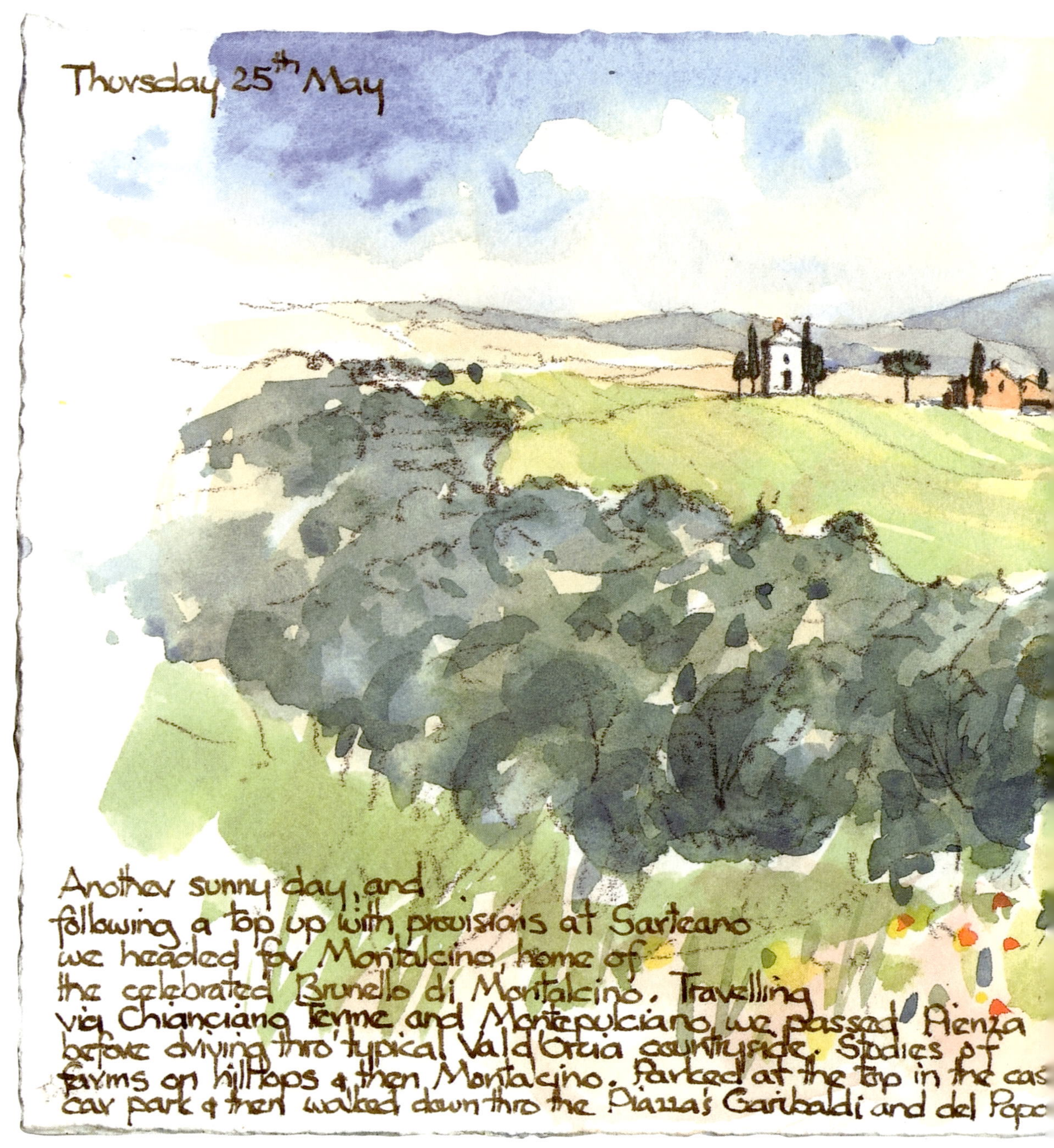

Diary Sketch 25th May, 2000 *Chiesina di Vitaleta* Conté w/c

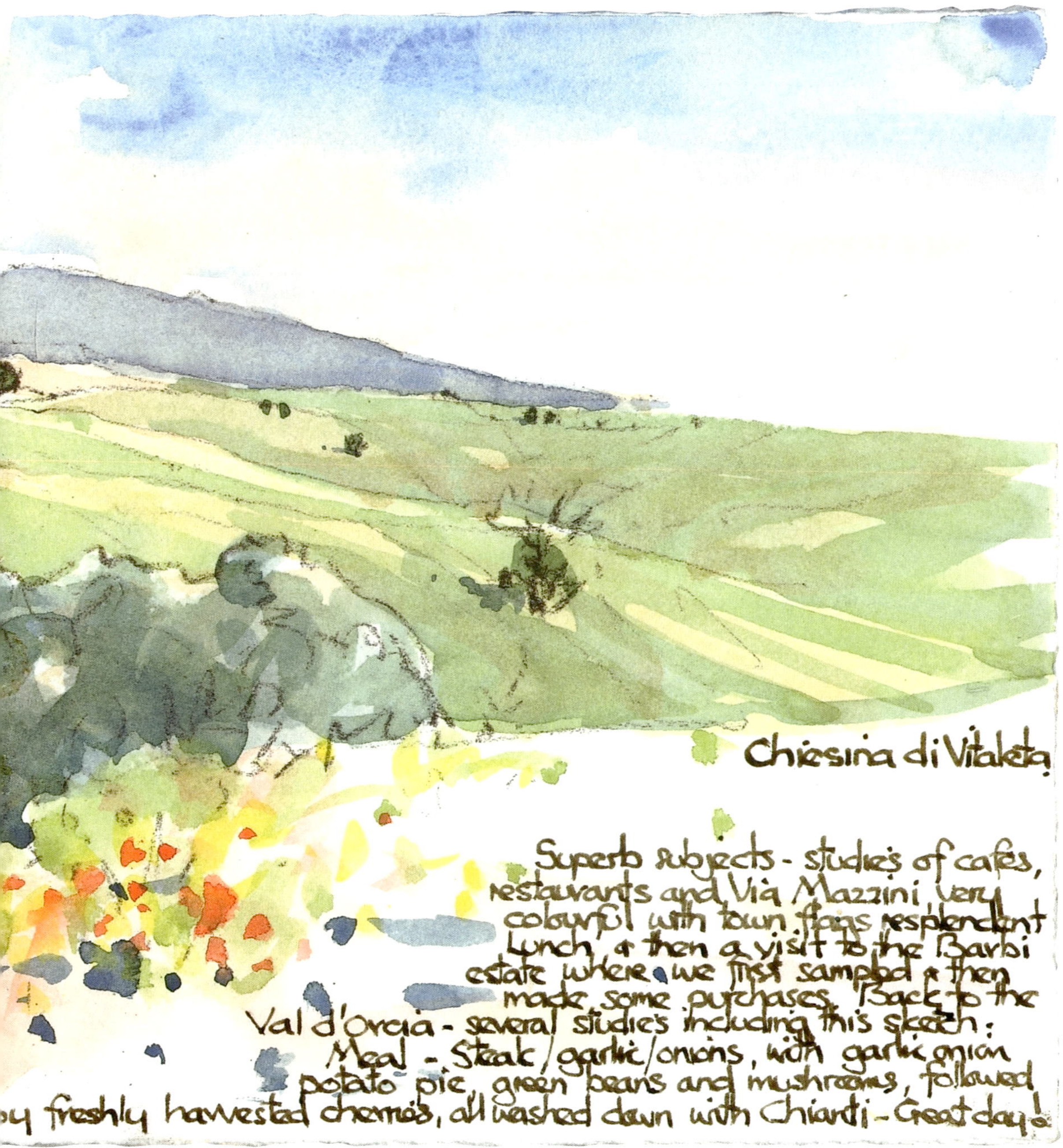
Chiesina di Vitaleta
Superb subjects - studies of cafes, restaurants and Via Mazzini very colourful with town flags resplendent. Lunch, & then a visit to the Barbi estate where we first sampled & then made some purchases. Back to the Val d'Orcia - several studies including this sketch:
Meal - Steak/garlic/onions, with garlic onion potato pie, green beans and mushrooms, followed by freshly harvested cherries, all washed down with Chianti - Great day!

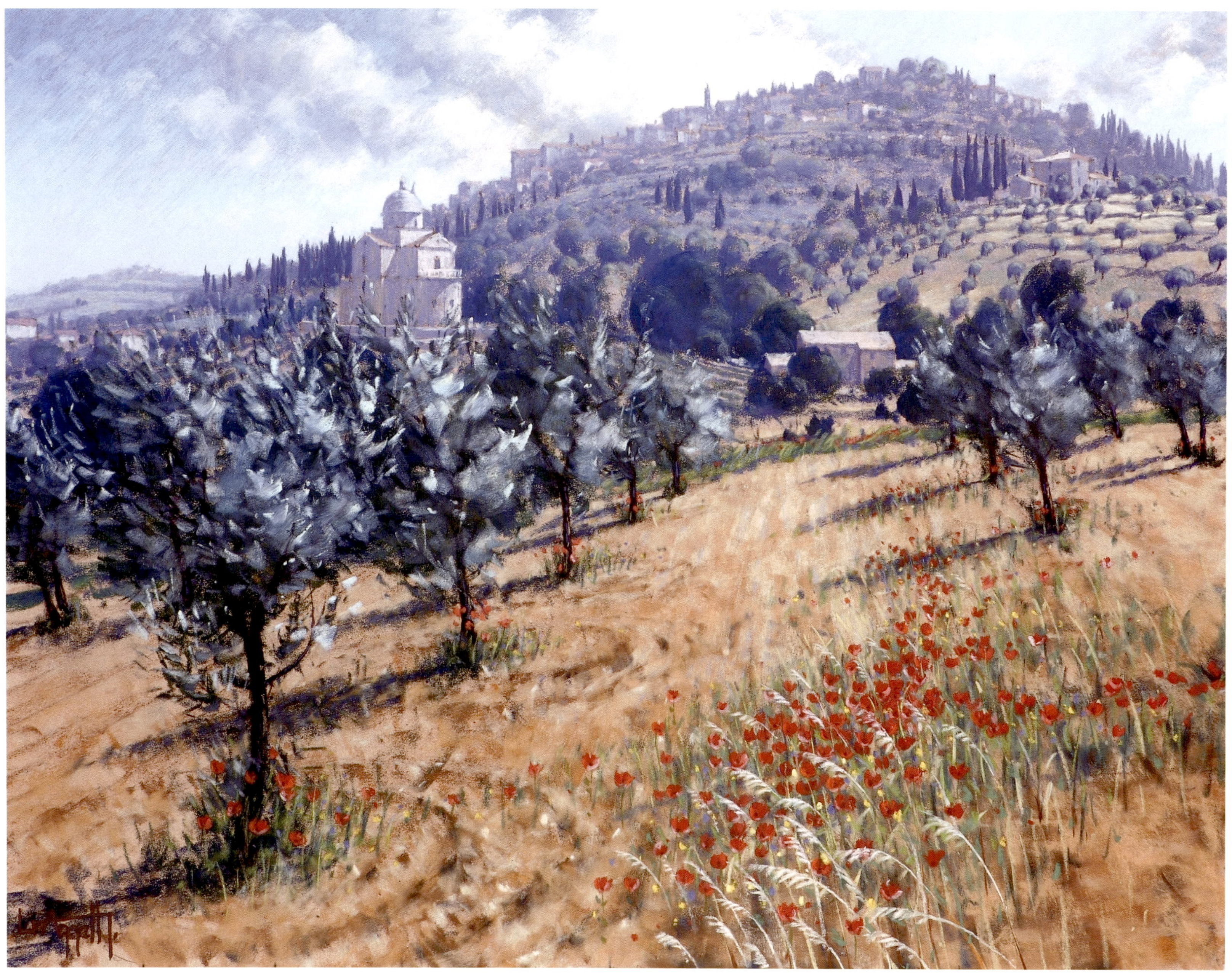

Montepulciano Pastel 500 x 650 mm

I have produced several paintings from this spot, which seems to change on each visit. Olive trees are beginning to mature now.

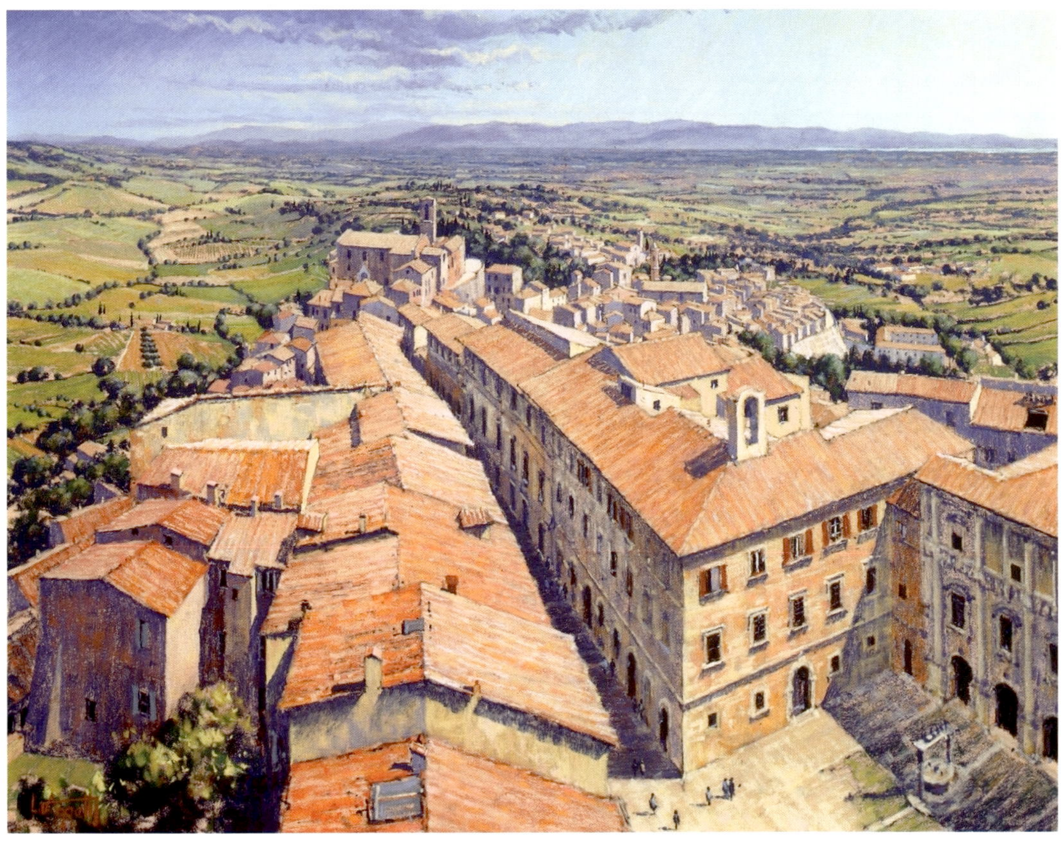

Rooftops, Montepulciano
Pastel   500 x 650 mm

A stunning view from the very top of this, the highest of the Tuscan hill towns.

Diary Sketch 26th May, 2000
Piazza Grande, Montepulciano
Conté w/c

SIENA AND THE CRETE SENESE

Siena has been used as our base camp for exploring the Crete Senese and Sienese hill towns. Campeggio, Siena Colleverde, to the north outside the walls, and within walking distance of the centre, is an excellently cared for site. There is a good bus service right outside, if you do not wish to take the exercise. Siena is stunningly beautiful, viewed from the outside, its skyline full of vigour and interest; and a painter's paradise inside. The early medieval character running right through the city, presents interesting subjects at almost every turn. The Piazza del Campo in the centre with the main streets leading to it, is the hub of the city. It is the most magical and theatrical of public spaces anywhere on earth. A perfect piece of organic planning, with its amphitheatre curve and nine segments of paving fanning down to the Palazzo Publico where the 97 m bell tower, the Torre del Mangia rises high above the city, the square, its buildings and people unknowingly participate in a continual theatrical performance.

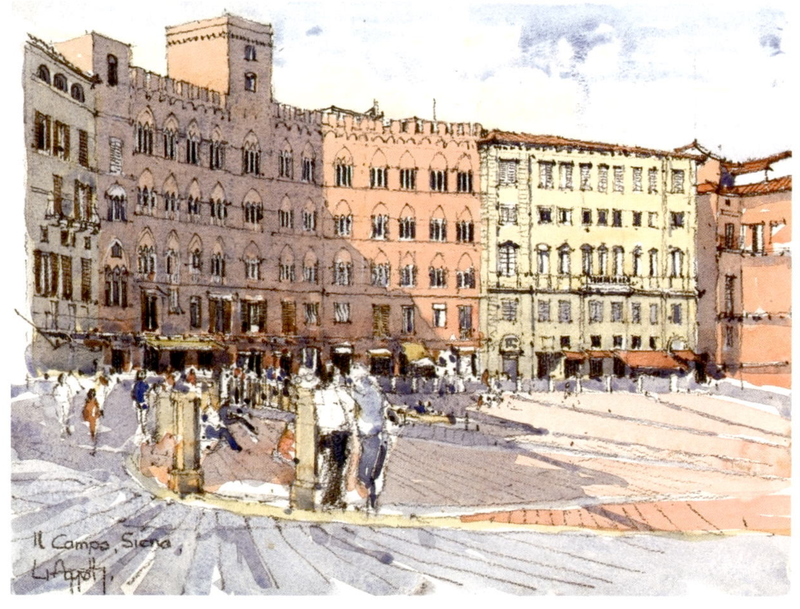

Il Campo, Siena Conté w/c 305 x 405 mm

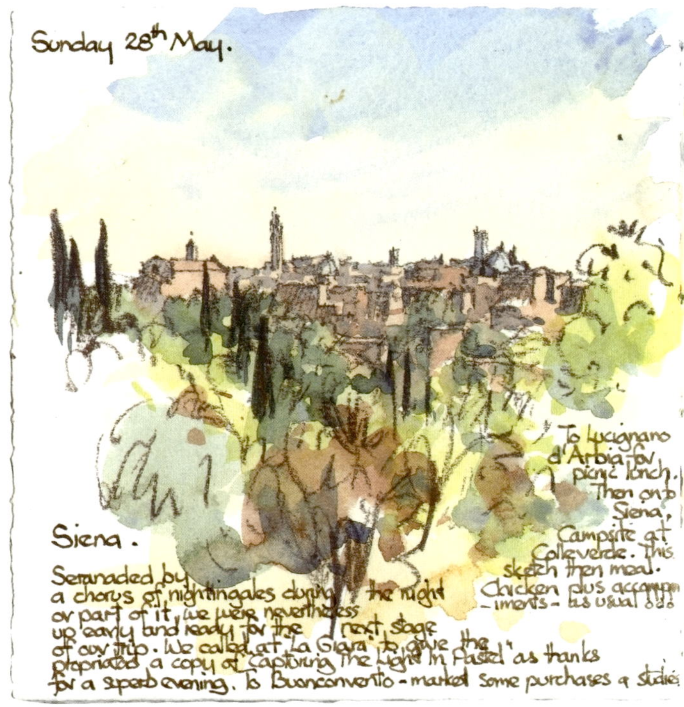

Diary Sketch 28th May, 2000 *Siena from Colleverde* Conté w/c

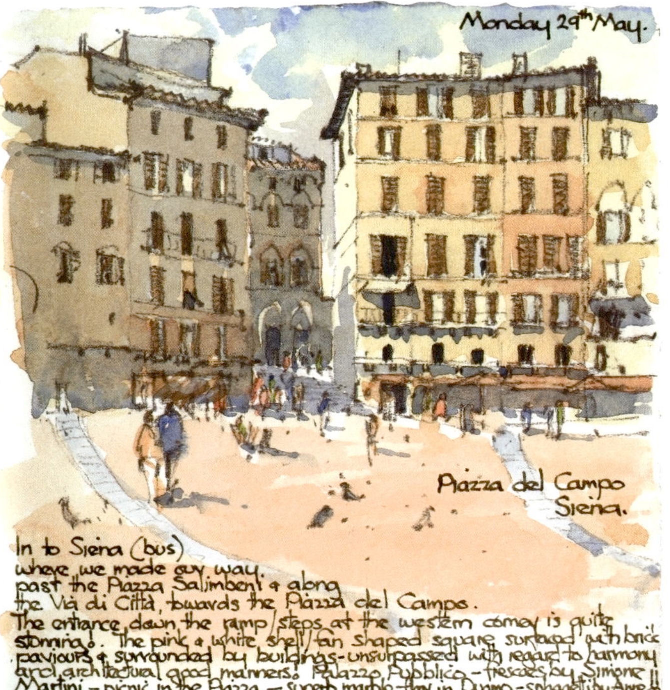

Diary Sketch 29th May, 2000 *Piazza del Campo, Siena* Conté w/c

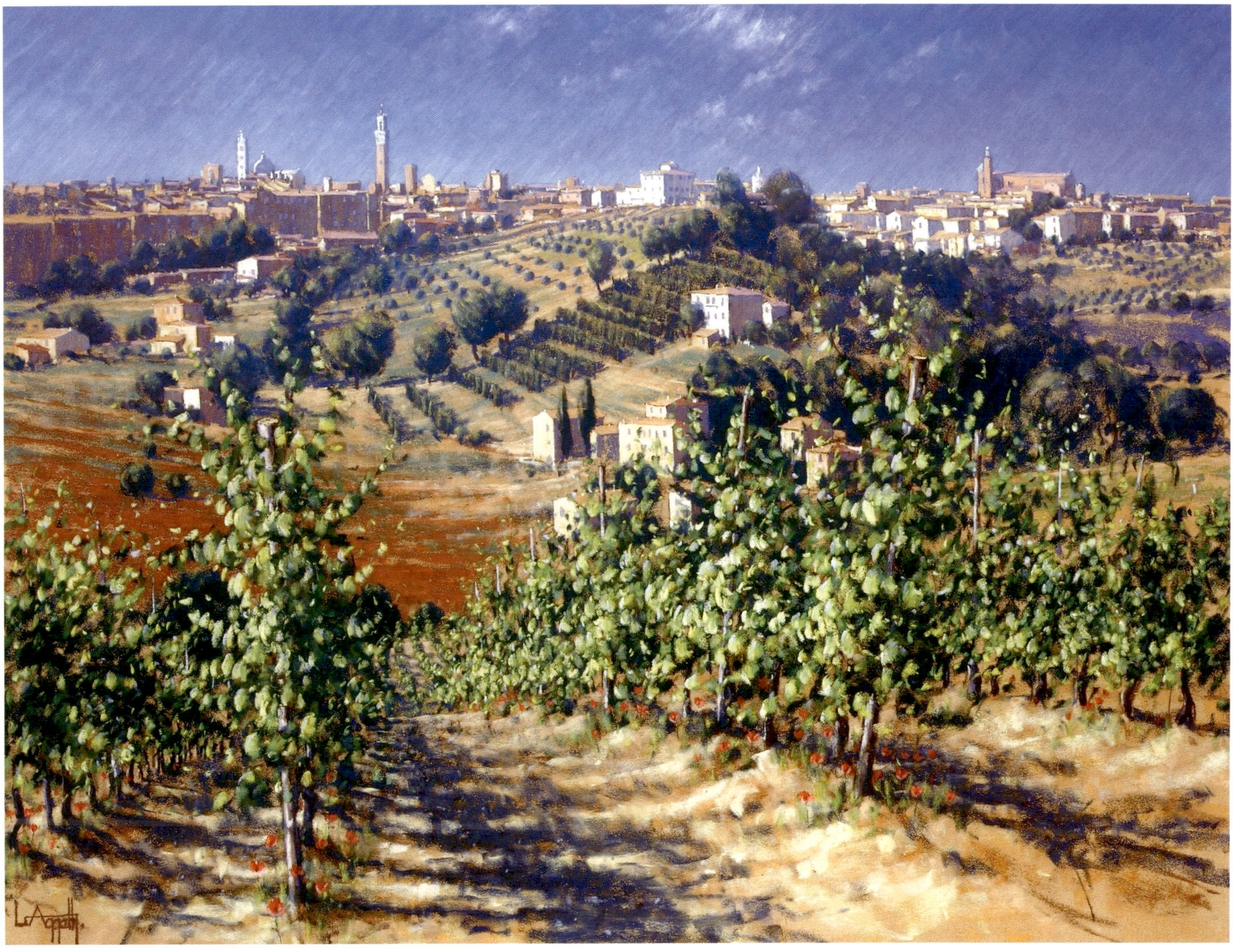

Vineyard outside Siena Pastel 600 x 800 mm

The vineyard takes the eye down and across to the magnificent skyline.

Painting *en plein air* in the Campo is an experience which will remain with me forever. There is no escape; you simply become part of the cast, many of whom in the immediate vicinity, are inclined to stand in front as well as behind you. The square is at its most atmospheric towards the end of the day, as the lowering sun casts longer shadows, the coach parties dwindle, and evening passeggiata (stroll) begins. Outside tables fill, and the constant chatter reverberates from wall to wall, producing a gloriously euphonic rallentando. Twilight turns to darkness, as lighting spills out across the paviours from cafés and restaurants, and the late evening performance begins …

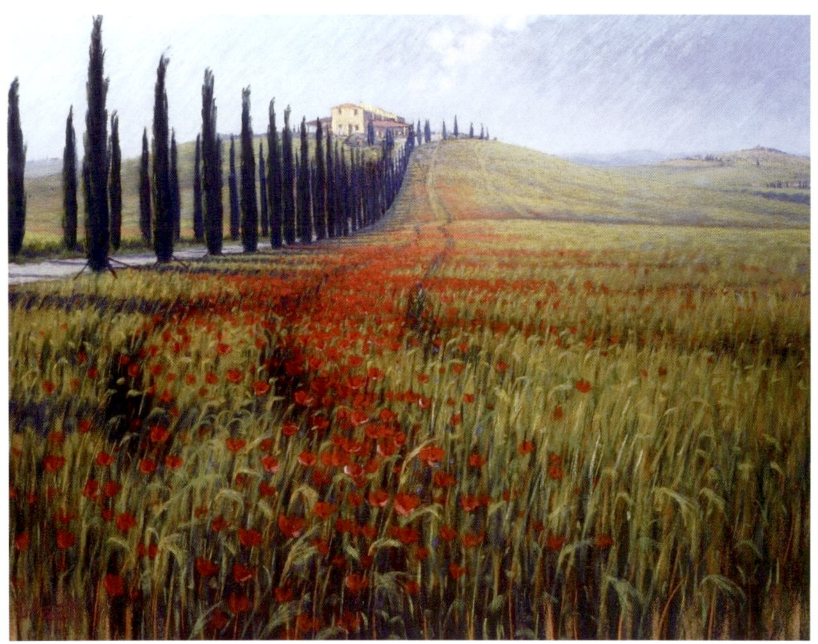

La Crete Landscape Pastel 500 x 650 mm

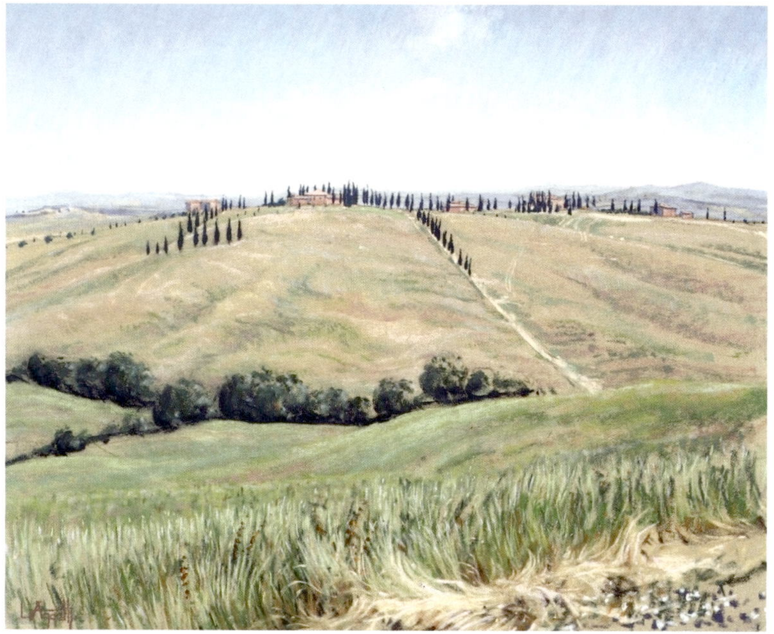

La Crete Pastel 400 x 500 mm

An en plein air *painting which defines the remoteness of the unchanged landscape.*

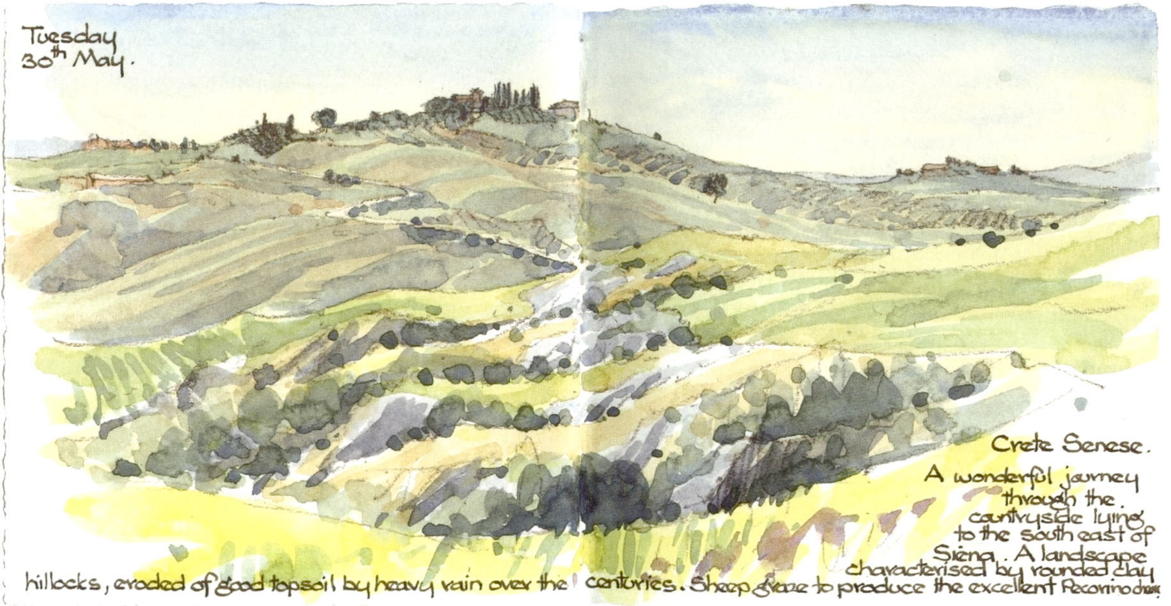

Diary Sketch 30th May, 2000 *La Crete* Conté w/c

The heartland of the Crete Senese lies to the south east of the city, where classic images of lonely cypresses on sun-baked clay hills and remote farmsteads atop crags, accessed by cypress lined tracks, are silhouetted against the Tuscan sky. The area is quite vast, with the epicentre around the Benedictine monastery of Monte Oliveto Maggiore, south of Asciano. There are countless subjects, unchanged over the centuries, and forays along the minor roads will take you to painting locations where you become part of the past as well as the present.

I have, when staying in Siena, ventured northwards into the southern part of the Chianti region, but this area is also conveniently accessed from the campsite at Barberino Val d'Elsa. The Sienese hill towns can also be comfortably reached from Siena, but these will be explored in the following pages, from the site at San Gimignano. The two *en plein air* Chianti paintings reproduced here, were, however, the result of successful excursions out of Siena.

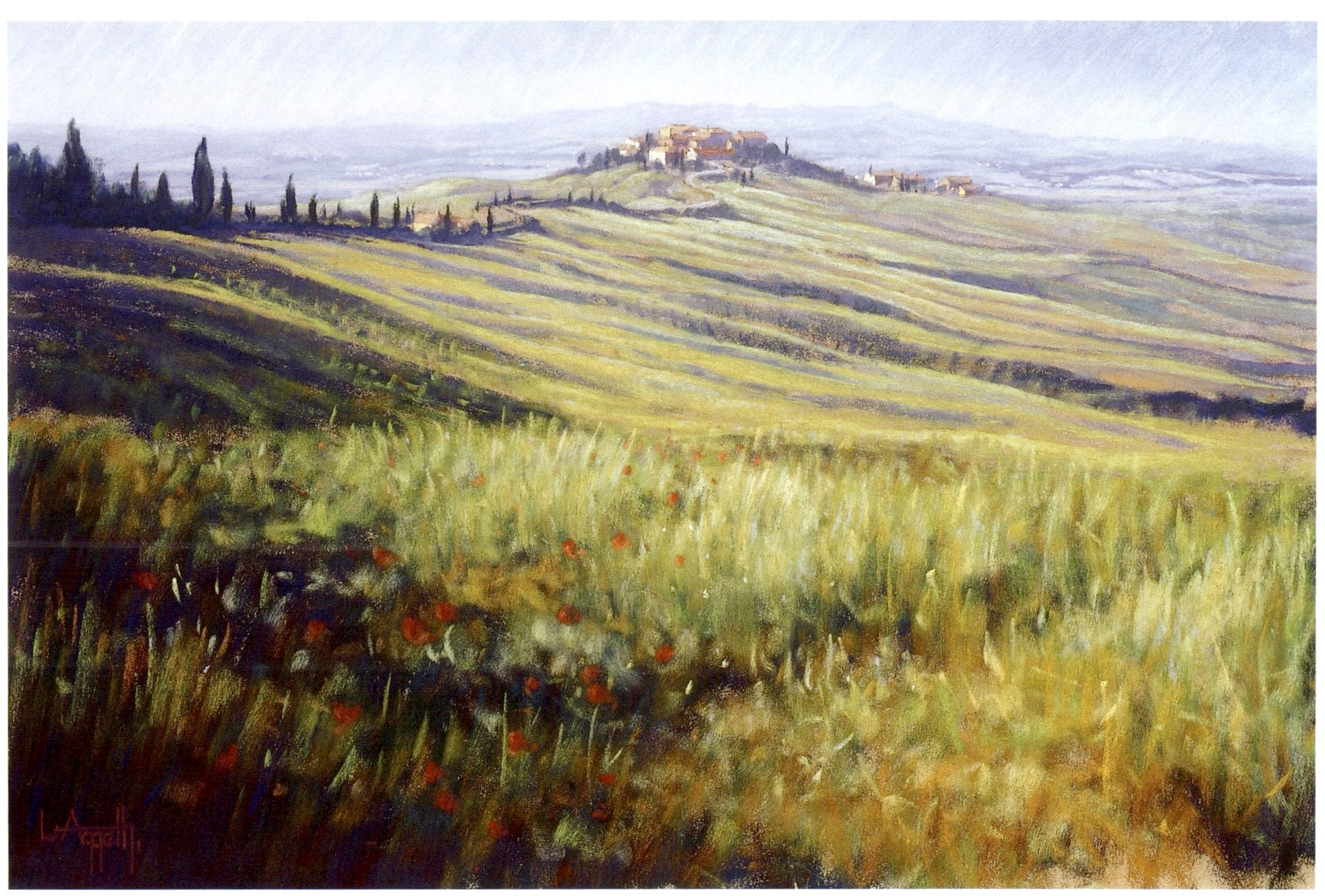

La Crete Pastel 325 x 500 mm

The painting of the prestigious Castello di Ama estate provided a most memorable experience. The fortified villa produces one of the most profound of all super-Tuscans, and a superb Chianti Classico. It is approached along an extremely dusty unmetalled track; our cream coloured VW received an additional off-white coating all over. The owners were delightful, and gave me permission to take the vehicle right up into the vineyards to the spot where I completed the painting illustrated. I was able to use the van's facilities, and for a change did not have to carry the rucksack, easel, board and stool, as I usually have to. I came away with some bottles of their excellent wine too.

Fonterutoli was also painted literally from the side of the VW, but on this occasion, a layby on the Strade Statali 222 from Siena to Castellina in Chianti was most conveniently placed for the view looking across vines and olives, over the hamlet, and back towards Siena. The Castello di Fonterutoli wines rate amongst Castellina's most brilliant.

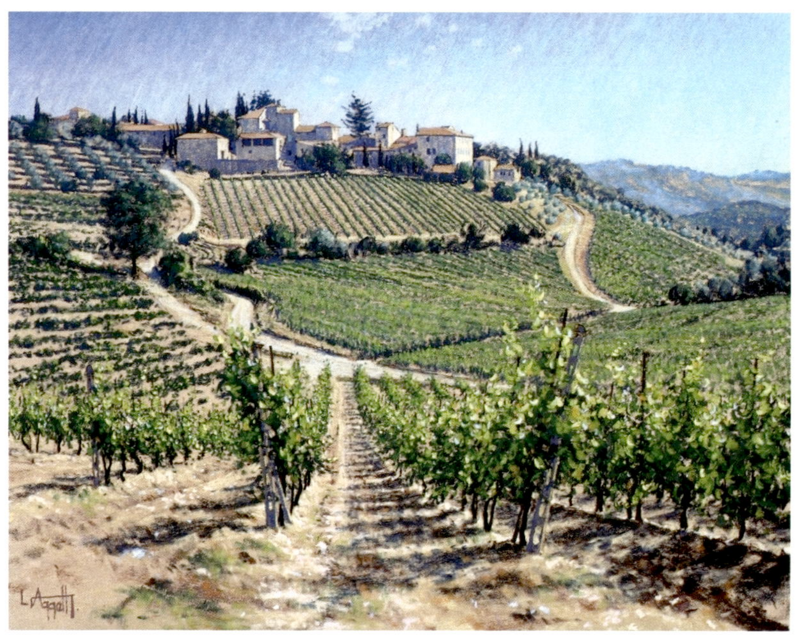

Castello di Ama, Chianti
Pastel 500 x 650 mm

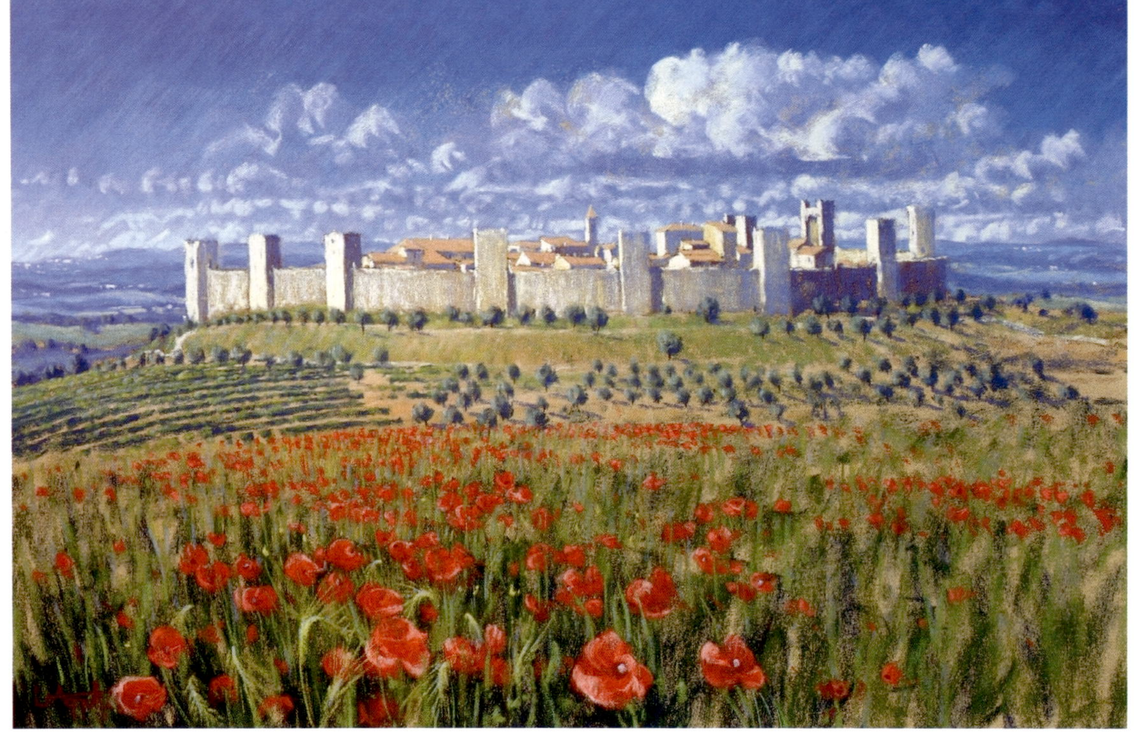

Monteriggioni Pastel
325 x 500 mm

Monteriggioni can be easily reached along the quieter Strade Statali 2, some 15 km to the north west of Siena. A perfectly preserved walled citadel, begun by the Sienese in 1213, it provides a striking subject when viewed from virtually any angle. During May, poppies flourish across the region, no more so than between Siena and Colle di Val d'Elsa, as featured in many of my *plein air* works.

The Boschetto Di Piemma campsite at Santa Lucia, San Gimignano, is ideally positioned for working in and around the Sienese hill towns. It is a one star site, and in need of a face lift, suffering as it does from tourist erosion, so popular is the town. It is ideal for a working visit however, being within easy walking distance of the town, and the marvellous surrounding countryside.

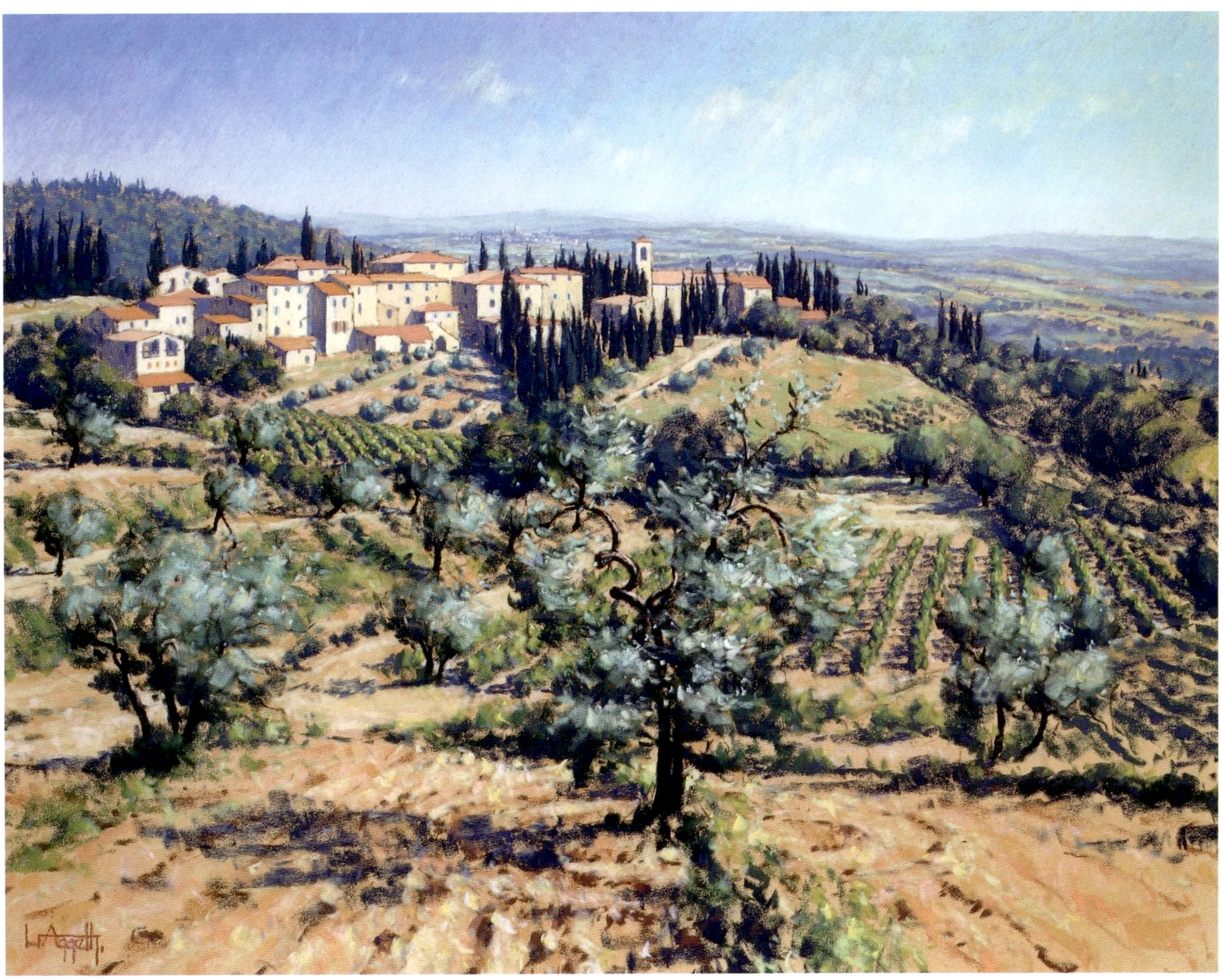

Fonterutoli Pastel 500 x 650 mm

SAN GIMIGNANO

My first visit to the town was in 1959 during the study tour with David Rhys mentioned earlier. We were on our way from Siena to Florence by means of walking and hitch-hiking, when we were given a lift by a local, driving a red open Alfa-Romeo sports car. He was visiting relatives just outside San Gimignano on his way to Florence and kindly offered to drop us in the town for three hours. We gladly accepted, and he took us right into the main square, the Piazza Della Cisterna. We hopped out, and with a wave he accelerated off, our laden rucksacks still on board. We spent an enjoyable if somewhat nervous three hours exploring the town, wondering if we would ever see him again. We finally returned to the square at the agreed time, our fears totally unfounded, to find our good friend already waiting for us, with a huge grin on his face, and hands on the steering wheel, waiting to whisk us through the delightful Chianti countryside to our destination.

I won't describe this miraculous hill town in detail here, guide books aplenty do that. Suffice to say that "delle Belle Torri" as San Gimignano is known, evokes the appearance of medieval Tuscany more than any other sight. The towers were built in aristocratic rivalry by the feuding nobles of the twelfth and thirteenth centuries. In the Middle Ages there were 70 such constructions, and there are just 14 remaining today, enclosed by the walls. Even so, they produce a stunning skyline. One theory for there being so many original towers, is that they were constructed when the town was a major textile centre, possessing the secret of saffron yellow dye, produced from a particular type of crocus. The towers were built to suspend the longer pieces of dyed cloth which commanded higher prices. The cloth had to be kept away from sunshine and dust, in order to facilitate the fixing of the colour. Lack of space prevented the required spaces from being provided horizontally. External staircases would have maintained uninterrupted hanging space inside, and the holes supporting these structures can be seen on the outside.

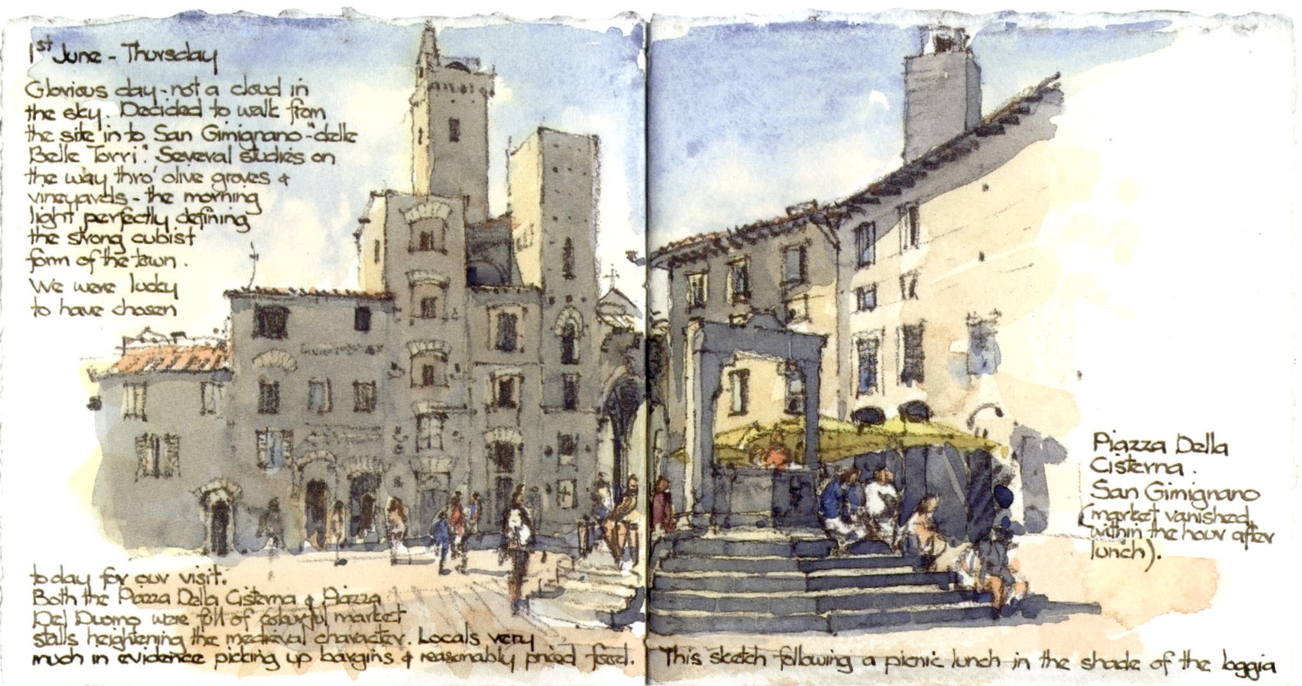

Diary Sketch 1st June, 2000 *Piazza Della Cisterna, San Gimignano* Conté w/c

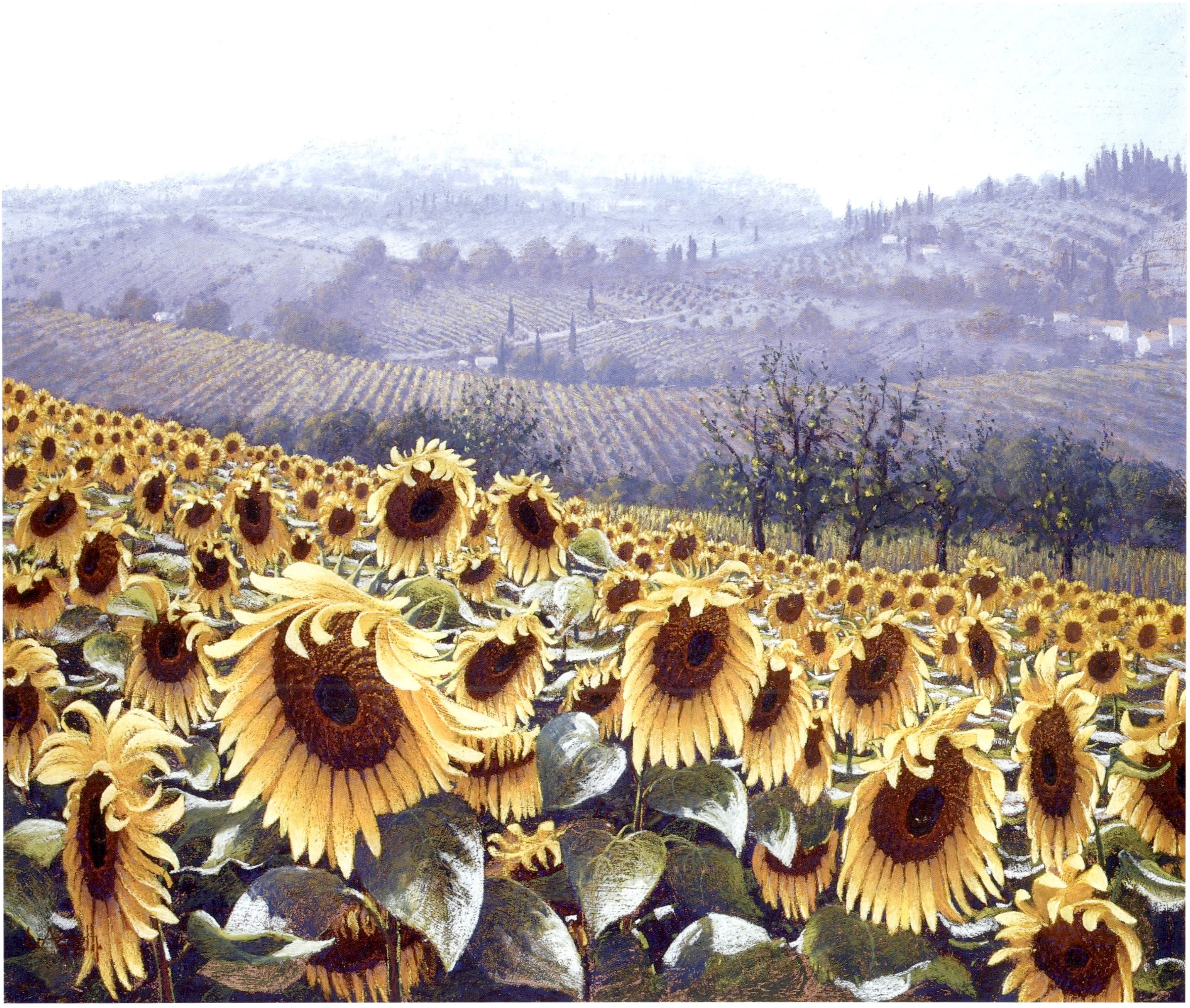

Tuscan Gold San Gimignano Pastel 1016 x 1220 mm

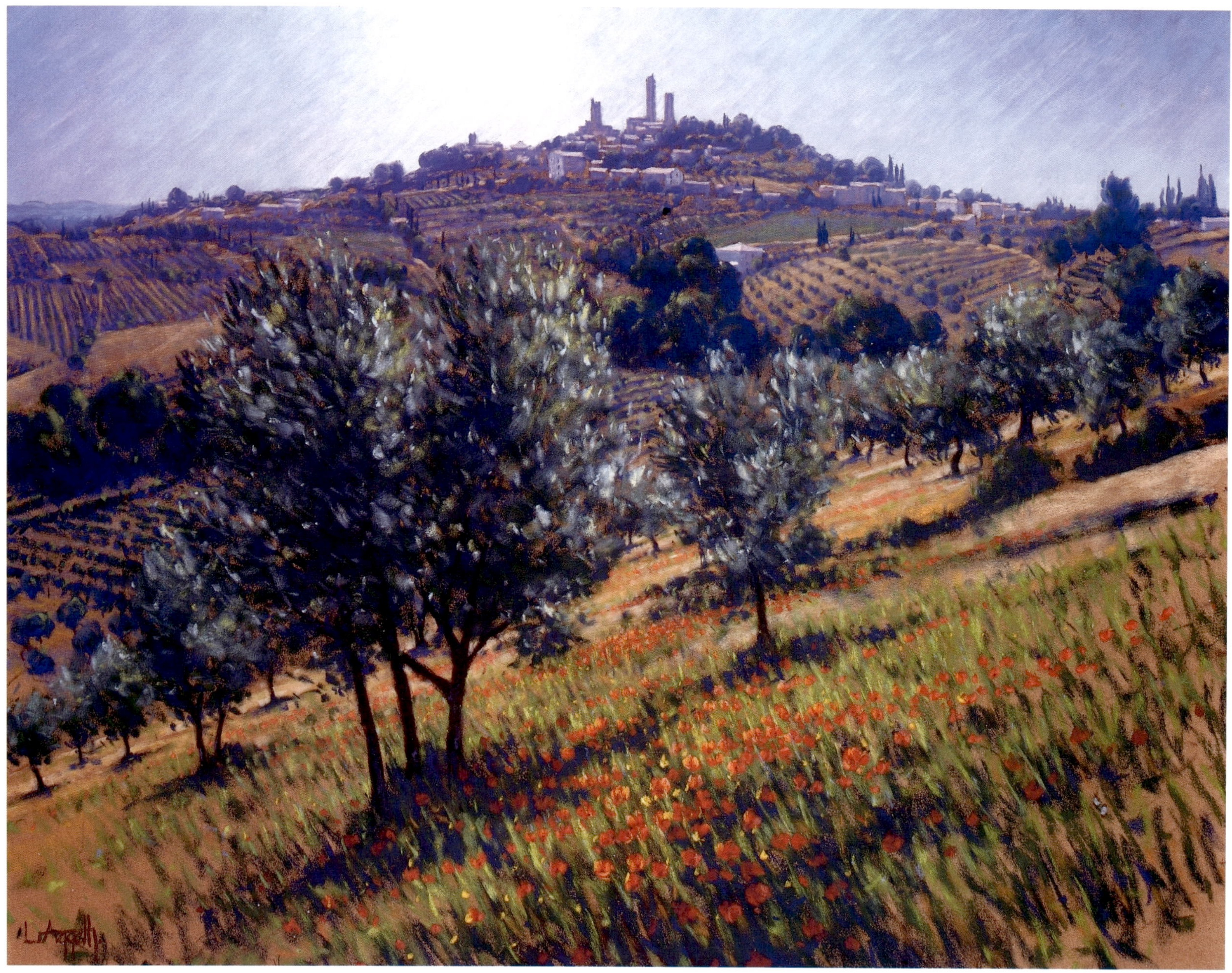

Poppies and Olives, San Gimignano Pastel 500 x 650 mm

The countryside surrounding San Gimignano is absolutely stunning, the town's remarkable skyline viewed from all aspects through wonderfully varied cultivation.

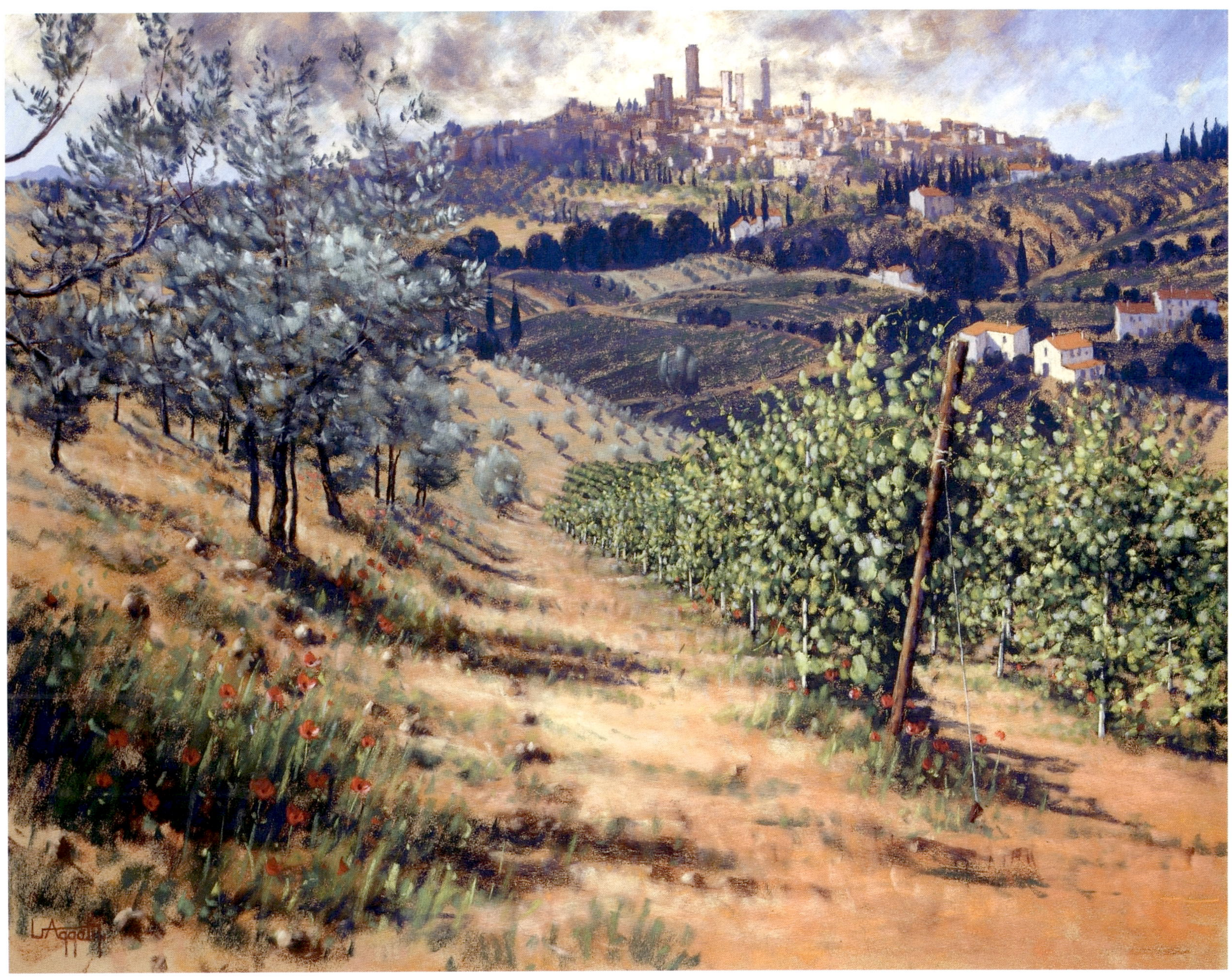

Olives, Poppies and Vines, San Gimignano Pastel 600 x 800 mm

A favourite view of mine, not far from the campsite, and on private land, to which I was kindly granted access.

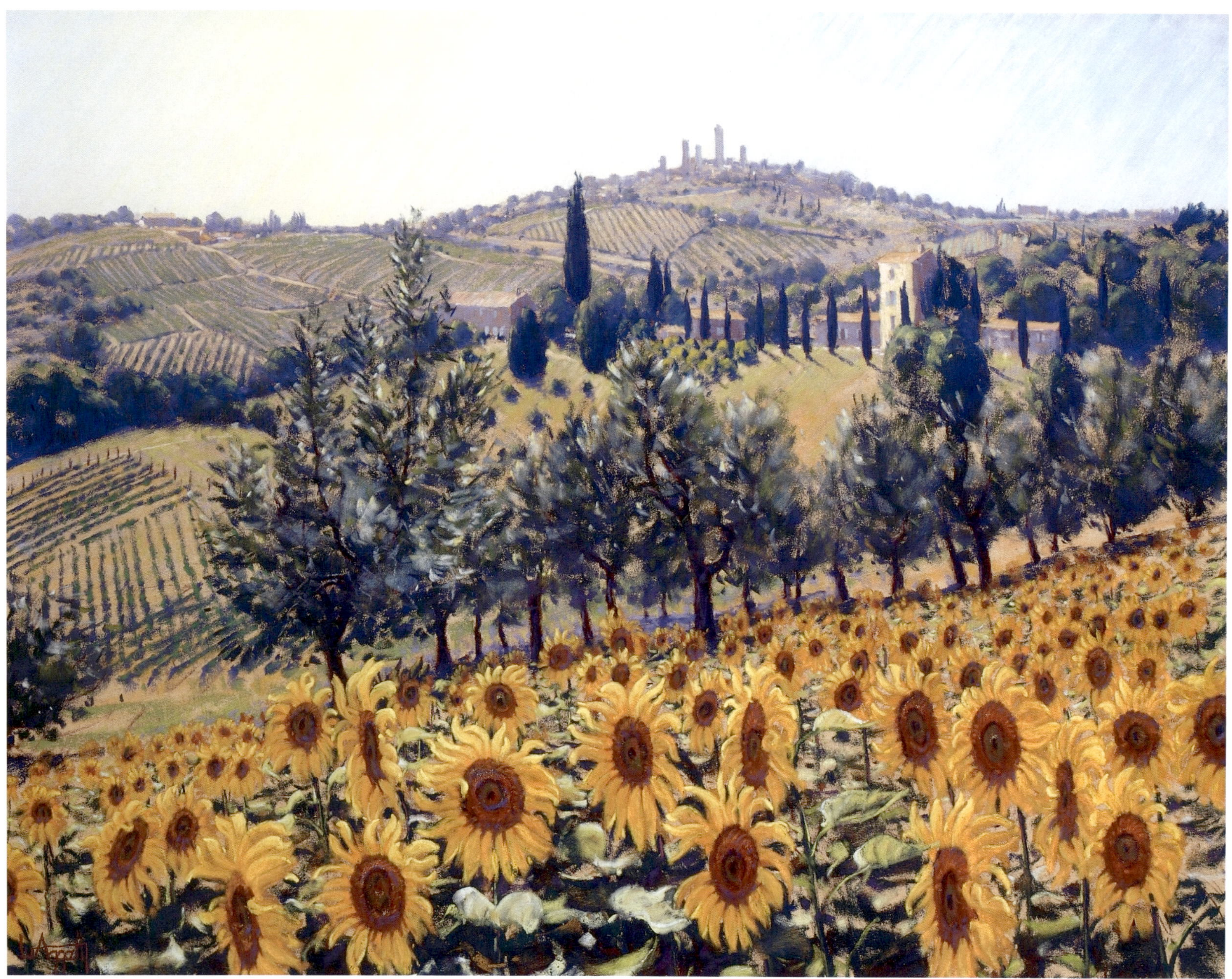

Sunflowers below San Gimignano Pastel 500 x 650 mm

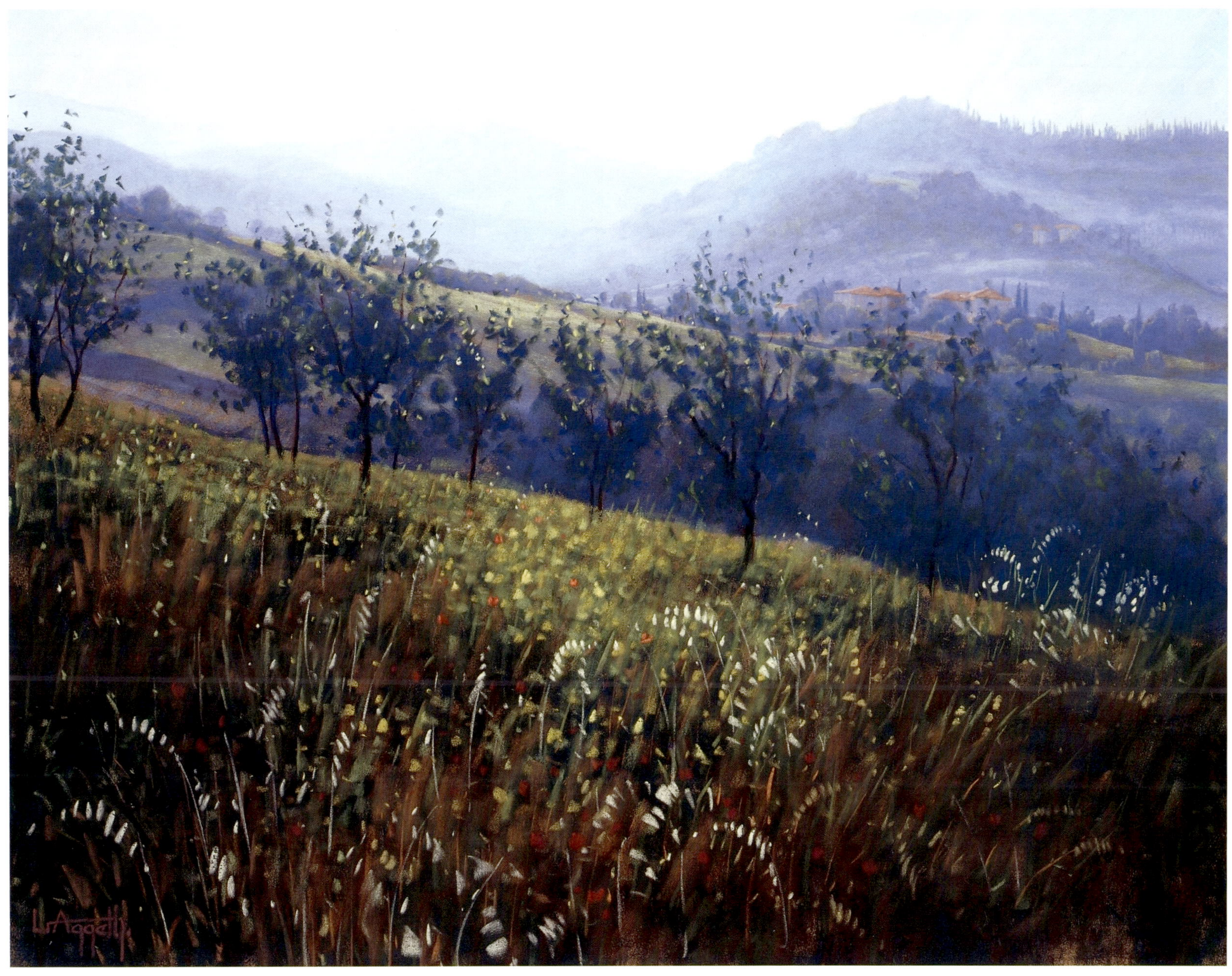

Evening Light, near San Gimignano Pastel 500 x 650 mm

Whatever the reason, the aesthetic result provides wonderful focal emphasis for landscape painting all around the town. The intensively cultivated land, supporting vineyards, olive groves, almonds, vegetables, cereals, fruit trees, and sunflowers all decorated with wild flowers, punctuated by cypress trees, and softly divided by swathes of deciduous woods, provides the multi-linear perspective which leads the viewer across the middle ground, towards this "Medieval Manhattan".

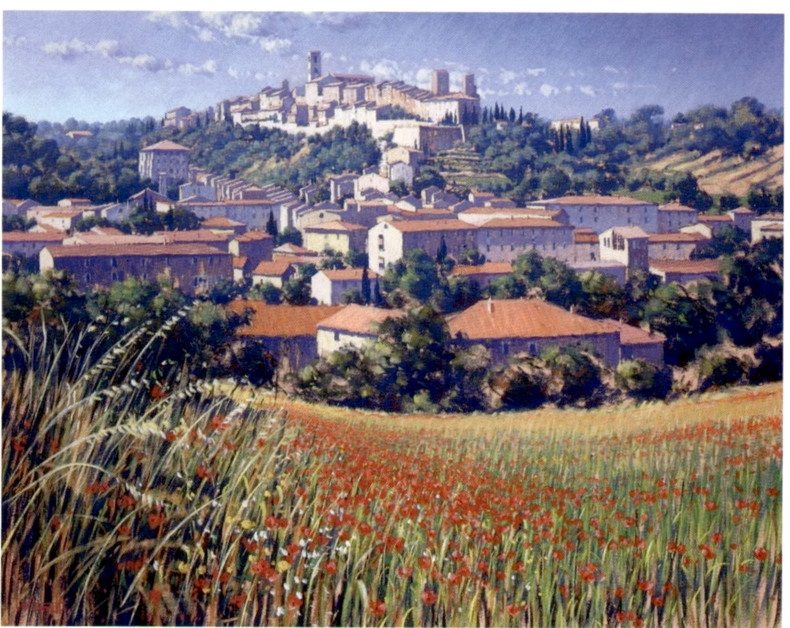

Poppies, Colle di Val d'Elsa Pastel 500 x 650 mm

Colle di Val d'Elsa, to the south east of San Gimignano, is another delight, although not so the lower town, a hotch-potch of light industry. The Colle Alta however, stretched out with medieval palazzi either side of the main street, along a ridge, is stunning. There are also good views to be found from below and away from the sprawl.

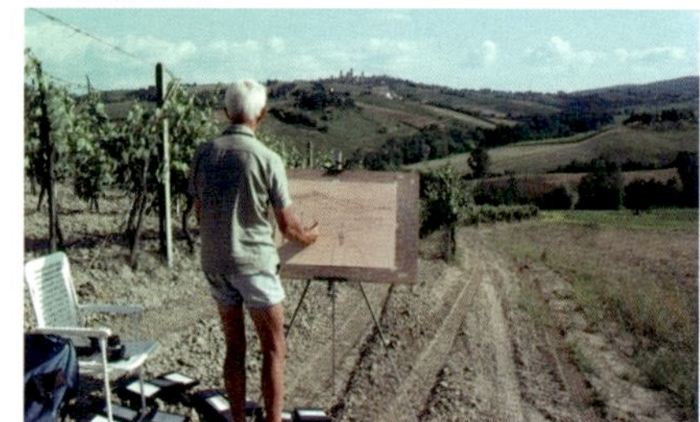

Vernaccia di San Gimignano.

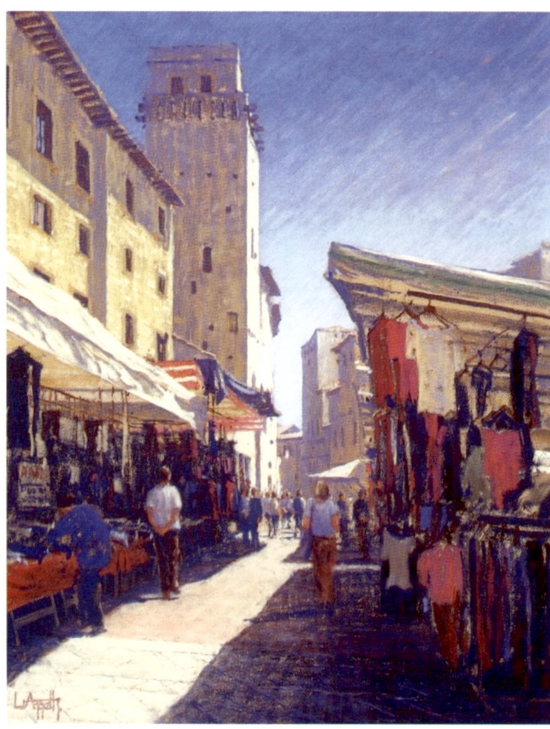

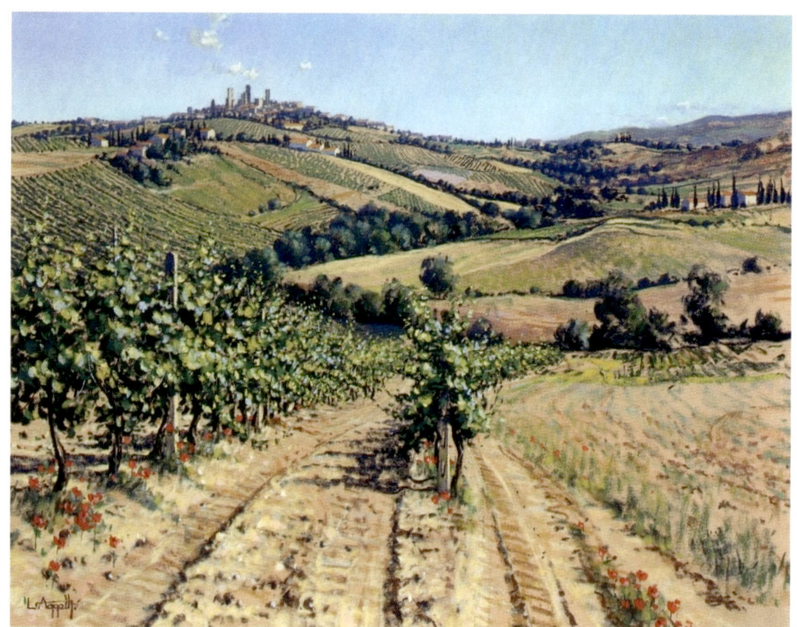

Vernaccia di San Gimignano Pastel 500 x 650 mm

Left: *Market, San Gimignano* Pastel 500 x 400 mm

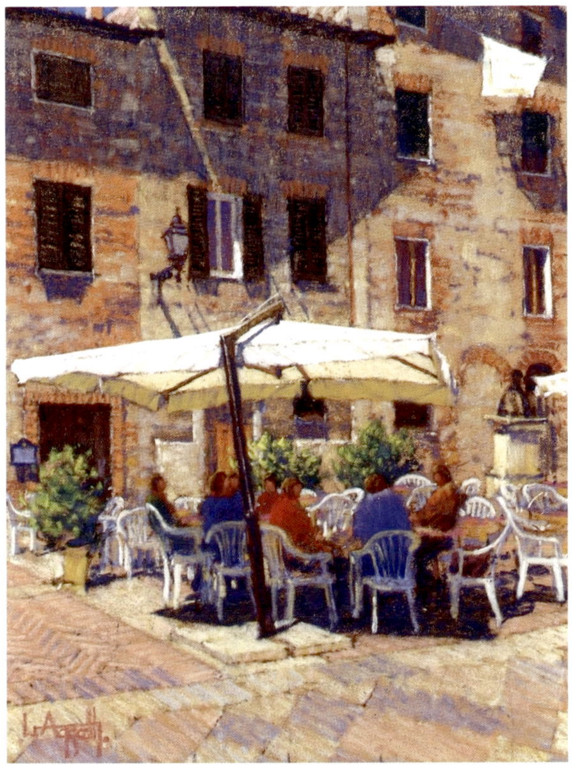

Café, Colle di Val d'Elsa Pastel 325 x 250 mm

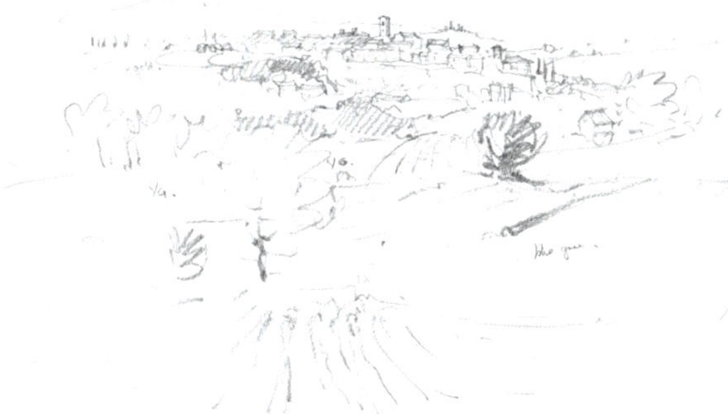

Colle di Val d'Elsa and San Gimignano
Pencil 210 x 300 mm

Right: *It was well worth the trek to find the location for this* en plein air *painting, thus avoiding the sprawl in front of the lower town.*

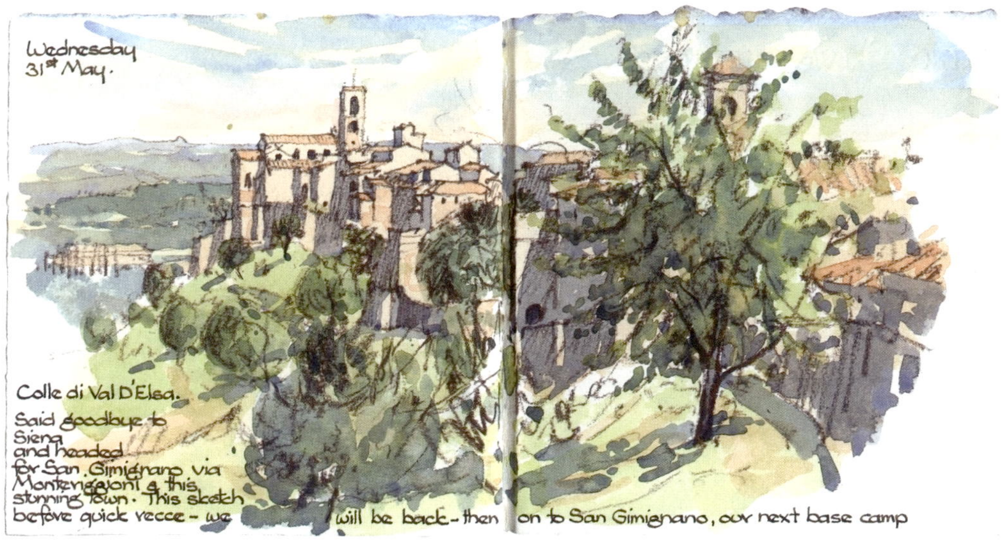

Diary Sketch 31st May, 2000 *Colle di Val d'Elsa* Conté w/c

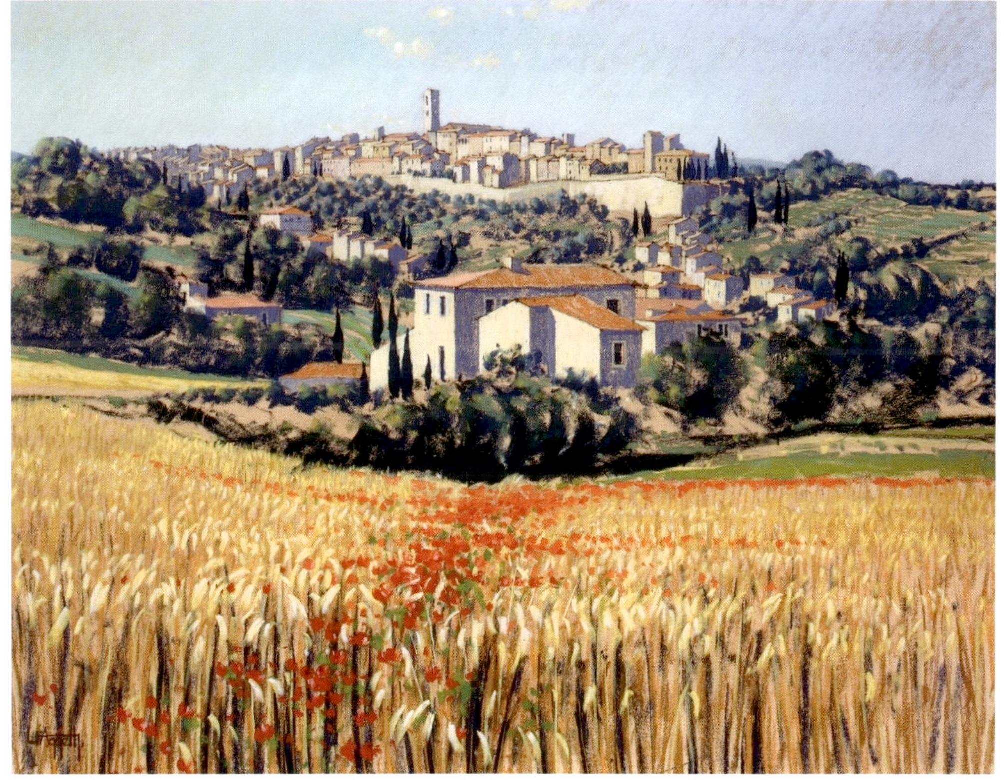

Colle di Val d'Elsa Pastel 500 x 650 mm

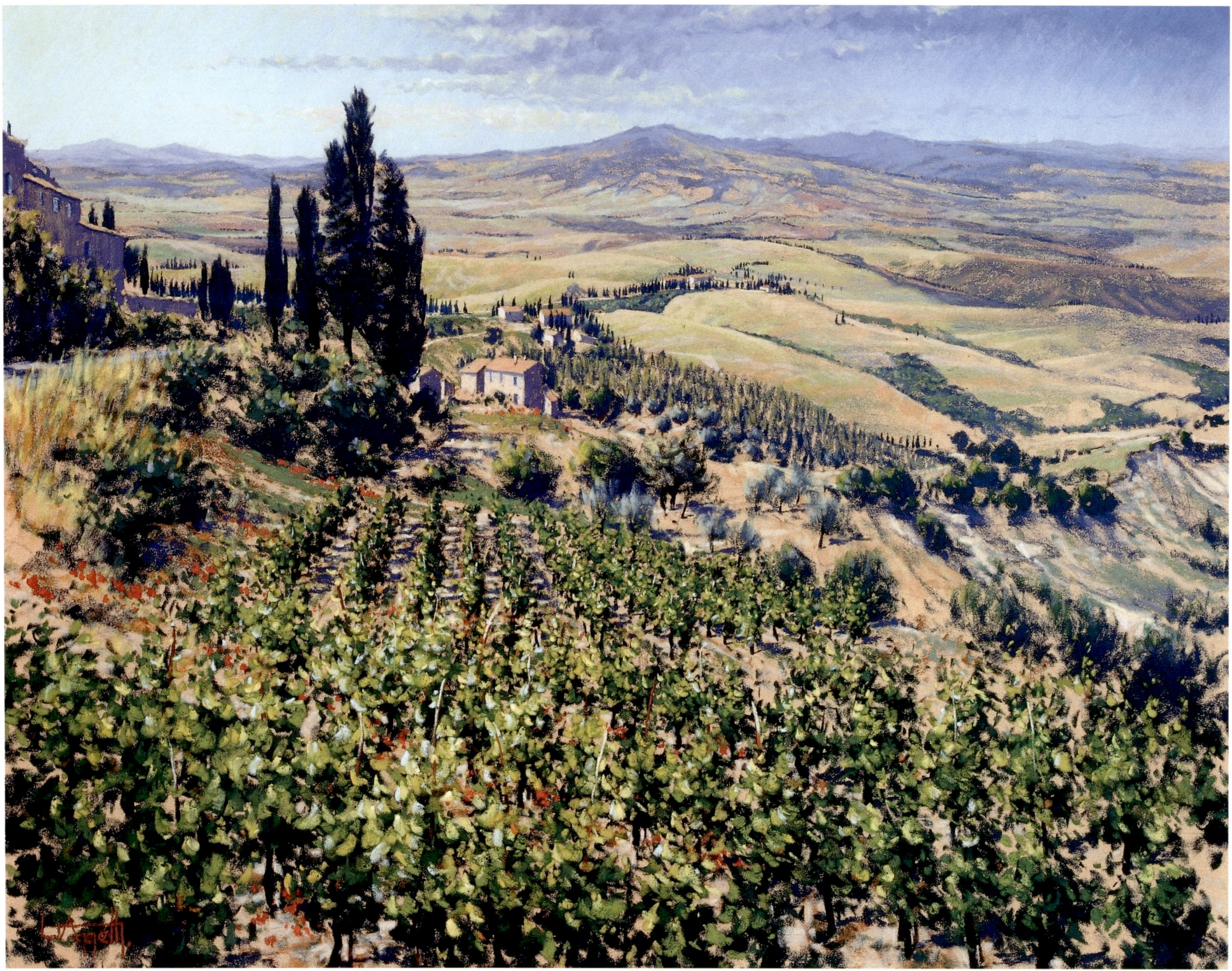

Volterra Pastel 600 x 800 mm

The views out from the Balze to the wild volcanic country on the west side of Volterra are breathtaking. Vineyards on the crumbling slopes take the eye out into the desolation along marching lines of cypress trees.

BARBERINO VAL D'ELSA AND CHIANTI

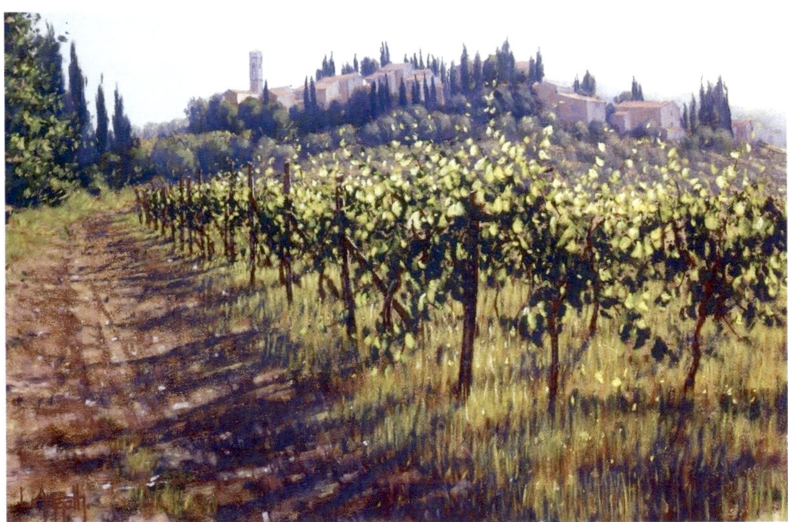

Evening Light, Cortine Pastel 325 x 500 mm

Volterra, over to the south west, and situated high on a plateau enclosed by grey volcanic hills, tinged with yellow, has a wild, bleak appearance. This has much to do with its position right on the edge of the eroded cliffs (Balze), where the walls of Etruscan Volterra drop away into the chasms, made more dramatic by alabaster mines, old and new, rather than the austere stone streets, dark stone palazzo and walled gateways of the town itself.

We move across north eastwards from San Gimignano to Barberino Val d'Elsa in the Chianti Region, where the Semifonte campsite, with its superb management makes an excellent base. There are some superb wines here on the westernmost fringe of the Classico zone, Monsanto being one of the largest estates. Another of these dynamic and brilliant estates, Isole e Olena lies outside the small stone hamlet of Cortine. We were shown over the Pasolini dall'Onda Borghese cellars in the town by Signor Pasolini, and I later painted in their vineyards, looking back towards Barberino Val d'Elsa. Olive groves, cereals and deciduous woodland too, surround this fortified hilltop village, named after a fourteenth century poet.

Diary Sketch 4th June, 2000
Barberino Val d'Elsa Conté w/c

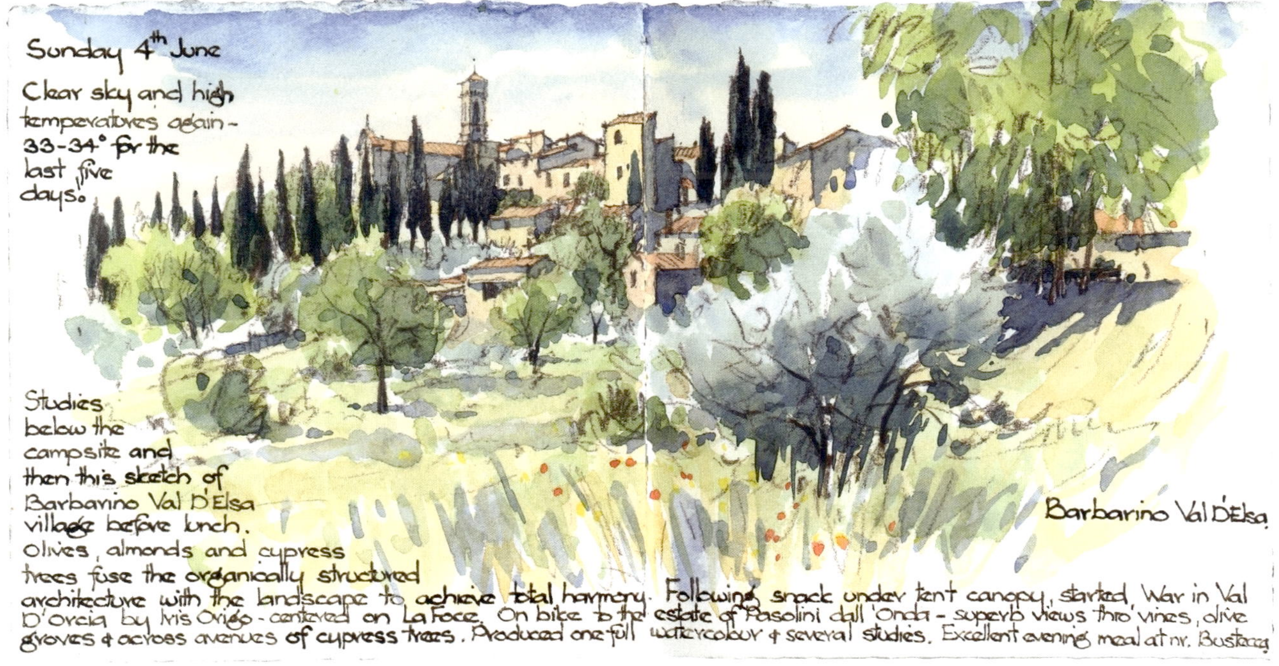

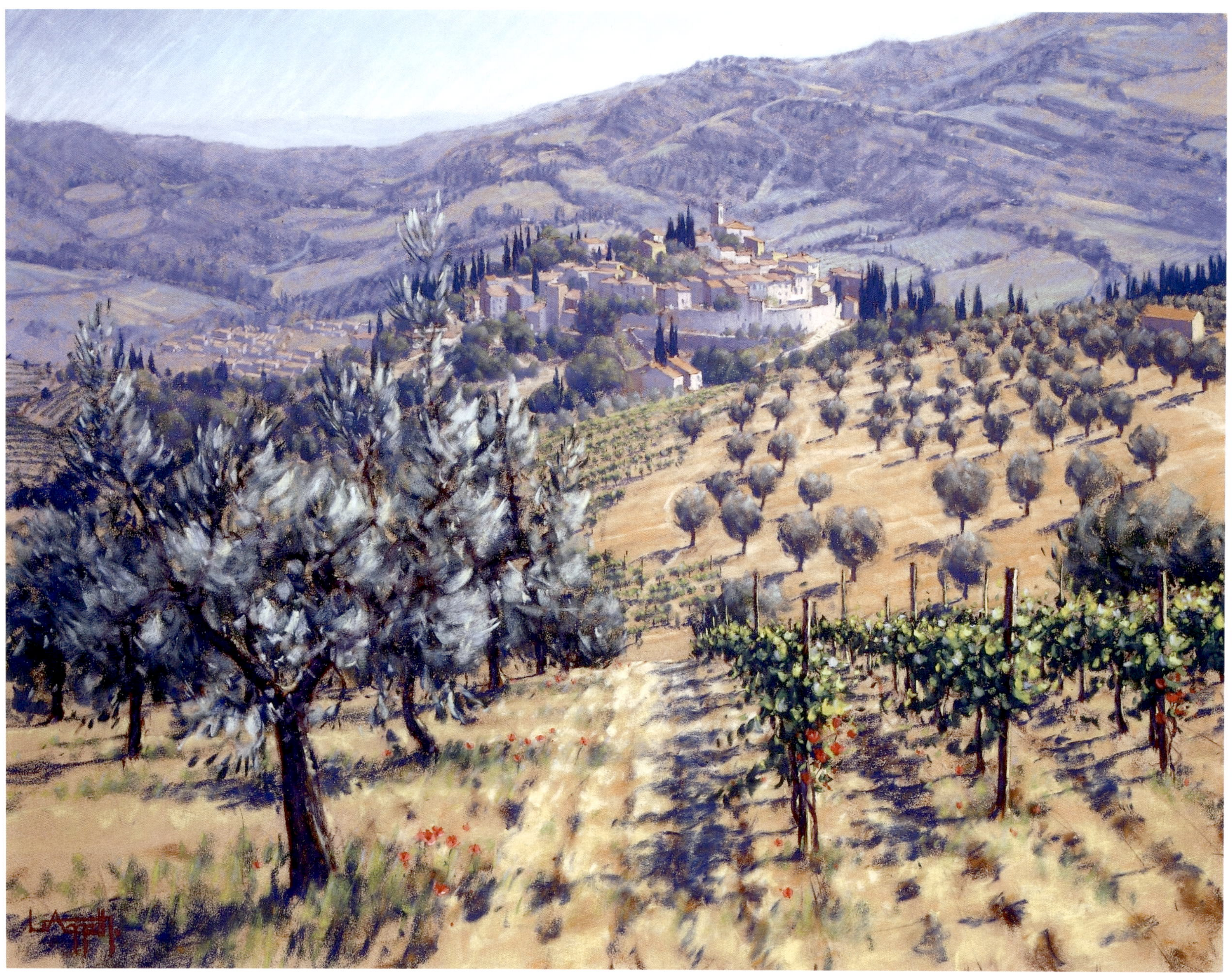

Chianti Spring, Montefioralle Pastel 500 x 650 mm

Elements of perspective, which are typically Tuscan, lead to this perfectly formed hamlet, where the buildings are accessed by a single elliptical street.

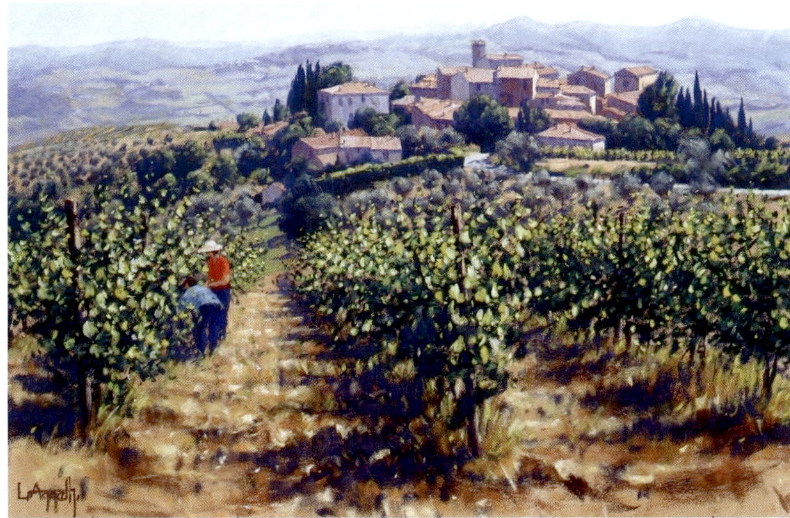

Castello di Volpaia Pastel 325 x 500 mm

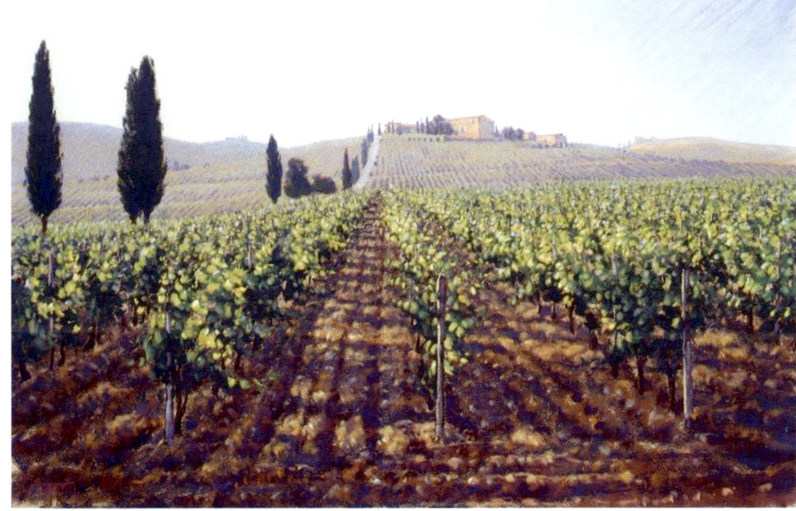

Chianti Classico Pastel 325 x 500 mm

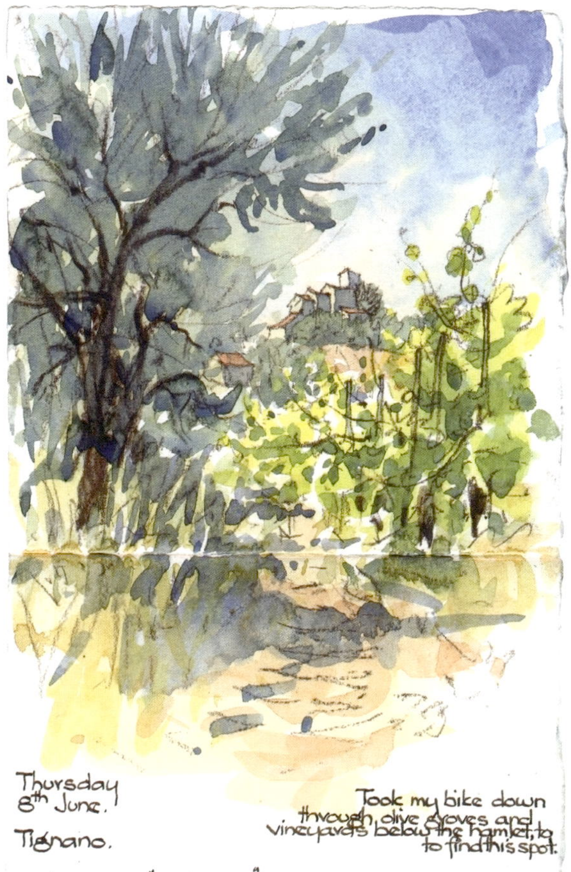

Diary Sketch 8th June, 2000 *Tignano* Conté w/c

The wine estates right across the Chianti region, their colour and atmosphere changing from season to season, provide wonderful subjects for paintings; their undulating, contour-hugging, roller-coaster rows of vines taking the eye towards exquisitely formed and sited Castellos, hamlets and villages; presenting a multitude of variable, and sometimes quite complex compositions.

Montefioralle, a fortified hill hamlet, and Castello di Volpaia, one of the highest hilltop hamlets, which produces wine of real refinement, are such examples, both in the heart of Chianti Storico – the area formed by the Lega del Chianti in the thirteenth century, and now vastly expanded to become the Chianti Classico wine zone.

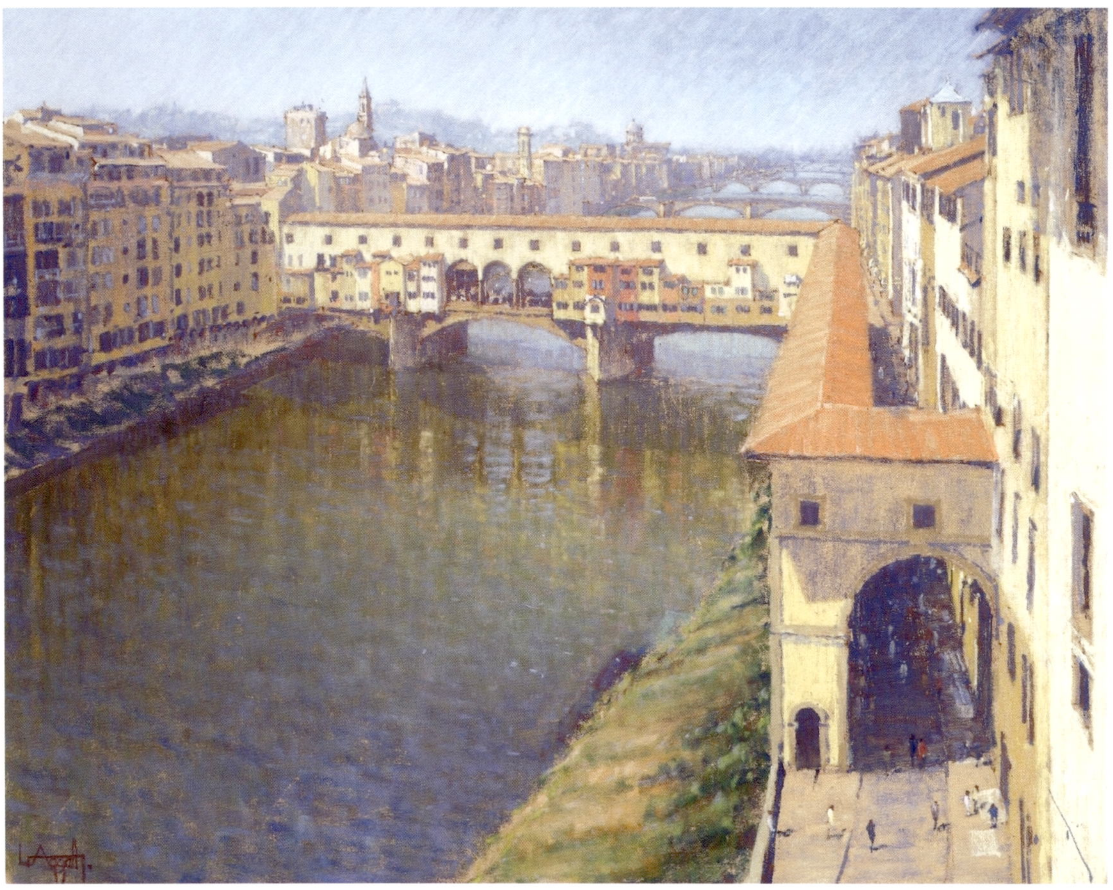

View from the Uffizi, Florence Pastel 500 x 650 mm

FLORENCE

We have visited Florence from Barberino Val d'Elsa by bus, leaving us with an everlasting recollection of an amusing experience which occurred on the return journey. An elderly character, sitting at the rear, and wearing a wide brimmed black hat with corresponding clerical cloak, sang in a musical, falsetto voice, the name of each stop, as the vehicle began to slow down. Many of the names were delivered with an operatic affetuoso, thus: - San Casciano in Vale di Pesa ... Tavernelle Val di Pesa ... and finally ... Barberino Val d'Elsa ... it was hilariously authentic!

For a working visit to this prestigious city of art, the terraced Michelangelo campsite, situated amongst olive trees below Viale Michelangelo, overlooking the Arno, and just east of the Piazzale Michelangiolo, is the perfect location. It is also within comfortable walking distance from the centre. My thoughts on Florence have been expressed at the beginning of this chapter, and these paintings show that I have spent much of my time above this beautiful city, during the morning, afternoon, evening, and eventually observing the sun set over the Arno, the light and atmosphere changing throughout the day. The paintings, frescoes and sculptures adorning the magnificent interiors will be fixed in my mind forever.

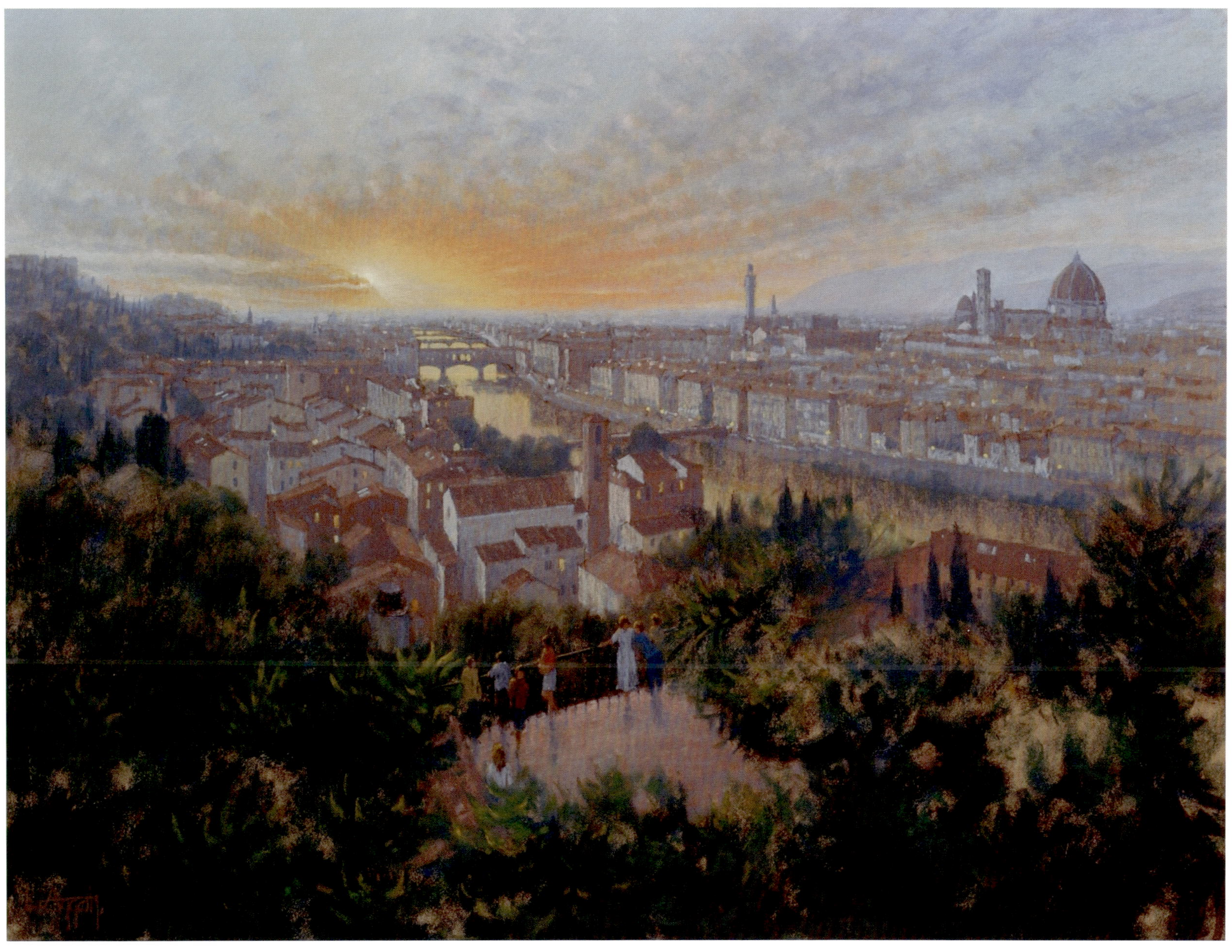

Sunset Over the Arno, Florence Pastel 600 x 800 mm

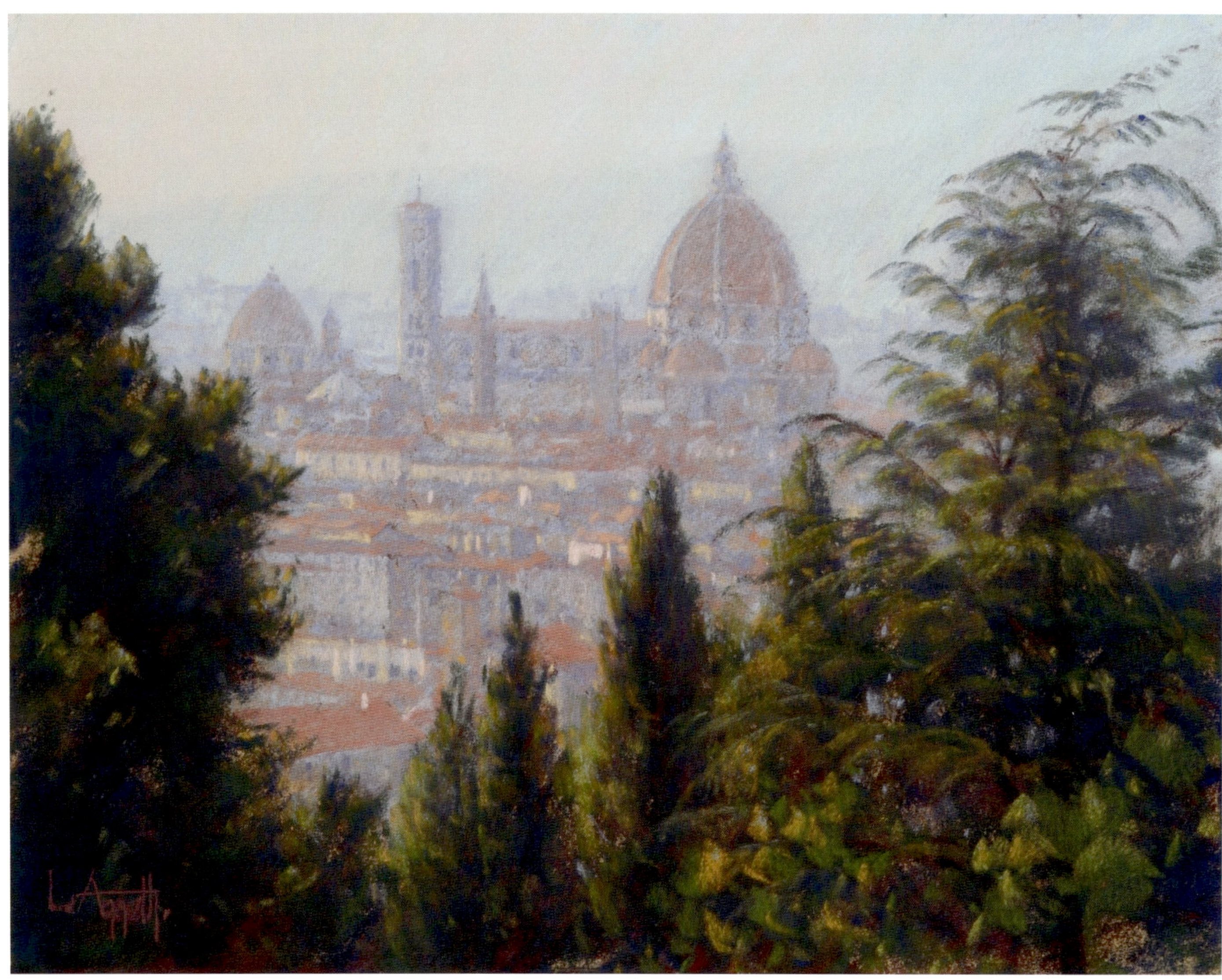

Evening Glow Pastel 250 x 325 mm

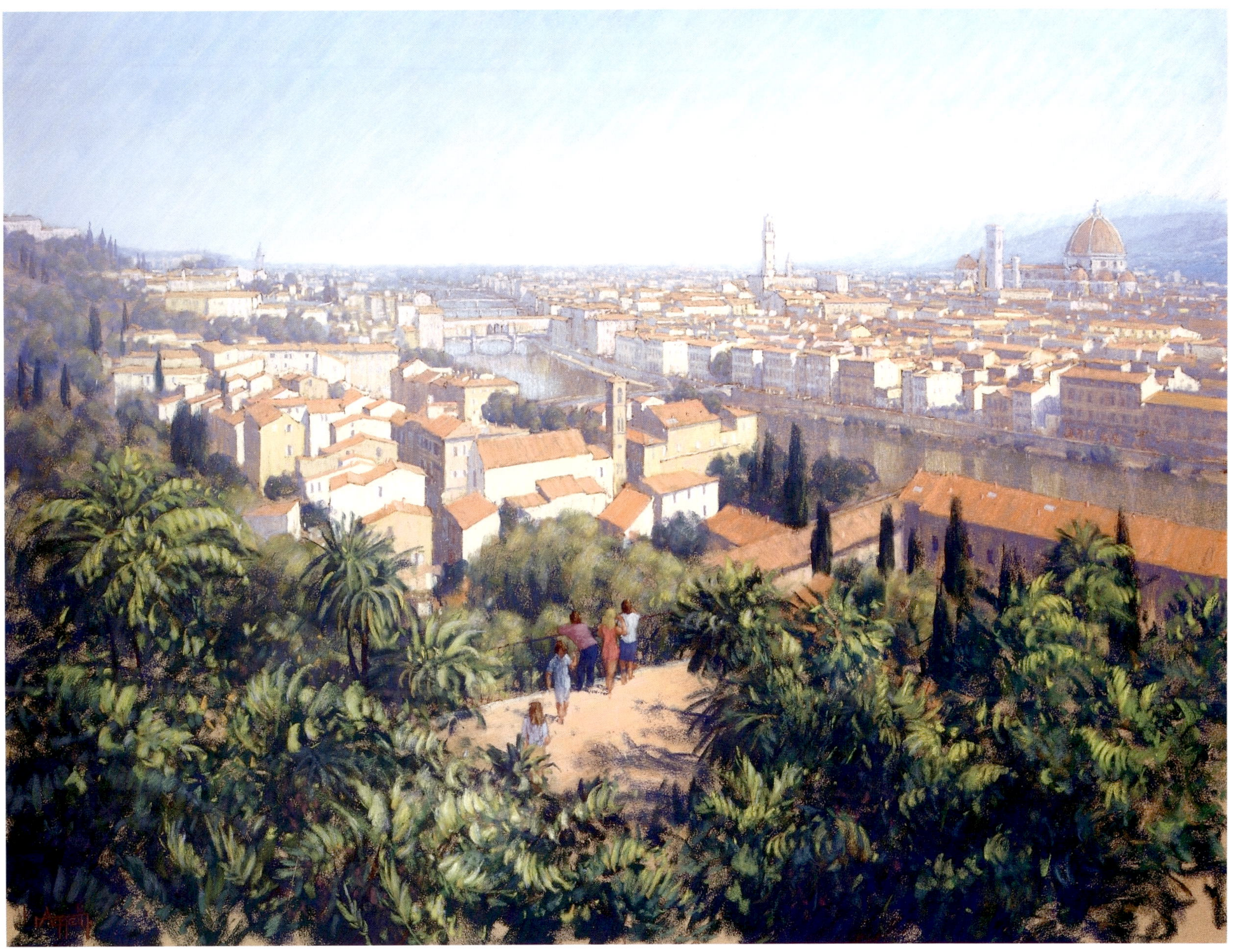

Florence from the Piazzale Michelangiolo Pastel 600 x 800 mm

A studio painting, from the western end of the Piazzale, capturing the morning light.

Venice

This amazing city is one of the few places on earth that always lives up to one's expectations; that never to be forgotten experience of the first visit when we were totally blown away by the spell-binding beauty of the place. Whether arriving by road (my only experience has been by scooter, in 1961, as already recounted), rail, air and/or by sea, the impact that this ethereal city has on the soul borders on the extreme, in terms of emotional excess. It is almost too much to bear if you land on the jetties at either San Marco, or San Zaccaria. Stay here for a month, two months or longer, and you will still not discover every nook and cranny. Many visitors get to know Venice through a series of short breaks, maximum one week, whereby something new can be discovered during each visit, and comfortably coped with. There are many corners I have yet to see and paint, and the sketches and paintings reproduced here have been selected from the fruits of my wanderings to date.

Despite the trauma of continual subjection to floods (the worst in 1966), this once powerful, commercial and naval force of the Mediterranean, has survived by changing roles. Still retaining the façades of 300 years ago, palazzi have become shops, hotels and apartments, warehouses have been converted into museums, and convents have been changed into centres for art restoration. One of the original monastery islands, San Servolo, was taken over by the Venice European Centre for the Trades and Professions of Conservation in 1980, and is now home to the Venice International University. Funds raised for the restoration of Venice are co-ordinated under the auspices of UNESCO, and the Venice in Peril foundation, originally known as the Italian Art and Archives Rescue Fund, works continually to restore and renovate the city, thus enabling us all to enjoy the city now, and to preserve it for future generations. W.H. Patterson held their 15th Venice in Peril Exhibition this year, an important event in London's January Calendar, for which I regularly and gladly provide paintings. The Gallery and exhibiting artists make a generous contribution towards the fund each year.

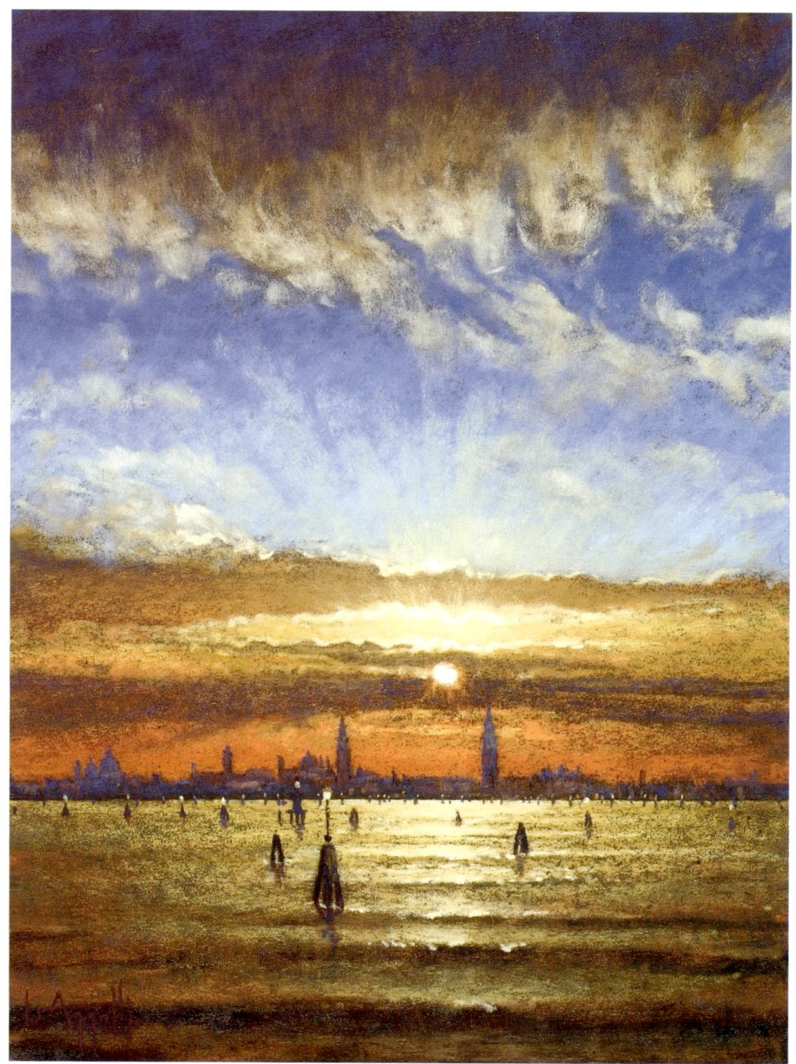

Venetian Red and Gold Pastel 650 x 500 mm

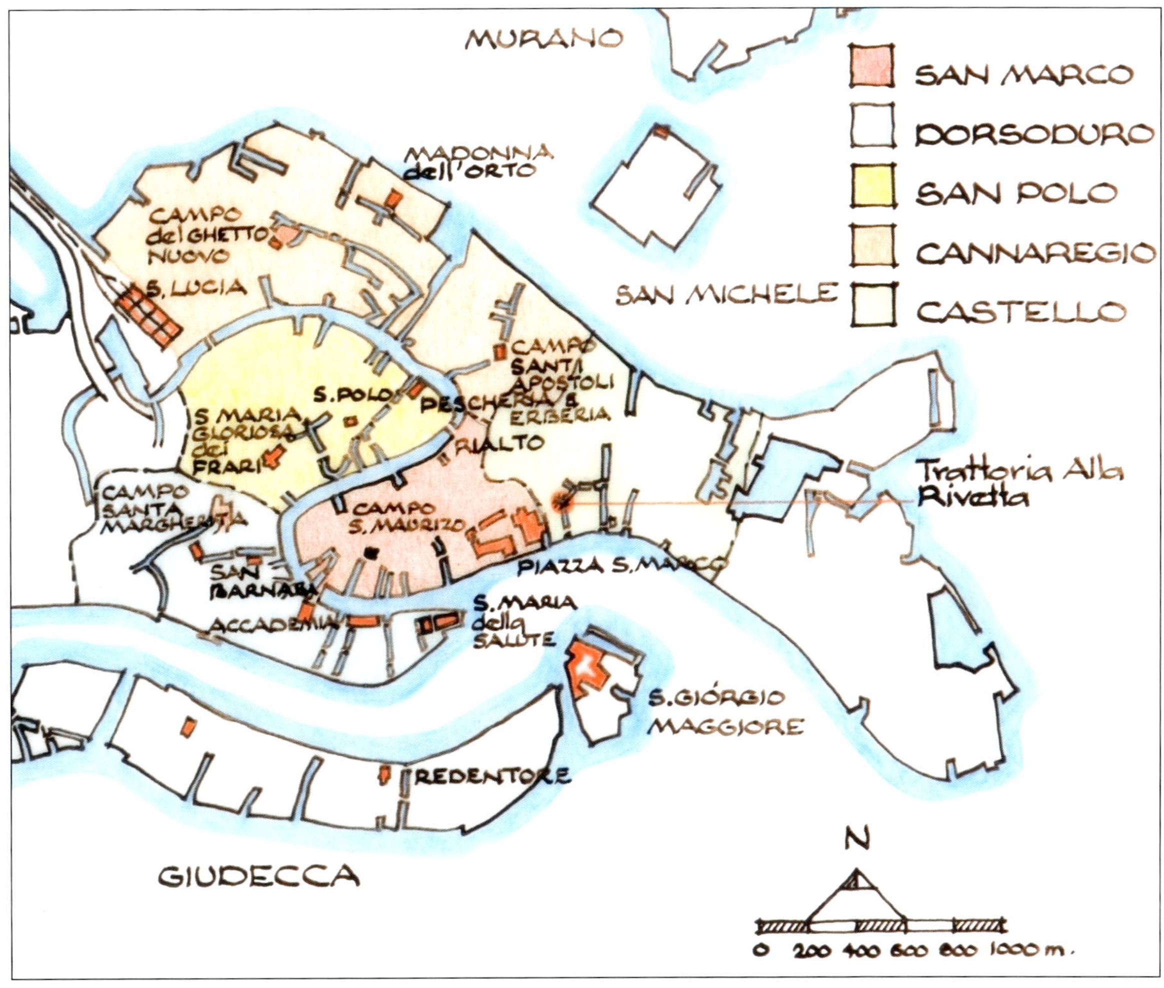

At the time of writing this book I have visited all six of the ancient administrative districts (sestieri) of Venice, and painted in four of them. So there is plenty of scope for further work here; practically an inexhaustible supply of material, I would say. I have worked in all directions from the two hotels used so far, both conveniently and centrally placed in San Marco; the small and excellent Hotel Novocento, along the Calle del Dose da Ponte, and the even smaller Hotel Diana in the Calle Specchieri just off the Piazza San Marco. I suspect we will try a self-catering arrangement next, the markets are so good! The restaurants are too, and we have a favourite which I will mention near the conclusion.

I have arranged the various diary sketches and paintings into a clockwise perambulation of the sestieri visited, beginning with San Marco.

SAN MARCO

It is great fun to work in the Piazza San Marco, although the ever inquisitive throng, are prone to repeatedly obstruct your view of the subject matter. If you are able to put up with this, and the inevitable questioning, then it is quite an experience, comparable to that of the Campo in Siena, mentioned earlier, and other popular arenas. Grand spaces such as these need people to bring them alive with movement and scale. The diary sketch shown here, slightly spoiled with watercolour seeping behind the binding from another sketch, was made under a warm grey sky, with spots falling, turning later to rain. I was just protected under the edge of the packed colonnade beside Quadri's Café.

An altogether different atmosphere arrives with nightfall. The Gran Caffè Quadri and Gran Caffè Lavena, alternate their musical offerings from beneath their lit canopies, vying with that emerging from the Caffè Florian opposite, which is far enough away for the notes not to clash. Under artificial lighting the mosaics of Basilica San Marco glowingly contrast with the night sky, and reflect beautifully in the rain-soaked stone and marble paving, or when the square is flooded from the Molo Quayside at acqua alta (high tide), or partially so, as depicted here.

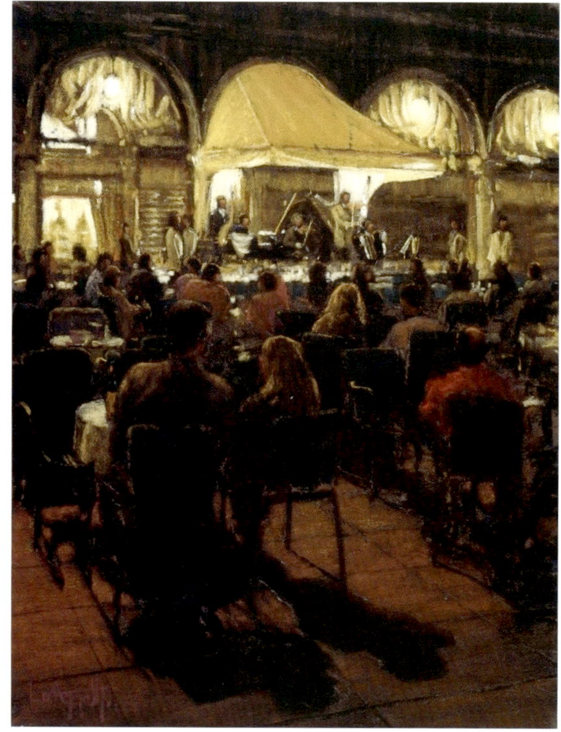

Night Serenade Pastel 325 x250 mm

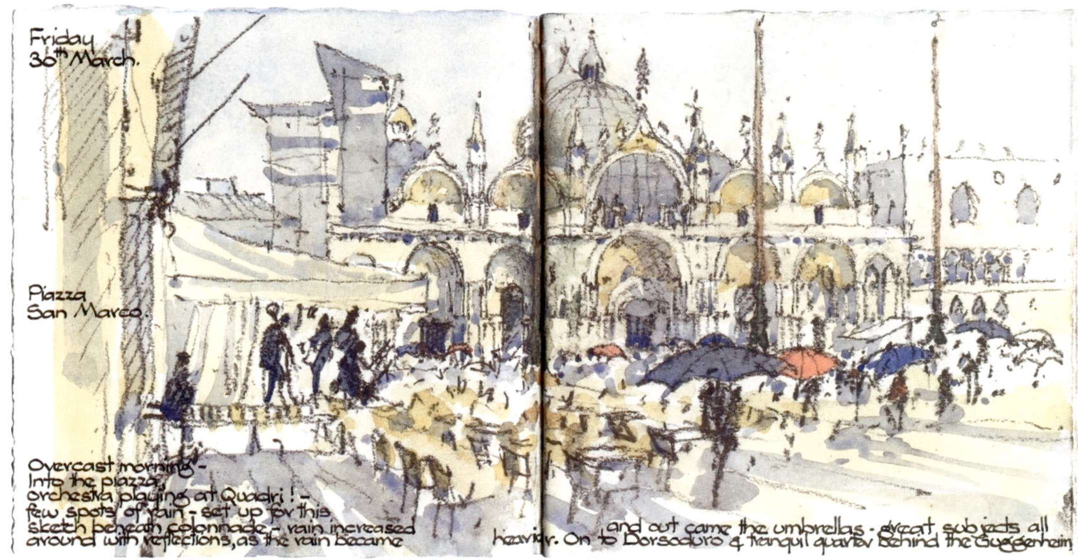

Diary Sketch 30th March, 2007 *Basilica San Marco from Gran Caffè Quadri* Conté w/c

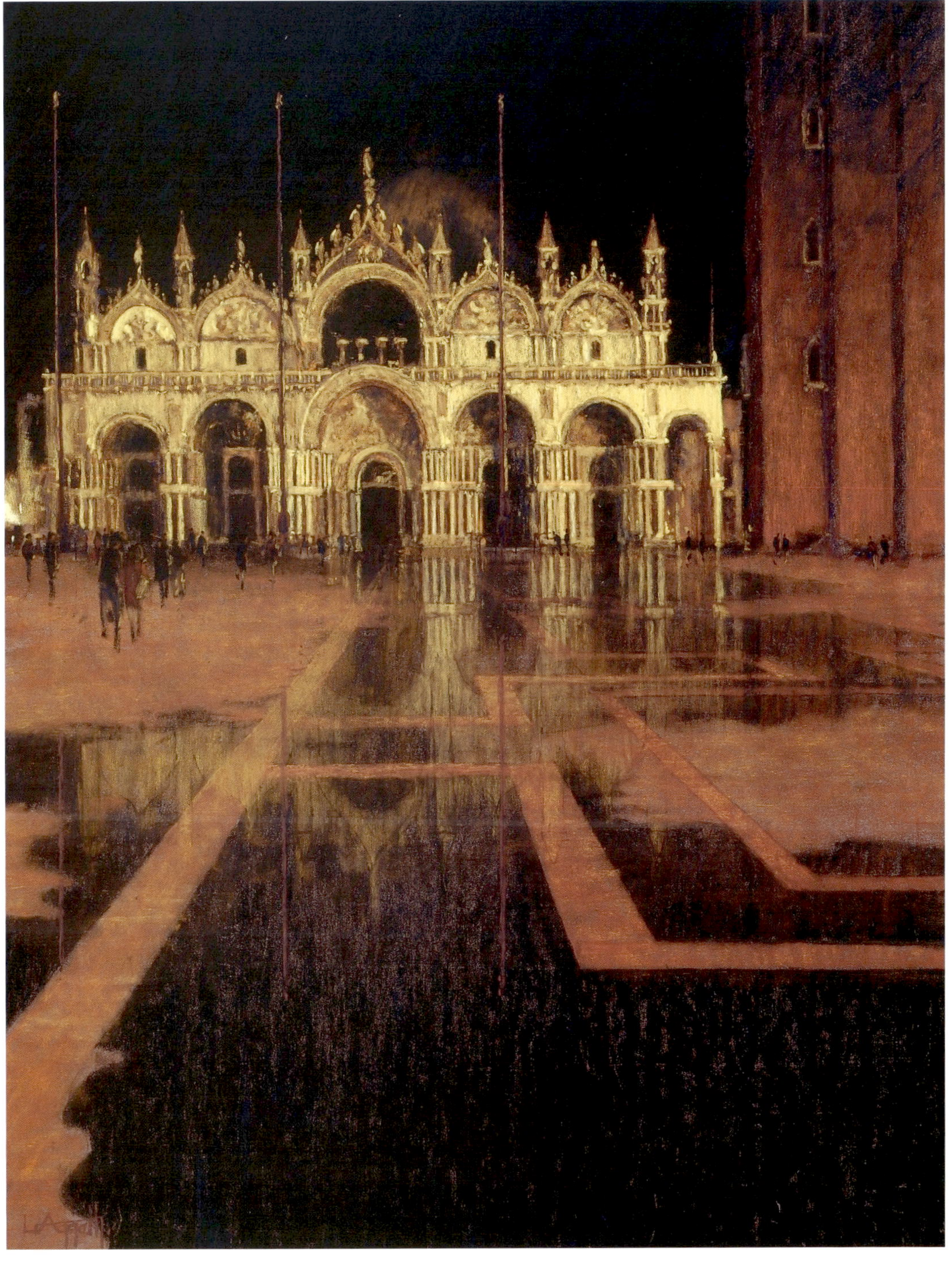

Night Reflections,
Piazza San Marco
Pastel 650 x 500 mm

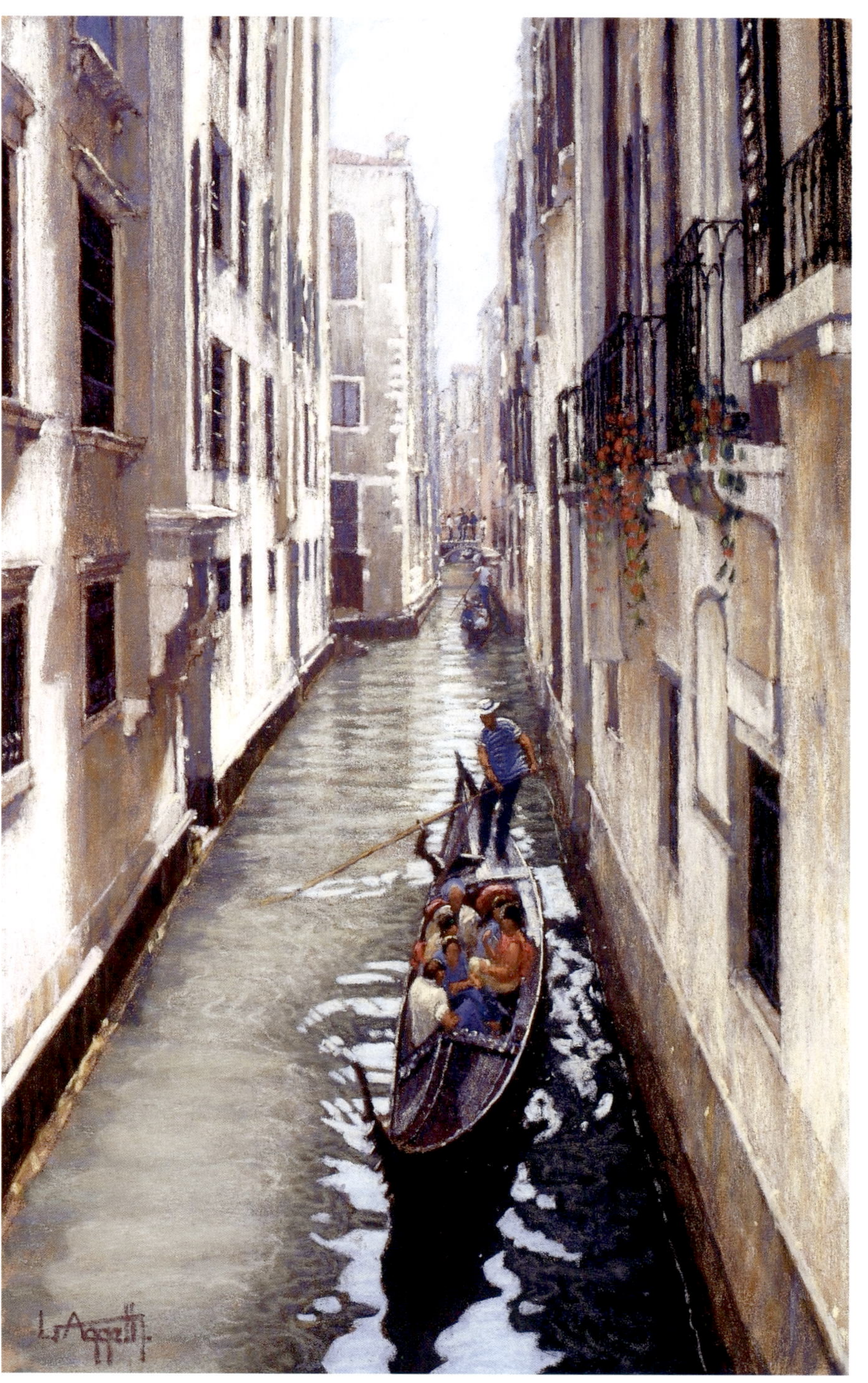

Venetian Jade Pastel 500 x 325 mm

One of the few paintings where I pay homage to the gondola. They are not so prevalent in the quieter backwaters, away from the touristy centre.

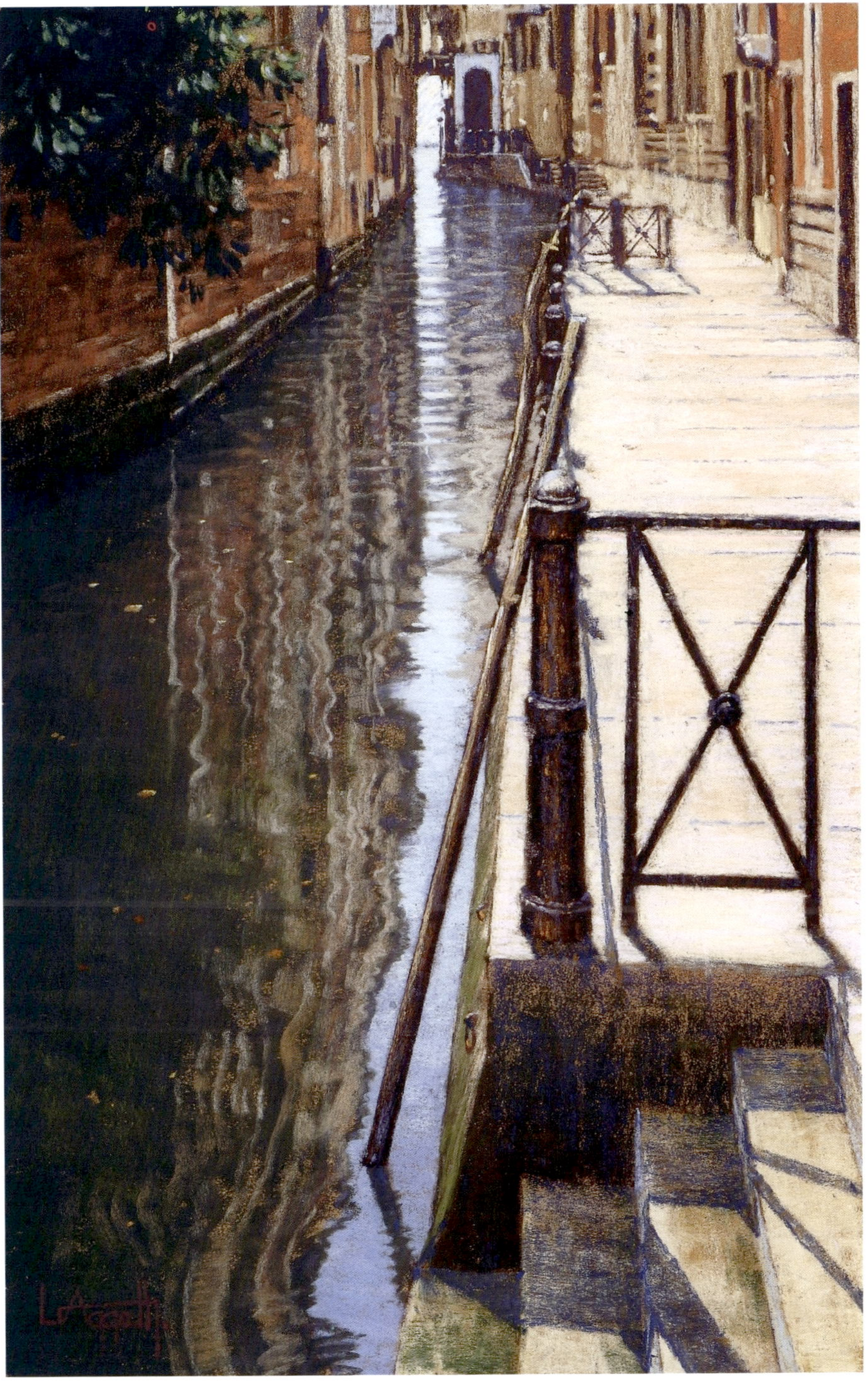

Reflections Pastel 500 x 325 mm

Typical fondamenta detailing, beautifully put together.

The views across the Canale, and Bacino di San Marco, from the Molo San Marco, to the island of San Giorgio Maggiore, just detached from the western end of Giudecca, are beautiful. Palladio's church and monastery, which are among his greatest architectural achievements, float like a stage set, so perfect is the composition. The island will become one, quite literally, this summer. As this book nears completion (May 2007), the island's renovated open air theatre will be reopening to host Venice's new open air opera festival. Performances of *A Night In Venice*, by Johann Strauss, will be performed from May to October, 2007.

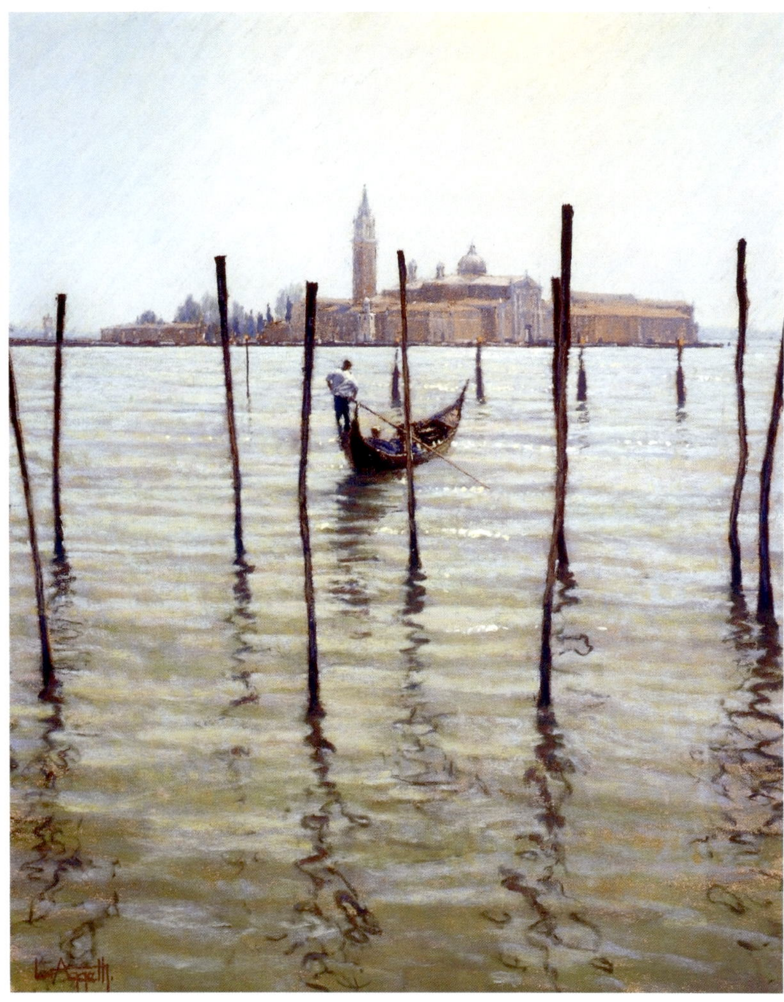

San Giorgio Maggiore, from Molo San Marco Pastel 500 x 400 mm

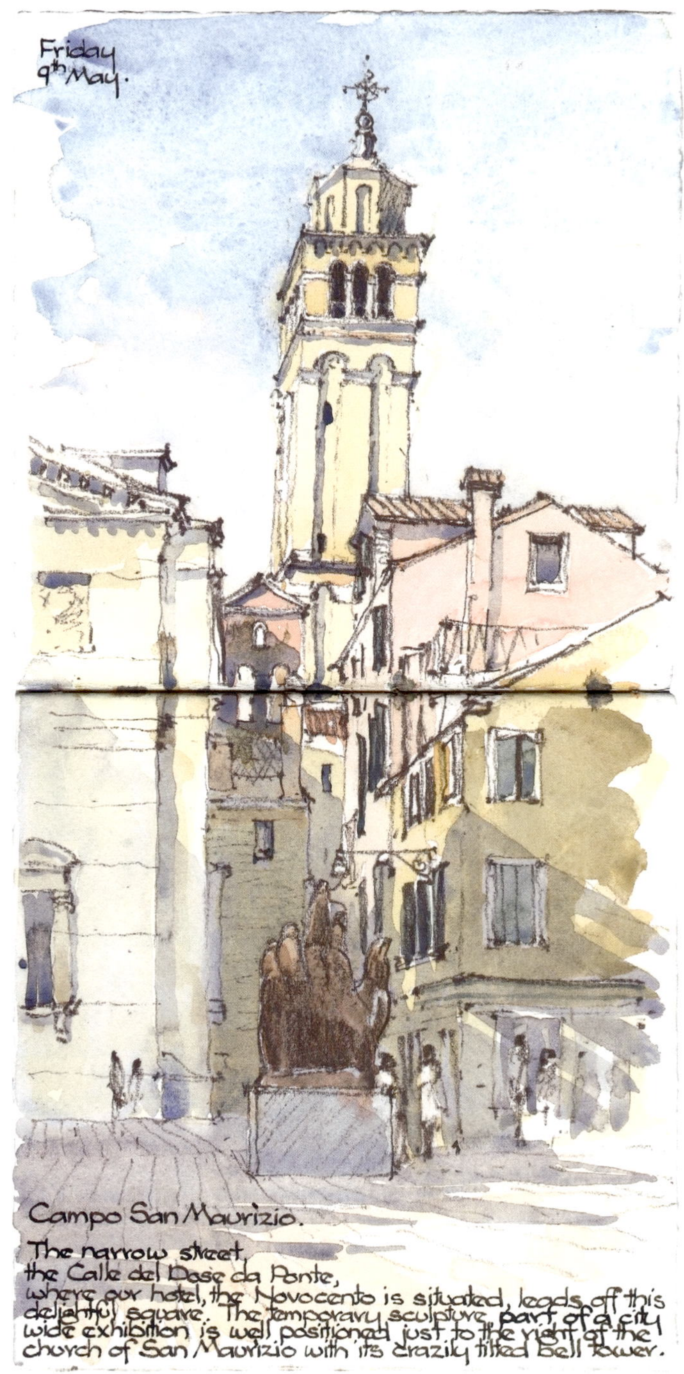

Diary Sketch 9th May, 2003 *Campo San Maurizio*

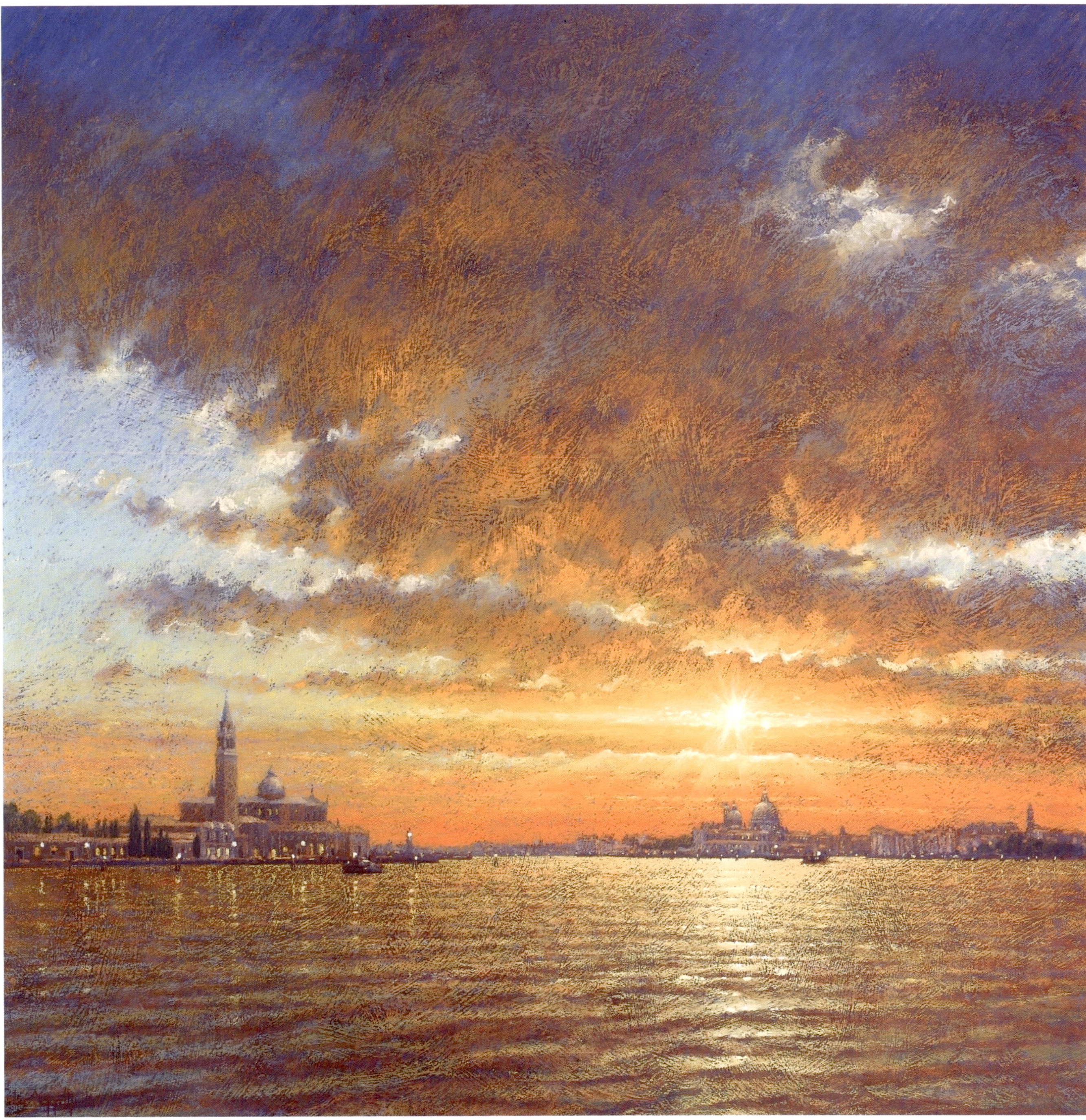

Venetian Gold, Canale di San Marco Pastel 1016 x 1016 mm

The dramatic oblique views across the Canale di San Marco, taking in Giudecca and the western end of Dorsoduro and capped by huge skies, have provided a rich source of material for many of my paintings.

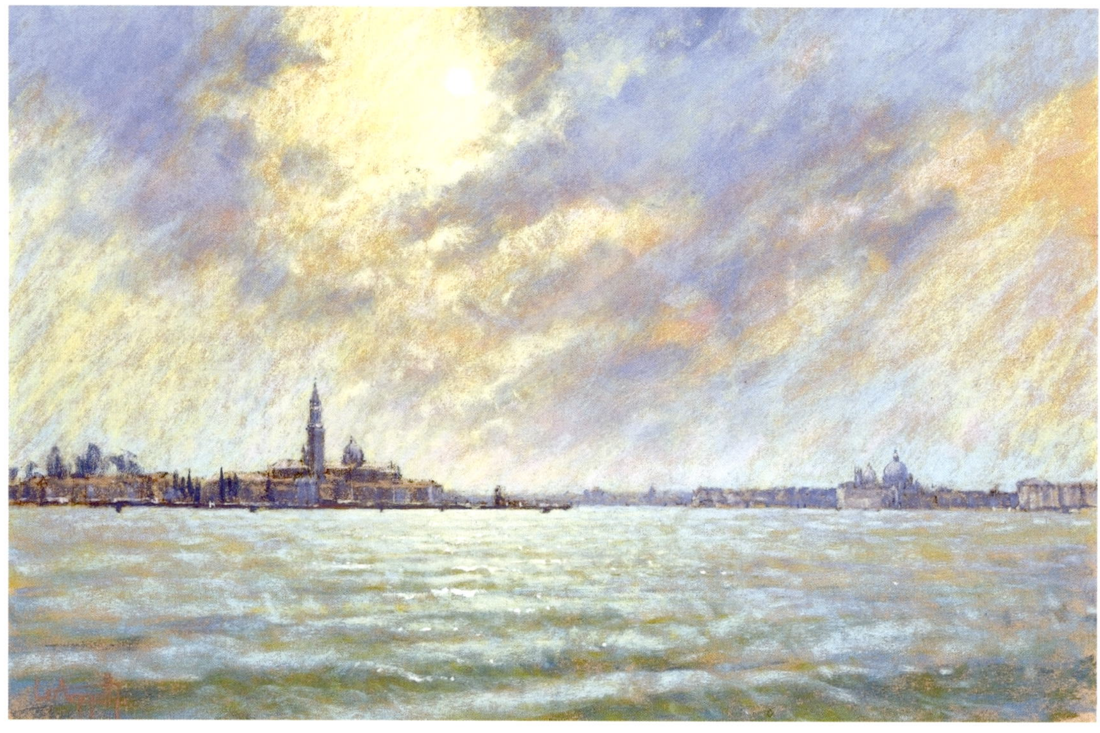

San Giorgio Maggiore and Giudecca, Canale di San Marco
Pastel 325 x 500 mm

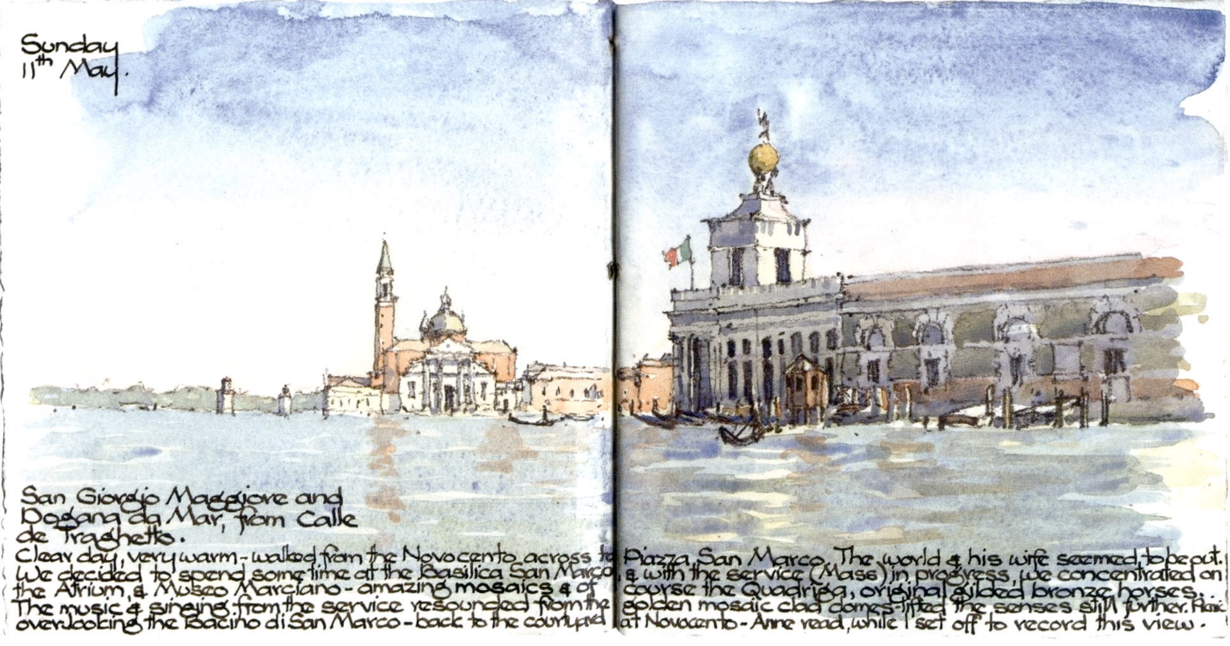

Diary Sketch
11th May, 2003
San Giorgio Maggiore and Dogana da Mar, from Calle de Traghetto
Conté w/c

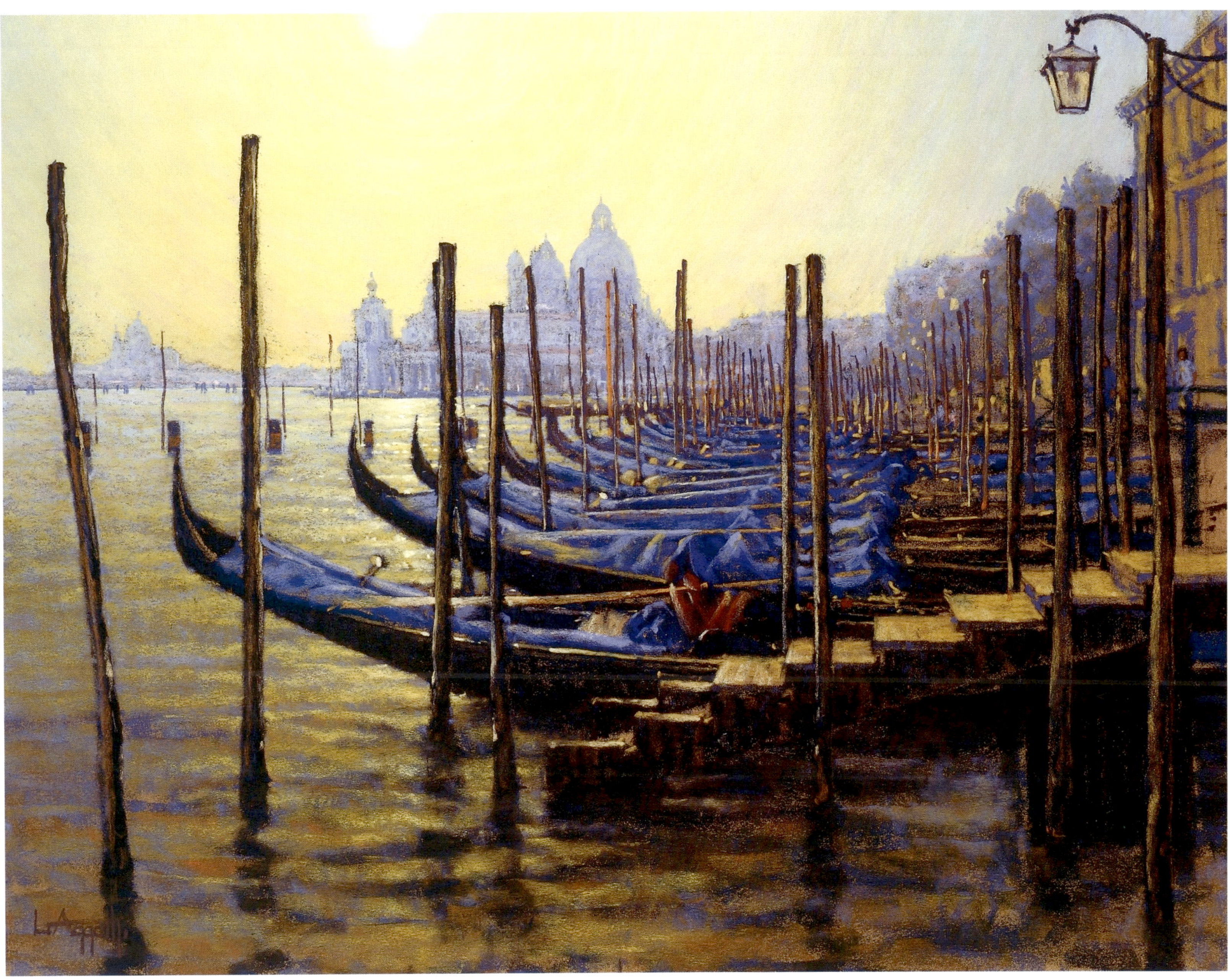

Blue and Gold, Molo San Marco Pastel 400 x 500 mm

DORSODURO

There are some real gems in this sestiere: wide-embracing views from the eastern tip near the Salute, and from the Zattere quay where wealthy Venetians who owned stately residences in this neighbourhood strolled up and down, gazing across to Giudecca. The majestic dome of Santa Maria della Salute stands proud at the entrance to the Grand Canal, with the Peggy Guggenheim Gallery, the Accademia Bridge, and the Accademia Galleries, together with smaller galleries along the fondamente behind, forming a strong cultural emphasis at this point. Quite fittingly, tranquil canals linking this area with the Zattere Quays, provide space and time for quiet contemplation, following enjoyment of these art treasures.

Further to the west the sestiere becomes more vibrant, where local inhabitants enjoy the small authentic restaurants and bars. The attractive San Barnaba floating barge, full of fruit and vegetables, provides a colourful scene on the Rio San Barnaba, flanked by the Fondamenta Gherardini. My favourite spot however, has to be the Campo Santa Margherita, a popular meeting place for locals, where the Causin Gelateria ice cream, gossip, and street football form part of the daily routine.

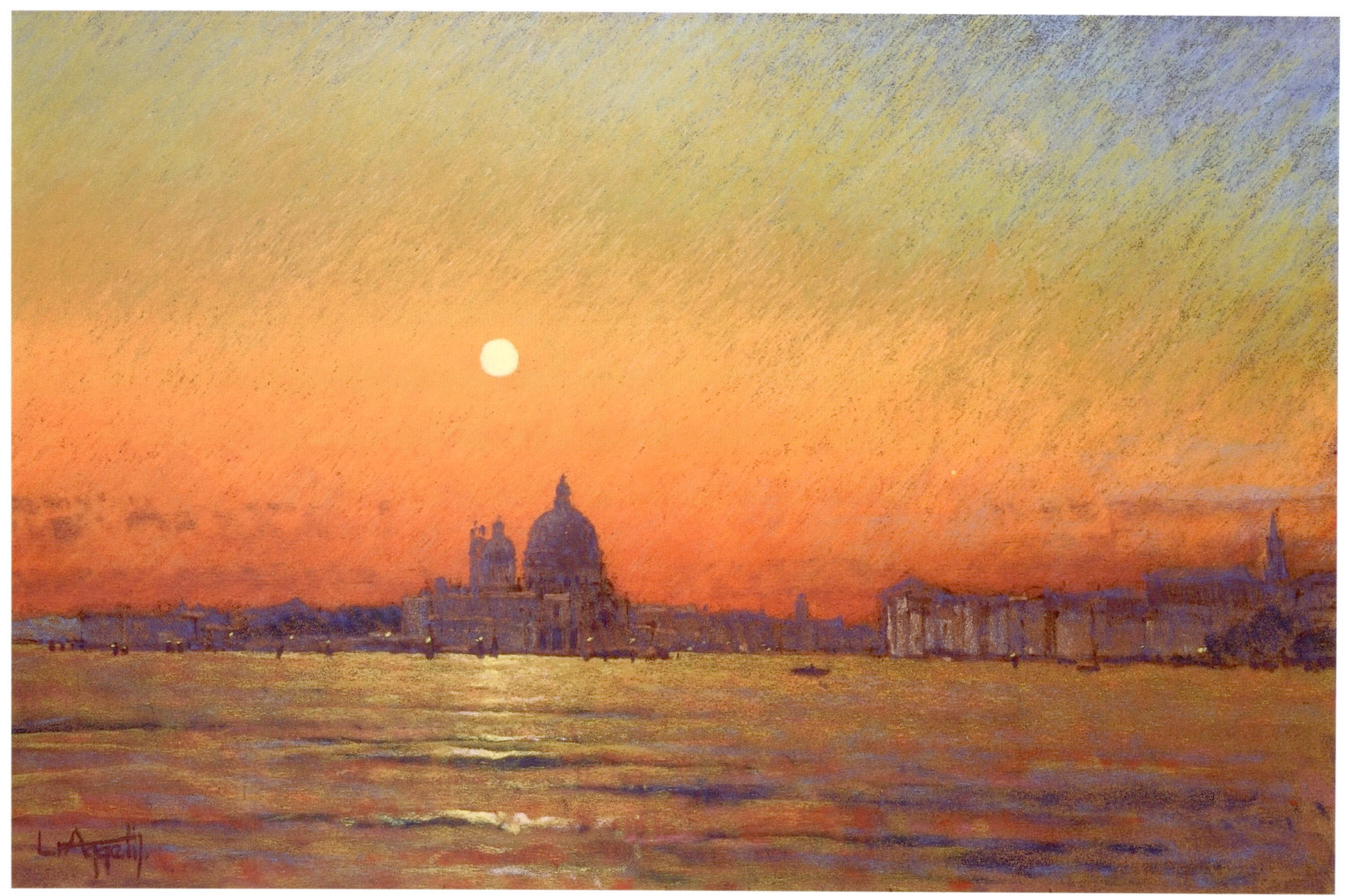

Sunset Over Dorsoduro Pastel 325 x 500 mm

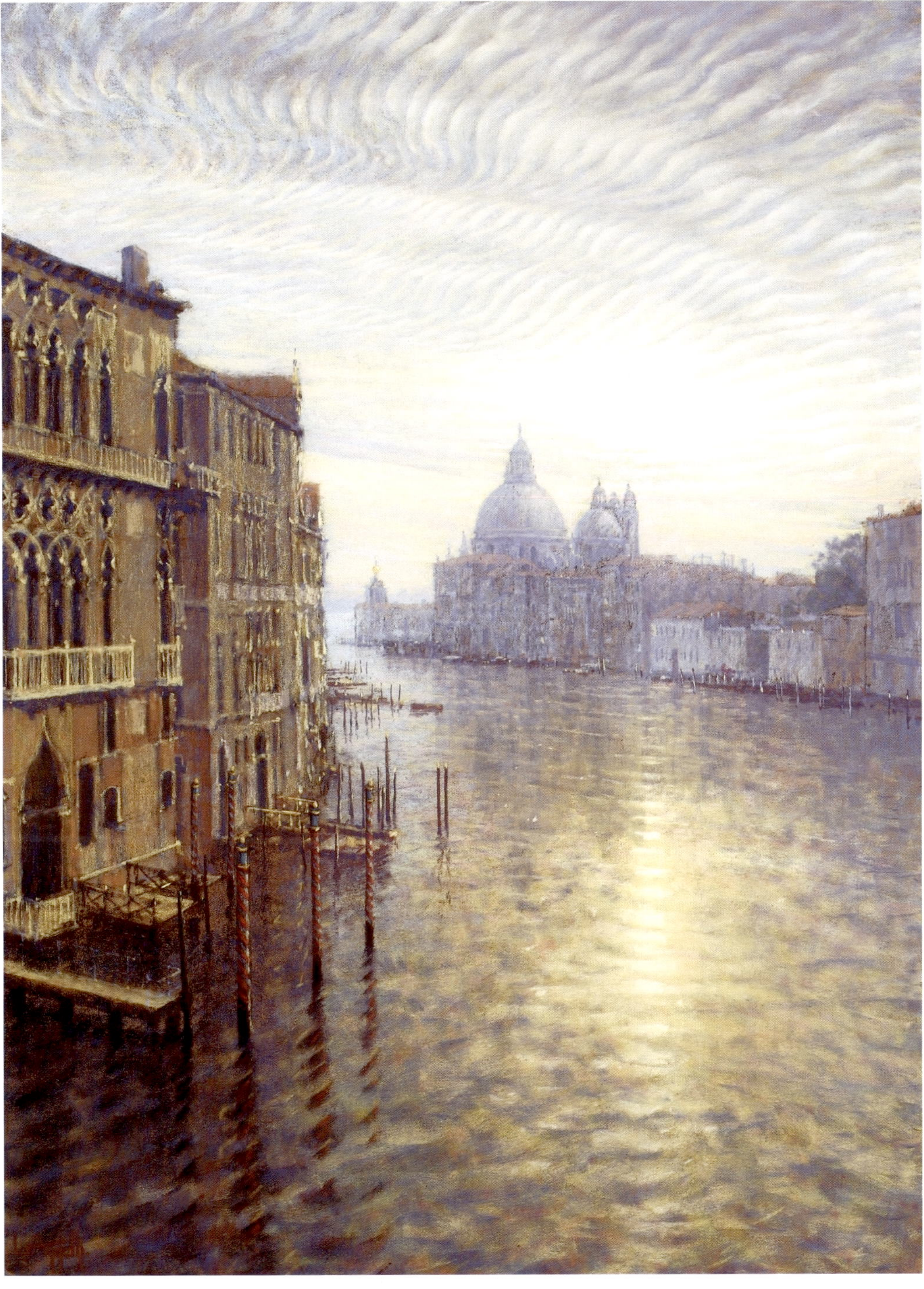

Morning Gold Pastel
800 x 600 mm

View from the Accademia Bridge before the day begins in earnest.

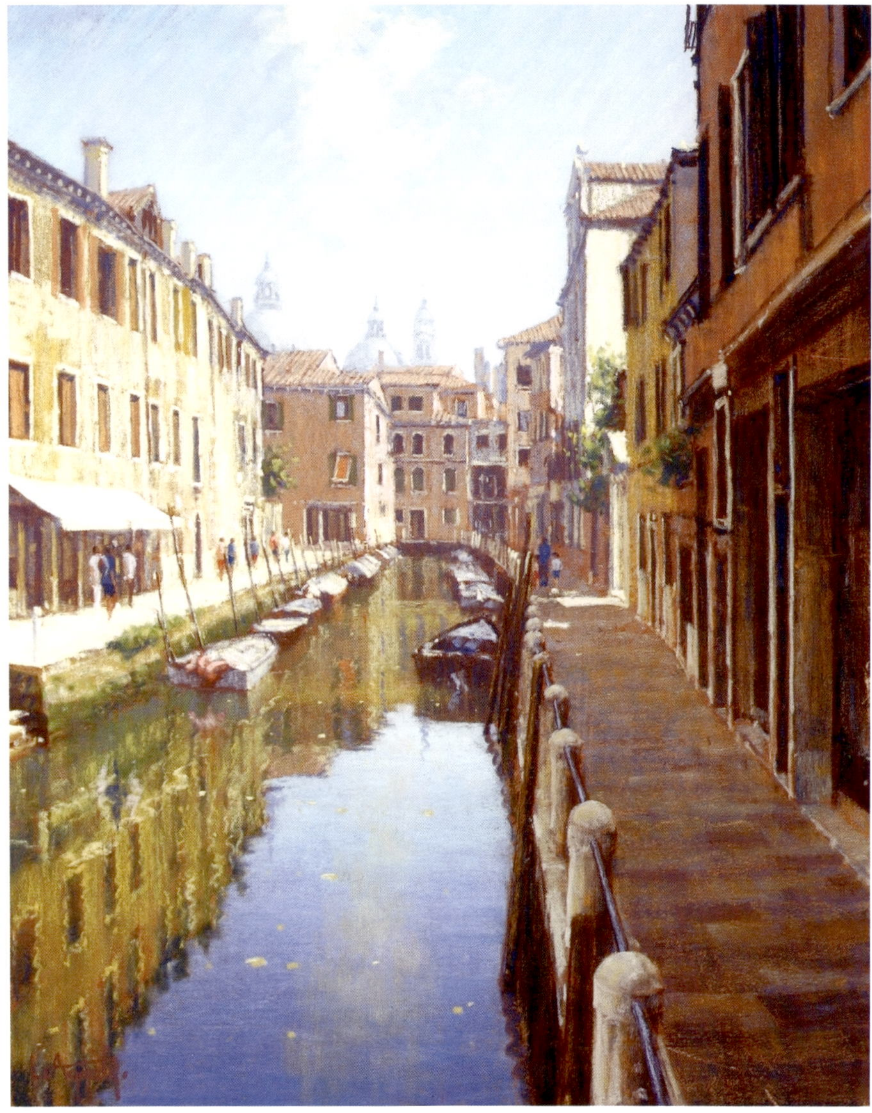

Fondamenta Zorzi Bragadin Pastel 500 x 400 mm

An area for quiet reflection, behind the cultural hotspots of the Guggenheim and Accademia Galleries.

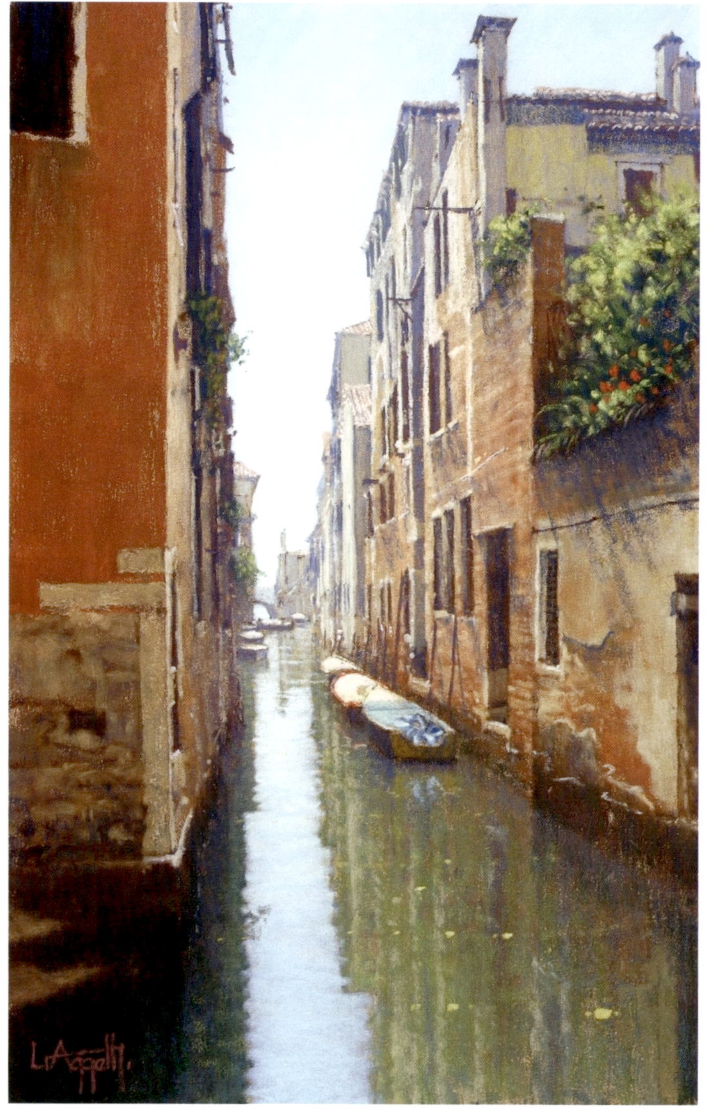

Venetian Red Pastel 500 x 325 mm

The epitome of Venetian backwaters, the Rio Piccolo del Legname, just behind, right, off the Fondamenta Zorzi Bragadin.

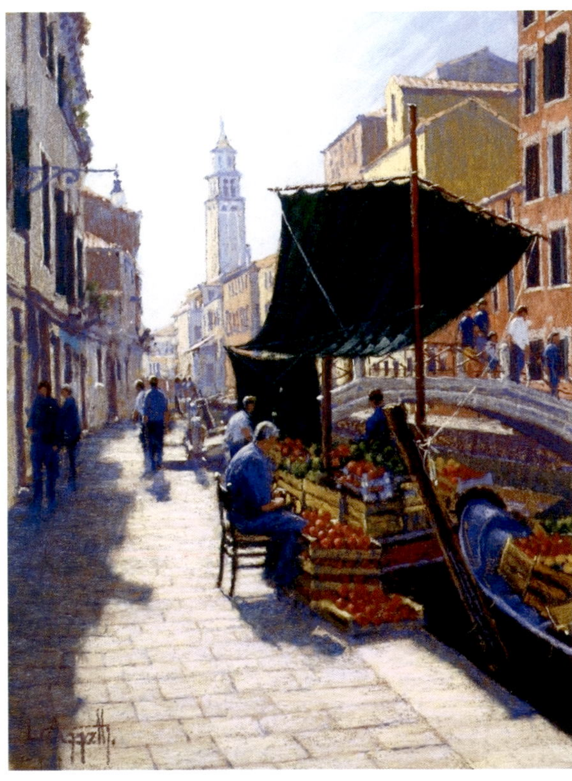

San Barnaba Pastel
325 x 250 mm

A popular spot, full of life, colour and chat.

Diary Sketch 31st March, 2007
San Barnaba Conté w/c

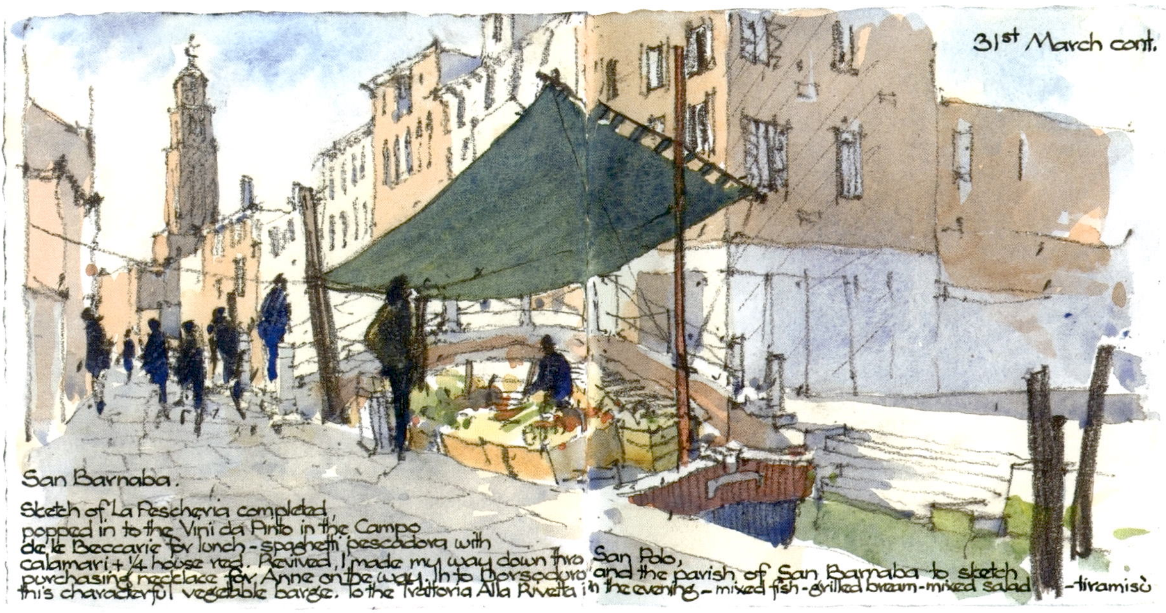

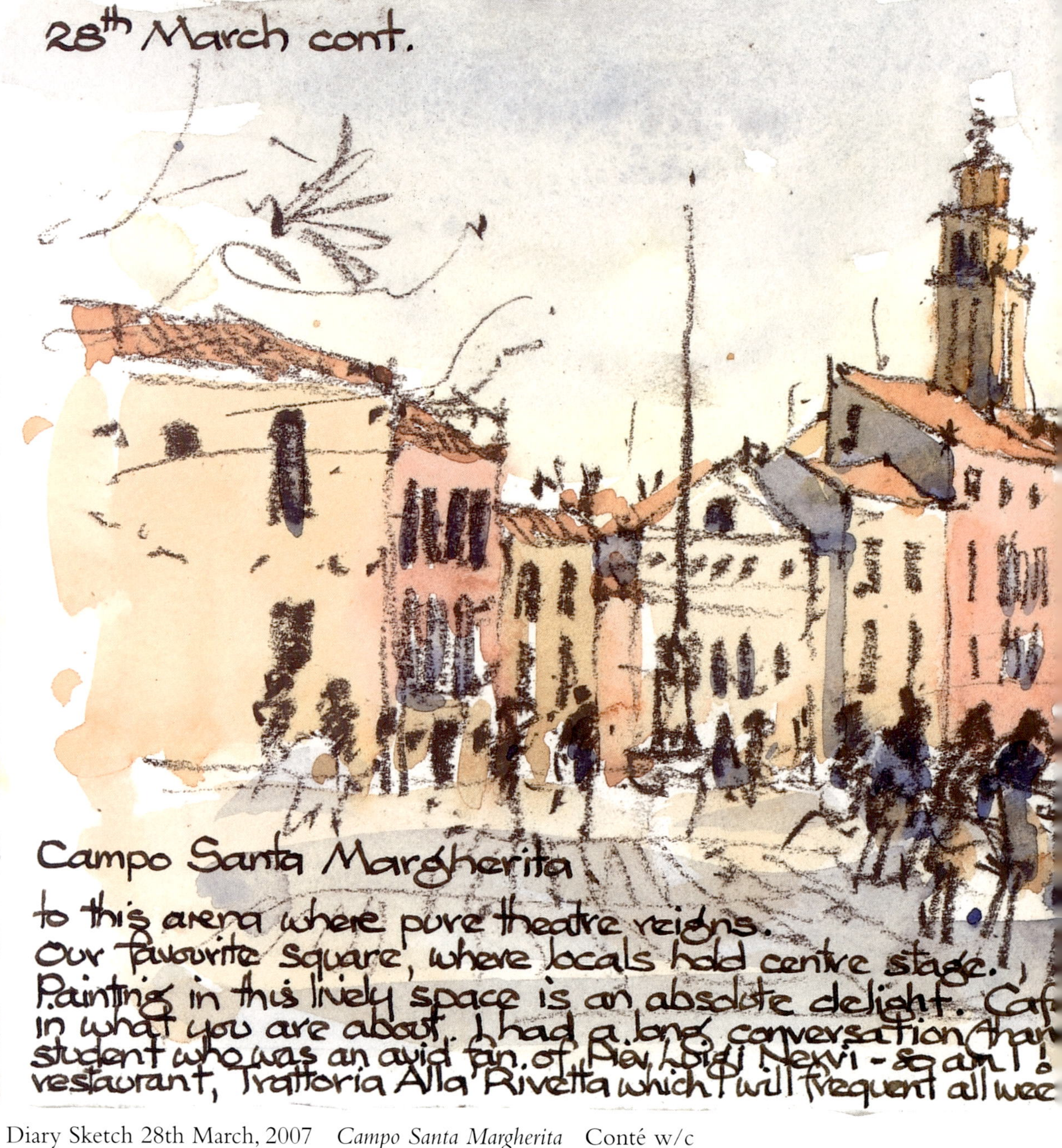

Diary Sketch 28th March, 2007 *Campo Santa Margherita* Conté w/c

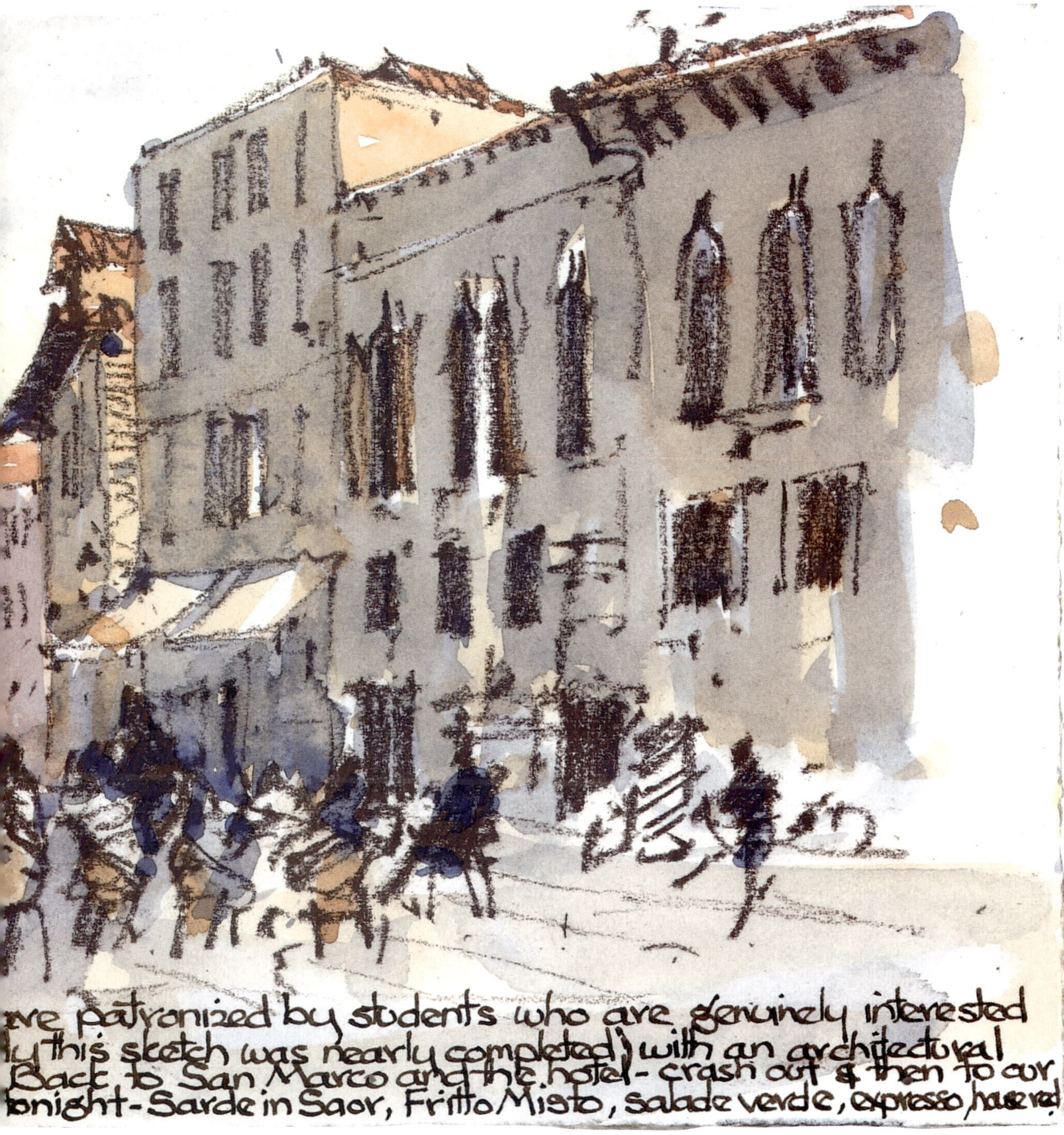
are patronized by students who are genuinely interested
ly this sketch was nearly completed) with an architectural
Back to San Marco and the hotel - crash out & then to our
tonight - Sarde in Saor, Fritto Misto, salade verde, expresso, house red

SAN POLO AND SANTA CROCE

These two sestieri are often linked together, due to their central position, but it is San Polo we are really concerned with, for I have yet to paint San Croce.

If western Dorsoduro, which we have just left, is lively, then San Polo is even livelier, due in no small part to the location of the fish, vegetable and fruit markets at the north-eastern end, flanking the Grand Canal. On our way there, via a delightful maze of small canals, criss-crossed by graceful bridges linking narrow fondamente, two spaces quite different in character provide interesting breaks. The Campo dei Frari and Campo San Rocco at the eastern end of Santa Maria Gloriosa dei Frari, form a wonderful L-shaped space enclosed by fine buildings including the Scuola Grande di San Rocco, patronized by Tintoretto for twenty-three years. The beautiful Santa Maria Gloriosa housing works by Titian and Bellini forms a serenely exquisite backdrop to the quiescent Rio dei Frari.

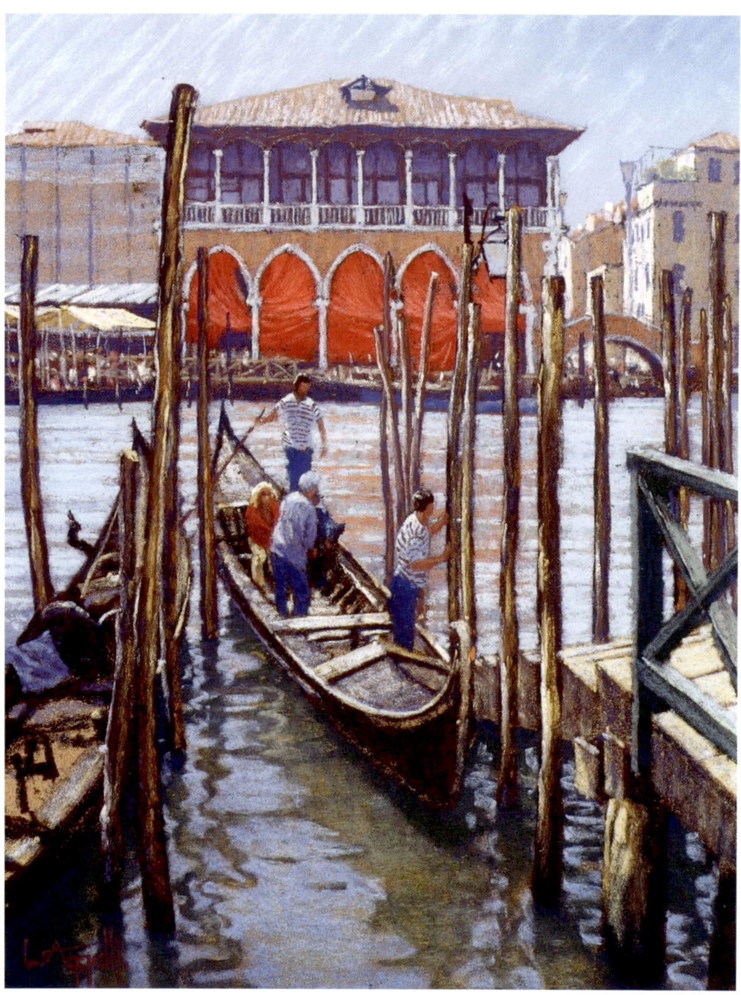

Pescheria Crossing Pastel 325 x 250 mm

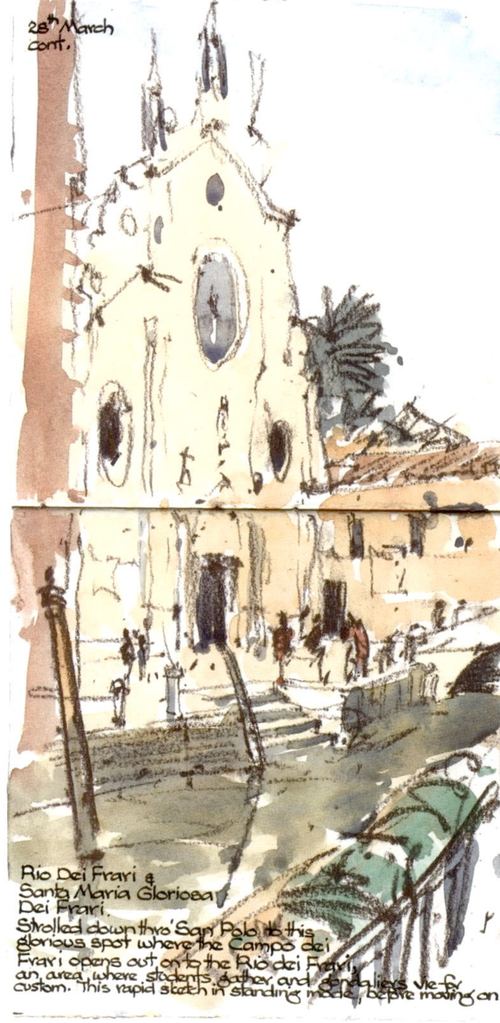

Diary Sketch
28th March, 2007
Rio dei Frari and Santa Maria Gloriosa dei Frari
Conté w/c

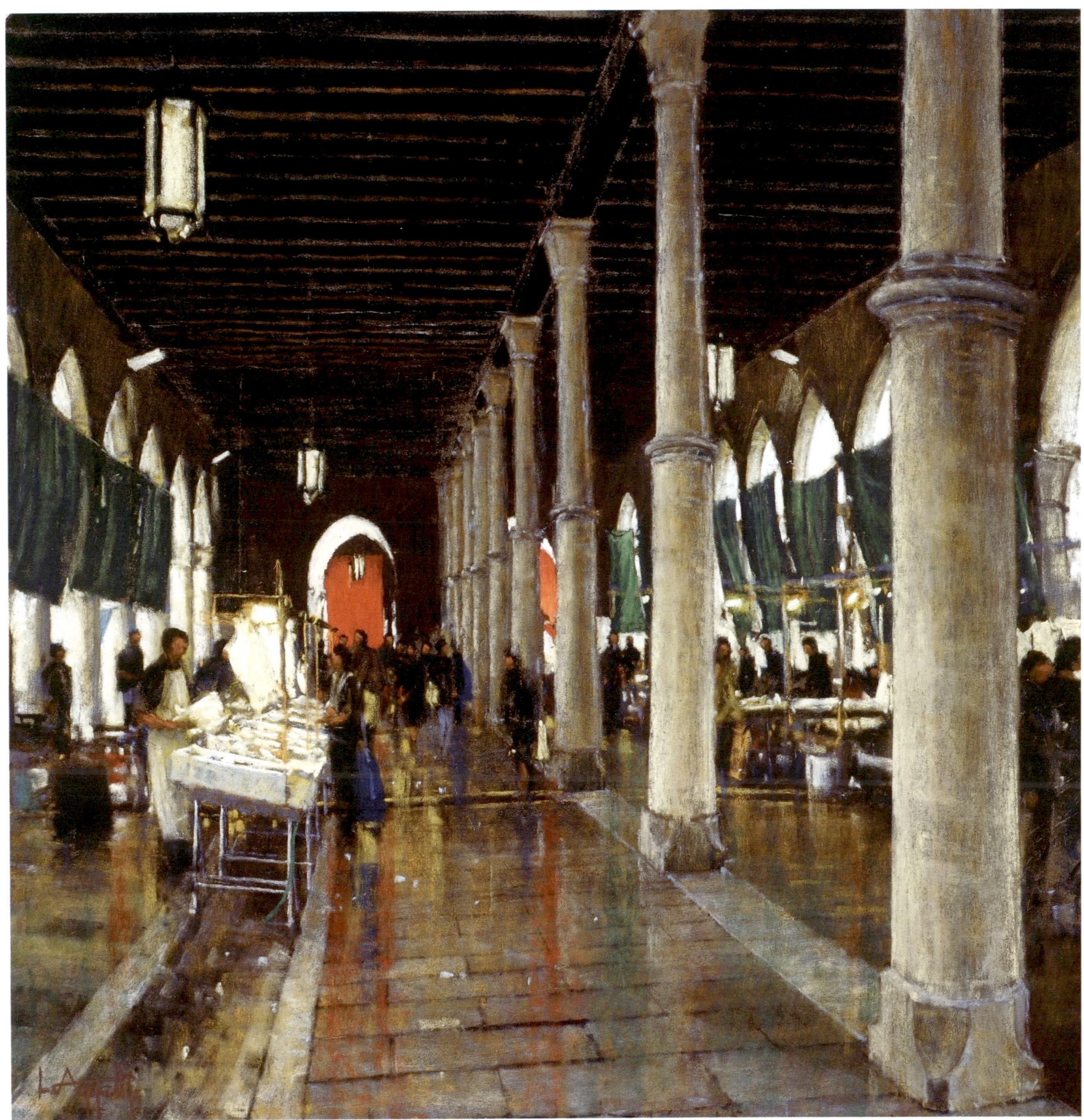

The Pescheria, Mercato del Pesce Pastel 500 x 500 mm

To the north east, in complete contrast to more narrow alleys and fondamente, we come to the Campo San Polo, a spacious square enclosed by fine buildings, and without a canal frontage. The Gothic Palazzo Soranzo is particularly beautiful. The square is a lively gathering point, and is used for Carnival festivities, and a haven for local youngsters who play football and ride bikes, or just gossip outside cafés.

The Pescheria with its strikingly decorative, wholly red or green sun shades is a bubble of activity from early morning until past noon. The sparkling fresh fish, squid, cuttlefish, and shellfish displayed on slabs are enhanced by spot lighting from low overhead rails, and the constant washing of surfaces, and movement of ice provides a shimmering scene, of vibrant colours, activity, people and reflections. The business is non stop, and the wonderful thing is that everyone enjoys it, retailers and customers alike. To paint and sketch in their company is a revelation. There are two halls, one with green shades and leading off the Campo de le Beccarie, and the other, next to it, directly facing the Grand Canal, and protected with red hangings. There is a Traghetto (gondola ferry crossing) directly outside this hall.

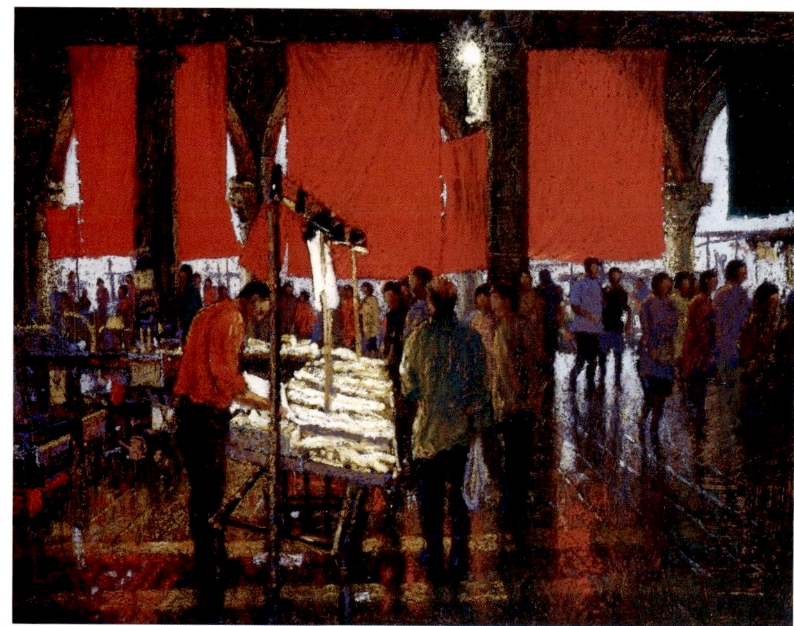

La Pescheria   Pastel   250 x 325 mm

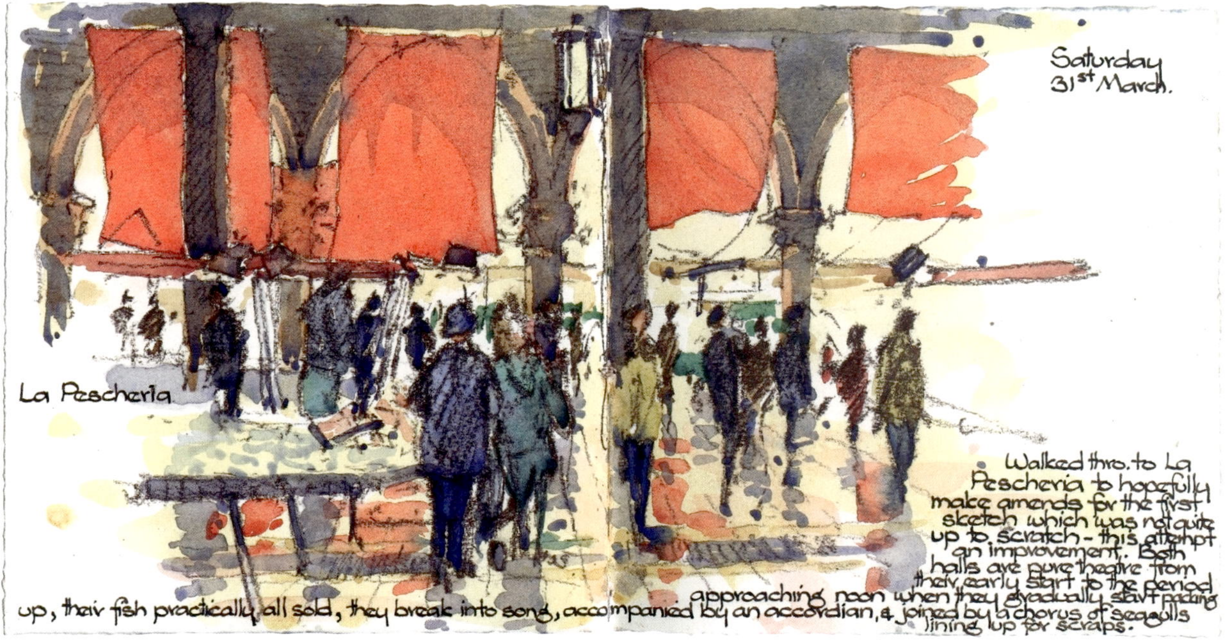

Diary Sketch 31st March, 2007   *La Pescheria*   Conté w/c

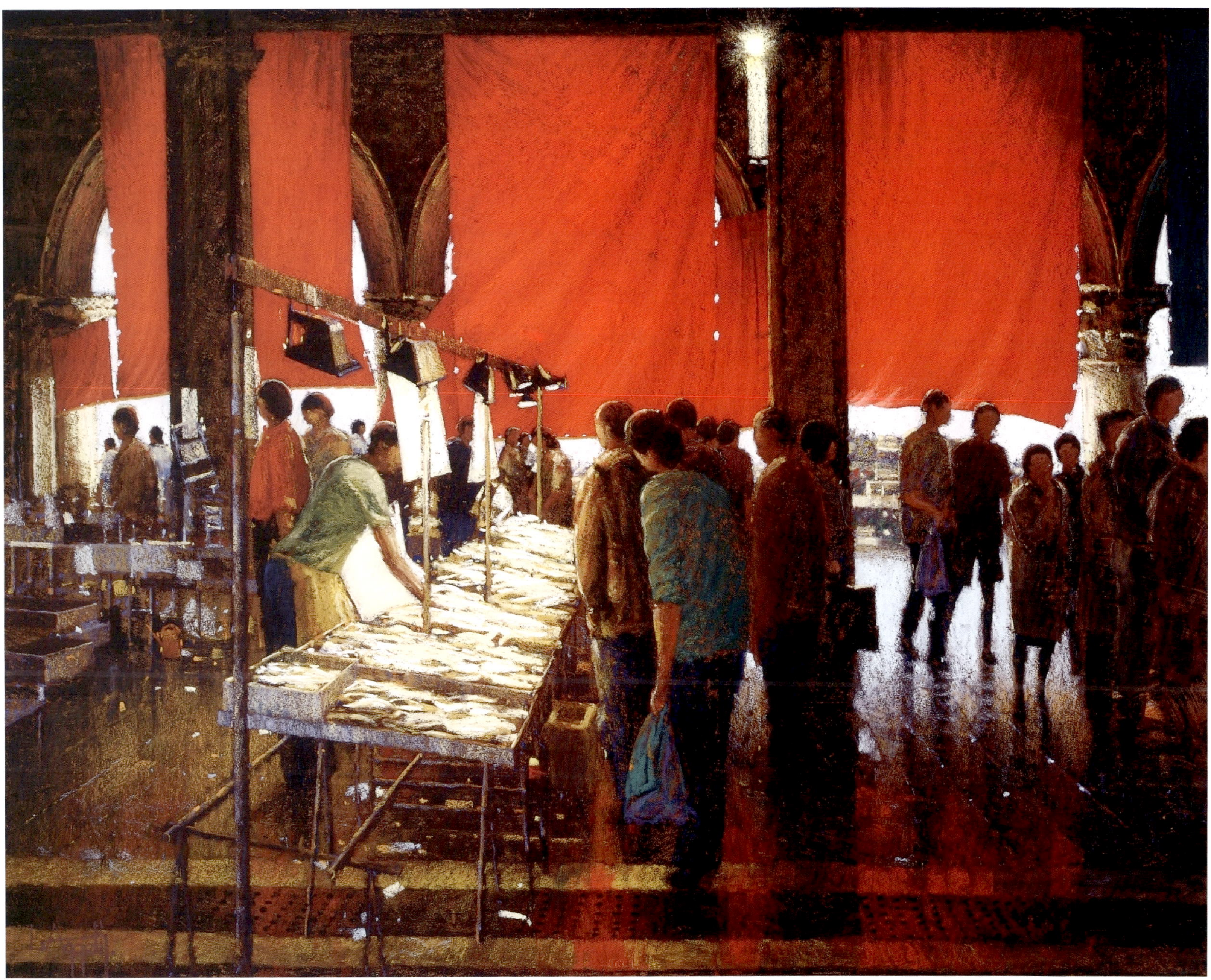

La Pescheria Pastel 1016 x 1220 mm

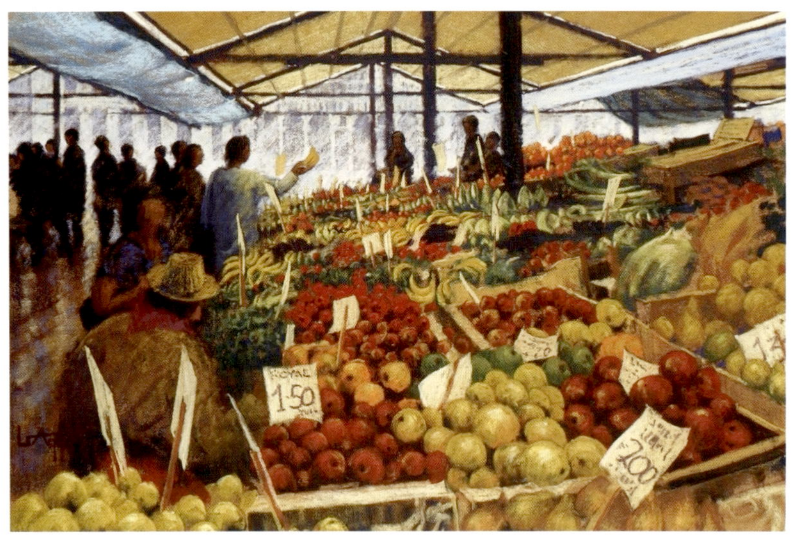

There is an unloading quay on the west side of the two halls where the Rio delle Beccarie enters the Grand Canal, and a similar facility along the Grand Canal frontage, which, further along, also serves the Erboria, the vegetable and fruit market alongside. This too is a colourful hive of activity, with views through the stalls across the Grand Canal to Cannaregio opposite. Access to this sestiere can be made via the Traghetto, a brief but cheap alternative to the "romantic cruise", or by walking through to the Ruga Degli Orefici, up the steps of the Rialto Bridge, down, and to the left, through Campo San Bartolomeo.

The Eboria Pastel 325 x 500 mm

Diary Sketch 28th March, 2007 *Rio delle Beccarie* Conté w/c

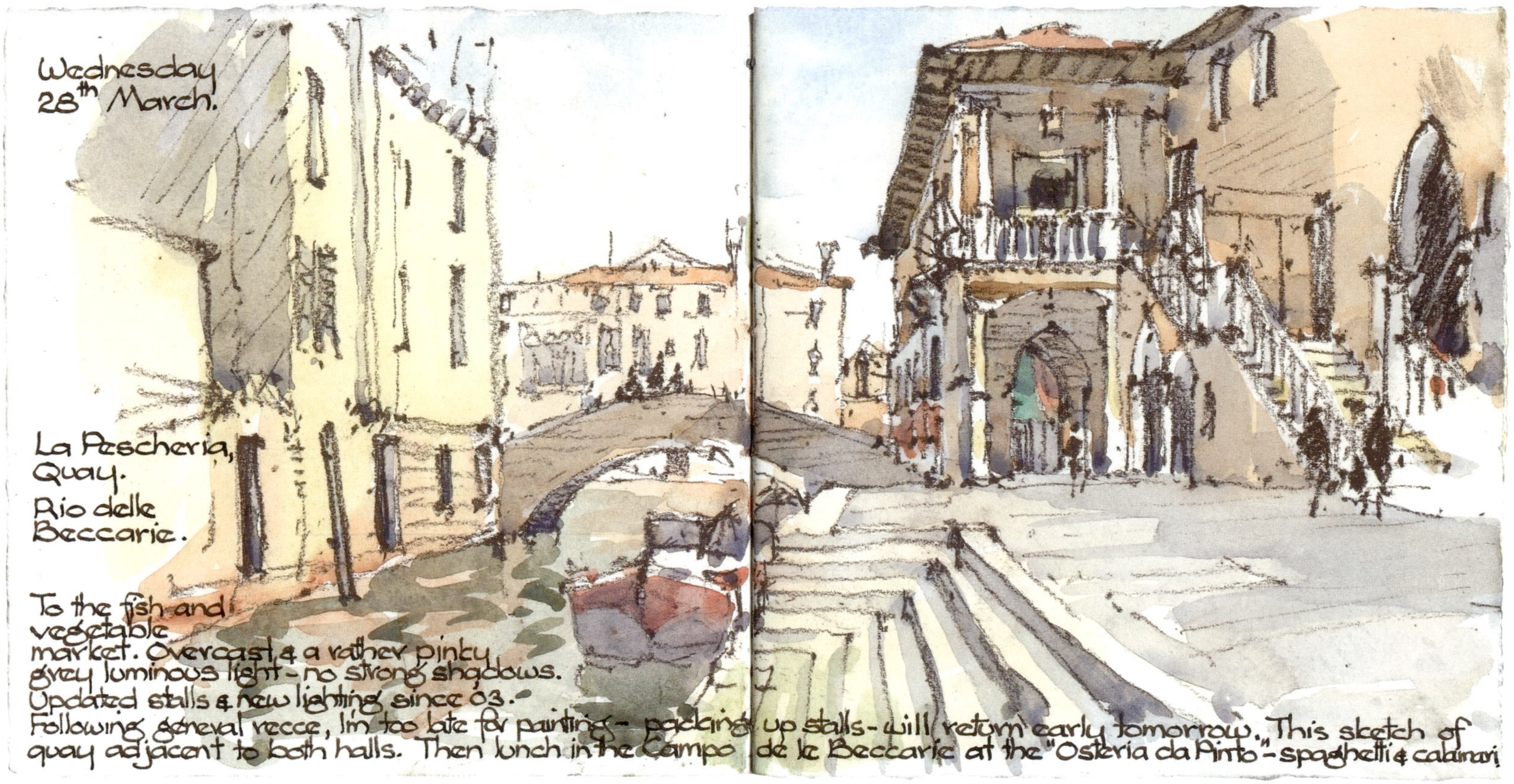

Wednesday
28th March.

La Pescheria,
Quay.
Rio delle
Beccarie.

To the fish and
vegetable
market. Overcast & a rather pinky
grey luminous light - no strong shadows.
Updated stalls & new lighting since 03.-
Following general recce, I'm too late for painting - packing up stalls - will return early tomorrow. This sketch of
quay adjacent to both halls. Then lunch in the Campo de le Beccarie at the "Osteria da Pinto" - spaghetti & calamari

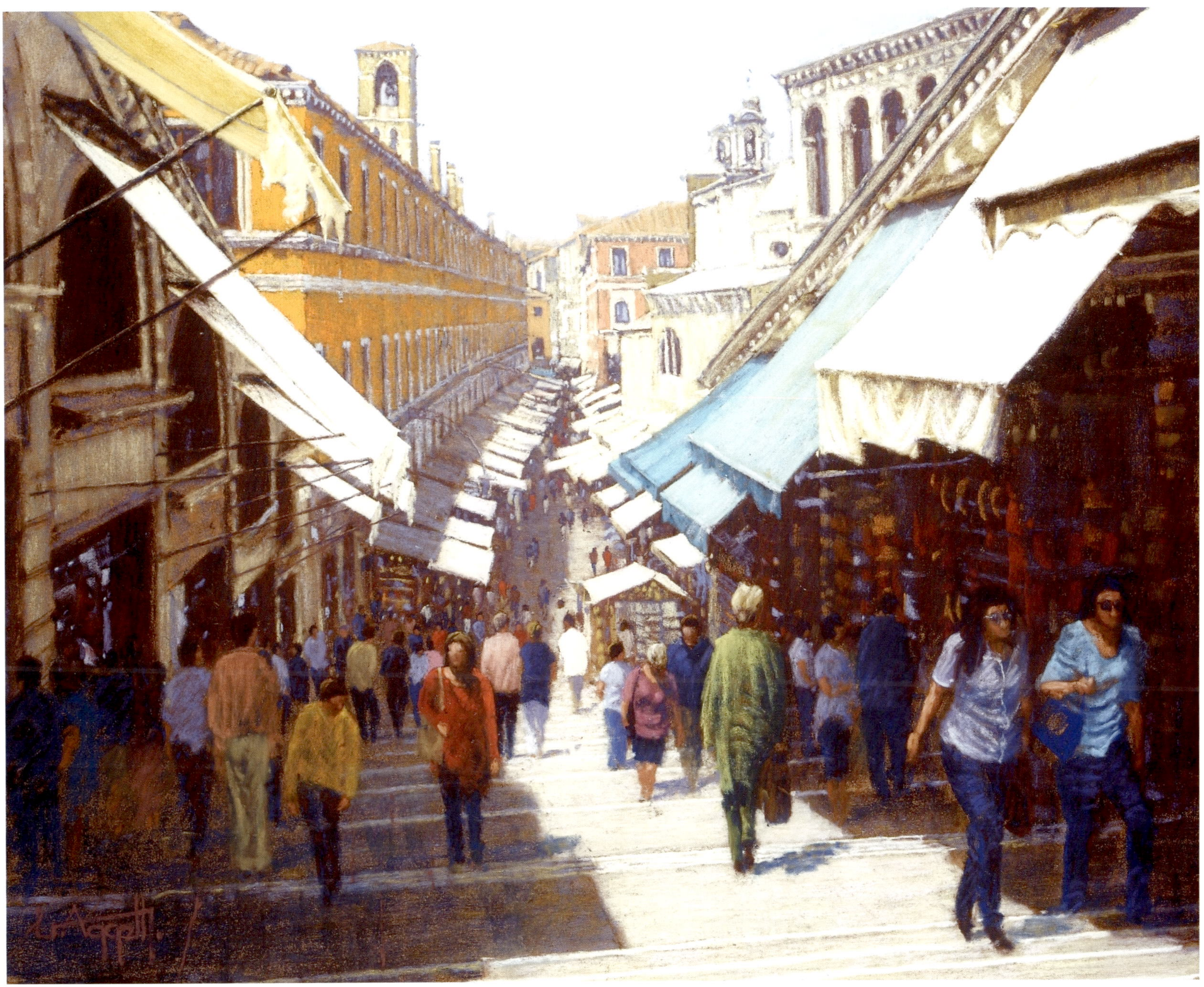

The Rialto Steps Pastel 400 x 500 mm

CANNAREGIO

This is the peaceful and more humble side of Venice, well worth the longer walk to get the lungs working a little (it is a flat city). The streets and fondamente of this unspoilt sestiere support shops and stores stocking basic groceries and other domestic requirements. Shuttered houses flank the waterways where clean washing is suspended from one side to the other, to be reflected in the jade still water. There is real life here, undisturbed by tourism, where the bars are always crowded with local Venetians, and children's voices are heard along the fondamente.

The Campo del Ghetto is the oldest part of the Jewish quarter. It was decreed in 1516 that all Jews in Venice be confined to the area that was once occupied by a foundry (geto). Thereafter ghetto was the name given to all Jewish enclaves throughout the world.

The cultural jewel in this sestiere is Tintoretto's parish church, the lovely Gothic, Madonna dell'Orto, containing a wealth of works by the artist, a poignant testimony to the genius of one of Venice's most famous sons, who was born, lived, worked and died here.

Making our way back via the Fondamenta dei Mori, along the Fondamenta della Misericórdia with its quiet backwaters, atmospheric bars and trattoria, to the Strada Nova, we come to the delightful Campo dei Santi Apostoli. This square always seems to be busy, partly due to its location at the hub of constant pedestrian traffic moving between San Marco, Cannaregio and Castello, The lofty bell tower stands high over the wonderfully articulated space which opens out on to the Rio dei Santi Apostoli, just before it enters the Grand Canal.

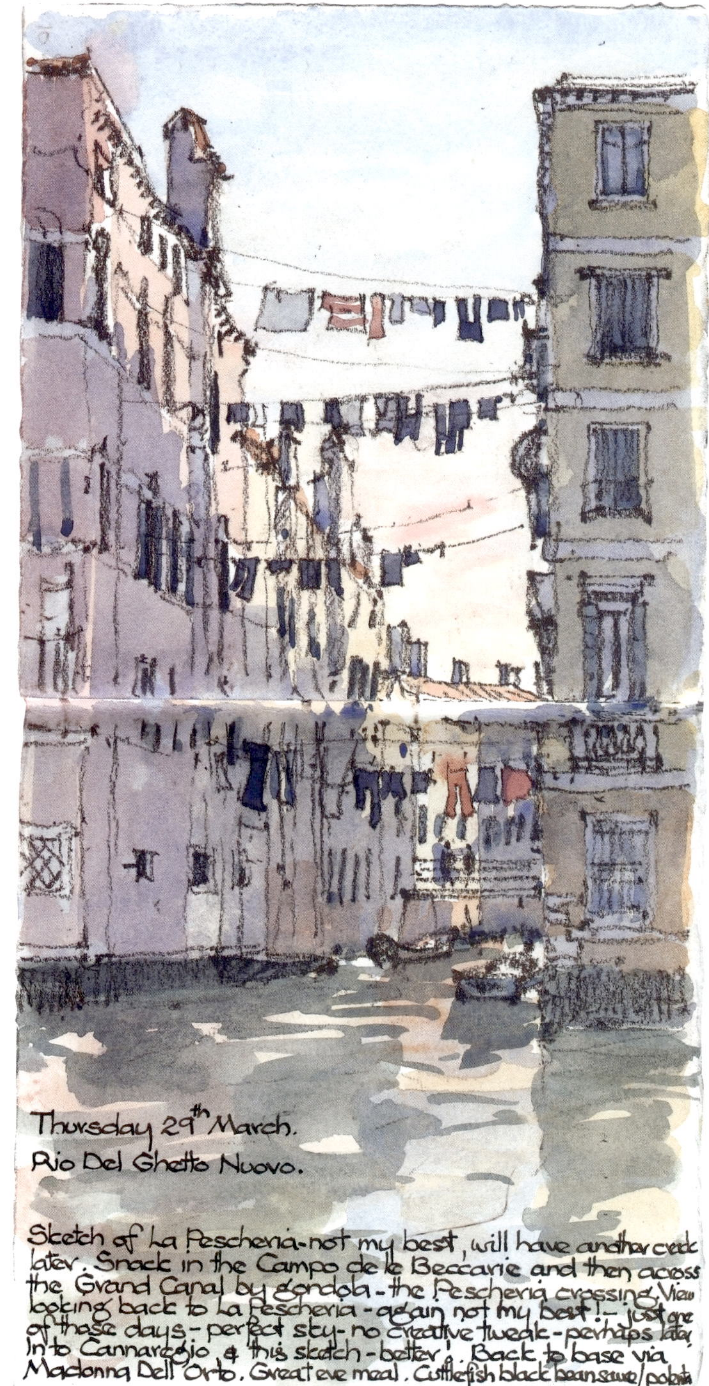

Diary Sketch 29th March, 2007
Rio del Ghetto Nuovo Conté w/c

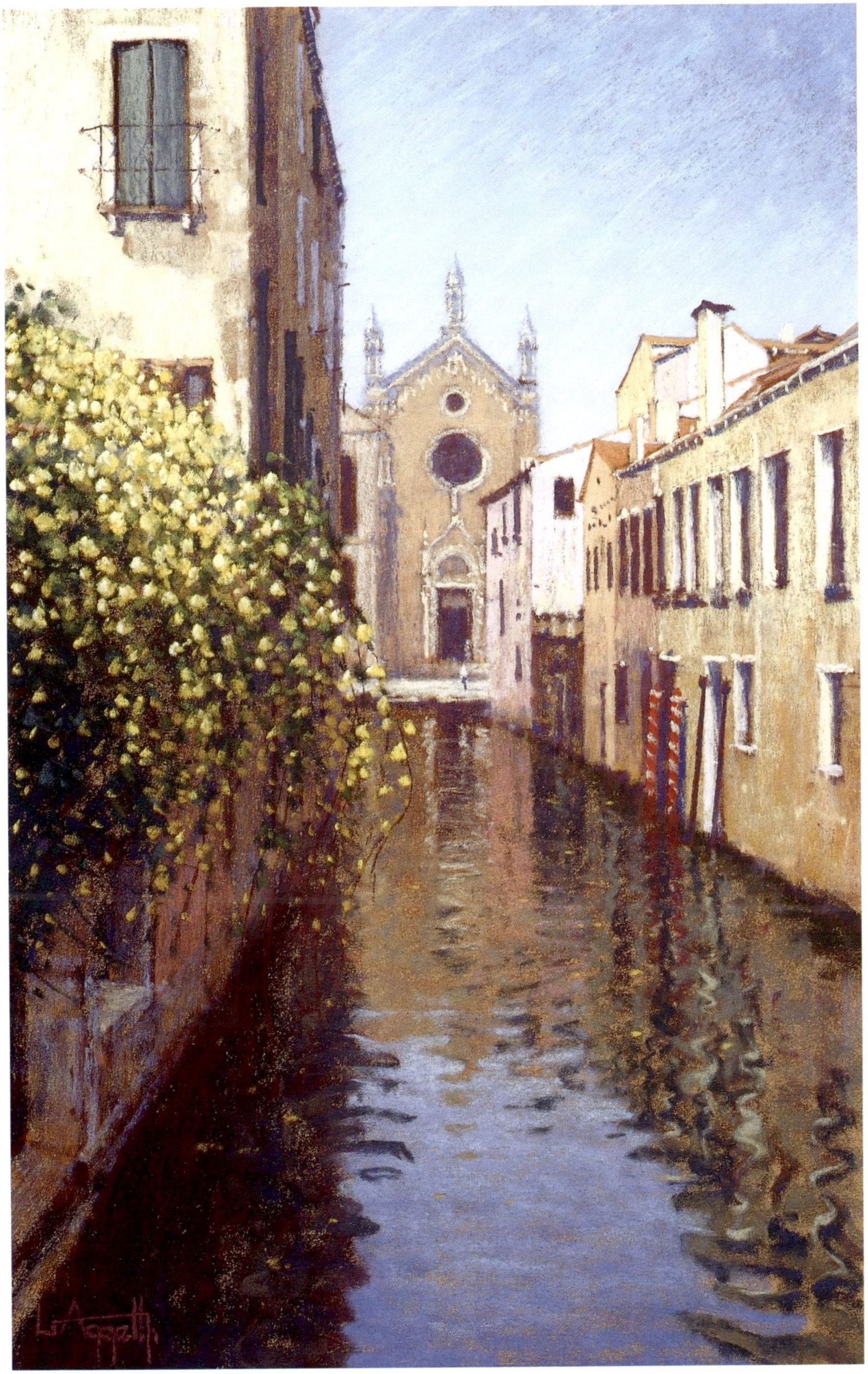

Madonna dell'Orto
Pastel 500 x 325 mm

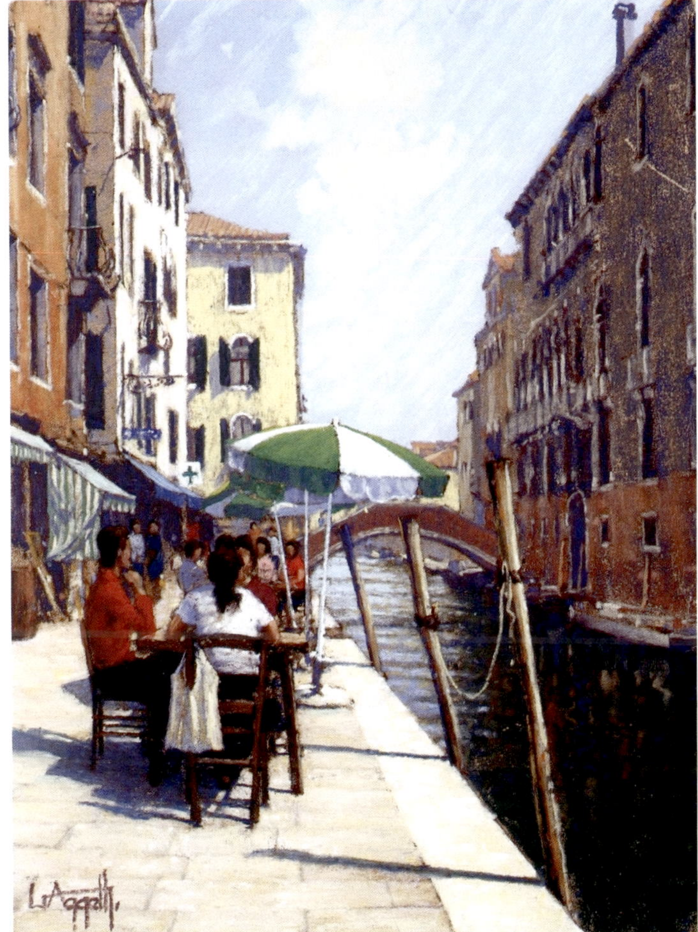

Rest Awhile, Fondamenta della Misericórdia Pastel 325 x 250 mm

Morning Calm Pastel
325 x 250 mm

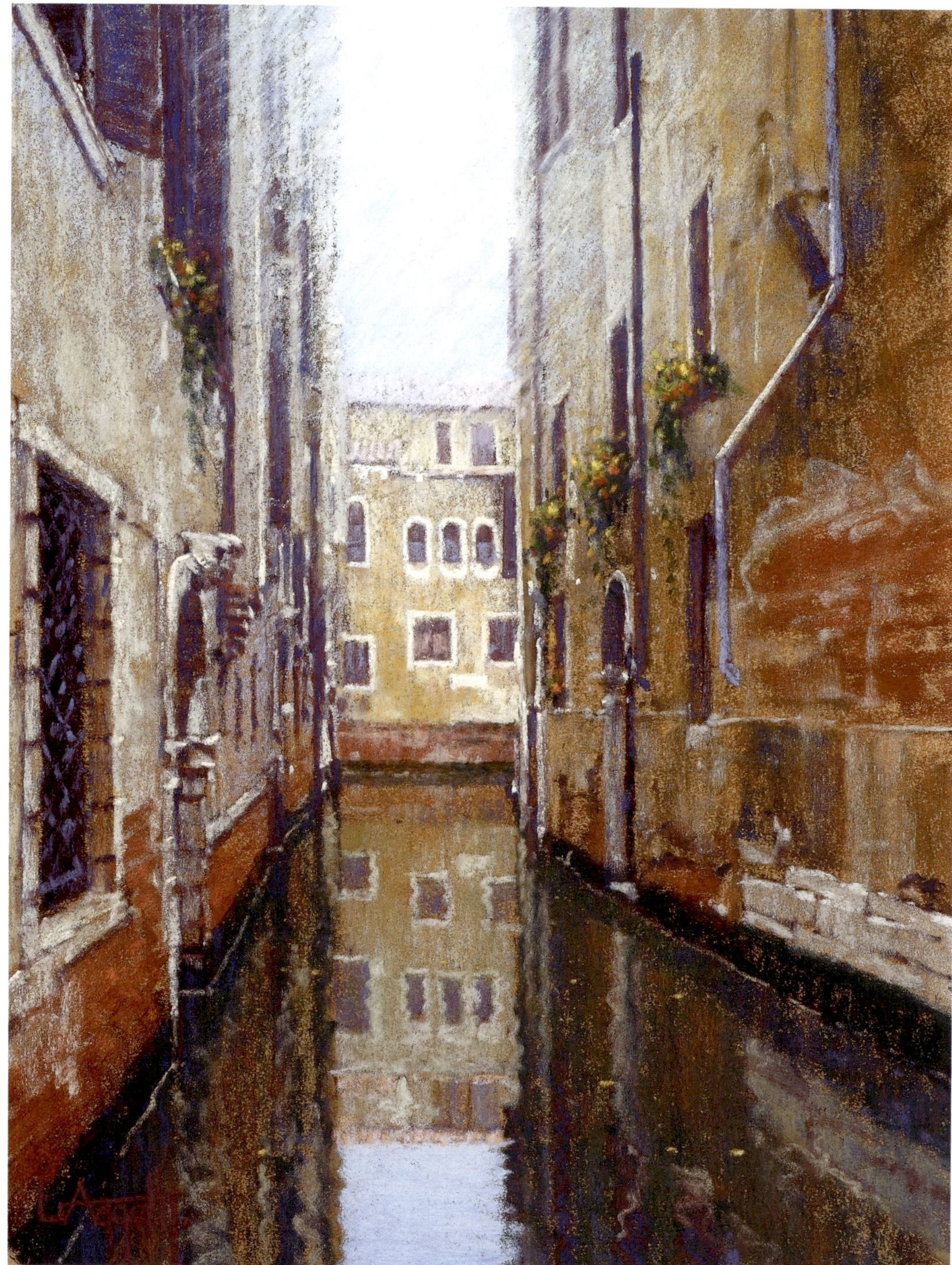

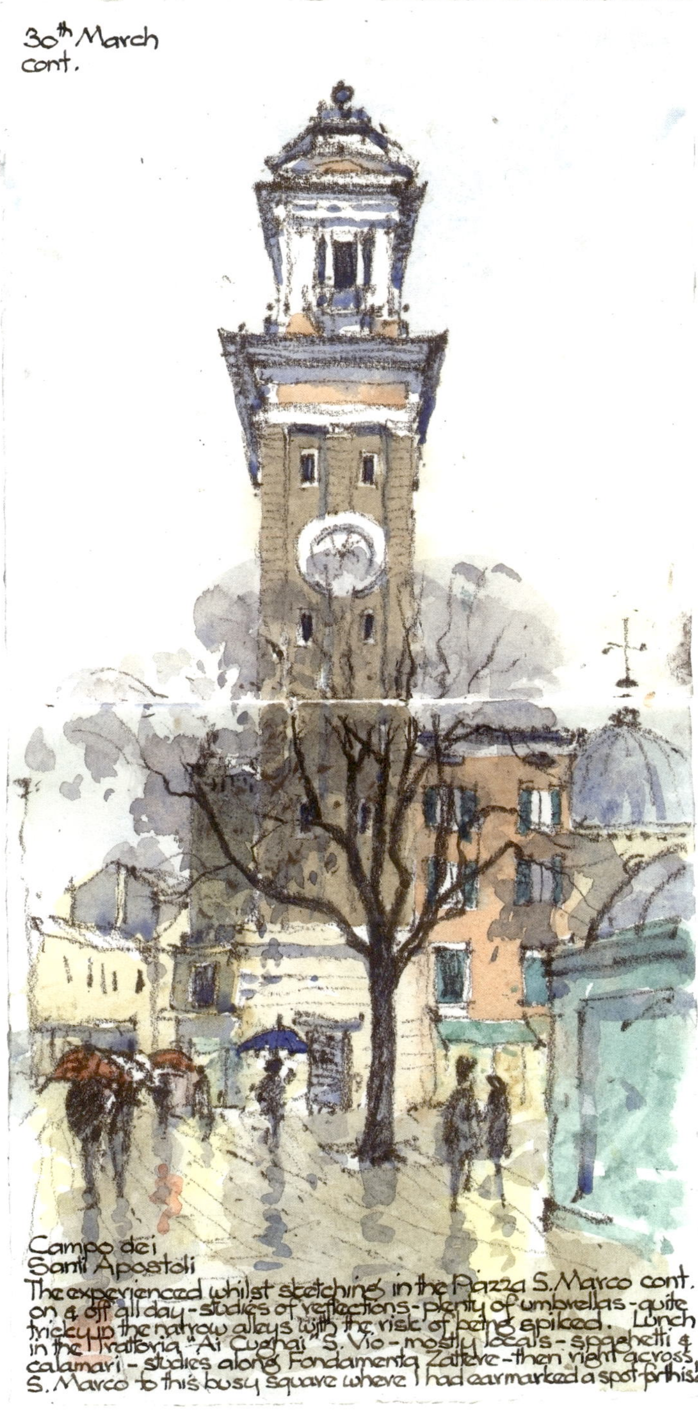

We complete our rather convoluted clockwise exploration by walking through to San Marco, and then east beyond the Basilica San Marco along the Sal San Provolo to our favourite restaurant, tucked in beside the steps of the Ponte San Provolo. Frequented by locals, and an increasing number of visitors following recommendations regarding the establishment's excellent food, and good value, the Trattoria Alla Rivetta, specializing in seafood, is an absolute gem. Do not come looking for "silver service", but if you enjoy honest, local and authentic Venetian fare, accompanied with cheerfully attentive service, then this is for you. I dined here every evening during my recent solo working visit, and have also eaten here with Anne. With tables shared (you are given the option), the ambience is fantastic.

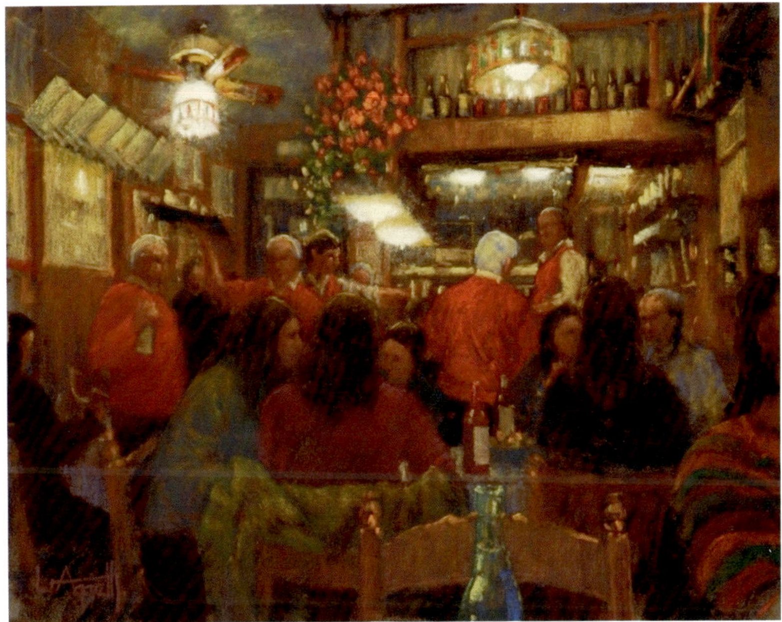

Trattoria Alla Rivetta Pastel 250 x 325 mm

Diary Sketch 30th March, 2007
Campo dei Santi Apostoli Conté w/c

VENICE LAGOON

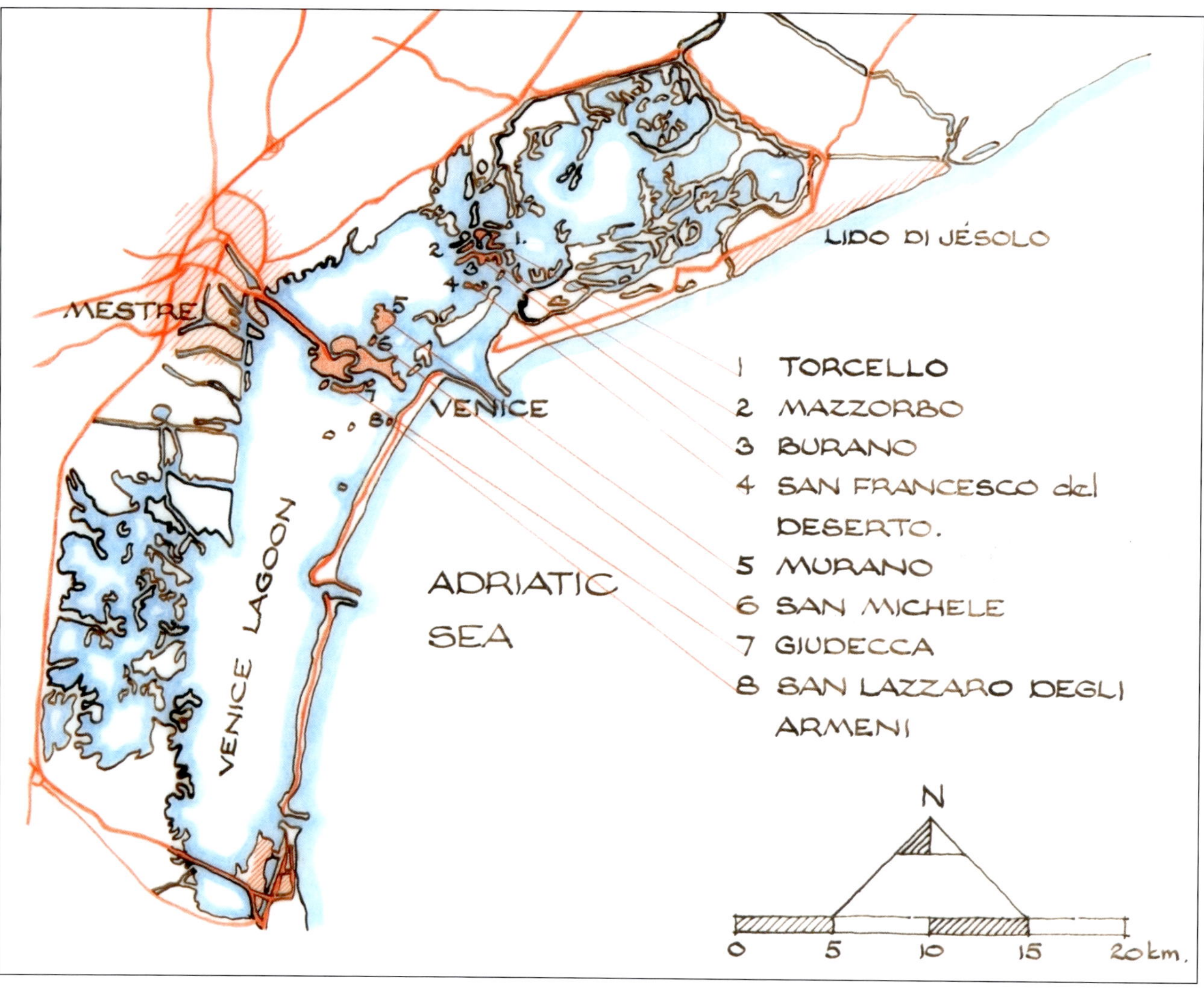

After rubbing shoulders with humanity in the narrow confined spaces of Venice Island, the vast open atmosphere to be experienced out on the Lagoon, provides an immensely contrasting relief. All of the islands are eminently paintable, and when viewed from the water they can sometimes, according to weather conditions, appear to be suspended between heaven and earth, and when the bell tower is tilted at an alarming angle, as is often the case, an almost unworldly atmosphere is created.

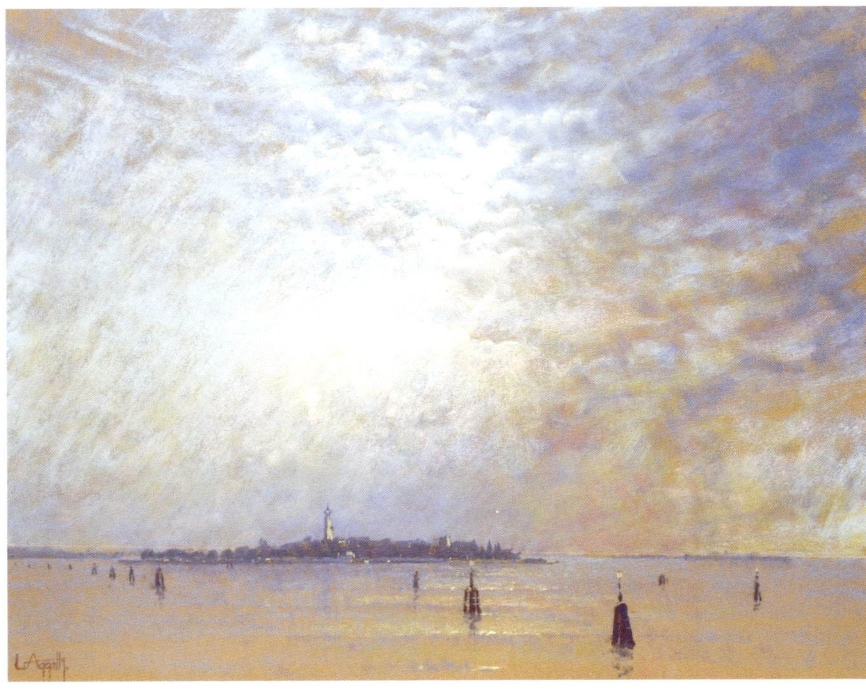

San Lazzaro degli Armeni
Pastel 500 x 650 mm

Lord Byron used to row across to this small Armenian monastery island just off the Lido to absorb Armenian culture.

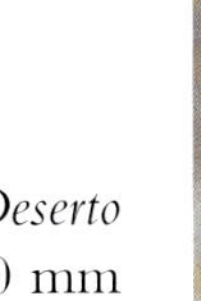

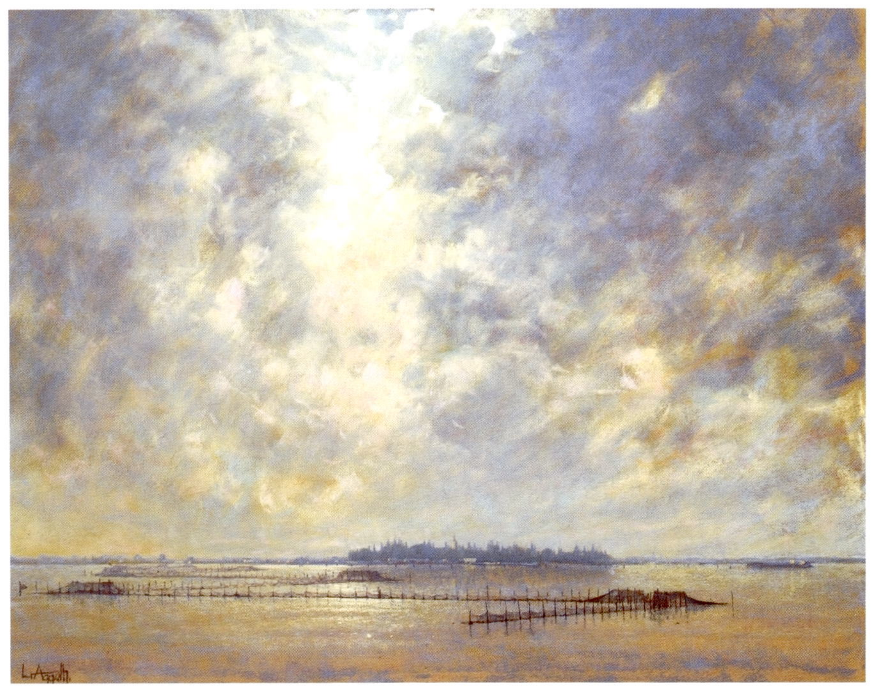

San Francesco del Deserto
Pastel 500 x 650 mm

Fishing nets/traps zig-zag their way towards this island, just south of Burano.

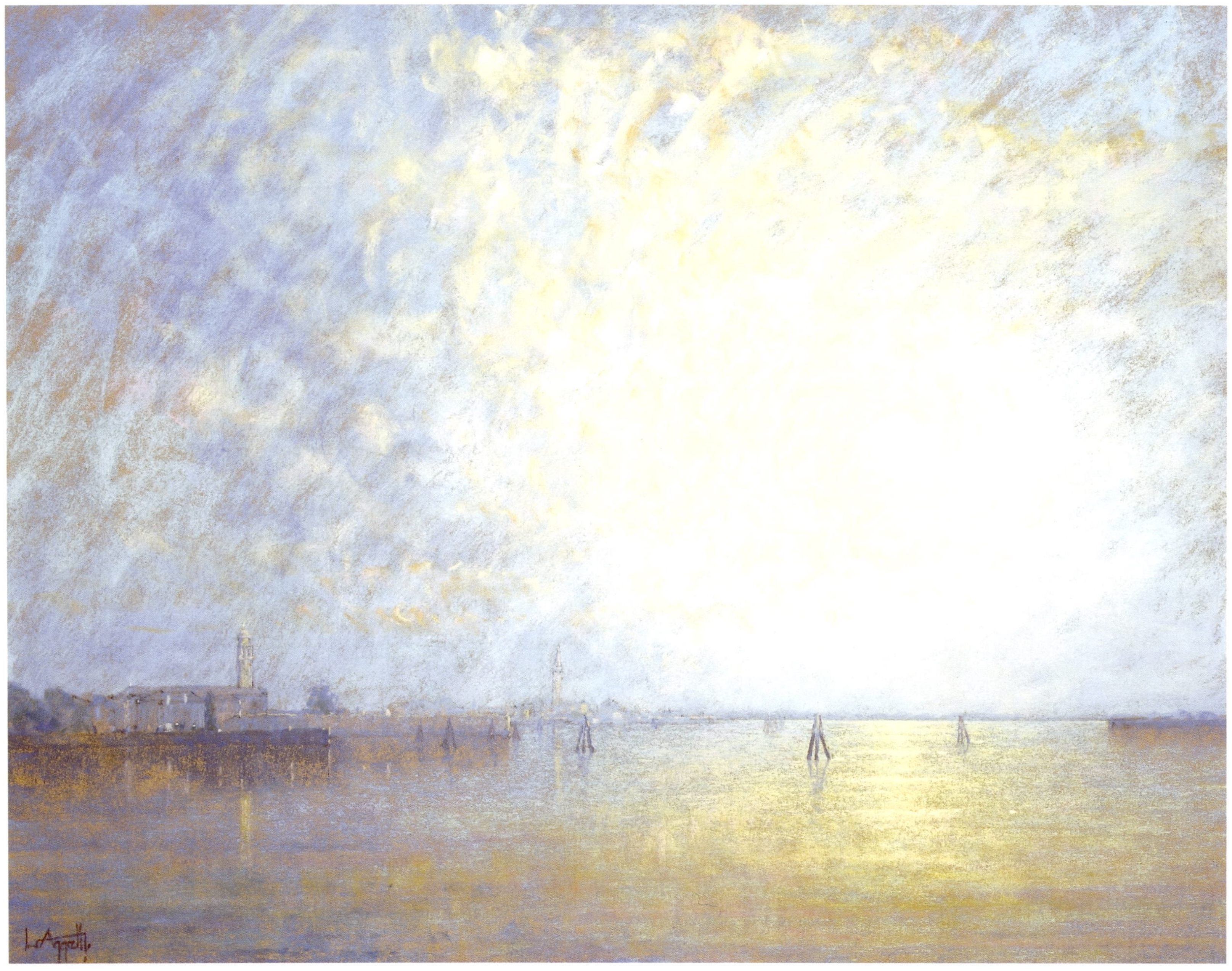

Sunrise Over Mazzorbo and Burano Pastel 500 x 650 mm

The dramatic sky and atmosphere are a mimesis of Burano's sixteenth-century "punto in aria" lace.

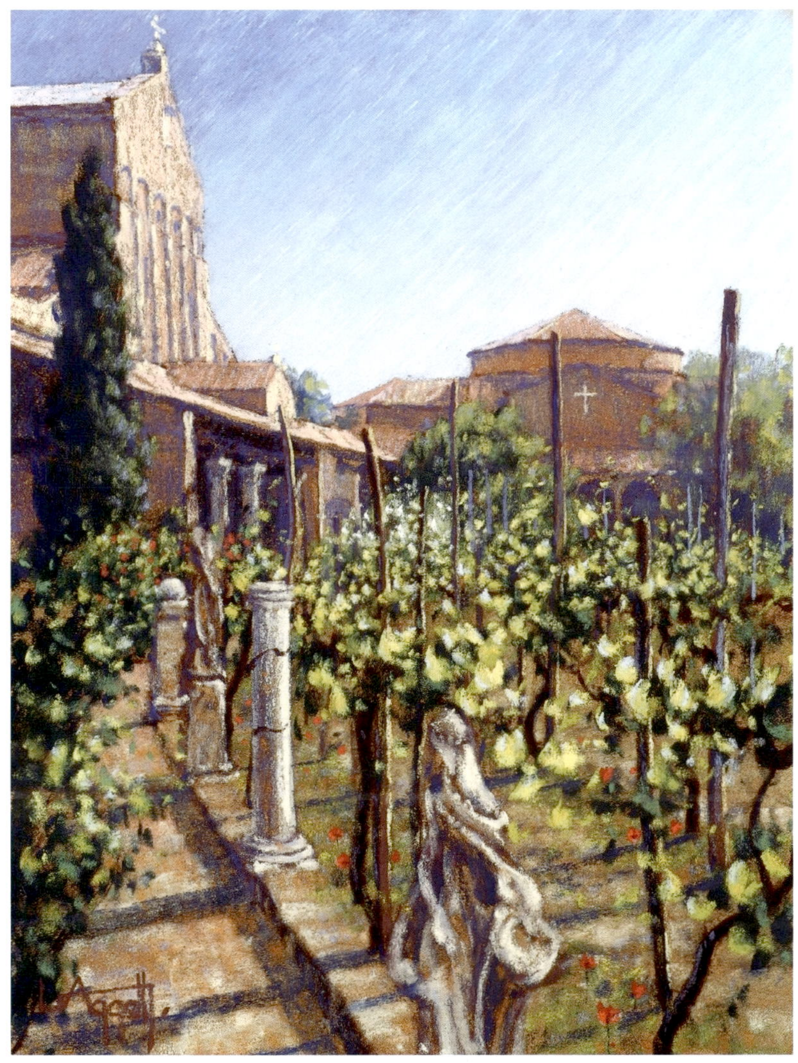

Vineyard, Torcello Pastel 325 x 250 mm

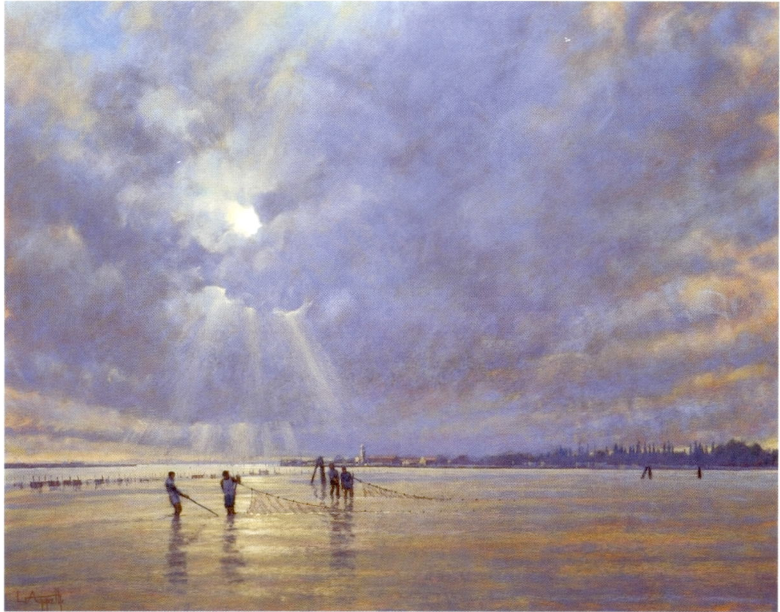

Approaching Storm, Burano Pastel 500 x 650 mm

Torcello, right at the northern end, is an absolute haven, or should be, depending on whether you manage to time your arrival in between large disgorged ferry loads. If you do, then you will enjoy the serene beauty of the remaining waterways, and the Byzantine cathedral of Santa Fosca, and surroundings. If you arrive with a large crowd, then hang back and wait for that mid-period.

Venice has much to do with water, and it is fitting perhaps, that this chapter, and the book, should be concluded with a view looking back towards this wondrous city, from the Laguna Veneta.

Lionel Aggett
RIBA, PS, SWAC

Lagoon Sunset
Pastel 650 x 500 mm

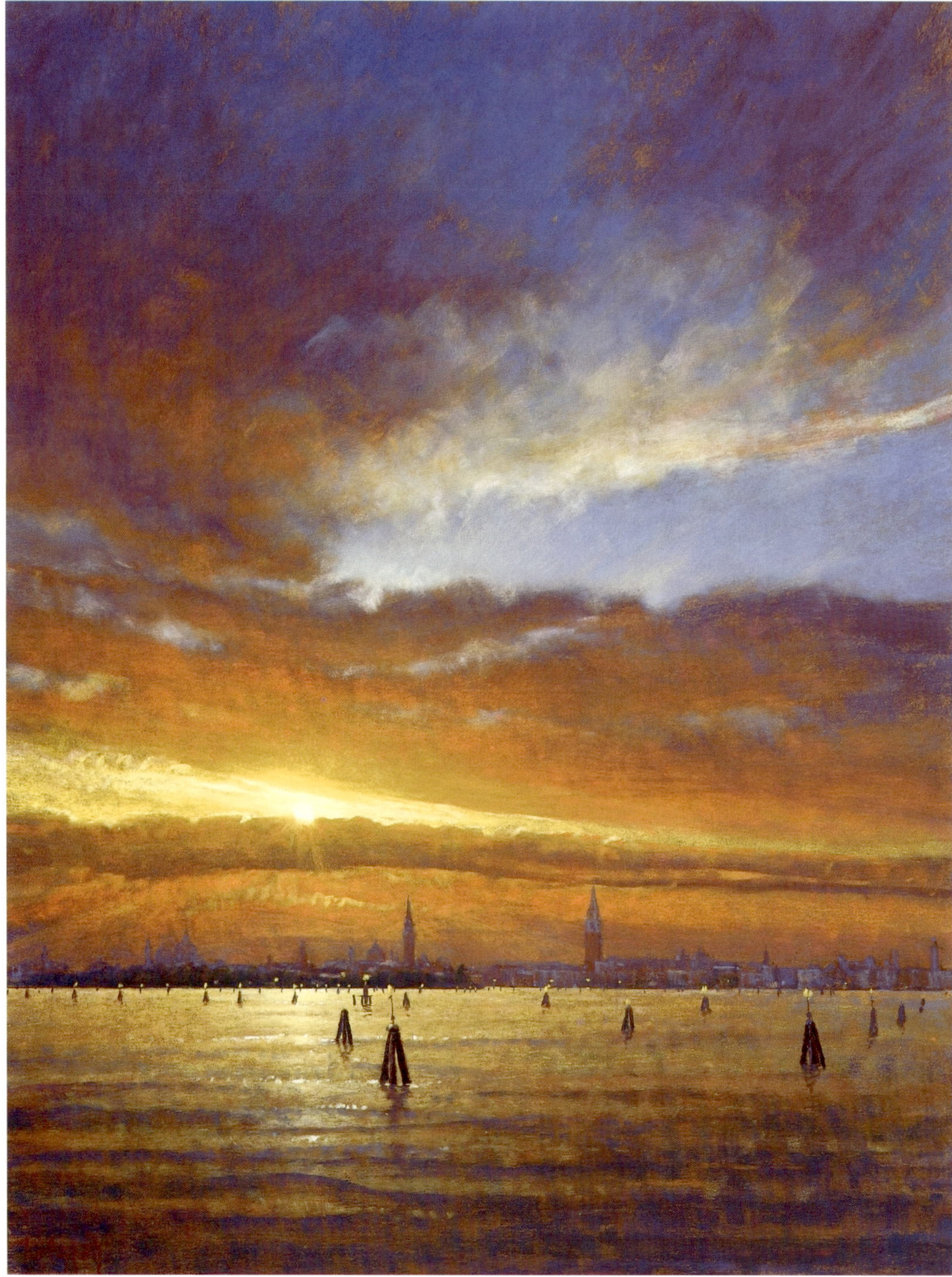